THE
OFFICIAL
ACT
ENGLISH GUIDE

THE
OFFICIAL
ACT

ENGLISH GUIDE

ACT

WILEY

Contents

Introduction

This guide will help you succeed on the ACT English test, which measures your understanding of what you've been taught in your core high school English courses. Reviewing all the grammar rules and writing skills you have learned during high school will take some time. This guide will help remind you of what you have learned and will likely teach you new skills and concepts as well. It covers the content of the ACT English and writing tests and the procedures you'll follow when you're actually taking the ACT English test. This guide also provides strategies for approaching the questions and content-specific test-taking tips.

The following chapters contain questions taken from actual ACT tests that are aimed at enhancing your understanding of the knowledge and skills you'll need to succeed on the test. Each question is followed by a detailed answer explanation. Chapters are organized by grammar and style concepts, which should help you see the patterns among the questions. Near the end of the guide, you will find a bank of real test questions and explanations as they appear on the test. This will give you practice switching gears between question types. A glossary is provided in the appendix to assist you in case you need reminders of common grammatical terminology.

If you already know your areas of strength and weakness when it comes to writing and grammar, you can look through the contents of this guide and focus on improving in those areas. If you are not yet aware of your weaknesses, take a diagnostic test. The Preparing for the ACT practice test is available for free online, and *The Official ACT Prep Guide* includes practice tests you can take. You should print the test if you plan to take it in hard copy so you can practice in the same manner in which you will take your actual test. Being able to cross out answer choices, underline, and star information can help you process the passages and questions.

We hope this guide helps you identify your strengths and improve areas of weakness so that you can show all that you know on your ACT English test.

Chapter 1:
An Overview of the ACT English and Writing Tests

Each ACT is different in its makeup and content. This chapter gives you an idea of what you can expect when you take the ACT English test and the ACT writing test.

The Structure of the English Test

The 45-minute ACT English test contains 75 questions in five passages. Each passage includes 15 questions, as follows:

Passage I   Questions 1–15

Passage II   Questions 16–30

Passage III Questions 31–45

Passage IV Questions 46–60

Passage V   Questions 61–75

If you divide your time evenly, you will spend 9 minutes per passage, and each question should take about 36 seconds to answer. The passages cover a wide variety of topics, ranging from texts about legendary athletes such as Roberto Clemente to scientific articles about exploring Mars.

At times, a concluding paragraph will be accompanied by questions about specific conventions and word choice, and then the final question will be a big-picture-meaning question, typically asking something like, "Suppose the writer's goal had been to write a brief essay concerning his experience with Miami time. Would this essay successfully fulfill that goal?" Since these types of questions are formatted differently from other questions, students may mistake them for directions and skip over them.

Remembering that each passage has 15 questions can help you realize that the last question related to a passage will end in a five or a zero. This should help you avoid accidentally skipping the last question.

In the following example, you will see how these questions will be formatted. Brackets are used to identify the number of a sentence within a paragraph and the paragraph numbers. Questions about an entire paragraph or passage will be identified by a box. Most question numbers appear below an underlined portion of a sentence. Be careful to replace *only* the underlined portion of the sentence as you test out the answer choices. Changes that have been made in previous sentences *should* be taken into account when answering subsequent questions. You will see this frequently in the chapter on subject-verb agreement. **Note:** The word *omit* means to delete or leave out.

Passage IV: Pinball and Chance

[1]

Doesn't anyone play pinball anymore? I was disappointed the other day when I took my kids to a game arcade. Afterwards, I went to the movies.
46
Not one of the many colorful machines with flashing lights were a pinball machine. Video games filled
47
the room.

[2]

[1] I can understand why video games might seem more attractive than pinball. [2] Video screens which have been populated by movie stars, monsters,
48
and heroes. [3] You can blow up cities, escape from dungeons, and battle all sorts of villains. [4] Pinball machines, on the other hand, are essentially all the same. [5] Some machines are bigger and fancier than others, but the object of pinball never changes: you have to keep a steel ball in play long enough to rack up a high score and win a free game. 49

46. Refer to the underlined portion of the passage at number 46, and choose the alternative you consider best.

   F. NO CHANGE

   G. I made my way to the movie theater after that.

   H. (The movie theater was my next stop.)

   J. OMIT the underlined portion.

47. Refer to the underlined portion of the passage at number 47, and choose the alternative you consider best.

   A. NO CHANGE

   B. was a

   C. were an actual

   D. would have been an actual

48. Refer to the underlined portion of the passage at number 48, and choose the alternative you consider best.

   F. NO CHANGE

   G. that are

   H. are

   J. OMIT the underlined portion.

49. For the sake of the logic and coherence of Paragraph 2, Sentence 4 should be:

   A. placed where it is now.

   B. placed after Sentence 1.

   C. placed after Sentence 5.

   D. OMITTED, because the paragraph focuses only on video games.

Some questions will ask about the passage as a whole. They will be formatted like number 15 in the following example.

By the time we found our way back to the car, the sun was high in the sky. We had taken three hours to complete a hike we usually finished in forty-five minutes. Yet the hike felt shorter then ever. As

14

we drove off, I remembered something else my grandmother used to say: "Miami time passes all too quickly."

14. F. NO CHANGE

   G. more shorter then

   H. the shortest than

   J. shorter than

Question 15 asks about the preceding passage as a whole.

15. Suppose the writer's goal had been to write a brief essay conveying a personal experience with "Miami time." Would this essay successfully fulfill that goal?

   A. Yes, because it presents the narrator's firsthand experience of a morning spent in Miami time.

   B. Yes, because it reveals that after a conversation with the grandmother, the narrator decided to live in Miami time.

   C. No, because it shares the views of more than one person with regard to the meaning of Miami time.

   D. No, because the term "Miami time" belonged to the grandmother, not to the narrator.

Content of the ACT English Test

The ACT English test measures your ability to use the Conventions of Standard English to edit passages, accomplish a certain task and purpose in writing, and create a style and tone through word choice. It focuses on three reporting categories that organize the types of questions you will answer and also make up the composite score you will receive. Each reporting category has a different number of questions associated with it on the ACT English test. You will not see the specific number of questions given in a category but rather the percentage of the total test score each will represent. Here is a brief description of the three reporting categories and their percentages in the total score of the English test.

- Conventions of Standard English (usage and mechanics): 51–56%

- Production of Writing (topic development, organization, unity, and cohesion): 29–32%

- Knowledge of Language (word choice, style, and tone): 13–19%

A reporting category is composed of a set of skills that you are expected to have; each question is based on one or more of these skills. For instance, for Conventions of Standard English questions, the skills range from correcting errors in grammar to recognizing the proper use of punctuation. You might find questions about subject-verb agreement, commas with coordinating conjunctions, and sentence fragments. Production of Writing questions might relate to logical transitions and evidence for arguments, and Knowledge of Language questions might ask about the mood and tone of a passage. The number of questions per category is not important. What matters is the percentage of each category in the test that will weight your final score. Following is a more detailed breakdown of the skills that fall under each category.

Conventions of Standard English

Conventions of Standard English test the following knowledge and skills:

- Determine when to use punctuation marks, including periods, colons, semicolons, dashes, and parentheses.

- Determine when to use subordinating and coordinating conjunctions to join clauses or revise awkward-sounding fragments or fused sentences.

- Use logical verb tenses in contexts.

- Recognize and correct disturbances in sentence structure, such as faulty placement of adjectives, participial phrase fragments, missing or incorrect relative pronouns, dangling or misplaced modifiers, faulty parallelism, run-on sentences, and weak conjunctions between independent clauses.

- Maintain consistent and logical verb tense and voice and personal pronouns within a paragraph or passage.

Production of Writing

Production of Writing questions test knowledge and skills in two areas of English composition.

Topic Development in Terms of Purpose and Focus

Examples of knowledge and skills tested in these questions include the following:

- Determine the relevance of material to the topic or the focus of the passage or paragraph.

- Identify the purpose of a word or phrase (for example, identify a person, define a term, or describe an object).

- Use a word, phrase, or sentence to accomplish a specific purpose, such as convey a feeling or attitude or illustrate a given statement.

Organization, Unity, and Cohesion

Examples of knowledge and skills tested in these questions include the following:

- Determine the need for transition words or phrases to define relationships in terms of time or logic.

- Determine the most logical place for a sentence in a paragraph.

- Provide a suitable conclusion for a paragraph or passage (for example, summarizing the main idea).

- Provide a suitable introduction for a paragraph or passage.

- Rearrange sentences in a paragraph or paragraphs to achieve a logical flow.

- Determine the most logical place to divide a paragraph to achieve a stated goal.

Knowledge of Language

Knowledge of Language questions test your ability to clearly and succinctly express yourself in written English. Knowledge and skills tested in these questions include the following:

- Revise unclear, clumsy, and confusing writing.

- Delete redundant and wordy material.

- Revise an expression to make it conform it to the style and tone used throughout the passage.

- Determine the need for conjunctions that create logical connections between clauses.

- Choose the most appropriate word or phrase in terms of the sentence content.

Questions assess your understanding of grammar and style rules in the context of the whole passage. You must pay attention not only to a single sentence with an error but also to the other sentences and paragraphs. The questions in the ACT English test never directly ask about grammar rules. For example, the test won't ask, "Can a subject of a verb be found within a prepositional phrase?" or "Which of the following is a relative clause?" Instead, you will be asked to revise sentences that include grammar and style errors. Spelling is not assessed in the ACT English test. At times, "NO CHANGE" will be the correct answer choice if the sentence was grammatically and stylistically correct in the first place.

The Content of the Writing Test

The optional writing test has important differences from the English test. It measures your ability to write a unified, coherent essay about an issue stated in the prompt. Rather than answering questions within reporting categories, you will follow each of the steps listed in the essay task. Your score, given from a low of 2 to a high of 12, depends on how well you have done each of the steps and completed the task. Here are the steps you will need to follow on the ACT writing test:

- Clearly state your own perspective on the issue and analyze the relationship between your perspective and at least one other perspective.

- Develop and support your ideas with reasoning and examples.

- Organize your ideas clearly and logically.

- Communicate your ideas effectively in Standard written English.

Chapters 8-13 of this guide will review each of these points, show samples of actual student essays, and explain the use of writing skills in their responses.

How to Use This Guide

This guide will give a brief description of each category followed by official sample questions associated with each category. It will review essential skills, present questions on those skills, and explain approaches to answering them. As you may notice, the English test covers many of the skills you need for writing. In the optional writing test, you respond to a prompt and compose an essay. This guide includes a review of both tests because they each call for such closely related skills.

2 Chapter 2: Taking the English Test

This chapter covers two common methods of navigating the questions in the English test. It also reviews how to thoughtfully check your work. Finally, this chapter describes several common question types and provides relevant sample questions with answer explanations.

Approaching the Questions

Before you take the ACT English test, you can use the practice questions in this guide to determine an approach for answering questions that works best for you. Most students like to read a passage until they see a question, finish that sentence, and then attempt the question asked. At times, reading past the underlined portion of the sentence will be necessary in order to gain a greater sense of context. This is particularly true of questions asking about transitions, verb tenses, pronouns, redundancy, or the content of a passage. Some students prefer to read one paragraph at a time. Those students then return to the individual questions within that paragraph.

Checking Your Answers

If you wish to double-check your work, you can do so either at the end of each passage while the content is still fresh in your memory or after finishing the complete English test. Mark questions that you are unsure about with a symbol like a question mark. On the online test, you will have a highlighting tool and will be able to use scrap paper for notes. If you are completing the test digitally, you can write out the letters of the answer choices (ABCD, for example) on scrap paper and cross them out as you eliminate wrong answers.

When checking your work, be sure to consider the context of the passage. Typically, you should read at least one sentence before and one sentence after the question. If you return only to the underlined questions themselves, you will likely answer the question incorrectly. Also, when changing an answer, try to consciously recognize the reason for the change by saying to yourself, "I am choosing answer B because I now realize_____. Answer C is incorrect because _____."

For example, when initially looking at question 23 in the following example, you might originally think that the correct sentence includes the plural word *artists* and therefore choose answer C. Later, you might realize that the word *artist* is singular. You should consciously justify your choice using the method just described. You would then say to yourself, "I am choosing answer B because I now realize that the word *artist* is singular and later in the sentence the singular pronoun *she* is used. Answer C is incorrect because *s'* is used for plural nouns and the word *artist* here is not plural. Using this explanation technique will help you be mindful of your thought process as you double-check your answers.

The artist Faith Ringgold has made a name for herself with her "story quilts," lively combinations of painting, quilting, and storytelling. One of these artworks, *The Sunflowers Quilting Bee at Arles*, depicts a scene of women at work on a quilt in a field of towering yellow <u>flowers that eight</u> African American
            22
 women sit around the quilt that covers their laps.
 	
    In reality, these women never met to piece together a quilt. The scene comes out of the <u>artists imagination</u> as a statement of the unity of purpose
   23
 that she perceives in their lives.
	23. A. NO CHANGE
	
	    B. artist's imagination
	
	    C. artists' imagination
	
	    D. artists imagination,

The best answer is B because Ringgold is the only artist being referred to at this point; the singular possessive form of the noun *artist's* is therefore required. Additionally, the sentence uses the singular pronoun she, which makes it clear that the word "artist" is singular.

The best answer is NOT:

A because *artists* is a plural noun, not the singular possessive form of the noun *artist's* that is required.

C because *artists'* is a plural possessive form of the noun, not the singular possessive form *artist's* that is required.

D because the phrase "artists imagination" uses the plural form of the noun *artists* instead of the singular possessive *artist's* that is required.

Types of Questions

Studying the qualities of the different types of questions on the ACT English test will help you navigate the questions more quickly on test day. For example, questions that include the words NOT or EXCEPT are not as straightforward as most ACT English test questions. Therefore, they require a particular approach. This chapter will review a wide range of question types that appear on the ACT English test. Identifying what type of question you are answering is often the first step to answering that question correctly.

Questions Are Multifaceted

It is helpful to keep in mind that most questions test multiple grammatical concepts simultaneously. Consider the following question.

The plan worked. By late morning, the crowd cheered as, welded to the two legs of the arch, the final section was hoisted up. Over three decades <u>and more than thirty years</u> of planning and building had <u>come to a conclusion</u>, and the tallest monument in the United States was now complete.	**12.** Refer to the underlined portion of the passage at number 12, and choose the alternative you consider best. **F.** NO CHANGE **G.** as the crowd cheered, the final section was hoisted up and welded to the two legs of the arch. **H.** as the crowd cheered, welded to the two legs of the arch, the final section was hoisted up. **J.** the final section was hoisted up as the crowd cheered and welded to the two legs of the arch.

This question primarily tests if you understand modifiers and how to create a clear and logical sentence. An overwhelming number of grammatical concepts are found in this question, including commas, nonessential clauses, subordinating conjunctions, coordinating conjunctions, and the placement of modifiers. You may know that nonessential information is information that can be cut out of a sentence without affecting the meaning and can be framed by commas. Accordingly, you should be able to eliminate the phrase "welded to the two legs of the arch," from the original sentence without affecting its meaning. Doing so yields the following: "By late morning, the crowd cheered as the final section was hoisted up." That is a complete sentence. Though the phrase "welded to the two legs of the arch," is placed appropriately immediately before the noun it modifies (the final section), it still does not create the clearest and most logical sentence. A modifier should come immediately before or after what it is modifying. In this case, the phrase "welded to the two legs of the arch," is appropriately describing the final section of the arch; however, answer choice **F** implies that the final section is welded to the arch *before* it is hoisted up, which isn't logical. The correct answer (**G**) creates a logical sentence through its use of the conjunction *and,* which clarifies the order of the events. The final section is hoisted first, and then it is welded to the arch. This question also demonstrates how important it is to read all of the answer choices because answer choice **F** properly implements several grammar rules, but it is still not the best answer choice.

The best answer is G because it provides the most logical and fluent arrangement of the possible parts of this sentence: an introductory dependent clause ("as the crowd cheered") followed by a main clause with a compound predicate ("the final section was hoisted up and welded to the two legs of the arch"). *As* is a subordinating conjunction, which means it will be followed by an independent clause + comma + subject + verb, as is the case here. The corrected sentence reads as follows:

> By late morning, *as* the crowd cheered, the final section was hoisted up and welded to the two legs of the arch.

The best answer is NOT:

> **F** because this arrangement of the pieces of information provides us with the nonsensical image of the final section being hoisted up after it had been welded to the legs of the arch.

> **H** because this arrangement of the pieces of information provides us with the absurd image of the crowd being welded to the legs of the arch.

> **J** because this arrangement of the pieces of information provides us with the confusing image of the crowd either doing some of the welding or being welded to the legs of the arch.

Sentences in the Context of Paragraphs

The following is an example of a paragraph from the ACT English test. Question 2 is an example of the type of question that requires an understanding of the context of that sentence within the paragraph as a whole. Questions are identified with a number under an underlined portion of text. Here, question 2 refers to the portion of the text identified with the number 2 under an underlined portion of the paragraph. The underlined portion is what would be replaced by the answer choices.

My family is part of the Miami <u>tribe a Native American people,</u> with strong ties to territory in
¹
present-day Ohio, Indiana, and Illinois. Growing up in the Midwest, I often heard my grandmother talk about "Miami time." When she was doing something she loved, whether it was <u>making freezer jam or researching tribal history,</u> she refused to be <u>rushed</u>
²
<u>in a hurry.</u>
³
	2. At this point, the writer would like to provide a glimpse into the grandmother's interests. Given that all the choices are true, which one best accomplishes this purpose?
	
	  F. NO CHANGE
	
	  G. being actively involved in her pursuits,
	
	  H. things I really hope she'll teach me one day,
	
	  J. historical research as well as domestic projects,

The best answer is F because "making freezer jam or researching tribal history" gives the most specific and vivid glimpse of what the grandmother was interested in.

The best answer is NOT:

> **G** because "being actively involved in her pursuits" is vague and gives no suggestion of what those pursuits are.

> **H** because "things I really hope she'll teach me one day" gives no suggestion of what those things are.

> **J** because "historical research as well as domestic projects" offers only a general notion of the interests that are more pointedly described in **F.**

EXCEPT and NOT Questions

Be aware that some questions will include the words EXCEPT or NOT. Though the words EXCEPT or NOT will be capitalized, students often overlook these words and therefore answer a question different from the one being posed. Here are some examples.

These eight women the story explains, strove in their various ways to support the cause of justice in the 21 world.	**21.** The underlined phrase could be placed in all the following locations EXCEPT: **A.** where it is now. **B.** after the word *support.* **C.** after the word *cause.* **D.** after the word *world* (ending the sentence with a period).

The best answer is C because placing the underlined portion after the word *cause* is the only one of the four choices that wouldn't be acceptable. This placement of the phrase "in their various ways" divides the phrase "the cause" from the prepositional phrase that describes the cause, "of justice." Therefore, all of the choices would be acceptable EXCEPT **C.**

The best answer is NOT:

> **A** because keeping the underlined portion where it is now creates a clear and correct sentence in English.

> **B** because placing the underlined portion after the word *support* creates a clear and correct sentence in English.

> **D** because placing the underlined portion after the word *world* (and before the period) creates a clear and correct sentence in English.

Notice that the following question 36 is identified differently than the majority of questions in the English section. Instead of the question number appearing under an underlined portion of the text, question 36 is identified by the number 36 appearing in a box because this question is not asking if a portion of the text should be replaced. It is asking why the preceding sentence should NOT be deleted. It is important to know that the word *preceding* means the sentence *before* the number 36. In other words, the question is asking about the following sentence and why it should be kept: "Méliès's magician's eye led him to discover the basics of special effects." The original sentence that follows the number 36 is not being replaced. That sentence has been reproduced here in order to clarify the way these questions function.

He experimented with effects such as speeding up and slowing down the action, reversing it for backward movement, and superimposing images of fantastic creatures over real people.

[1] Undaunted, Méliès honed his photographic skills to tell fantasy stories instead. [2] Méliès, a French magician, was fascinated by the workings of the new motion picture camera. [3] Specializing in stage illusions, he thought the camera offered potential to expand its spectacular magic productions. [4] By
33
1895, he was working with the new invention. [5] He found out, however, that the public preferred
34
live magic acts to filmed versions. 35

Méliès's magician's eye led him to discover the basics of special effects 36 . He experimented with effects such as speeding up and slowing down the action, reversing it for backward movement, and superimposing images of fantastic creatures over real people. Using overhead pulleys and trapdoors, he was able to do interesting things.

36. The writer is considering deleting the preceding sentence from the essay. The sentence should NOT be deleted because it:

F. describes Méliès's ability as a magician, which is important to understanding the essay.

G. begins to explain the techniques of trick photography that Méliès eventually learned.

H. creates a transition that provides a further connection between Méliès the magician and Méliès the filmmaker.

J. indicates that Méliès's interest in learning about trick photography existed before his interest in magic.

The best answer is H because the sentence under consideration should NOT be deleted; it creates a transition between the preceding paragraph, about Méliès the magician, and this paragraph, which focuses on Méliès's exploration of special film effects.

The best answer is NOT:

F because the sentence under consideration mentions Méliès's "magician's eye" but doesn't otherwise describe his ability as a magician.

G because the sentence under consideration mentions "the basics of special effects" but doesn't begin to explain any of the techniques of trick photography.

J because the sentence under consideration doesn't indicate "that Méliès's interest in learning about trick photography existed before his interest in magic." The preceding paragraph, in fact, describes Méliès's interests as beginning with magic, then moving into filmmaking.

LEAST Questions

Some questions ask about what answer choice would be LEAST acceptable. These questions can typically be reworded as follows: "Eliminate acceptable alternatives." For these questions, typically three of the answers are quite similar to each other. The correct answer tends to be the answer that differs the most from the others. For example, three of the words might have a positive or neutral connotation while the fourth may have a negative connotation. The connotation of a word is its implied meaning. For example, the word *frugal* describes a person who is conscientious about spending. The connotation of this word is positive, while the word *miserly* describes a person who hoards money out of selfishness. Though *frugal* and *miserly* have similar denotations, or literal meanings, their connotations are quite different from one another.

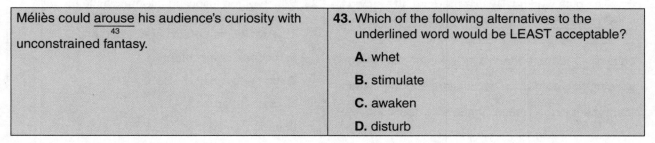

| Mélès could <u>arouse</u> his audience's curiosity with
⁴³
unconstrained fantasy. | **43.** Which of the following alternatives to the underlined word would be LEAST acceptable?

A. whet

B. stimulate

C. awaken

D. disturb |

The best answer is D because *disturb* is the only one of the four alternatives that, in the context of the sentence, can't reasonably be used as a substitute for the underlined word (*arouse*). "Disturb his audience's curiosity" is neither a conventional expression in standard English nor an appropriate innovation here. Therefore, *disturb* is the LEAST acceptable alternative to *arouse*.

The best answer is NOT:

A because the word *whet,* meaning here to stimulate or excite curiosity, is an acceptable, idiomatically appropriate alternative to the word *arouse.*

B because the word *stimulate,* meaning here to encourage or increase curiosity, is an acceptable, idiomatically appropriate alternative to the word *arouse.*

C because the word *awaken,* meaning here to stir up or stimulate curiosity, is an acceptable, idiomatically appropriate alternative to the word *arouse.*

| He or she learns where the hazards lurk and the special weapons are hidden. Pinball, <u>though,</u> can't
⁵²
be predicted with such accuracy. | **52.** Which of the following alternatives to the underlined portion would be LEAST

acceptable?

F. therefore,

G. however,

H. by contrast,

J. on the contrary, |

The best answer is F. Notice that this question asks for the LEAST acceptable answer. In other words, the best answer is the weakest choice. If you read the paragraph carefully, you will see that the idea presented in this sentence (pinball is unpredictable) is meant to contrast with the idea in the preceding sentence (video games are predictable). Given this context, using the transitional word *therefore* at this point is illogical and confusing.

The best answer is NOT:

> G because *however,* is an acceptable alternative to *though,* providing the same logical transition.

> H because *by contrast,* also provides an acceptable alternative to *though.*

> J because, along with **G** and **H,** *on the contrary,* provides an acceptable alternative to *though.*

The plan worked. By late morning, the crowd cheered as, welded to the two legs of the arch, the final section was hoisted up. Over three
27
decades and more than thirty years of planning and
28
building had come to a conclusion, and the tallest
29
monument in the United States was now complete.

29. Which of the following alternatives to the underlined portion would be LEAST acceptable in terms of the context of this sentence?

   F. reached completion,

   G. come to a halt,

   H. come to an end,

   J. ended,

The best answer is G because this is the LEAST acceptable alternative to the underlined portion. The sentence with the underlined portion reads, "Over three decades … of planning and building had come to a conclusion, and the tallest monument in the United States was now complete." Replacing the word *conclusion* with *halt* creates a meaning problem in the context of this sentence because "coming to a halt" expresses the idea of stopping or suspending before or without completion.

The best answer is NOT:

> F because it provides an acceptable wording. The phrase "reached completion," works in the context of this sentence just as well as "come to a conclusion," does.

> H because it provides an acceptable wording. The phrase "come to an end," works in this sentence just as well as "come to a conclusion," does.

> J because it provides an acceptable wording. The word "ended" works in this sentence just as well as "come to a conclusion" does.

General Strategies for Adding or Deleting Words or Phrases

The ACT hopes that students will communicate clearly and concisely. To assess this skill, some questions will ask if a sentence or a sentence fragment should be added or deleted. This requires understanding the context surrounding the portion of the passage in question. The following is one approach to answering these types of questions.

1.   Paraphrase the excerpt in question.

2.   Take notice of any pronouns such as *he, she, it, they, them.* Try to determine to what/to whom these pronouns refer.

3.   Predict what you think would come before and after the sentence in question. You may wish to jot down a brief note about this.

4.   Look at the paragraph as a whole. Ask yourself, "Are there some sentences that need to stay together in order to maintain the logical flow of the passage?" This is often the case when one sentence employs a pronoun (*he, she, it, they*) that refers back to a common noun in the sentence prior.

5.   Compare your predictions to the sentences within the passage. Consider if the new content fits logically into the flow of the existing paragraph.

Some questions will ask you what would be *lost* if a portion of the original passage were deleted. These questions are actually asking you what that content *adds* to the passage. Therefore, it is best to read the sentence or detail in question and paraphrase to yourself what it adds to the passage. That will provide the answer to the question of what would be lost if that portion of the text were deleted.

Adding Information for Clarity

The following is an example of a question that asks what information should be included for clarity. The strategies for this type of question are similar to those for a question asking if a sentence should be added or deleted.

The Save-U has a neon sign out front that says "Friendly 24-Hour Service," but as far as I can tell, no one really works there. The washers and dryers are lime green, and the paneling on the walls has been painted to match, although it was later varnished with some kind of artificial wood grain finish. [23] I often stare at that paneling when I don't have a magazine or newspaper to read and don't want to do my schoolwork. Deep in thought, I contemplate the competence of the laundromat's interior designer.

23. At this point, the writer wants to add a sentence that would further describe the laundromat's paneling. Which of the following sentences would best accomplish this?

A. I guess the brush strokes are intended to resemble wood grain, but they don't.

B. I know that the varnish provides some protection for the wood paneling.

C. To me, it seems that lime green was a bizarre choice for an interior wall paint.

D. I imagine that the person who chose that color scheme must be a unique individual.

The best answer is A because it provides the added detail asked for in the question. Pay close attention to the stated question. It asks for the sentence that would best accomplish the writer's wish to "further describe the laundromat's paneling." **A** is the only choice that accomplishes this goal. It further describes the "artificial wood grain finish" by showing that it was intended to resemble wood grain but doesn't.

The best answer is NOT:

B because it does not provide a detail that further describes the paneling. Although **B** mentions the paneling, it does not offer a further description of it. Rather, it adds a detail that is irrelevant to the paragraph.

C because it, too, fails to further describe the paneling. Instead, it offers an opinion about the color of the paneling.

D because it is incorrect in the same way that **C** is. It offers an opinion about the person who "chose that color scheme," but it does not further the description of the paneling.

The following question asks about adding the most relevant content. This is just another way of asking what content would logically fit if added into the context of the passage.

In reality, these women never met to piece
_____
  22
together a quilt. The scene comes out of the artists
imagination as a statement of the unity of purpose
_____
  23
that she perceives in their lives. Sojourner Truth and
Harriet Tubman fought to abolish slavery and, later,
was active in the crusade for suffrage. Newspaper
_____
  24
journalist Ida B. Wells courageously spoke out for
                                _____
social and racial justice in the late nineteenth and
_____
early twentieth centuries.
_____
           25

25. Given that all the choices are true, which one provides the most relevant information at this point in the essay?

A. NO CHANGE

B. married Ferdinand Barnett, editor of the first Black newspaper in Chicago, the *Chicago Conservator.*

C. wrote for newspapers in Memphis, New York City, and finally, Chicago.

D. was born in Holly Springs, Mississippi, in 1862, the eldest of eight children.

The best answer is A because information about Wells speaking out for social and racial justice is highly relevant, given that the paragraph focuses on the causes championed by the women, including Wells, depicted in Ringgold's artwork.

The best answer is NOT:

B because information about the man Wells married is only marginally relevant to the topic of the paragraph: the historical reality behind Ringgold's artwork.

C because information about which newspapers Wells wrote for isn't as relevant to the topic of the paragraph as the information in **A.**

D because information about Wells's birthplace, birth year, and siblings is only marginally relevant to the topic of the paragraph.

[5]

The company's name reflects this African American focus as well. Glory is meant to evoke
                                                      _____
                                                         41
both the exultant spirit of gospel churches and the movie during the Civil War of the same name, which
          _____
                 42
tells the story of a black regiment. [43]

[6]

With twenty full-time employees in its administrative offices, Glory Foods has come a long way from its beginnings. America's dinner tables were the beneficiaries of Bill Williams's drive,
       ____
        44
determination, and culinary expertise. [45]

43. At this point, the writer is considering adding the following sentence: The actor Denzel Washington starred in the film, which earned several awards. Should the writer make this addition?

A. Yes, because the additional detail explains why the film *Glory* was so inspiring.

B. Yes, because if readers understand that the film *Glory* earned awards, they will also understand why the company was named "Glory Foods."

C. No, because the information distracts the reader from the focus of the essay.

D. No, because the essay does not say if Bill Williams had ever met the actor Denzel Washington.

The best answer is C because it clearly explains why the writer should not add the information about the actor who starred in the film *Glory*. This information is not in keeping with the main point of the paragraph, which is to explain how the company got its name. Adding information about an actor distracts the reader from the focus of the paragraph and the essay as a whole.

The best answer is NOT:

A because it suggests that the sentence belongs in the paragraph when it clearly does not. Information about the actor who starred in *Glory* is not relevant at this point in the essay.

B because it, too, wrongly suggests that the sentence belongs in the paragraph.

D because even though it does indicate that the writer should not add the sentence, the reason given for not making this addition makes no sense. Including additional information saying that Bill Williams had met the actor Denzel Washington would also be irrelevant to the essay.

> When I was a girl in the 1960s, my friends and I loved Nancy Drew. [55] We loved her loyal companions, her bravado, and there was a love for her freedom to do what she wanted.
> 56
> We also loved how smart she was and how pretty,
> 57
> how confident and successful. We were surprised and delighted that eighteen-year-old Nancy was so accomplished at so many things. She was able to
> 58
> solve crimes, win golf tournaments, kick bad guys in the shins, and impress her father's distinguished clients. She did it all—and without scuffing her shoes or losing her supportive boyfriend, Ned.

55. At this point, the writer is thinking about adding the following true statement:

One of a number of series that have featured the young female detective, the Nancy Drew Mystery Story series was begun in 1930 and now totals 173 books. Should the writer make this addition here?

A. Yes, because it supports statements about the longevity and popularity of this series.

B. Yes, because it helps to explain why the narrator "loved Nancy Drew."

C. No, because it distracts the reader from the main focus of this paragraph.

D. No, because it fails to include relevant information about the author of the series.

The best answer is C because the proposed sentence, concerning how many books are in one of the series featuring Nancy Drew, shouldn't be added at this point in the essay because it distracts the reader from the main point of the paragraph, which is about why the narrator and her childhood friends loved Nancy Drew so much.

The best answer is NOT:

A because although the proposed sentence does attest to the longevity and popularity of the Nancy Drew Mystery Story series, the sentence is out of place and largely irrelevant at this point in a paragraph mainly about the place Nancy Drew held in the narrator's childhood and that of her friends.

B because the proposed sentence, with its facts and figures, addresses the history of the Nancy Drew Mystery Story series, not why the narrator loved Nancy Drew, which is why the sentence is out of place and largely irrelevant at this point in a paragraph mainly about the place Nancy Drew held in the narrator's childhood and that of her friends.

D because although the proposed sentence shouldn't be added at this point, adding in information about the author of the Nancy Drew Mystery Story series would only make the sentence more out of place and irrelevant, given that the paragraph is mainly about the place Nancy Drew held in the narrator's childhood and that of her friends.

Recent reports suggest that the cost of a human voyage to Mars could run as high as 100 billion dollars. This is a startling number, especially in light of the fact that the International Space Station, the most ambitious NASA project yet, carried a
67
projected price tag of "only" 17 billion dollars. In the end, NASA overspent on the International Space Station. [68] One can only imagine if the final price
69
of a human voyage to Mars would be.

68. The writer is considering adding the following true information to the end of the preceding sentence (placing a comma after the word *Station*): with a final construction cost of almost 30 billion dollars. Should the writer make this addition?

F. Yes, because it strengthens the assertion made in this sentence by adding explicit detail.

G. Yes, because it proves space flight will be more affordable in the future.

H. No, because it weakens the point made in the paragraph about the cost of human flight to Mars.

J. No, because it detracts from the essay's focus on the human experience in travel to Mars.

The best answer is F because the information should be added to the sentence; the explicit detail about the amount of money actually spent on constructing the space station—nearly double the already high projected cost of $17 billion—strengthens the sentence's assertion that "NASA overspent on the International Space Station."

The best answer is NOT:

G because although the information should be added to the sentence, nothing in the information suggests, let alone proves, that space flight will be more affordable in the future.

H because the information would strengthen, rather than weaken, the point made in the paragraph about the high cost of human flight to Mars. If the actual cost of constructing the International Space Station was almost double the projected cost, it's reasonable to worry about the accuracy of the already high projections of the cost of sending humans to Mars. Thus, the information should be added to the sentence.

J because the essay's focus isn't on the human experience in travel to Mars but rather on the costs of manned and unmanned missions to the planet. The information isn't a digression but instead strengthens the point made in the paragraph about the high cost of human flight to Mars. Thus, the information should be added to the sentence.

As with all diseases, the best cure is prevention.
70
Experts suggest that you avoid borrowing flash drives because they might contain viruses. They warn that many of these viruses are quite sophisticated in their programming. They also say
71
that you should make copies of your computer files, so that if a virus does strike and you must delete your infected files, you will at least have backup copies. Experts also point out that using the Internet and World Wide Web has led to new risks of infection in the form of viruses hidden in programs downloaded from these resources.

71. In this paragraph, the writer intends to recommend a number of specific ways to protect computer data against viruses. This is to be the second recommendation. Given that all of the choices are true, which one would best accomplish the writer's intention?

A. NO CHANGE

B. propose adding software that checks the spelling in the papers you write on your computer.

C. advise you to give your system frequent checkups with antivirus programs.

D. suggest that in order to protect your computer, you must be aware of the various ways to prevent viruses.

The best answer is C because the question states that the writer's intention is to recommend "ways to protect computer data against viruses." **C** provides a recommendation by advising the reader to use antivirus programs frequently.

The best answer is NOT:

A because stating that many "viruses are quite sophisticated" does not provide a recommendation and, thus, does not accomplish the writer's stated intention.

B because it does provide a recommendation of sorts, but not the recommendation stated in the question. Adding software that checks spelling does not "protect computer data against viruses."

D because although this choice makes a broad recommendation ("be aware of the various ways to prevent viruses"), it does not recommend "specific ways to protect to protect computer data," which is the writer's stated intention.

PASSAGE V: When a Computer Gets Sick

[1]

Imagine sitting in front of a computer monitor, filling the screen with your mind's jumbled thoughts. Tomorrow's assignment is slowly materializing before your eyes. Suddenly, without warning, each of the letters, in front of you tumbles to the bottom
61
of the screen. Is this a bad dream? Not exactly. The computer is probably sick, unless the diagnosis may
62
be that the computer has a virus.

(continued)

PASSAGE V: When a Computer Gets Sick (*continued*)

[2]

Analogous to a biological virus that takes over a living cell, a computer virus is a program, or set of instructions, that invades a computer either to create mischief or do real damage. The type of computer virus mentioned above is more mischievous than harmful. Eventually, the letters reorder themselves on the screen. Not all <u>viruses however,</u> straighten themselves out.
                        63

[3]

<u>Computer viruses range from being temporary annoyances to permanently destroying data.</u>
                        64
Computer vandals rig these viruses to go off at a preset time. These bombs can permanently destroy data, and that can be <u>disastrous to the operation</u> of a computer.
                        65

[4]

<u>Detection programs</u> are available that <u>searches</u>
        66
for and then <u>destroys</u> computer viruses. Evidence that
        67
some software writers have played up the medical <u>analogy being</u> found in the names of their <u>programs:</u>
        68   69
Vaccine, Checkup, Antitoxin, and Disinfectant.

[5]

<u>As with</u> all diseases, the best cure is prevention.
        70
Experts suggest that you avoid borrowing flash drives because they might contain viruses. <u>They warn that many of these viruses are quite sophisticated in their programming.</u> They also say
                        71
that you should make copies of your computer files, so that if a virus does strike and you must delete your infected files, you will at least have backup copies. Experts also point out that using the Internet and World Wide Web has led to new risks of infection in the form of viruses hidden in programs downloaded from these resources.

[6]

If there is a virus in your system, you had hope that it <u>better</u> responds to the appropriate treatment
        72
and therapy. Otherwise, you could be in for a long night at the computer.

73. The following question asks about the passage as a whole. Upon reviewing this essay and realizing that some information has been left out, the writer composes the following sentence, incorporating that information: Names like these suggest that the problem is serious. The most logical and effective place to add this sentence would be after the last sentence of Paragraph:

A. 2.

B. 3.

C. 4.

D. 5.

74. Paragraphs 1, 5, and 6 of this essay are written in the second person (*you, your*). If these paragraphs were revised so that the second-person pronouns were replaced with the pronouns *one* and *one's,* the essay would primarily:

F. gain a more polite and formal tone appropriate to the purpose of the essay.

G. gain accessibility by speaking to a broader and more inclusive audience.

H. lose the sense of directly addressing and advising the reader.

J. lose the immediacy of its setting in terms of time and place.

The best answer for question 73 is C because the most logical and effective placement for this sentence is after Paragraph 4. The last sentence of this paragraph lists the names of the virus detection programs; the new sentence, which refers to those names, logically follows. Also, this new sentence states that the "Names … suggest that the problem is serious." The names identified in Paragraph 4 (Vaccine, Checkup, Antitoxin, and Disinfectant) do imply a level of seriousness.

The best answer is NOT:

A because Paragraph 2 provides a description of what a computer virus can do and does not refer to any "names" of viruses. Adding the sentence here makes no sense.

B because the main topic of Paragraph 3 is computer "bombs." As with **A,** there is no reference to particular "names."

D because it, too, would be an illogical placement. Although there are "names" in the last sentence of Paragraph 5 (Internet and World Wide Web), these names do not use the medical analogy which shows how destructive computer viruses can be.

The best answer for question 74 is H because the second-person pronouns (*you, your*) do directly address the reader. Revising the essay so that it used the third-person pronouns *one* and *one's* would sacrifice that sense of addressing and advising the reader.

The best answer is NOT:

F because, although shifting to the third-person pronouns *one* and *one's* may change the tone of the essay, a polite and formal tone is clearly not appropriate to the purpose of this piece.

G because changing the pronouns in the essay from second to third person would not suggest that the writer is "speaking to a broader and more inclusive audience."

J because, in this essay, the setting is not a prominent element, and a shift in pronouns from second to third person would not change the sense of that setting.

My grandfather is not known for embracing technological <u>change. He still drives</u> his '59 Chevy
₆₆
Impala. (He <u>says,</u> he can't imagine needing frivolous
₆₇
options like automatic transmission or power steering.) So, when he has <u>went</u> to buy a new color
₆₈
television—<u>owing to the knowledge that</u> his old
₆₉
black-and-white model had finally quit—and the salesperson tried to talk him into buying a model with a remote control, he resisted. He said that he had two good legs and was perfectly capable of getting out of his chair. [70]

70. Given that all are true, which of the following additions to the preceding sentence (replacing "chair.") would be most relevant?

A. chair that was made of black leather.

B. chair when he wanted to change the channel.

C. chair by the south window in the family room.

D. chair where he liked to sit.

The best answer is B because it adds an appropriate and relevant detail here. In this sentence, the writer is expressing that the grandfather believed he was still healthy and had no need of a remote control for his television—"He said that he had two good legs and was perfectly capable of getting out of his chair." The addition of "when he wanted to change the channel" fits with the point of the rest of the sentence.

The best answer is NOT:

A because the fact that the chair "was made of black leather" is irrelevant to the writer's purpose here.

C because the fact that the chair is located "by the south window in the family room" is a pointless digression in this sentence.

D because, again, the fact that the grandfather "liked to sit" in his chair is an insignificant detail here. Because it was "his chair," he would presumably like to sit there.

PASSAGE VI: Grandpa's Remote Control

[1]

My grandfather is not known for embracing technological change. He still drives his '59 Chevy Impala. (He says, he can't imagine needing frivolous options like automatic transmission or power steering.) So, when he has went to buy a new color television—owing to the knowledge that his old black-and-white model had finally quit—and the salesperson tried to talk him into buying a model with a remote control, he resisted. He said that he had two good legs and was perfectly capable of getting out of his chair. [5]

[2]

However, the salesperson was persistent and, appealing to Grandpa's TV-viewing habits, described the various functions on the remote. However, my grandpa could punch in the time, and the channel of his favorite daily news program, and the TV would turn on that program at the proper time. In the end, Grandpa did buy the remote, and it has since become something he uses all the time.

[3]

Grandpa is intrigued by the various uses for that remote. He has confided in me that the volume control is perfect for turning up the sound whenever Grandma asks him to take out the garbage. For example, he says, the button that mutes the sound lets him cut them off in midsentence.

This question asks about the passage as a whole.

14. The writer is considering deleting the first sentence from Paragraph 3. If the writer removed this sentence, the essay would primarily lose:

A. information about the intriguing uses of the remote.

B. details supporting the fact that Grandpa liked using the remote.

C. a humorous blend of descriptive details and relevant information.

D. a transition from the first two paragraphs to the rest of the essay.

[4]

Grandpa's favorite feature on the remote is the sleep function. This option automatically turns the TV off after a preset amount of time, which is very convenient when he falls asleep while watching a

10

show. For him, Grandpa says what he wants his TV doing, even when he sleeps, is to know a source of both pleasure and power.

11

[5]

[1] As for the programming function, Grandpa not only uses it for the news but also for playing jokes on his youngest grandchildren. [2] Explaining to the unsuspecting child that he has a remote control implanted in his little finger, Grandpa points his

12

finger at the TV and, to the child's amazement, seemingly turns it on. [3] I suppose Grandpa hasn't learned all the possible uses of the remote control, but I don't doubt he will continue to discover new and creative ways of using it. [14]

13

The best answer is D because it provides an effective transition from the first part of the essay to the second part. The opening paragraphs focus on Grandpa's resistance to but eventual acquisition of a new TV with a remote control. The last sentence of Paragraph 2 indicates that Grandpa overcame his resistance to technology and began to use the remote. The first sentence of Paragraph 3 points out that Grandpa has actually grown interested in the uses of the remote, and this leads into the rest of the essay's description of the uses that he discovers, many of which wouldn't be found in that 200-page manual.

The best answer is NOT:

   A because the first sentence of Paragraph 3 is "Grandpa is intrigued by the various uses for that remote." This sentence suggests that the remote control might have intriguing uses, but it doesn't provide any information about those uses.

   B because, again, the sentence does suggest that Grandpa liked using the remote, but it doesn't provide any details that support that as a fact.

   C because it would be a vast overstatement to say that this sentence is "a humorous blend of descriptive details and relevant information."

Deleting Information

The ACT English test often asks if information should be added to or deleted from a passage. Information that should be deleted or not included in a passage will fall into one of these three categories: random, redundant, or disruptive.

1. A sentence should be deleted if it is **random.** This includes facts that do not advance the argument or description. This could mean needless definitions, historical connections, or tangents. To some extent, gauging if a sentence is random depends on outside knowledge. For example, if a passage about global climate change included a sentence about the invention of the steam engine, this may strike some students as random when, in fact, it is connected to global climate change. Steam engines run on fossil fuels and thus emit carbon dioxide into the atmosphere, which contributes to global climate change.

   Sometimes determining if a piece of information is relevant will depend on outside knowledge. For example, it would *not* be random if the invention of the steam engine were mentioned in an article about asthma rates in cities that discussed the role factory pollution plays in exacerbating this medical condition. That same information would be random if it were found in an article about how artists are knitting sweaters and placing them on prominent statues.

2. A sentence should be deleted if it is **redundant.** You should delete or not add information that has already been stated earlier in the passage in the exact same manner. This can be difficult to evaluate, particularly given that the introduction of a passage typically gives an overview of the points that will appear in the body paragraphs. Ask yourself if the sentence in question adds more specific information than what is offered already. If it does, then this information should likely be included in the passage. For example, if the introduction talks broadly about women who have contributed to science and then later goes into depth about several specific female scientists, then that is useful information that expands on the general overview provided in the introduction. When a passage provides specific examples of a broader concept stated earlier in the passage, that is not considered redundant or random. It is considered to be useful elaborating detail.

Examples

Broad	Specific
News sources	Magazines, newspapers, and the Internet
Uncommon sports	Curling, polo, and chess boxing
Life's milestones	Getting a driver's license, graduating college, getting a job, and buying a home

3. A sentence should be deleted if it is **disruptive.** For example, sometimes adding a new sentence will make a new illogical noun serve the antecedent for a pronoun such as *he, she, it, they, them,* or *their.*

Let's look at a section from a passage.

Among the more serious viruses are those referred to as "bombs." Tech companies hire what are known as white-hat hackers in order to ensure the security of their systems. Computer vandals rig
16
these viruses to go off at a preset time.

Notice that the phrase "these viruses" does not have a logical antecedent in the sentence directly prior to it. Look in the sentence before the pronoun *these* for a plural noun that *these* could refer back to. The only plural noun in that sentence is "white-hat hackers," and they cannot be logically referred to as *viruses*. In most cases, the noun that agrees with the pronoun should come in the sentence directly before the pronoun. Let's look at a correct use of a pronoun in the following to see how this works.

> Among the more serious viruses are those referred to as "bombs." South Korea was recently struck by a bomb that temporarily disabled automatic teller machines across the country. Computer vandals rig **these kinds of viruses** to go off at a preset time.
>
> 17

Notice that the phrase "these kinds of viruses" *does have* a logical antecedent. The previous sentence gives an example of a specific bomb, which is a virus, and the phrase "these kinds of viruses" refers to the type of virus that created a problem in South Korea.

The results indicated a problem that threatened to postpone the topping-out ceremony marking the placement of the final section between the two freestanding legs of the St. Louis Gateway Arch. [20]	**20.** The writer is considering deleting the following from the preceding sentence: marking the placement of the final section between the two freestanding legs of the St. Louis Gateway Arch. If the writer were to delete this phrase, the essay would primarily lose: **A.** a minor detail in the essay's opening paragraph. **B.** an explanation of the term "topping-out ceremony." **C.** the writer's opinion about the significance of the topping-out ceremony. **D.** an indication of the topping-out ceremony's importance to the people of St. Louis.

Strategy: For this kind of question, read the portion that is up for consideration and try to paraphrase it. This will help you further reflect on the meaning of this piece of information. For example, the phrase "marking the placement of the final section between the two freestanding legs of the St. Louis Gateway Arch" describes what the "the topping-out ceremony" is. How could this information be characterized? Could this information be cut out? If not, why not?

The best answer is B because this sentence explains that the topping-out ceremony being referred to here is "the placement of the final section between the two freestanding legs of the St. Louis Gateway Arch." Without this phrase, we wouldn't be able to figure out what "topping out" meant until we were halfway into the essay. Key terms are frequently defined in the introductory paragraph of a passage.

The best answer is NOT:

A because the essay would not lose a minor detail if this phrase were deleted. This is a key piece of information.

C because the wording of this phrase is straightforward and factual—there's nothing to suggest that the writer is expressing his or her opinion on the significance of anything.

D because the phrase does not state the ceremony's importance to St. Louis residents. Readers might draw a conclusion about the ceremony's importance based on the essay as a whole, but that's something else entirely.

PASSAGE II: Faith Ringgold's Quilting Bee

The artist Faith Ringgold has made a name for herself with her "story quilts," lively combinations of painting, quilting, and storytelling. Each artwork consists of a painting framed by quilted squares of fabric and story panels. One of these artworks, The Sunflowers Quilting Bee at Arles, depicts a scene of women at work on a quilt in a field of towering yellow <u>flowers that eight</u> African American women
                       16
sit around the quilt that covers their laps. Who are these people stitching among the flowers? What brings them so close that their shoulders touch?

    <u>Thus, the</u> answers to these questions can be
       17
found in the artwork itself. Ringgold has told <u>the story of this gathering on two horizontal panels of text.</u> One
                                                18
panel is sewn into the piece's top border, the other into <u>it's</u> bottom border. These eight <u>women the story</u>
           19   20
<u>explains,</u> strove <u>in their various ways</u> to support the
                            21
cause of justice in the world.

    In <u>reality,</u> these women never met to piece
          22
together a quilt. The scene comes out of the <u>artists</u>
                                               23
<u>imagination</u> as a statement of the unity of purpose that she perceives in their lives. Sojourner Truth and Harriet Tubman fought to abolish slavery and, later, <u>was active</u> in the crusade for suffrage.
                24
Newspaper journalist Ida B. Wells <u>courageously spoke out for social and racial justice in the late</u>
                                     25
<u>nineteenth and early twentieth centuries.</u>

Establishing her own hair products <u>business, herself</u>
<u>in the first decade of the twentieth century,</u>
₂₆
<u>millions of dollars were later bequeathed by</u>
₂₇
Madam C. J. Walker to charities and educational
institutions. Among the schools that benefited from
this <u>generosity, were</u> those that Mary McLeod
₂₈
Bethune opened and ran in order to provide a
better education for Black students. And Fannie
Lou Hamer, Ella Baker, and Rosa Parks showed
leadership and strength during the civil rights
<u>movement, it happened</u> in the 1950s and 1960s.
₂₉
   In the artwork, Ringgold has surrounded these
women with bright sunflowers. The flowers seem to
celebrate the women's accomplishments and the
beauty of their shared vision. [30]

30. If the writer were to delete the preceding sentence, the essay would primarily lose:

F. an interpretation of the artwork that serves to summarize the essay.

G. a reflection on the women depicted in the artwork that compares them to Ringgold.

H. a description of a brushwork technique that refers back to the essay's opening.

J. an evaluation of Ringgold's artistic talent that places her in a historical context.

The best answer is F because the sentence under consideration interprets what the flowers represent ("seem to celebrate") and makes a concluding reference to the main focus of the essay ("the women's accomplishments and the beauty of their shared vision.").

The best answer is NOT:

G because the sentence under consideration makes no comparison of Ringgold to the women depicted in the artwork.

H because the sentence under consideration says nothing about a brushwork technique.

J because the sentence under consideration offers no evaluation of Ringgold's artistic talent, only an interpretation of what the flowers represent ("seem to celebrate").

There are many regular customers whose faces have become familiar—<u>mostly older people from</u>
<u>around the neighborhood.</u> Usually a crowd of
₂₆
thirteen-year old <u>kids that</u> is gathered around the
₂₇
video machines, regardless of the time of day.

26. The writer is considering deleting the following phrase from the preceding sentence: "mostly older people from around the neighborhood." If the writer were to make this deletion, the essay would primarily lose:

F. specific descriptive material.

G. detail providing a logical transition.

H. foreshadowing of the conclusion.

J. an understatement of important information.

Strategy: For this kind of question, read the portion that is up for consideration and try to paraphrase it. This will help you further reflect on the meaning of this piece of information. For example, the phrase "mostly older people from around the neighborhood" describes the age of the majority of people who are regular customers. How could this information be characterized? What does it contribute to the passage?

The best answer is F because the phrase "mostly older people from around the neighborhood" specifically describes the group of "regular customers" mentioned in the first part of the sentence. If the phrase were deleted, specific descriptive material about the regular customers' age would be lost.

The best answer is NOT:

G because the phrase is not a detail that provides a logical transition because the sentence that follows describes a different group of customers.

H because the phrase does not foreshadow the conclusion. The writer does not conclude the essay with "older people from around the neighborhood"; rather, the essay ends with all the people who frequent the laundromat.

J because this information is not understated. Also, it is not "important information"—essential to the essay—but, rather, an interesting and relevant side note.

Thirty-two years of planning and effort resulted in this moment. In 1933, <u>attorney and civic leader</u> 21 Luther Ely Smith envisioned a memorial that would recognize St. Louis's major role in the westward expansion of the United States. 22

22. If the writer were to delete the preceding sentence, the paragraph would primarily lose:

A. an explanation of why St. Louis had a major role in the westward expansion of the United States.

B. details about what Luther Ely Smith thought the memorial he envisioned should look like.

C. background information about the history leading to the Gateway Arch.

D. biographical information about Luther Ely Smith.

Strategy: First read the sentence in question and paraphrase it in your own words. Then think about what would be lost if this sentence were not included in the passage. Finally, compare your thoughts to the answer choices. Completing this inductive reasoning will help you avoid becoming drawn toward the incorrect answers.

The best answer is C because this sentence states, "In 1933, attorney and civic leader Luther Ely Smith envisioned a memorial that would recognize St. Louis's major role in the westward expansion of the United States." It does provide some helpful background about the history leading up to the construction of the Gateway Arch, and it's the only place in the essay where such background is provided.

The best answer is NOT:

A because the sentence does state that St. Louis played a role in the westward expansion, but it does not explain why St. Louis played that role.

B because the sentence does state that Smith envisioned a memorial, but it does not mention what the memorial that he envisioned might look like.

D because the sentence does provide some biographical facts about Smith—he was an attorney and a civic leader, and he had an idea about a memorial. However, this information is not particularly crucial. The information that is most relevant and meaningful to this paragraph is that a memorial to St. Louis's role in the US westward expansion (that is, the Gateway Arch) was first envisioned in 1933.

Sentence Placement

Some questions also ask about the placement of a sentence within a paragraph. You can use the same basic approach to answer those types of questions. Reread the sentence in question. Think about what ideally should come before and after that sentence. Then compare your ideas about what should come before and after the sentence to the options provided within the paragraph. Also think about which sentences need to remain together. Typically, this will be based on pronouns, possessive adjectives, and demonstrative adjectives. Pronouns include words such as *he, she, it,* and *they*. Possessive adjectives include *my, your, his, her, its, their, our, your,* and *whose.* Demonstrative adjectives include *these, those, this* and *that*. One challenge of this type of question is that the sentences before and after the sentence in question will contain grammatical errors themselves. In order to demonstrate that challenge, the next example shows how this passage appears in the ACT English test first and then how the passage looks when corrected.

The following example assesses your ability to understand logical organization, which would fall under the English reporting category of Production of Writing (organization, unity, and cohesion).

Original Passage

[1] Down the street from <u>the college, I attend, the</u>
₁₆
Save-U Laundromat is always open, and someone
is always there. [2] It <u>was</u> on a corner, across the
₁₇
<u>street; from</u> a drugstore on one side and a big
₁₈
park on the other. [3] The park isn't really a park
at all but part of the grounds of a private boarding
school. [4] But no one is ever around to enforce the
threats, and in the summer everyone enjoys the
benches, the grass, and the <u>coolly magnificence</u> of
₁₉
the shade trees. [5] Signs are posted all over the
lawn threatening every sort of drastic action against
<u>trespassers who wrongfully enter the property.</u> [21]
₂₀

Revised Passage

[1] Down the street from the college I attend, the
Save-U Laundromat is always open, and someone
is always there. [2] It was on a corner, across the
street from a drugstore on one side and a big
park on the other. [3] The park isn't really a park
at all but part of the grounds of a private boarding
school. [4] But no one is ever around to enforce the
threats, and in the summer everyone enjoys the
benches, the grass, and the cool magnificence of
the shade trees. [5] Signs are posted all over the
lawn threatening every sort of drastic action against
trespassers. [21]

21. For the sake of logic and coherence, Sentence 5 should be placed:

A. where it is now.

B. before Sentence 1.

C. after Sentence 1.

D. after Sentence 3.

Repeated Question from Above

21. For the sake of logic and coherence, Sentence 5 should be placed:

A. where it is now.

B. before Sentence 1.

C. after Sentence 1.

D. after Sentence 3.

The best answer is D because placing Sentence 5 after Sentence 3 makes the paragraph logical and coherent. If you read Sentences 3, 4, and 5 carefully, you will notice that Sentence 4 does not logically follow Sentence 3. The opening clause in Sentence 4, "But no one is ever around to enforce the threats," has no antecedent to connect it back to Sentence 3. The threats in Sentence 4 refer to the "signs … posted all over the lawn" that are referred to in Sentence 5. Therefore, Sentence 4 makes the best sense when it follows Sentence 5 rather than precedes it.

The best answer is NOT:

A because leaving Sentence 5 where it is now is not logical because sentence 4 refers to the concept of "threats," which are not introduced in Sentences 1, 2, or 3. Sentence 5 must be moved before Sentence 4 so that Sentence 5 can introduce the idea of the signs that "threaten every sort of drastic action against trespassers."

B because Sentence 5 would be a poor and illogical introduction to this paragraph because the reader would not know to what lawn the writer was referring. In addition, the paragraph would make no sense if Sentence 1 followed Sentence 5.

C because this arrangement of the sentences is also illogical and would confuse the reader. Placing Sentence 5 after the description of the laundromat in Sentence 1 makes no sense because the signs on the lawn are on the grounds of a school and are not part of the laundromat.

---

[2]

[1] I can understand why video games might seem more attractive than pinball. [2] Video screens which have been populated by movie stars, monsters,
___
48

and heroes. [3] You can blow up cities, escape from dungeons, and battle all sorts of villains. [4] Pinball machines, on the other hand, are essentially all the same. [5] Some machines are bigger and fancier than others, but the object of pinball never changes: you have to keep a steel ball in play long enough to rack up a high score and win a free game. [49]

49. For the sake of the logic and coherence of Paragraph 2, Sentence 4 should be:

A. placed where it is now.

B. placed after Sentence 1.

C. placed after Sentence 5.

D. OMITTED, because the paragraph focuses only on video games.

The best answer is A because it provides the most logical sequence of sentences for this paragraph. Sentence 4 provides a necessary link between the description of the video games in Sentences 1 through 3 and the description of the pinball machines in Sentence 5. In Sentence 4, the phrase "on the other hand" signals that this sentence is going to provide a contrasting point of view. In this case, the writer contrasts video games and pinball machines.

The best answer is NOT:

B because if Sentence 4 were placed right after Sentence 1, the paragraph would be incoherent, illogical, and confusing. Placing Sentence 4 here would interrupt the description of the video games with a comment about pinball machines.

C because placing Sentence 4 after Sentence 5 would confuse readers. They would not understand that the phrase "Some machines" in Sentence 5 actually refers to pinball machines. Also, the transitional phrase "on the other hand" in Sentence 4 does not logically follow the information in Sentence 5.

D because omitting Sentence 4 would confuse readers. The transition that Sentence 4 provides is a necessary link between the description of the video games in Sentences 1 through 3 and the description of the pinball machines in Sentence 5.

---

[5]

[1] As for the programming function, Grandpa not only uses it for the news but also for playing jokes on his youngest grandchildren. [2] Explaining to the unsuspecting child that he has a remote control implanted in his little finger, Grandpa points his
___
14

finger at the TV and, to the child's amazement, seemingly turns it on. [3] I suppose Grandpa hasn't learned all the possible uses of the remote control, but I don't doubt he will continue to discover new and creative ways of using it. [16]
___
15

16. Upon reviewing Paragraph 5 and realizing that some information has been left out, the writer composes the following sentence:

He programs the TV to turn on at a time when a grandchild will be visiting. The most logical placement for this sentence would be:

F. before Sentence 1.

G. after Sentence 1.

H. after Sentence 2.

J. after Sentence 3.

The best answer is G because the placement that creates the most logical order is between Sentences 1 and 2. First, the statement that Grandpa likes to use the programming function to play jokes on his grandchildren. Then, the explanation of how he does it: he programs the TV to turn on at a certain time; in the grandchildren's presence, he points his finger at the TV when it's programmed to turn on.

The best answer is NOT:

F because it is not the most logical place to add this information. It doesn't make sense to explain Grandpa's TV programming trick before the reader even knows that Grandpa likes to use the programming function to play jokes on his grandchildren.

H because it reverses the chronological order of how Grandpa's joke works. He can't play the trick on the grandchildren and then program the TV to turn on at a certain time.

J because it is incorrect for the same reason that **H** is. The chronological order of the setup of the remote control–finger joke is out of whack.

---

[1] Undaunted, Méliès honed his photographic skills to tell fantasy stories instead. [2] Méliès, a French magician, was fascinated by the workings of the new motion picture camera. [3] Specializing in stage illusions, he thought the camera offered potential to expand its spectacular magic productions. [4] By ¯¯33 1895, he was working with the new invention. [5] He found out, however, that the public preferred live ¯¯34 magic acts to filmed versions. [35]

35. For the sake of the logic and coherence of this paragraph, Sentence 1 should be placed:

A. where it is now.

B. after Sentence 2.

C. after Sentence 3.

D. after Sentence 5.

The best answer is D because Sentence 1 explains what Méliès did after he was undaunted by the discovery that people didn't like filmed magic acts (Sentence 5). He began instead to tell fantasy stories.

The best answer is NOT:

A because keeping Sentence 1 where it is now would weaken the logic and coherence of the paragraph. The paragraph would begin with a reference to Méliès being undaunted and turning to fantasy stories instead before Méliès had been formally described in Sentence 2 and before the incident that caused him to turn away from filmed magic acts had been related (Sentences 3 to 5).

B because placing Sentence 1 after Sentence 2 would weaken the logic and coherence of the paragraph. The words *undaunted* and *instead* in Sentence 1 would make no sense, because there's nothing in Sentence 2 to suggest that Méliès had met with any problems.

C because placing Sentence 1 after Sentence 3 would weaken the logic and coherence of the paragraph. The words *undaunted* and *instead* in Sentence 1 would make no sense, because there's nothing in Sentences 2 or 3 to suggest that Méliès had met with any problems.

When she was doing something she loved, whether it was <u>making freezer jam or researching tribal history,</u> she refused to be <u>rushed in a hurry.</u> "I'm
2   3
on Miami time today," she would say. Conversely, if we were running late for an <u>appointment. She</u>
4
would chide us by saying, "Get a move on. We're not running on Miami time today, you know."

   <u>It was a difficult concept for me to grasp.</u> My
5
grandmother tried to explain that "Miami time" referred to those <u>moments, when</u> time seemed
6
to slow down or stand still. Recently, the meaning of her <u>words</u> started to sink in. One morning, my
7
son and I <u>will inadvertently slip</u> out of the world
8
measured in seconds, minutes, and hours, and into one measured by curiosity and sensation.

5. Given that all the choices are true, which one provides the best opening to this paragraph?

  A. NO CHANGE

  B. I remember being late for a doctor's appointment one day.

  C. My grandmother lived with us, and as a result she and I became close over the years.

  D. My son asks me about my grandmother, whom he never met.

The best answer is A because it opens this paragraph with a general statement about the concept of Miami time and serves as the most logical link between the preceding paragraph and the subject of this paragraph.

The best answer is NOT:

    B because the reference to the doctor's appointment is only loosely related to the end of the preceding paragraph and to the subject of this paragraph, which is defining and describing the concept of Miami time.

    C because the general reference to the relationship between the narrator and the grandmother is only loosely related to the subject of this paragraph, which is defining and describing the concept of Miami time.

    D because the general reference to the son being curious about and having never met the grandmother is only loosely related to the subject of this paragraph, which is defining and describing the concept of Miami time.

3

Chapter 3:
Conventions of Standard English: Sentence Structure, Formation, and Usage

This chapter reviews several grammar concepts that relate to real test questions you will see later in the guide in the sample questions section. You may not get a question directly asking about these grammar concepts, but knowledge of these concepts will help you answer other questions that focus more specifically on grammar concepts that will be explained in the later sections that include sample test questions.

Sentence Structure

One of the most frequently tested concepts on the ACT English test is the concept of what constitutes a sentence. If your English teacher has ever written "comma splice" or "run-on sentence" on your essays, then you may have devoted some thought to what makes a sentence a sentence.

Each of the following statements is, in fact, a sentence.

A. What is that smell?	A. This is a question.
B. Take out the trash.	B. This a command. The implied subject is *you*.
C. I wish I did not have to ask.	C. This is a wish.
D. It stinks!	D. This is an exclamation.
E. The curtain unfolded.	E. This includes a subject and a verb. It is a sentence.
F. The baby seems tired.	F. The verb *seems* describes a state of being.
G. Running is my favorite hobby.	G. *Running* is the noun form of the verb "to run."
H. She is.	H. This could be a complete thought in response to a question such as, "Is she planning to attend the party?"

In simplest terms, a sentence is a complete thought. It must contain a subject and a verb. A subject is typically the doer of the action. Subjects are usually nouns such as *woman, dog,* or *apartment,* and pronouns such as *he, she, it,* and *they.* Subjects can also be nouns that refer to abstract concepts such as *creativity, education,* or *freedom.* Subjects can be gerunds, which are the noun form of an action such as *singing, jumping,* or *cooking.* **Common nouns** refer to people, places, and things, and **proper nouns** refer to specific people, places, and things such as *Abraham Lincoln, New York,* or *the Constitution.* Notice that proper nouns are capitalized. A **noun phrase** describes a person, place, or thing in more than just one word. Typically, a noun phrase is made up of an adjective and a noun. A noun phrase can include other modifiers such as articles (*a, an, the*) or prepositional phrases. Nouns and noun phrases are typically the subject of the sentence.

Examples

The season finale <u>was</u> disappointing.

The final act of the musical <u>was</u> powerful.

A kind stranger <u>helped</u> me parallel park.

Verbs and Verb Phrases

Verbs are often easier to identify because they are typically action words. A verb phrase includes the main verb and helping verbs such as *is, was, are, must, shall, will, should, would, can, could, may,* and *might.*

The following are examples of verbs in their infinitive form.

Examples

To consider to think about something

To eat to consume food

To defenestrate to throw out a window

To meditate to focus the mind

To throw to launch in the air

The following are examples of <u>verb phrases</u>.

1.   He <u>might run</u> for class president.

2.   You <u>should get</u> eight hours of sleep each night.

Some <u>verb phrases</u> function as modifiers or as introductory clauses. Consider the following:

3.   <u>When the train arrived,</u> we packed up our bags.

4.   <u>Taking a selfie,</u> the young woman did not notice her purse was being stolen.

5.   <u>As we crossed the finish line,</u> we were greeted by our families.

Confusingly, the same word can be a different part of speech depending on the context of the sentence. For example, the word *run* can function as a verb as it does in the sentence, "I <u>run</u> a mile each day." In the following sentence, however, the word *run* is part of a relative clause and therefore does not function as a verb. Relative clauses offer further information about a noun and begin with a relative pronoun such as *who, whom, whose, which, that, where, when* and *why.*

Example

Social media influencers who run contests <u>do</u> so in order to increase their followers.

The word *run* functions as part of the relative clause "who run contests," which describes the noun phrase "social media influencers." The who clause specifies a certain subset of influencers. The verb in this sentence is *do.* Notice also that the phrase "do so" is used to reiterate that these particular influencers run contests. It would be redundant to say "**Social media influencers** who run contests *run contests* in order to increase their followers."

In the following sentences the **subjects** have been identified in bold and the <u>verbs</u> have been underlined.

Examples

1. **Neil Armstrong** <u>walked</u> on the moon in 1969.

2. **Neil Armstrong** <u>loved</u> seeing the curvature of the earth from outer space.

3. **Walking** on the moon <u>was</u> Neil Armstrong's most famous achievement.

4. **Neil Armstrong** <u>was</u> the first man to walk on the moon.

5. **Neil Armstrong and Buzz Aldrin** <u>were</u> the first men to walk on the moon.

6. **Neil Armstrong and Buzz Aldrin** <u>took</u> photographs, <u>collected</u> specimens from the surface, and <u>conducted</u> a solar wind experiment.

7. There <u>is</u> **a conspiracy theory** that the moon landing was a hoax and that the footage was actually shot in a film studio.

Explanations

1. "**Neil Armstrong**" is the subject of the first sentence, and *walked* is the verb in this sentence. Some grammar textbooks will also use the word predicate to refer to the verb phrase of a sentence that includes the main verb along with its auxiliaries, modifiers, and objects.

2. In the second sentence, *loved* is the verb. Some verbs such as *hate* or *admire* describe emotions.

3. In the third sentence, *walking* is the subject. It is the noun form, or gerund, of the verb *to walk*. Gerunds end in -ing.

4. In the fourth sentence, "**Neil Armstrong**" is still the subject of the verb; however, the verb in the fourth sentence is not an action word. Some verbs, called linking verbs, describe states of being. The verb *to be* is the most common verb used to describe states of being. Here are several other verbs used to describe states of being:

appear	feel	stay	smell	taste
become	remain	seem	sound	turn

   Linking verbs connect adjectives with the subject of the sentence that they modify. For example, in the following sentence, the word *friendly* describes the dog: "The dog seems friendly."

5. In the fifth sentence, "**Neil Armstrong and Buzz Aldrin**" are a compound subject. Therefore, the verb <u>were</u> must be plural.

6. The sixth sentence includes a compound predicate. The sentence describes several actions taken by the compound subject "**Neil Armstrong and Buzz Aldrin**".

7. In the seventh sentence, the subject and verb are inverted. Notice that the subject "a conspiracy theory" follows the verb *is*. This flipping of the subject and the verb can make it difficult to identify the subject of the verb.

   Strategy: to identify the subject, turn the statement into a question, asking yourself, "What is there?" The answer is, "There is a conspiracy theory," so "conspiracy theory" must be the subject of the sentence.

Indefinite Pronouns

The subject of a sentence is not always easy to identify. Each of the following sentences includes a subject that students often have difficulty recognizing. *Each* and *none* are singular indefinite pronouns, and therefore they should agree with singular verbs. When conjugating verbs to agree with indefinite singular pronouns, it can be helpful to remember the rule that the subject (a noun) of a verb cannot be in a prepositional phrase. The most common prepositional phrases begin with the prepositions *to, for, from,* and *of.* Consider the following sentences with pronouns that correctly agree with the verbs in these sentences:

Each of the students <u>is</u> prepared for the test.

Some of the students <u>are</u> prepared for the test.

Many of the students <u>are</u> prepared for the test.

A number of students <u>are</u> skipping school this Friday.

The number of teachers getting their masters' degrees <u>is</u> increasing.

Strategy

One strategy for completing these questions involves crossing out the entire prepositional phrase in order to see that the subject must be found elsewhere in the sentence.

<u>**Each**</u> ~~of the students~~ is prepared for the test.

<u>**Some**</u> ~~of the students~~ are prepared for the test.

<u>**Many**</u> ~~of the students~~ are prepared for the test.

Singular indefinite pronouns such as the following do not refer to a specific individual: *another, anybody, anyone, anything, each, enough, everybody, everyone, everything, less, little, much, nobody, no one, nothing, one, other, somebody, someone,* and *something.*

Examples

1. **The number** of teachers who remain in the profession for over ten years <u>is</u> declining.

2. **Anyone** <u>can learn</u> a second language if he or she invests adequate effort.

3. **No one** <u>is saying</u> that high school is easy.

4. **Somebody** <u>needs</u> to volunteer to present first.

Collective Nouns

Collective nouns refer to groups of people, animals, or things and are treated as a singular unit. Some examples of collective nouns include the following:

army	audience	band	board	committee	class	faculty
family	flock	group	herd	panel	staff	team

Collective nouns are singular and therefore take singular verbs. In the following examples, the collective noun has been highlighted in bold and the verb has been underlined. Notice that collective nouns are often followed by a prepositional phrase beginning with the word *of*.

Examples

1. The **collection** of gems and minerals at the Natural History Museum <u>is</u> extensive.

2. The **heap** of laundry in my bedroom <u>continues</u> to grow each day.

3. A **fleet** of police cars <u>surrounds</u> the robbers.

Relative Clauses

Relative clauses begin with relative pronouns such as *who, whose, where, when, which,* and *that.* They are often used in incorrect answers to questions testing if you know what a complete sentence is. This is because these words tend to make the verb of the sentence no longer function as a verb in relation to the subject of the sentence. Instead, they weave the verb into a clause that essentially functions like an adjective to describe the noun immediately before the relative pronoun.

Relative clauses help provide additional information such as timing or location. The following examples demonstrate how relative clauses can provide elaboration that builds off of the main idea of a sentence. The relative clauses have been underlined. Notice that the clauses beginning with *which* are framed by commas. This will be addressed further in the chapter on comma usage.

Example 1

Sentence 1$_A$ The teacher is always prepared for class.

Sentence 1$_B$ She is one of the teachers at the school <u>who is always prepared for class</u>.

Sentence 1$_C$ One of the teachers, <u>who is always prepared for class,</u> was surprisingly late today and forgot her book.

Example 2

Sentence 2$_A$ Nachos are delicious.

Sentence 2$_B$ Nachos, <u>which are delicious</u>, should be served regularly in the dining hall.

Sentence 2$_C$ The dining hall regularly serves nachos, <u>which are delicious</u>.

Example 3

Sentence 3$_A$ Professional photographers capture stunning images.

Sentence 3$_B$ Photographers <u>who have telephoto lenses</u> can capture incredible images of birds in flight.

Sentence 3$_C$ Wedding photographers, <u>who capture once-in-a-lifetime moments</u>, must own sophisticated backup equipment.

Using the Relative Pronoun "Which"

On the ACT English test, clauses beginning with *which* are typically framed by commas. This is because a which clause provides a defining property of the noun it modifies. Which clauses can also come at the end of a sentence as is shown in Example 4. Rarely the word *which* may appear at the beginning of a sentence, as shown in Example 5.

Examples

1. Red hair, <u>which is a product of recessive genes</u>, can appear in children whose parents do not have red hair.

2. Jeans, <u>which are pants made of denim or other cotton fabric</u>, are the most comfortable pants.

3. Corgis, <u>which are quite short</u>, were used as cattle herders in the tenth century.

4. I love jeans, <u>which are pants made of denim or other cotton fabric</u>.

5. *Exception:* <u>Which college you attend</u> could have a major impact on your future career.

In Example 5, the phrase "which college you attend" functions like the subject of the verb phrase "could have," and therefore it should not have a comma after it because that would mean separating the subject from the verb with a single comma, which is not allowed.

Which versus That

Questions on the ACT English test often ask you to choose between the words *which* and *that*. The word *which* is the right choice if the information that comes next defines all members of the noun that comes before it. For example, in the previous Example 2, **all** jeans are "made of denim or other cotton fabric." In the following Example 6, the information that follows the word *that* is narrowing the scope of the broader category **jeans.** Acid-washed jeans are a subcategory of the noun *jeans.* In the previous Example 3, all corgis are short; therefore, a *which* clause is appropriate. In the following Example 6, not all dogs are purebreds; therefore, a *that* phrase appropriately narrows the scope of the category **dogs.** Phrases that begin with *that* should typically not be framed by commas.

6.   Jeans <u>that are acid washed</u> are sometimes in style.

7.   Dogs <u>that are purebred</u> are more likely to be adopted.

In order to demonstrate this point, the sentences above have been reproduced with the nonessential information crossed out. Then the sentences have been reproduced with the nonessential information removed.

1.   Red hair, ~~which is a product of recessive genes,~~ can appear in children whose parents do not have red hair.
     Red hair can appear in children whose parents do not have red hair.

2.   Jeans, ~~which are pants made of denim or other cotton fabric,~~ are the most comfortable pants.
     Jeans are the most comfortable pants.

3.   Corgis, ~~which are quite short,~~ were used as cattle herders in the tenth century.
     Corgis were used as cattle herders in the tenth century.

4.   I love jeans, ~~which are pants made of denim or other cotton fabric.~~
     I love jeans.

You should always be able to cut out nonessential information from a sentence by including framing commas around it. This rule also applies to words that function as asides or emphasizers when they occur in the middle of a sentence. Consider the following list of asides and emphasizers. Notice how these words can be removed from sentences 8 and 9 without affecting the meaning of the sentences.

indeed	nevertheless	though
however	for instance	regardless

Examples

8.   It is difficult to be vegetarian at my college. At the largest dining hall on campus, **in fact,** there are rarely meatless entrees.

It is difficult to be vegetarian at my college. At the largest dining hall on campus, ~~in fact,~~ there are rarely meatless entrees.

It is difficult to be vegetarian at my college. At the largest dining hall on campus, there are rarely meatless entrees.

9.   Many tasty alternatives to dairy exist. Cashew milk, **for instance**, is delicious.

Many tasty alternatives to dairy exist. Cashew milk, **~~for instance~~** is delicious.

Many tasty alternatives to dairy exist. Cashew milk is delicious.

4

Chapter 4:
Conventions of Standard English Concepts and Sample Questions: Sentence Structure and Usage

This chapter reviews information about common sentence structures found on the ACT English test. The chapter begins with a review of parallel structure and correlative conjunctions. It examines how relative pronouns, adjectives, adverbs, and prepositional phrases can provide elaborating detail. Several common grammatical errors including sentence fragments, run-ons, and dangling modifiers are also reviewed.

Parallel Structure

Parallelism in writing means that similar grammatical structures are used within one or more sentences. For example, you wouldn't say, "I like drawing, painting, and **to knit**." You would say, "I like drawing, painting, and knitting" or "I like to draw, paint, and knit." Notice that in the first example, the list includes the noun forms of verbs. In the second example, the infinitive forms of each verb are used. Try to keep the part of speech consistent in your writing.

Logical Comparisons

Parallelism also involves comparing like with like. For example, you should compare paintings by one artist to paintings by another artist. You should not compare a painting to a painter, a novel to a novelist, or a building to an architect. When making a comparison, it is important that the two people, places, or things being compared can be logically compared to one another. To correct an illogical comparison without being redundant, you should use the phrases "that of" and "those of." This should make sense if you look at the following correct answers:

WRONG My test score was higher than the valedictorian.

CORRECT My test score was higher than **that of** the valedictorian.

Explanation

This sentence is comparing one person's score to another. It is not appropriate to compare a test score to a person. Therefore, the original sentence contained a grammatical error.

WRONG Pablo Picasso's abstract art is more widely known than Mark Rothko.

CORRECT Pablo Picasso's abstract art is more widely known than **that of** Mark Rothko.

WRONG My short film received more votes than Doug.

CORRECT My short film received more votes than **that of** Doug.

WRONG The call of a cardinal is more widely recognized than a screech owl.

CORRECT The call of a cardinal is more widely recognized than **that of** a screech owl.

WRONG Today's knee surgeons are more skilled in robotics than thirty years ago.

CORRECT Today's knee surgeons are more skilled in robotics than **those of** thirty years ago.

We spent the rest of the morning veering from the trail to investigate small snatches of life. Lizards lazing in the sun and quail <u>rustled</u> through grasses surprised us.
                   12
	12. F. NO CHANGE
	
	  G. rustling
	
	  H. were rustling
	
	  J. DELETE the underlined portion.

The best answer is G because the word *rustling* is parallel in form to *lazing* previously in the sentence. Together, these two words help form the compound subject of the verb *surprised* ("Lizards lazing … and quail rustling … surprised us.").

The best answer is NOT:

F because *rustled* isn't parallel in form to *lazing* previously in the sentence, and this lack of parallelism creates an ungrammatical sentence ("Lizards lazing in the sun and quail rustled through grasses surprised us.").

H because *were rustling* isn't parallel in form to *lazing* previously in the sentence, and this lack of parallelism creates an ungrammatical sentence ("Lizards lazing in the sun and quail were rustling through grasses surprised us.").

J because deleting the underlined portion creates an ungrammatical, nonsensical sentence ("Lizards lazing in the sun and quail through grasses surprised us.").

I know that I could go in there anytime, and someone would look up from playing pinball or folding clothes and <u>nods and smiles</u> at me. 　　　　　　　　　　　　　　　29	**29.** Refer to the underlined portion of the passage at number 29, and choose the alternative you consider best. **A.** NO CHANGE **B.** nod and smile **C.** nodding and smiling **D.** nods to smile

The best answer is B because it is grammatically correct, and the verbs in the sentence are parallel (maintain the same verb tense). The appropriate verbs here are "nod and smile" because they correctly follow the auxiliary (helping) verb *would*: "someone would look up … and [would] nod and smile at me." Although the helping verb *would* is not repeated before "nod and smile," it is implied.

The best answer is NOT:

A because the sentence is ungrammatical. It incorrectly uses the third-person singular verb form ("nods and smiles") after the implied helping verb *would*.

C because the use of the present participle ("nodding and smiling") after the helping verb *would* is ungrammatical. Note also that that sentence lacks parallelism: "someone would look up … and nodding and smiling at me." There is an illogical tense shift from the present tense ("would look") to the present participle ("nodding and smiling").

D because the sentence is ungrammatical. In addition, it results in an illogical statement.

I was sure that girls growing up today would have more up-to-date role models and my generation's favorite sleuth <u>would of been</u> retired to the <u>library's</u>
47
<u>dusty,</u> back rooms.
	47. A. NO CHANGE
	   B. would have been
	   C. would of
	   D. DELETE the underlined portion.

The best answer is B because the context calls for the auxiliary verb *would* to express the presumption expressed by "I was sure" (and to parallel *would have* previously in the sentence) and calls for the present perfect verb *have been retired* in the passive voice to indicate the idea that the "sleuth" received the action of being "retired" to the library's back rooms.

The best answer is NOT:

    A because *would of been* is an improperly formed verb that uses the word *of* instead of *have.*

    C because *would of* is an improperly formed verb that uses the word *of* instead of *have.*

    D because deleting the underlined portion leaves just the simple past tense verb *retired,* which isn't parallel to the other verb in the sentence, *would have.*

The attractions of video games, however, are superficial and short-lived. As you guide your character through the game's challenges, you come to know exactly how the <u>machine that's built</u>
to last will respond to your every move.
50
<u>He or she learns</u> where the hazards lurk and the
51
special weapons are hidden.
	51. A. NO CHANGE
	   B. We learn
	   C. You learn
	   D. People learned

The best answer is C because it maintains the second-person (*you*) perspective that is used throughout this paragraph. Note that the writer is using the second-person point of view in this paragraph to speak directly to and draw in the reader. Consider the sentence preceding this one: "As you guide your character through the game's challenges, you come to know how the machine will respond to your every move."

The best answer is NOT:

    A because it fails to maintain a consistent viewpoint. It makes an illogical shift from the second person (*you*) to the third-person singular (*he* or *she*).

    B because it makes an illogical shift from the second person (*you*) to the first-person plural (*we*).

    D because it not only shifts from second person (*you*) to third person (*people*) but also illogically shifts from present tense (*learn*) to past tense (*learned*).

> When I was a girl in the 1960s, my friends and I loved Nancy Drew. [55] We loved her loyal companions, her bravado, and <u>there was a love for her freedom to do what she wanted.</u>
> ₅₆

56. F. NO CHANGE

G. a love for her freedom to do what she wanted.

H. her freedom to do what she wanted.

J. the freedom to do as one wants.

The best answer is H because "her freedom to do what she wanted" is clear and is parallel with "her loyal companions" and "her bravado," used previously in the sentence to identify two other things the narrator and her friends loved about Nancy Drew.

The best answer is NOT:

F because "there was a love for her freedom to do what she wanted" is not parallel with the two similar structures in the sentence ("her loyal companions," "her bravado") and is awkward, wordy, and redundant with "we loved."

G because "a love for her freedom to do what she wanted" is not parallel with the two similar structures in the sentence ("her loyal companions," "her bravado") and is awkward and redundant with "we loved."

J because "the freedom to do as one wants" is not parallel with the two similar structures in the sentence ("her loyal companions," "her bravado") and because the impersonal and rather formal pronoun one is stilted and out of place in a sentence focused on Nancy Drew's qualities.

> She <u>was able to solve crimes,</u> win golf tournaments,
> ₅₈
> kick bad guys in the shins, and impress her father's distinguished clients. She did it all—and without scuffing her shoes or losing her supportive boyfriend, Ned.

58. F. NO CHANGE

G. was capable of solving crimes,

H. was good at crime solving,

J. solved crimes,

The best answer is F because the phrase "was able to solve crimes" effectively sets up a grammatically parallel list of notable things Nancy Drew was able to do: "solve crimes," "win golf tournaments," "kick bad guys in the shins," and "impress her father's distinguished clients."

The best answer is NOT:

G because the phrase "was capable of solving crimes" doesn't set up a parallel list of notable things Nancy Drew was able to do, because *solving* isn't parallel with *win, kick,* and *impress,* nor is it standard to say that Drew "was capable of … win golf tournaments," and so on.

H because the phrase "was good at crime solving" doesn't set up a parallel list of notable things Nancy Drew was able to do, because *solving* isn't parallel with *win, kick,* and *impress,* nor is it standard to say that Drew "was good at … win golf tournaments," and so on.

J because the phrase "solved crimes" doesn't set up a parallel list of notable things Nancy Drew was able to do, because *solved* isn't parallel with *win, kick,* and *impress.*

Correlative Conjunctions

Correlative conjunctions are sets of words that connect parallel parts of a sentence: nouns with nouns, modifiers with modifiers, and so forth. Table 4.1 provides some of these conjunctions and shows how they're used in sample sentences.

Table 4.1 Conjunctions and Sentence Examples

Correlative Conjunctions	Sentence
both/and	Being left-handed was **both** a blessing **and** a curse.
either/or	Jaime wants to adopt **either** a golden retriever **or** a chocolate lab.
neither/nor	The restaurant called *Surf and Turf* served **neither** seafood **nor** beef.
not/but	I see myself **not** as a lecturer **but** as a facilitator.
not only/but also*	Corey is **not only** brilliant **but also** humble.
more/than	I always bring **more** snacks **than** I could ever eat.
as/as	Brian is **as** tall **as** his dad.
such/that	The Milky Way was **such** an awe-inspiring sight **that** we tried to find it again the next day.
Scarcely/when	Ishaan had **scarcely** made it home **when** his children began asking for dinner.
as many/as	We will admit **as many** people **as** we can until the ride is full.
no sooner/than	**No sooner** had the job been posted **than** Carmen applied.
rather/than	I would **rather** miss a day of work **than** drive in this ice storm.
between/and	It is difficult to decide **between** renting an apartment **and** owning a home.
it was not until/that	**It was not until** she worked on a farm **that** Kathryn committed to becoming a vegetarian.

* note that *also* is not always required

My older sister had gotten married the summer before, so not only did we have a room for Ligia, and we all admitted that the house had seemed too quiet lately.	**11. A.** NO CHANGE **B.** but **C.** while **D.** yet

The best answer is B because it correctly uses the correlative conjunctions *not only* and *but*. Correlative conjunctions connect similar ideas and are always used in pairs. In this sentence, the pair is "not only did we have a room … but … the house had seemed too quiet." The conjunctions *not only* and *but* logically connect the two reasons that the family agreed to host Ligia.

The best answer is NOT:

A because "not only … and" does not logically connect the two reasons, and it is not idiomatic (it does not conform to Standard written English).

C because "not only … while" does not logically connect the two reasons, and it is not idiomatic (it does not conform to Standard written English).

D because "not only … yet" does not logically connect the two reasons, and it is not idiomatic (it does not conform to Standard written English).

With its distinctive red tint and its polar ice caps, the planet Mars has fascinated humans for thousands of years. <u>There were</u> ancient Babylonian

61
astronomers who associated Mars with their war god Negral, to twentieth-century science fiction writers <u>whose works become best-sellers, this</u>

62
planet has often been a symbol of ill will and danger.

61. A. NO CHANGE

   B. When

   C. From

   D. Those

The best answer is C because the preposition *from* effectively sets up the long introductory phrase "From ancient Babylonian astronomers … to twentieth-century science fiction writers" that begins the sentence.

The best answer is NOT:

A because the words *there were* introduce another independent clause into the sentence, resulting in ungrammatical and confusing sentence structure.

B because the subordinating conjunction *when* creates a nonsensical introductory phrase and an ungrammatical sentence.

D because the adjective *those* creates a nonsensical introductory phrase and an ungrammatical sentence.

Pronouns and Antecedents

Pronouns are words that take the place of nouns, proper nouns, and noun phrases such as *he, she, they,* and *it*. Each pronoun should have a clear antecedent, which is the word that the pronoun takes the place of. The antecedent may also be called the referent. Sometimes it can be difficult to identify what word a pronoun is referring back to.

Strategy: A pronoun refers to the noun that is in agreement with and nearest to it, found before the pronoun. Therefore, in most cases, you can look at the noun immediately before the pronoun to determine what the pronoun should be. Still, you should devote some time to considering the logic of the sentence because this strategy does not work every single time.

Example

> The student liked his erasable **pens** because <u>they</u> wrote smoothly and erased completely.

Strategy: Look for the noun that comes before the pronoun *they*. Does the description that follows fit the *pens*? Yes. It is the pens that write smoothly and erase completely. The pronoun *they* refers back to the plural pens.

In a nonfiction passage, after a person is mentioned for the first time, his or her last name is used in each subsequent reference. So, for example, if the first paragraph introduces a doctor named Jada Russell, she would be referred to as Russell throughout the remainder of the passage. Still, feminine pronouns such as *she* and *her* should be used when referring to Jada Russell. For example, the passage might say, "Jada Russell was eighteen years old when <u>she</u> graduated from high school."

Table 4.2 shows pronouns organized by their various functions. It is not important for you to memorize the names of the different types of pronouns, but it is important for you to understand their functions.

Table 4.2 Pronouns and Their Functions

	Subject Pronouns	Object Pronouns	Possessive Adjectives	Possessive Pronouns	Reflexive Pronouns
1st person	I	me	my	mine	myself
2nd person	you	you	your	yours	yourself
3rd person male/female	he/she	him/her	his/her	his/hers	himself/herself
3rd person	it	it	its	N/A	itself
1st person plural	we	us	our	ours	ourselves
2nd person plural	you	you	your	yours	yourselves
3rd person plural	they	them	their	theirs	themselves
Any person or number	who	whom		whose	

Reflexive Pronouns

Reflexive pronouns are used when the subject and object are one in the same. In other words, the doer of the action is also the receiver of the action. Consider this example.

Example 1

You should take care of **yourself** before helping other passengers adjust their oxygen masks.

The subject of the sentence is *you*. The word *yourself* emphasizes that you are the one who is "taking care" of yourself.

Reflexive pronouns are also used in order to emphasize who has completed the action. Sometimes these pronouns are called emphatic or intensive pronouns for that reason.

Example 2

Though the seventh-grade student's father worked for the National Aeronautics and Space Administration (NASA), she assured her teacher that she created her solar-powered car for the science fair entirely by **herself.**

Example 3

She completed the group project by **herself** because she did not trust her classmates.

Example 4

I prefer to cook dinner **myself** instead of going out to a restaurant.

Let's take a look at some real ACT questions that incorporate pronouns.

Establishing her own hair products business, <u>herself</u> in the first decade of the twentieth century, millions of dollars were later bequeathed by Madam C. J. Walker to charities and educational institutions. Among the schools that benefited from this <u>generosity, were</u> those that Mary McLeod Bethune opened and ran in order to provide a better education for Black students.	**26. F.** NO CHANGE **G.** business belonging to her **H.** business, herself, **J.** business

The best answer is J because the word *business* is sufficient, together with the words "her own" previously in the sentence, to indicate that Madam C. J. Walker established her own business.

The best answer is NOT:

F because the intensive pronoun *herself* is awkward and redundant with "her own" and because the comma between the noun *business* and the intensive *herself* is unnecessary and confusing.

G because the phrase "belonging to her" is awkward and redundant with "her own".

H because the intensive pronoun *herself* is awkward and redundant with "her own" and because an intensifier, even when appropriate in a sentence, doesn't need to be set off by commas from the rest of the sentence.

Every year my high school hosts international exchange <u>students, those teenagers</u> join our senior class.
                                  1
	1. A. NO CHANGE
	
	    B. students, he or she is invited to
	
	    C. students who
	
	    D. students they

The best answer is C because it appropriately uses the relative pronoun *who* to introduce the clause that modifies students—"who join our senior class." Besides introducing that clause, the pronoun *who* also functions as the subject of the clause.

The best answer is NOT:

A because it creates a comma splice (two or more complete sentences separated only by a comma). The phrase "those teenagers" is the subject of the second complete sentence.

B because it produces a comma splice. In addition, it creates grammatical disagreement between the plural *students* and the singular *he or she*.

D because it creates a run-on, or fused, sentence. There is no punctuation or conjunction (connecting word) between the two statements.

Glory Foods' president and founder, <u>Bill Williams,</u>
                                           32
explains the unusual slogan by admitting that while he knows that his foods can't beat the taste of real home cooking, <u>it does</u> come very close.
                                    33
	33. A. NO CHANGE
	
	      B. it has
	
	      C. they do
	
	      D. and that they

The best answer is C because the third-person plural pronoun *they* clearly refers back to the plural noun *foods*.

The best answer is NOT:

A because the singular pronoun *it* has no logical antecedent. An antecedent is the word or phrase to which a pronoun refers. In this sentence, the antecedent *foods* is plural and requires a plural pronoun (*they*).

B because *it has* has no logical antecedent.

D because it creates faulty coordination and a confusing statement. The phrase "and that they" does not effectively coordinate with "that while he knows."

Nancy Drew, the teenaged heroine of heaps of 49 young adult mystery novels, is alive and well and 50 still on the job. I know because my niece, Liana, and her friends were reading that all summer long. 51	**51. A.** NO CHANGE **B.** the mysteries **C.** up on that **D.** it over

The best answer is B because the phrase "the mysteries" makes clear that the girls were reading Nancy Drew novels all summer long.

The best answer is NOT:

A because the pronoun *that* has no clear, logical antecedent. Though *that* is obviously intended to refer to the Nancy Drew novels the girls were reading all summer long, *that* is singular and *novels* is plural.

C because the pronoun *that* has no clear, logical antecedent. Though *that* is obviously intended to refer to the Nancy Drew novels the girls were reading all summer long, *that* is singular whereas novels is *plural*. Furthermore, "reading up on that" is an idiomatic phrase but one that doesn't work in this context. To "read up on" something means to learn about a topic, not to read a number of novels for pleasure.

D because "Liana and her friends were reading it over all summer long" is confusing in more than one way. First, we again have to ask what they were reading, because it doesn't logically refer to anything in the preceding sentence. Then "over all summer long" is a redundant phrase, with *over* being an extra, or superfluous, word.

Grandpa is intrigued by the various uses for that remote. He has confided in me that the volume control is perfect for turning up the sound whenever Grandma asks him to take out the garbage. For example, he says, the button 8 that mutes the sound lets him cut them off in 9 midsentence.	**9. A.** NO CHANGE **B.** advertisers **C.** it **D.** its function

The best answer is B because *advertisers* is a specific noun that clearly communicates who Grandpa wants to be able to cut off in midsentence. If you simply chose the word *them*, there would not be a logical referent for the pronoun *them*. To determine if a logical referent exists, look for a plural noun prior to the use of the pronoun *them*. The only plural noun in the sentence is *uses*, and it doesn't make sense to talk about cutting off *uses* for the remote. The noun *grandma*, which also appears in this paragraph, is not plural, and therefore cannot be replaced by the pronoun *them*.

The best answer is NOT:

A because the pronoun *them* does not have a clear antecedent (a noun that it refers to and stands in for). The plural noun that is closest to *them* is "uses for the remote control," which is not logical in context.

C because the pronoun *it* seems to refer back to the noun *sound*, but that is nonsensical. How do you "cut sound off in midsentence"?

D because the possessive pronoun *its* might refer back to the noun *sound* or to the noun *button*, but both of those would be nonsensical. "The button that mutes the sound lets him cut the button's function off in midsentence" doesn't make sense.

Sentence Fragments

A sentence fragment is an incomplete sentence. Often relative pronouns, subordinating conjunctions, and participial phrases create sentence fragments because they use a word that could function as a verb but instead use it as a different part of speech such as an adjective in the form of a participial phrase. For example, the phrase "**following** a specific process of chemical bonding" functions like an adjective in the following sentence: Snowflakes form from tiny water droplets, **following** a specific process of chemical bonding as they freeze.

Below you will find several examples of sentence fragments. Students often have trouble identifying that these types of fragments are not sentences because the examples do each contain a subject and a word that can function like a verb given the appropriate context.

Examples

1. Students who love to read

2. Students who would prefer to watch a film

3. Because we already booked the flight

4. Such as knitting, crocheting, and sewing

5. Creating a perfect storm

6. Which is the reason I no longer participate in holiday gift swaps

The incorrect answers for the following question create sentence fragments.

I can recall students from Costa Rica, Italy, Norway, and Nigeria. Last year, one of our school's exchange <u>students being</u> Ligia Antolinez, <u>who came</u> from Bucaramanga, Colombia.	**2.** **F.** NO CHANGE **G.** students was **H.** students, named **J.** students,

The best answer is G because it provides the predicate *was,* which produces a complete sentence. Remember that a statement that has no predicate verb is a sentence fragment (an incomplete sentence).

The best answer is NOT:

F because it uses the verb form *being,* which is a participle. Because it is a verb form, a participle is often mistaken for the main verb in a sentence. This statement has no predicate, so it is a sentence fragment.

H because it has no predicate verb. Without a predicate, the statement is a sentence fragment and does not express a complete thought.

J because it lacks a verb and therefore creates another sentence fragment.

Some ACT English test questions offer only one answer choice that creates a grammatically correct and complete sentence. Take this next question for example.

Usually a crowd of thirteen-year-old <u>kids that is</u> ₂₇ gathered around the video machines, regardless of the time of day.	**27. A.** NO CHANGE **B.** kids who **C.** kids, and they **D.** kids

The best answer is D because it results in a complete sentence. The complete subject of the sentence is "a crowd of thirteen-year-old kids." The predicate *is* immediately follows this subject.

The best answer is NOT:

A because it creates an incomplete sentence. It improperly inserts the pronoun *that* between the subject and predicate, which results in a sentence fragment.

B because it creates an incomplete sentence. It inserts the relative pronoun *who* between the subject and the predicate and creates a sentence fragment. The verb *is* no longer functions as a verb in this context.

C because the use of the comma and the conjunction *and* generally indicates that the sentence contains two independent clauses, but in this case, there is only one independent clause. "Usually a crowd of thirteen-year old kids" is a phrase, not a clause, because it has no verb. Meanwhile, in the main clause, the predicate *is* disagrees in number with the subject *they.*

Recent reports suggest that the cost of a human voyage to Mars could run as high as 100 billion dollars. This is a startling number, especially in light of the fact that the International Space Station, the most ambitious NASA project <u>yet,</u> ₆₇ carried a projected price tag of "only" 17 billion dollars. In the end, NASA overspent on the International Space Station. 68 One can only imagine if the final price of a human voyage to Mars would be. ₆₉	**69. A.** NO CHANGE **B.** what **C.** how **D.** DELETE the underlined portion.

The best answer is B because *what* is the logical introductory word in the noun clause functioning as the direct object of the verb *imagine,* resulting in "what the final price of a human voyage to Mars would be."

Strategy: Turning this clause around reinforces the idea that *what* is the best answer: "The final price of a human voyage to Mars would be *what*?"

The best answer is NOT:

A because *if* is an illogical introductory word in the noun clause functioning as the direct object of the verb *imagine.*

C because *how* is an illogical introductory word in the noun clause functioning as the direct object of the verb *imagine.* Turning the clause around makes this clear: "The final price of a human voyage to Mars would be *how*?"

D because deleting the underlined portion results in an illogical, incomplete-sounding sentence: "One can only imagine the final price of a human voyage to Mars would be."

Architect Eero Saarinen, <u>who created</u> the design that symbolized the memorial's theme of St. Louis as the "Gateway to the West." ₂₃	**23. F.** NO CHANGE **G.** Saarinen, creator of **H.** Saarinen created **J.** Saarinen creating

The best answer is H because it is the only choice that makes this a complete sentence.

The best answer is NOT:

F because it creates a sentence fragment—a noun phrase ("Architect Eero Saarinen") and a dependent clause that modifies the noun phrase ("who created the design that symbolized the memorial's theme").

G because it creates a sentence fragment—a noun phrase ("Architect Eero Saarinen") and an appositive phrase that renames the noun phrase ("creator of the design that symbolized the memorial's theme").

J because it creates a sentence fragment—a noun phrase ("Architect Eero Saarinen") and a participial phrase modifying the noun phrase ("creating the design that symbolized the memorial's theme").

Being

The word ***being*** is almost always wrong in ACT English test questions because it often creates a sentence fragment. Typically, the word *being* can be replaced with a clearer word choice. It is often best replaced with *because,* a comma, an appositive phrase, a colon, or a simple present or past tense form of the verb *to be* such as *is* or *was*. Sometimes choosing the word *being* rather than *is* or *was* leads a sentence to not have a verb. That is the case in the next sample question.

Evidence that some software writers have played up the medical <u>analogy being</u> found in the names 68 of their <u>programs</u>: Vaccine, Checkup, Antitoxin, and 69 Disinfectant.	**68. F.** NO CHANGE **G.** analogy is **H.** analogy, having been **J.** analogy,

The best answer is G because it provides a predicate verb ("is found") for the main clause of this sentence. ("Evidence … is found in the names of their programs.")

The best answer is NOT:

F because it creates an incomplete sentence, a fragment. The participle "being found" cannot function as the predicate verb of the main clause of this sentence.

H because it creates a fragment; the participle "having been found" cannot function as a predicate verb.

J because, in this case, the verb form *found* reads as if it were a past participle, not a predicate verb. This too is a sentence fragment because it lacks a predicate for the sentence's main clause.

Who versus Whom

The ACT English test often assesses if students know the difference between when to use *who* and *whom*. As a general rule, *who* and *whoever* function as the subject of the sentence. This means that they refer to the person doing the action (verb) of the sentence. *Whom* or *whomever* typically function as direct objects, which means they are the receiver of the verb. To determine the direct object, ask yourself, what or whom is affected by the subject's action. *Whom* and *whomever* can also function as indirect objects or as the objects of prepositions. Indirect objects are the receivers of the direct object. For example, in the following sentence *pie* is the direct object and *me* is the indirect object.

Grandma <u>passed</u> me the pie.

You can determine the direct object by asking yourself "What did Grandma pass?" You can determine the indirect object by asking yourself "To whom did Grandma pass the pie?" Looking at several examples will help these concepts make more sense. Below the verbs have been underlined.

Example A:	**Who** Subject	<u>threw</u>	the water balloon? direct object	
Example B:	**Who** Subject	<u>ran</u>	the mile direct object	the fastest?

Example C: Studies show that one of the most important factors in children's math education is the educational background of the instructor **who** teaches them.

Example D: Frederick Douglass was a former slave **who**, after years of studying in secrecy, became a famous orator in support of the abolitionist movement.

Notice here that the nonessential clause that is framed by commas can be cut out of the sentence in order to clearly see that *who* is followed by a verb.

Example E:	To **whom**	<u>did</u>	you	<u>give</u>	the gift?
	Indirect object	Helping verb	subject		direct object

Example F: The trophy goes to **whomever** wins the most points at Field Day.

Example G: For **whom** did you bake these cookies?

In this case, whom is the object of the preposition *for*.

Example H: Cassie has a soccer coach **whom** she dislikes because he is always yelling.

Strategy: A strategy for choosing between *who* and *whom* is to replace the word in question with *he* or *him* to see which sounds better.

Who is like *he* because both typically function as the subject of a sentence.

Whom is like *him* because both typically function as the direct object of a sentence.

Who and *whoever* typically come before an action verb or after linking verbs such as *is* or *appears*. See the glossary for a more complete list of linking verbs, also known as state-of-being verbs.

Whom and *whomever* typically come after a preposition such as *to, for, from, of,* or *with*.

Let's take a look at one of our examples to test this strategy.

Who threw the water balloon? **He** threw the water balloon. OR **Him** threw the water balloon.

Which sounds better? "He threw the water balloon" should sound better. It also fits the general pattern of *who* coming before a verb.

Exceptions

The phrases "some of whom," "most of whom," "all of whom," and "both of whom" break the general rule that *whom* should not come directly before a verb. Each of the following sentences is grammatically correct. Notice that a verb follows *whom* in these sentences.

1. Redheads, <u>some of whom</u> are pale, make up less than 1 percent of the population.

2. Albinos, <u>all of whom</u> are pale, make up less than 1 percent of the population.

3. I know a set of twins, <u>both of whom</u> dislike dressing alike.

Who's and Whose

Who's is the contraction of *who is*. **Whose** is the possessive form of *who*.

Examples

Who's to say why the college suddenly became so popular?

Who's to blame for the mess in the kitchen?

Who's picking up the pizza?

Who's responsible for paying for the heat?

Whose responsibility is it to pay for the heat?

Whose gray fleece is this?

The Songbird Forest Reserve is a region in Brazil **whose** flora and fauna support the rarest living bird: the Stresemann's Bristlefront.

Note: *Whose* can be used to describe nouns that are not people.

The following table provides a helpful guide to knowing when to use *who*, *whom*, and *whose*.

	Subject Pronouns	Object Pronouns	Possessive Adjectives	Contraction
3rd person male/female	he/she	him/her	his/her	he's = he is she's = she is
	who	whom	whose	who's = who is

Let's take a look at some real ACT questions that draw on these concepts.

Every year my high school hosts international exchange <u>students, those teenagers</u> join our senior class. 　　　　　　　　　　　　1	1. **A.** NO CHANGE **B.** students, he or she is invited to **C.** students who **D.** students they

The best answer is C because it appropriately uses the relative pronoun *who* to introduce the clause that modifies *students*—"who join our senior class." Besides introducing that clause, the pronoun *who* also functions as the subject of the clause.

The best answer is NOT:

A because it creates a comma splice (two or more complete sentences separated only by a comma). The phrase "those teenagers" is the subject of the second complete sentence.

B because it produces a comma splice. In addition, it creates grammatical disagreement between the plural *students* and the singular *he or she*.

D because it creates a run-on, or fused, sentence. There is no punctuation or conjunction (connecting word) between the two statements.

I can recall students from Costa Rica, Italy, Norway, and Nigeria. Last year, one of our school's exchange <u>students being</u> Ligia Antolinez, <u>who</u> came ₂ ₃ from Bucaramanga, Colombia.	**3.** **A.** NO CHANGE **B.** whom **C.** which **D.** she who

The best answer is A because it correctly uses the pronoun *who* to introduce the clause that describes Ligia Antolinez. In this sentence, *who* is required because it refers to a person. The pronoun *who* is also appropriate because it functions as the subject of the clause.

The best answer is NOT:

B because it uses the object pronoun *whom* instead of the subject pronoun *who*.

C because it uses the pronoun *which* when the personal pronoun *who* is required. In general, *who* refers to people and *which* refers to objects, events, or animals.

D because it inserts an unnecessary pronoun, *she*. Because *who* is the subject of the descriptive clause, the pronoun *she* has no function in this sentence.

Run-on, or Fused, Sentences

A run-on sentence means that two complete sentences have no proper punctuation separating them. These are also called fused sentences.

Examples

WRONG The bird of paradise lives primarily in New Guinea it performs an elaborate mating dance to attract a partner.

CORRECT The bird of paradise lives primarily in New Guinea. It performs an elaborate mating dance to attract a partner.

CORRECT The bird of paradise, which performs an elaborate mating dance to attract a partner, lives primarily in New Guinea.

My grandfather is not known for embracing technological <u>change. He still drives</u> his '59 Chevy Impala. 76	**76. A.** NO CHANGE **B.** change he still drives **C.** change still driving, **D.** change, and still driving

The best answer is A because it provides punctuation (in this case, a period) that appropriately separates these two complete thoughts or statements: "My grandfather is not known for embracing technological change" and "He still drives his '59 Chevy Impala."

The best answer is NOT:

B because it creates a run-on, or fused sentence. There is no punctuation or conjunction (connecting word) between the two statements.

C because the phrase "still driving his '59 Chevy Impala" is not a complete statement (because there is no stated subject). It could work in this sentence if it were set off from the main clause with a comma. It would then modify "My grandfather," the subject of the main clause, but this answer doesn't provide that punctuation.

D because the conjunction and that connects the phrase "still driving his '59 Chevy Impala" to the main clause creates confusion by linking groups of words that are not grammatically parallel.

They don't need to be reminded that girls can be <u>successful they know</u> that. 59	**59. A.** NO CHANGE **B.** successful they already know **C.** successful; they know **D.** successful, knowing

The best answer is C because the semicolon after the word *successful* is appropriately used to divide this sentence into two closely related independent clauses.

The best answer is NOT:

A because the lack of appropriate punctuation and/or a conjunction between the words *successful* and *they* creates a fused sentence.

B because the lack of appropriate punctuation and/or a conjunction between the words *successful* and *they* creates a fused sentence.

D because *successful, knowing* creates a confusing, possibly redundant sentence, as it's not clear who knows what.

Modifiers

Modifiers such as adjectives, participial phrases, and adverbs provide further information and/or clarifying details.

Adjectives

Adjectives are modifiers that describe nouns. Most questions regarding adjectives on the ACT English test assess whether you know that a comma should not separate an adjective from the noun it modifies. Other adjective questions check to see if you know when to use adjectives and when to use adverbs.

Examples

1. Today I <u>wore</u> my **purple cashmere** sweater.

2. Yesterday I <u>wore</u> a **black leather** jacket.

3. In cold weather, I <u>wear</u> **two** layers.

4. In the winter, the mountain <u>is</u> covered with **beautiful white** snow.

5. It <u>was</u> a **cold, gloomy** day.

6. The blobfish's **pink, gelatinous** flesh <u>allows</u> it to easily float.

If two successive adjectives come before a noun, you may be asked to decide if a comma should separate the two adjectives.

Strategy: Read the sentence, stating the two adjectives with the word *and* in between them. If this sounds good, then you *should* have a comma between the two adjectives. When a comma or the word *and* can be placed between two adjectives, those are known as **coordinate adjectives.** Coordinate adjectives have equal weight and modify the same noun. Another strategy is to reverse the order of the adjectives. Coordinate adjectives are interchangeable because they have equal weight. **Cumulative adjectives** sound awkward when the word *and* appears between them. Their order cannot be reversed.

Example 1: Coordinate Adjectives

CORRECT It was a cold, gloomy day.

CORRECT It was a cold and gloomy day.

CORRECT It was a gloomy and cold day.

Example 2: Cumulative Adjectives

CORRECT Today I wore my **purple cashmere** sweater.

WRONG Today I wore my **purple, cashmere** sweater.

WRONG Today I wore my **purple and cashmere** sweater.

"Today I wore my purple and cashmere sweater" sounds awkward. Therefore, you should not place a comma between *purple* and *cashmere*. Likewise, it sounds awkward if you reverse the order of the adjectives. "Today I wore my cashmere purple sweater" does not sound quite right. The correct sentence should be "Today I wore my purple cashmere sweater." Most students can hear that it is awkward when cumulative adjectives are reversed.

Here is a question that tests this concept.

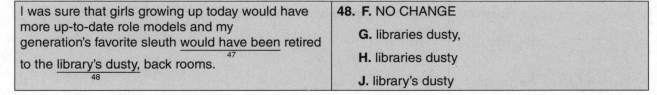

I was sure that girls growing up today would have more up-to-date role models and my generation's favorite sleuth <u>would have been</u> retired ₄₇ to the <u>library's dusty,</u> back rooms. ₄₈	**48. F.** NO CHANGE **G.** libraries dusty, **H.** libraries dusty **J.** library's dusty

The best answer is J because the possessive form of the word *library* (*library's*) is needed to indicate "the dusty back rooms of the library" and because no comma is needed between the words *dusty* and *back*. The phrase "back rooms" functions as a single unit (a compound noun) and *dusty* and *back* aren't coordinate adjectives. If you insert *and* between *dusty* and *back*, it sounds awkward, which can help you realize that these are not coordinate adjectives.

The best answer is NOT:

F because the comma between *dusty* and *back* is unnecessary because "back rooms" functions as a single unit (a compound noun) and *dusty* and *back* aren't coordinate adjectives. (You couldn't say "the library's dusty and back rooms," for example.)

G because the plural form *libraries* is incorrectly used in place of the possessive form *library's* and because the comma between *dusty* and *back* is unnecessary because "back rooms" functions as a single unit (a compound noun) and *dusty* and *back* aren't coordinate adjectives.

H because the plural form *libraries* is incorrectly used in place of the possessive form *library's*.

Did you know that you are supposed to list adjectives in a certain order? Table 4.3 lists the correct order.

Table 4.3 Types of Adjectives

Type of Adjective	Examples
quantity	one, twenty, many, few, all
opinion	beautiful, quaint, interesting, itchy, confusing
size	giant, small, diminutive
age	old, new, ancient, young, youthful
shape	circular, rectangular, square, curved
color	red, orange, maroon, black
nationality/origin	Thai, Chinese, Italian
material	velvet, plastic, gold
purpose	dessert spoon, yoga pants, coin purse

Comparative and Superlative Adjectives

Comparative adjectives are used when comparing two things; they often end in *-er*. Superlative adjectives are used when comparing three or more things; they often end in *-est*.

Comparative Examples

1. Simone de Beauvoir scored <u>better</u> than Paul Nizan on the philosophy exam at École Normale, which was impressive considering it was her first attempt to pass.

2. I am <u>older</u> than my brother.

Superlative Examples

1. Jean-Paul Sartre performed <u>the best</u> on the philosophy exam at École Normale.

2. James Madison was the <u>shortest</u> president, standing 5 feet and 4 inches tall.

3. Simone de Beauvoir was the <u>youngest</u> student to pass the philosophy exam at École Normale.

The following table provides examples of comparative and superlative adjectives.

Table 4.4 Comparative versus Superlative Adjectives

Comparative	Superlative
clearer	clearest
worse	worst
more popular	most popular
farther	farthest
fewer	fewest
less	the least

Note: The word *fewer* is used with countable nouns, and the word *less* is used with uncountable nouns. Similarly, the word *many* is used for countable nouns, and the word *much* is used for uncountable nouns.

An **adjective of quantity** is used when what is being quantified cannot be counted. For example, at an ice cream shop, you might be asked, "How **much** chocolate sauce do you want?" <u>Chocolate sauce</u> is not a countable noun, and therefore an adjective of quantity must be used. Alternately, <u>pumps of chocolate sauce</u> can be counted, so you might be asked, "How **many** pumps of chocolate sauce do you want? Countable nouns take an **adjective of number** (many) and uncountable nouns take an adjective of quantity (much). Similarly, the word *fewer* refers to countable nouns, as in "She has fewer cookies than I do." The word *less* can be used with uncountable nouns, as in "She has less cookie dough than I do."

Table 4.5 shows several examples of countable and uncountable nouns.

Table 4.5 Countable versus Uncountable Nouns

Countable	Uncountable
fewer	less
many	much
dollars	money
research papers	research
sugar packets	sugar
scoops of ice cream	ice cream

Here are several examples of these nouns in the context of a sentence.

Examples

1. Writing skills are relevant in **many** <u>professions</u>.

2. How **many** <u>hours</u> did you spend writing this paper?

3. How **much** <u>effort</u> did you put into this essay?

4. I didn't eat that **much** <u>ice cream</u> at the party.

5. I ordered **fewer** <u>boxes of cookies</u> than my sister did.

6. I have **less** <u>cookie dough</u> than I need for five dozen cookies.

Note: *Than* is used for comparison. *Then* is used to refer to sequence.

Let's look at some real ACT English test questions that address these rules about adjectives.

This laundromat has three soda machines, two candy machines, two pinball machines, five video machines, and a machine that eats dollar bills and spits out too <u>much or too few</u> quarters.
25
	25. **A.** NO CHANGE
	
	  B. many or too fewer
	
	  C. many or too few
	
	  D. much or few

The best answer is C because it provides the correct adjectives *(many, few)* to describe the quarters. The phrase "too many or too few quarters" describes a relationship of number.

The best answer is NOT:

  A because it is ungrammatical. It incorrectly uses an adjective of quantity *(much)* when an adjective of number *(many)* is required.

B because it incorrectly adds the modifier *too* to the comparative adjective *fewer*.

D because it is ungrammatical. It incorrectly uses an adjective of quantity (*much*) when an adjective of number (*many*) is required.

Nouns Functioning Like Adjectives

In some cases, a noun can function like an adjective. In most of these cases, the noun is a job and the noun being modified is a proper noun. When this happens, the noun should not be separated from the proper noun that it modifies with a comma. Notice that the following examples do not include a comma.

Examples

1.   *Singer* **Ella Fitzgerald** sold millions of albums.

2.   *Immigrant* **Albert Einstein** made valuable contributions to the field of physics.

3.   *Twenty-five-year-old* **Elizabeth Cady Stanton** omitted the word *obey* from her wedding vows.

By contrast, if the proper noun comes second, a comma is needed. Notice that in these cases articles such as *a, an,* and *the* are typically used.

Examples

1.   **Ella Fitzgerald,** a famous jazz singer, sold millions of albums.

2.   **Albert Einstein,** an immigrant from Germany, made valuable contributions to the field of physics.

3.   **Elizabeth Cady Stanton,** a twenty-five-year-old bride and women's rights activist, omitted the word *obey* from her wedding vows.

My family is part of the Miami <u>tribe a Native American people,</u> with strong ties to territory in present-day Ohio, Indiana, and Illinois.	**1.** **A.** NO CHANGE **B.** tribe, a Native American, people **C.** tribe, a Native American people **D.** tribe; a Native American people

The best answer is C because the comma after *tribe* sets off what follows as a nonrestrictive appositive that describes what "the Miami tribe" is: "a Native American people with strong ties to territory in present-day Ohio, Indiana, and Illinois."

The best answer is NOT:

A because it is missing the comma needed after *tribe* to set off the following nonrestrictive appositive from the noun *tribe* and because it places an unnecessary and confusing comma between the noun *people* and the series of prepositional phrases starting with "with strong ties" that follows and describes people.

B because it pointlessly separates with a comma the adjective *Native American* from the noun *people.*

D because it misuses the semicolon. The semicolon inappropriately implies that what will follow is an independent clause, as in "My family is part of the Miami tribe; we are a Native American people...."

Participial Phrases

A **participial phrase** is a phrase that typically begins with a word ending in *-ing* on *-ed*. It functions like an adjective to describe the noun immediately before it. Notice how "powering lights across town" elaborates on the solar panels, which is the noun right before the participial phrase in the following example.

Example

The town has installed many solar panels, <u>powering lights across the town.</u>

Let's take a look at a question that incorporates a participial phrase. Notice that what comes before the participial phrase is a complete sentence. Notice that the *-ing* word comes immediately after a comma. This is a common correct sentence structure on the ACT English test and in mature writing in general.

<u>The United States has competed with other countries to explore space.</u> By 2003, the National Aeronautics and Space Administration (NASA) <u>would of sent</u> thirty spacecraft to the red planet, ₆₄ <u>speculation has been prompted</u> that a human voyage may no longer be the stuff of fiction.	**65. A.** NO CHANGE **B.** to which speculation has prompted **C.** prompting speculation **D.** which is speculation

The best answer is C because the participial phrase "prompting speculation" modifies in a clear way the preceding clause: by sending thirty spacecraft to Mars by 2003, NASA had led people to think seriously about the possibility of a human mission to Mars.

The best answer is NOT:

A because the subject *speculation* and the verb *has been prompted* begin a second independent clause joined to the first by only the comma after the word *planet,* creating a comma splice.

B because the words "to which speculation has prompted" create a confusing and ungrammatical construction, partly because "speculation has prompted" isn't a conventional, idiomatic expression and partly because the pronoun *which* has no logical antecedent.

D because the words "which is speculation" create a confusing construction because the pronoun *which* has no logical antecedent.

Adverbs

Adverbs provide information about location, timing, reason, manner, and extent. You have likely been taught that adverbs modify verbs, but did you know that they can also modify adjectives and other adverbs? Adverbs often end in *-ly*. Consider the following examples.

Examples

1.   Bring the laundry **downstairs.**

2.   Recycling bins have been **strategical**ly placed throughout the stadium.

3.   I take a vitamin **daily.**

4.   You need to finish your three essays **in two hours.**

5.   The substitute teacher shouted **loudly** when the students did not follow directions.

6.   The horses waited **patiently** to be fed apples.

7.   I **quickly** smelled that the gas stove was left on.

8.   I **always** look both ways before crossing the street.

Remember that linking verbs are modified by **adjectives** not adverbs.

appear	feel	stay	smell	taste
become	remain	seem	sound	turn

Examples

9.   The horses' stalls smell **bad** before they are cleaned.

10.   The dahlias look **beautiful**.

11.   I felt **sad** when I learned that this would be the **final** season of my favorite television show.

12.   It soon became **clear** that the defendant was guilty.

Note: The words *smell* and *look* are examples of verbs that can function as action verbs or linking verbs depending on the context. See Examples 7–10.

The following question tests if you know when to use an adjective and when to use an adverb.

But no one is ever around to enforce the threats, and in the summer everyone enjoys the benches, the grass, and the <u>coolly magnificence</u> of the shade trees. 19	**19. A.** NO CHANGE **B.** cool magnificence **C.** magnificently cool **D.** cool magnificent

The best answer is B because it is grammatically correct. In this sentence, *cool* is used as an adjective to modify the noun *magnificence*.

The best answer is NOT:

> **A** because *coolly* is an adverb, and an adverb cannot be used to modify a noun. (Adverbs generally modify verbs or adjectives.)

> **C** because it uses an adjective phrase—"magnificently cool"—where a noun is required. The complete phrase "The magnificently cool of the shade trees" is both ungrammatical and confusing.

> **D** because it uses an adjective phrase—"cool magnificent"—where a noun is called for. The phrase "the cool magnificent of the shade trees" is ungrammatical.

No matter how many games you play on any pinball machine, <u>the various times of each</u> game 58 is different. That's what makes pinball a <u>continually</u> challenge. 59	**59. A.** NO CHANGE **B.** continuously **C.** continual **D.** continue

The best answer is C because it provides an adjective (*continual*) for the noun that it precedes (*challenge*).

The best answer is NOT:

> **A** because the adverb *continually* lacks a neighboring sentence element that it can modify (a verb or an adjective).

> **B** because the adverb *continuously* faces the same problem of lacking something to modify.

> **D** because the verb form *continue* is simply out of place here between the article *a* and the noun *challenge*.

The interplanetary travel film that he created, *A Trip to the Moon,* had production costs of $4,000, <u>highly excessively</u> for its time. In this film, a space capsule 38 <u>that is fired and thereby launched and projected</u> 39 from a cannon lands in the eye of the Man in the Moon.	**38. F.** NO CHANGE **G.** exceeding highly **H.** high excessively **J.** exceedingly high

The best answer is J because the phrase "exceedingly high" appropriately uses the adverb *exceedingly* in front of the adjective it modifies, *high,* which in turn modifies the noun *costs.*

The best answer is NOT:

F because an adjective is needed to modify the noun *costs,* whereas the phrase "highly excessively" consists of two adverbs.

G because an adjective is needed to modify the noun *costs,* whereas the phrase "exceeding highly" consists of a participle and an adverb.

H because the phrase "high excessively" reverses conventional word order.

Misplaced Modifier

A **dangling modifier** occurs when a modifier is not appropriately placed or when the noun being modified is not logical. This can be fixed by changing the order of the sentence or by making sure that the noun being modified comes immediately before or after the modifier. In the following examples, the modifier has been underlined and the noun being modified is bolded. Often, correcting this kind of error requires using the passive voice, meaning that the noun that is doing the verb is not the subject of the sentence. Remember that passive voice often includes the word *by.*

Examples

WRONG <u>Made from walnuts and mushrooms</u>, my father served the **veggie burgers.**

CORRECT <u>Made from walnuts and mushrooms</u>, **the veggie burgers** were served by my father.

WRONG <u>Featuring stunning photographs</u>, **the website**'s user was impressed.

CORRECT <u>Featuring stunning photographs</u>, **the website** was impressive.

The second half of my junior year was anything but quiet. <u>Introduced by me to my favorite music, at top volume, I started being taught by Ligia the most popular Colombian dance steps.</u> 12	**12. F.** NO CHANGE **G.** Introducing Ligia to my favorite music, at top volume, she started teaching me the most popular Colombian dance steps. **H.** Teaching me the most popular Colombian dance steps, Ligia was introduced by me to my favorite music, at top volume. **J.** I introduced Ligia to my favorite music, at top volume, and she started teaching me the most popular Colombian dance steps.

The best answer is J because it is the clearest and most logical, and it is the most structurally sound. The two clauses in this sentence are parallel and logically follow one another. The second clause, "she started teaching me … dance steps," logically follows "I introduced Ligia to my favorite music."

The best answer is NOT:

F because using the passive voice ("I started being taught by Ligia") makes the sentence confusing. It is difficult for the reader to tell what the subject and object of this sentence are. The arrangement of the sentence elements is also confusing and garbled.

G because it has an incorrect modifier. When a modifying phrase containing a verb comes at the beginning of a sentence, the phrase is followed by a comma. The word that the phrase modifies should immediately follow the comma. In this case, the modifying phrase "Introducing Ligia to my favorite music, at top volume," is followed by the pronoun *she,* instead of the pronoun *I* (to refer to the narrator).

H because the modifying word after the introductory phrase is correct, but the rest of the sentence is weak because it relies on the passive voice ("was introduced by me"). In addition, the phrase at the end of the sentence, "at top volume," is misplaced.

Establishing her own hair products <u>business, herself in the first decade of the twentieth century,</u> 26 <u>millions of dollars were later bequeathed by Madam C. J. Walker</u> to charities and educational institutions. Among the schools that benefited from 27 this <u>generosity, were</u> those that Mary McLeod 28 Bethune opened and ran in order to provide a better education for Black students.	**27. A.** NO CHANGE **B.** Madam C. J. Walker later bequeathed millions of dollars to charities and educational institutions. **C.** charities and educational institutions later received millions of dollars from Madam C. J. Walker. **D.** millions of dollars were later bequeathed to charities and educational institutions by Madam C. J. Walker.

The best answer is B because this sentence structure makes "Madam C. J. Walker" the subject of the sentence, which is necessary in order to have the introductory participial phrase "establishing her own hair products business in the first decade of the twentieth century" refer clearly to Walker.

The best answer is NOT:

    A because this sentence structure makes the introductory participial phrase a dangling modifier that refers to "millions of dollars," which doesn't make sense.

    C because this sentence structure makes the introductory participial phrase a dangling modifier that refers to "charities and educational institutions," which doesn't make sense.

    D because this sentence structure makes the introductory participial phrase a dangling modifier that refers to "millions of dollars," which doesn't make sense.

Imagining all these people, it is that I know they remain there even after I have left.
28
	28. F. NO CHANGE
	
	  G. It being that I imagine all these people, they
	
	  H. Imagining all these people, they
	
	  J. I imagine that all these people

The best answer is J because it is clear, concise, and structurally sound. It clearly expresses the idea that it is the writer who is imagining.

The best answer is NOT:

    F because it has an ineffective sentence structure that results in a dangling modifier. When a modifying phrase containing a verb comes at the beginning of a sentence, the phrase is followed by a comma ("Imagining all these people,"). Following the comma is the word that this phrase modifies. Notice in this sentence that the pronoun *it* incorrectly follows the introductory phrase. The modifying word should be the pronoun *I*.

    G because it creates a confusing and unclear statement. In the clause "It being that I imagine all these people," the reader does not know to what the pronoun *It* refers.

    H because it has a dangling modifier. The pronoun *I* should follow the introductory clause, not the pronoun *they*, because *I* should be the subject of "imagining all these people."

Even as a child, Williams loved to prepare food, and as a young adult, he refined his cooking skills
34
at the prestigiously acclaimed Culinary Institute of America.
35
	34. F. NO CHANGE
	
	  G. his cooking skills were refined
	
	  H. his skill in cooking was refined
	
	  J. the refinement of his cooking skills occurred

The best answer is F because it provides the clearest, most concise statement, and it uses modifiers correctly. Note that the pronoun *he* directly follows and correctly modifies the adjective phrase "as a young adult."

The best answer is NOT:

    G because it creates a dangling modifier. The phrase "as a young adult" does not logically refer to or modify the noun phrase it precedes ("his cooking skills"). This arrangement of sentence elements results in a confusing statement.

H because although the wording is somewhat different, the problem creates a dangling modifier. Here, "his skill" is not "a young adult."

J because the choice creates a dangling modifier. In this statement, "the refinement of his cooking skills" is not "a young adult."

In 1989, he came up with his idea for a line of Southern-inspired cuisine,₃₆ a time when there were no convenience foods designed for African American consumers.	**36. F.** NO CHANGE
	
	   G. He came up with his idea for a line of Southern-inspired cuisine in 1989,
	
	   H. He came up in 1989, with his idea for a line of Southern-inspired cuisine,
	
	   J. The idea came to him in 1989, that a line of Southern-inspired cuisine should be marketed,

The best answer is G because the sentence parts are arranged in a logical order so that they modify the appropriate elements. This results in the clearest word order for this sentence. Because what comes after the underlined portion describes "a time," the noun that comes immediately before it needs to be a time word such as 1989.

The best answer is NOT:

F because the clauses are put together in a way that confuses the reader. The noun phrase "a line of Southern-inspired cuisine" doesn't connect logically with the noun and the clause that immediately follows it: "a time when there were no convenience foods designed for African American consumers."

H because it is ambiguous. It is unclear what is meant by the opening clause "He came up in 1989."

J because it strings clauses together in a confusing way.

In a strange terrain filled with hostile creatures,₄₀ the space travelers experience many adventures. They escape back to Earth in the capsule by falling off the edge of the moon, landing₄₁ in the ocean, they bob around until a passing ship finally rescues them.	**41. A.** NO CHANGE
	
	   B. moon after landing
	
	   C. moon. Landing
	
	   D. moon, after landing

The best answer is C because for clarity this sequence of events should be divided into two sentences, the first indicating that the travelers fall off the edge of the moon to escape and the second establishing that the travelers land in the ocean and are eventually rescued.

The best answer is NOT:

A because using only a comma after the word *moon* to join two independent clauses creates a comma splice. (Alternatively, it's possible to see the error here as a comma splice created by the comma after the word *ocean*.)

B because the phrase "moon after landing" creates a fused sentence. (Alternatively, it's possible to see the error here as a comma splice created by the comma after the word *ocean,* with the sentence then suggesting illogically that the space travelers fell off the edge of the moon after landing in the ocean.)

D because using only a comma after the word *moon* to join two independent clauses creates a comma splice. (Alternatively, it's possible to see the error here as a comma splice created by the comma after the word *ocean.*)

As for the programming function, Grandpa not only uses it for the news but also for playing jokes on his youngest grandchildren. Explaining to the unsuspecting child that he has a remote control implanted in his little finger, <u>Grandpa points</u> his finger at the TV and, to the child's amazement, seemingly turns it on.	**12.** Refer to the underlined portion of the passage at number 12, and choose the alternative you consider best. **F.** NO CHANGE **G.** pointing **H.** having pointed **J.** Grandpa has pointed

The best answer is F because it provides a main clause for this sentence: "Grandpa points his finger at the TV and … seemingly turns it on." Notice that the phrase introducing the sentence (which is often called a participial phrase) cannot be a main clause because it has no stated subject. "Explaining to the unsuspecting child that he has a remote control implanted in his little finger," describes "Grandpa."

The best answer is NOT:

G because it creates a sentence fragment. There is no stated subject and no main clause.

H because it creates a sentence fragment. There is no stated subject and no main clause.

J not because of a fragment problem but because of a tense shift problem. Both the verb in the preceding sentence (*uses*) and the second verb in the compound predicate in this sentence (*turns*) express action in the present. It doesn't make sense to place a verb here (*has pointed*) that expresses action that began in the past and continues in the present.

Prepositions

Prepositions most often show the relationships of time, space, and direction. They connect words in a sentence to prepositional phrases that act as modifiers.

Examples

1.   The train **on** the northbound track left the station.

2.   The train left the station **in** a cloud of smoke.

The following are examples of prepositions:

about	from
before	in
during	to
for	of

The company's name reflects this African American focus as well. *Glory* is meant to evoke both the exultant spirit of gospel churches and the movie <u>during the Civil War</u> of the same name, which tells the story of a black regiment.	**42.** The best placement for the underlined portion would be: **F.** where it is now. **G.** after the word *name* (but before the comma). **H.** after the word *story*. **J.** after the word *regiment* (ending the sentence with a period).

The best answer is J because it is the clearest, most logical statement. The prepositional phrase "during the Civil War" clearly modifies "a black regiment." Modifying phrases should be placed as near as possible to the words they modify, which is why "during the Civil War" is best placed at the end of this sentence.

The best answer is NOT:

F because the phrase "during the Civil War" appears to modify "the movie." This placement wrongly suggests that the movie was filmed and shown during the Civil War. In addition, the phrase "of the same name" appears to modify "the Civil War" instead of "the movie."

G because the phrase "during the Civil War" appears to modify "the same name," which makes no sense.

H because the phrase "during the Civil War" appears to modify "of a black regiment." Again, the resulting statement "which tells the story during the Civil War of a black regiment" reads as though the movie was shown during the war.

<u>Detection programs</u> are available that <u>searches for</u> and then destroys computer viruses. ₆₆ ₆₇	**67. A.** NO CHANGE **B.** searches for and destroys **C.** search for and destroys **D.** search for and destroy

The best answer is D because both verbs in the subordinate, or dependent, clause of this sentence agree in number with the subject programs, which the clause modifies. The subject *programs* is plural, so the verbs search and destroy must also be plural.

The best answer is NOT:

   A because the singular verb forms (*searches, destroys*) do not agree with their plural subject, *programs*.

   B because the singular verb forms (*searches, destroys*) do not agree with their plural subject, *programs*.

   C because it is ungrammatical. Although the verb *search* is plural and agrees with the subject *programs,* the verb *destroys* is singular and does not agree.

By the time we found our way back to the car, the sun was high in the sky. We had taken three hours to complete a hike we usually finished in forty-five minutes. Yet the hike felt <u>shorter then</u> ever. As ₁₄ we drove off, I remembered something else my grandmother used to say: "Miami time passes all too quickly."	**14. F.** NO CHANGE **G.** more shorter then **H.** the shortest than **J.** shorter than

The best answer is J because "shorter than" is the correct comparative form to use to contrast how long the three-hour hike seemed to take with how long the normal-length hike usually seemed.

The best answer is NOT:

   F because the adverb *then* is incorrectly used instead of the preposition *than* to introduce the second part of the comparison.

   G because *more shorter* is an incorrectly formed comparative term and because the adverb *then* is incorrectly used instead of the preposition *than* to introduce the second part of the comparison.

   H because *shortest* is a superlative term used here incorrectly to compare two things. *Shortest* should only be used when comparing three or more things.

Subject-Verb Agreement

Proper subject-verb agreement depends on properly identifying the subject of the sentence. This can be difficult to do when a subject has many modifiers. One strategy is to identify the verb in the sentence because this is arguably simpler, particularly if the verb is an action word. You can test if a word is a verb by seeing if it sounds logical when the word *to* is placed before it. For example, does *to swim* sound like an action? Does *to exist* sounds like a state-of-being? It is more difficult to identify verbs that describe emotions or states of being. Once you have identified the verb, ask yourself, "Who or what is doing this verb?" Practice identifying the verb in the following sentence.

Tamika gives a gift to her twin brothers each year for their birthday.

The verb in this sentence is the action word *gives*. Who gives the gift? Tamika gives the gift. Therefore, Tamika is the subject of the sentence, and therefore the verb should be singular.

Plural Indefinite Pronouns

Creating agreement can be difficult when the subject of a sentence is an indefinite pronoun. The following information clarifies which indefinite pronouns are plural, which are singular, and which can be either depending on the context.

Both, few, fewer, many, some, others, and *several* are examples of plural indefinite pronouns.

Examples

1.   **Some** do not <u>believe</u> it is ethical to experiment with gene editing.

2.   **Both** <u>curve</u> tests.

3.   **Few** <u>enjoy</u> being forced to complete community service.

Indefinite Pronouns That Can Be Singular or Plural

In the cases of indefinite pronouns—*all, any, more, most, some, none*, and *percents*—the verb agreement is typically determined by the noun that follows the indefinite pronoun and the word *of*. See Examples 5 and 6. Notice that Example 5 includes a plural verb to agree with *teachers*, and Sentence 6 includes a singular verb to agree with *cake*. Notice that in Example 8, a plural verb *were* is used to agree with the plural noun *tee shirts*, and in Example 9, the singular verb *makes* is used to agree with the singular noun *population*. Though *population* refers to multiple people, the word itself is singular.

Examples

4.   **Most** students <u>love</u> when teachers bring candy to class.

5.   **Some** of the teachers <u>give</u> time in class to read for pleasure.

6.   **Some** of the cake <u>was</u> left at the end of the party.

7.   **Two-hundred students** <u>take</u> sophomore English. **None** of them <u>ask</u> for extra credit until the last week of the semester.

8.   **Thirty percent** of the **tee shirts** we ordered <u>were</u> too small.

9.   **One percent** of the **population** <u>makes</u> at least $421,926 per year in America.

Note: Some grammar books will say that *none* is singular because it means "not one." ACT reading and science test passages have included sentences in which *none* is treated as plural. For example, one science passage says, "**None** of the cells <u>were</u> able to divide."

Strategy: Which One Is Different?

Sometimes you can answer a question correctly without even looking at the original passage if you know what to look for. This typically works only for questions about subject-verb agreement, verb tense, and punctuation use. Let's take a look at several questions you could tackle with this approach. If three answers are all quite similar to each other, then you should gravitate toward the answer that is different. For example, if three of the answers are singular, then the correct answer is probably plural. If all three answers are past tense, the correct answer is likely present tense. If you are offered a period, semicolon, a colon, and a comma, the comma is likely correct because a period, semicolon, a colon, and even a conjunction with a comma before it can all separate two independent clauses. See the section on conjunctions for more information.

The washers and dryers are lime green, and the paneling on the walls <u>has been</u> painted to match, 22 although it was later varnished with some kind of artificial wood grain finish.	**22. F.** NO CHANGE **G.** have been **H.** were **J.** are

Sometimes you can determine the right answer choice simply by noticing which answer choice differs the most from the rest. In the case of this question, answers **G, H,** and **J** are each plural. Answer **F** is the only singular verb. This should actually lead you to be drawn to answer **F.** Plug it in, and see if it agrees with the subject of the sentence. What was painted to match? The paneling was painted to match, and "the paneling" is a singular subject, so it agrees with a singular verb like *has been*. Remember that the word *walls* cannot be the subject in this sentence because it is within a prepositional phrase "on the walls."

The best answer is F because the singular verb *has* agrees with the singular noun *paneling*. Remember that the verb must agree in number with its subject (in this case, *paneling*) and not the object of the preposition (in this case, the plural noun *walls*).

The best answer is NOT:

G because the plural verb *have* does not agree in number with the singular noun *paneling*.

H because it has an agreement problem. The plural verb *were* does not agree in number with the singular noun *paneling*.

J because it has an agreement problem. The plural verb *are* does not agree in number with the singular noun *paneling*.

Our technologically advanced times <u>has allowed</u>
                                                               ₃₁
filmmakers to create spectacular science fiction
films to intrigue us with worlds beyond our
experience. Imagine the excitement in <u>1902 when</u>
                                                     ₃₂
audiences first saw *Le Voyage dans la lune* (*A Trip to the Moon*), a groundbreaking movie produced by Georges Méliès.
	31. A. NO CHANGE
	  B. have allowed
	  C. allows
	  D. was allowing

The best answer is B because the plural present perfect verb *have allowed* agrees with the plural subject *times* and indicates appropriately that the creation of spectacular science fiction films continues.

The best answer is NOT

  A because the singular present perfect verb *has allowed* doesn't agree with the plural subject *times.*

  C because the singular verb *allows* doesn't agree with the plural subject *times.*

  D because the singular past progressive verb *was allowing* doesn't agree with the plural subject *times* and incorrectly indicates that the creation of spectacular science fiction films ended in the past.

[1] On a familiar trail near our house, I was pushing Jeremy in his stroller and <u>were thinking</u> of the
                                                      ₉
day ahead and the tasks I had to complete. [2] Suddenly, he squealed with pure delight and pointed toward a clearing. [3] There, two <u>does and three fawns</u> stood watching us. [4]
                    ₁₀
Five pairs of ears flicked like antennae seeking a signal. [5] After a few moments, the deer lowered their heads and began to eat, as if they had decided we were harmless. [6] By then, my son's face was full of wonder. 11
	9. A. NO CHANGE
	  B. were having thoughts
	  C. thinking
	  D. DELETE the underlined portion.

The best answer is C because thinking is the second half of a compound verb (*was pushing and … thinking*). The words *I was* are implied in front of *thinking.*

The best answer is NOT:

  A because the plural verb *were thinking* doesn't agree with the singular subject *I.*

  B because the plural verb *were having* doesn't agree with the singular subject *I.*

  D because deleting the underlined portion would leave the second part of the sentence without a verb ("I was pushing Jeremy in his stroller and of the day ahead …").

Verb Tense

Most verb tense questions will ask you to determine when simple present and past tense should be used. It is rare for other tenses like past progressive to be the correct answer. For these questions, look at the surrounding context to determine the appropriate tense for the verb.

Regular Verbs

Regular verbs follow a specific pattern. The past tense of a regular verb, for example, is formed by adding *-ed, -d, -t, -en,* or *-n.* Table 4.6 shows the different forms of *to ask.*

Table 4.6 Regular Verb Tenses

	Past	Present	Future
Simple	I asked a question.	I ask questions.	I will ask a question.
Continuous	I was asking questions.	I am asking questions.	I will be asking questions.
Perfect	I had asked a question.	I have asked questions.	I will have asked questions about the test by the time I take it.
Perfect continuous	I had been asking questions.	I have been asking questions.	I will have been asking questions.

Table 4.7 shows the present tense conjugations of *to ask.* As you can see, only the singular he/she/it form ends in *-s.*

Table 4.7 Conjugation of a Regular Verb

Singular	Plural
I ask	We ask
You ask	You ask
He/She/It asks	They ask

Notice that many verb tenses are created using the verbs *to have* and *to be.* Tables 4.8 and 4.9 show the different forms of the verb *to have* and *to be,* respectively.

Table 4.8 Conjugation of To Have

Singular	Plural
I have	We have
You have	You have
He/she/it has	They have

Table 4.9 Conjugation of To Be

Singular	Plural
I am	We are
You are	You are
He/She/It is	They are

You will need to use past participles to form the following verb tenses: the past perfect, future perfect, and present perfect tenses. Past participles usually end in the following: *ed, -d, -t, -en,* or *-n*.

Examples

1. I had <u>woken</u> up early that morning.

2. At the end of the month, I will have <u>cooked</u> breakfast for myself for twenty-one days.

3. I have <u>taught</u> this book for five years.

Some past participles are irregular such as the following:

had awakened	had slain
had bidden	had sneaked *or* snuck
had dived	had sought
had leaped *or* leapt	had swum
had ridden	had drunk
had sung	had begun
had shone	had run

Other Verb Forms

This section will review real questions and the format of several verb forms that are not commonly tested on the ACT English test. Typically, when these verb forms are offered, they are not the correct answer. Still, it should be helpful to understand when these verb forms should be used.

Present Progressive

This verb tense refers to continuous present actions.

Present tense of *to be* + the present participle (*-ing*) of the verb

Examples

1.   **I** <u>am making</u> apple pies for the bake sale.

2.   **We** <u>are preparing</u> for the debate.

Past Progressive

This verb tense refers to continuous past actions.

Past tense of *to be* + the present participle (*-ing*) of the verb

Examples

1.   As **we** <u>were waiting</u> for the train, we ate our breakfast.

2.   **He** <u>was studying</u> for his test when his friends invited him to get pizza.

3.   **We** <u>were catching up</u> on the television show when my friend told us spoilers.

4.   **We** <u>were cooking</u> dinner while watching a lesson about how to complete each step.

5.   In the 1990s, the widespread **availability** of the internet <u>was allowing</u> individuals to connect with people across the country. **People** <u>were able to</u> realize, sometimes for the first time, that **they** <u>were</u> not alone in their passion for obscure hobbies like competitive duck herding or extreme ironing.

Strategy: In the rare cases when the past progressive is the correct answer, the sentence typically has a date or another past tense event within it. Typically, the wrong answers will not have proper subject-verb agreement. The past progressive tense tends to emphasize that one past tense event is ongoing and begins before another past tense event. That can be seen in the first example. Eating breakfast occurs *after* the start of the wait for the train. The past tense events can also occur simultaneously as is the case in the second sentence. Sentences that include the past progressive often include words such as *as, when,* and *while* to emphasize the relationship between two past tense events.

Past Perfect

This verb tense refers to actions completed in the past.

had + the past participle of the verb

Examples

1.   **Mr. Robinson** <u>was surprised</u> to learn that **Gus** <u>had won</u> the class officer election given his lack of experience in student government.

2.   If **I** <u>had planned</u> my time better, I would have been done with the project by now.

Strategy: In the rare cases when the past perfect is the correct answer, the sentence typically also includes the phrase "would have." The past perfect emphasizes one past tense event's relation to another. In the first example, Gus wins first, and then Mr. Robinson is surprised to learn this news. In the second example, if the planning had been done earlier, then the project would be done. Each of these sentences emphasizes the relationship between two past tense events. Typically, the simple past tense won't be offered along with the past perfect tense. Assessing subject-verb agreement should also help you eliminate some wrong answers. "I would have been done" is written in a mood called the conditional perfect progressive. It is not necessary to address this mood further because it is so rarely tested. When it is tested, it helps signal that the past perfect tense should be used previously in the sentence. It is also not necessary for you to understand the difference between mood and tense in order to do well on the ACT English test.

Future Perfect

The future perfect tense is also rarely correct on the ACT English test, but it is sometimes offered. This tense describes a future action that will be completed prior to another future action.

The formula for the future perfect is the following:

will have + past participle

Examples

1.   By the end of high school, **I will have taken** the ACT three times.

2.   By the time the children arrive home from school, their father **will have hidden** all the holiday presents he just bought.

3.   My teacher says I cannot drop my science fair project off at school at 4:30 p.m. because she **will have left** already.

My grandmother tried to explain that "Miami time" referred to those <u>moments, when</u> time seemed
₆
to slow down or stand still. Recently, the meaning of her <u>words</u> started to sink in. One morning, my
₇
son and I <u>will inadvertently slip</u> out of the world
₈
measured in seconds, minutes, and hours, and into one measured by curiosity and sensation.

[1] On a familiar trail near our house, I was pushing Jeremy in his stroller and <u>were thinking</u> of the
₉
day ahead and the tasks I had to complete. [2] Suddenly, he squealed with pure delight and pointed toward a clearing. [3] There, two <u>does and three fawns</u> stood watching us.
₁₀

8. F. NO CHANGE
   G. inadvertently slip
   H. are inadvertently slipping
   J. inadvertently slipped

The best answer is J because the past tense verb *slipped* appropriately describes an event that occurred in the past and is consistent with the other past tense verbs used throughout the essay.

The best answer is NOT:

   F because the verb *will* slip describes a past event in future tense.

   G because the verb *slip* describes a past event in present tense.

   H because the verb *are slipping* describes a past event in present progressive tense.

Nancy Drew, the teenaged heroine of <u>heaps</u> of
₄₉
young adult mystery <u>novels, is alive</u> and well and
₅₀
still on the job. I know because my niece, Liana, and her friends were reading <u>that</u> all summer
₅₁
long. By the time Liana went back to <u>school and</u>
₅₂
<u>had</u> followed Nancy Drew on a safari to <u>solve</u> *The*
₅₃
Spider Sapphire Mystery and had explored Incan ruins for clues to *The Secret of the Crossword Cipher.*

52. F. NO CHANGE
   G. school, she had
   H. school, having
   J. school, she

The best answer is G because the main clause of the sentence must have a subject (*she*) and a verb (*had followed*), and the verb must be in past perfect tense to indicate that Liana had already read the Nancy Drew novels *The Spider Sapphire Mystery* and *The Secret of the Crossword Cipher* before she went back to school.

The best answer is NOT:

    F because "school and had" leaves the sentence without a main clause, creating an inappropriate sentence fragment.

    H because "school, having" leaves the sentence without a main clause, creating an inappropriate sentence fragment.

    J because "school, she" creates an inappropriate verb tense shift. The phrases "By the time" and "went back" signal that the past perfect verb had followed, rather than the simple past form followed, is needed to indicate that Liana had already read the Nancy Drew novels *The Spider Sapphire Mystery* and *The Secret of the Crossword Cipher* before she went back to school.

Verb tense questions typically rely on the context of the sentences before and after the sentence in question. Look at least one sentence before and at least one sentence after the sentence you will be correcting. Look at the tenses of other verbs in the paragraph. One challenge of this type of question is that the sentences before and after the sentence in question will contain grammar errors. In order to help you manage that challenge, in some of the examples that follow, you will find a corrected version of the paragraph with the verbs highlighted in bold font.

Original Passage	**13. A.** NO CHANGE
The second half of my junior year was anything but quiet. <u>Introduced by me to my favorite music, at top volume, I started being taught by Ligia the most popular Colombian dance steps.</u> My father spoke fondly of the days before two teenagers <u>taken</u> over₁₃ the phone, the stereo, the kitchen—well, most of the house, really. My mother helped Ligia with her math homework, and Ligia taught Mom beginning Spanish.	**B.** took **C.** had took **D.** begun to take
Revised Passage	
The second half of my junior year **was** anything but quiet. I **introduced** Ligia to my favorite music, at top volume, and she **started** teaching me the most popular Colombian dance steps. My father **spoke** fondly of the days before two teenagers <u>taken</u> over₁₃ the phone, the stereo, the kitchen—well, most of the house, really. My mother **helped** Ligia with her math homework, and Ligia taught Mom beginning Spanish.	

The best answer is B because it uses the correct verb form. The entire essay is in the past tense, so the past tense took is required here.

The best answer is NOT:

A because it uses an incorrect verb form here—the past participle *taken* without an auxiliary (*helping*) verb (for example, *had*).

C because *had took* is an incorrect verb form.

D because it uses an incorrect verb form—the past participle *begun* without an auxiliary verb (*had*).

Original Passage	24. **F.** NO CHANGE
In reality, these women never met to piece <u>22</u> together a quilt. The scene comes out of the <u>artists imagination</u> as a statement of the unity of purpose <u>23</u> that she perceives in their lives. Sojourner Truth and Harriet Tubman fought to abolish slavery and, later, <u>was active</u> in the crusade for suffrage. Newspaper <u>24</u> journalist Ida B. Wells <u>courageously spoke out for social and racial justice in the late nineteenth and</u> <u>25</u> <u>early twentieth centuries.</u>	**G.** was actively engaged **H.** was engaged **J.** were active
Revised Passage	
In reality, these women never met to piece together a quilt. The scene comes out of the artist's imagination as a statement of the unity of purpose that she perceives in their lives. Sojourner Truth and Harriet Tubman fought to abolish slavery and, later, <u>was active</u> in the crusade for suffrage. Newspaper <u>24</u> journalist Ida B. Wells courageously spoke out for social and racial justice in the late nineteenth and early twentieth centuries.	

The best answer is J because the plural verb *were* agrees with the plural compound subject, "Sojourner Truth and Harriet Tubman."

The best answer is NOT:

F because the singular verb *was* doesn't agree with the plural compound subject "Sojourner Truth and Harriet Tubman."

G because the singular verb *was* doesn't agree with the plural compound subject "Sojourner Truth and Harriet Tubman."

H because the singular verb *was* doesn't agree with the plural compound subject "Sojourner Truth and Harriet Tubman."

Original Passage	17. **A.** NO CHANGE
[1] Down the street from the <u>college, I attend, the</u> ^{16} Save-U Laundromat is always open, and someone is always there. [2] It <u>was</u> on a corner, across the ^{17} street; from a drugstore on one side and a big park ^{18} on the other.	**B.** is
	C. had been
	D. was located
Revised Passage	
Down the street from the college I **attend,** the Save-U Laundromat **is** always open, and someone **is** always there. It <u>was</u> on a corner, across the street ^{17} from a drugstore on one side and a big park on the other. The park **isn't** really a park at all but part of the grounds of a private boarding school.	

The best answer is B because it appropriately uses the present tense to describe an event that is happening in the present time. Notice that the writer begins the essay in the present tense ("the Save-U Laundromat is always open").

The best answer is NOT:

A because it makes a confusing tense shift from present (*is*) to past (*was*).

C because it makes another confusing tense shift—this time from the present tense to the past perfect tense.

D because it makes a confusing tense shift from present to past.

The company's name reflects this African American focus as well. *Glory* is meant <u>to evoke</u> both ^{41} the exultant spirit of gospel churches and the movie of the same name, which tells the story of a black regiment during the Civil War.	41. **A.** NO CHANGE
	B. at evoking
	C. in evoking of
	D. OMIT the underlined portion

The best answer is A because it correctly uses the infinitive form of the verb (*to evoke*) after the verb of intention (*is meant*).

The best answer is NOT:

  B because the verb phrase "is meant at evoking" is not an idiom of Standard written English and confuses the reader.

  C because it is incorrect because the verb phrase "is meant in evoking of" is not idiomatic English and results in an unclear statement.

  D because omitting the infinitive *to evoke* also results in a phrase that is not Standard written English. The verb is meant needs to be followed by an infinitive verb form—in this case *to evoke*.

In a strange terrain filled with hostile <u>creatures</u>, the ₄₀ space travelers experience many adventures. They escape back to Earth in the capsule by falling off the edge of the <u>moon, landing</u> in the ocean, they ₄₁ bob around until a passing ship finally rescues them. Producing the film long before interplanetary explorations <u>had began</u>, Méliès could <u>arouse</u> his ₄₂ ₄₃ audience's curiosity with unconstrained fantasy.	**42. F.** NO CHANGE **G.** would of begun, **H.** have began, **J.** had begun

The best answer is J because the past perfect verb had begun is made up of the past tense form *had* and the past participle *begun*. Past perfect is called for here because Méliès produced a movie long before interplanetary explorations had taken place.

The best answer is NOT:

  F because *had began* is an improperly formed past perfect verb that uses the past tense form *began* instead of the past participle *begun*.

  G because *would of begun* is an improperly formed verb that uses the word *of* instead of *have*.

  H because *have began* is an improperly formed present perfect verb that uses the past tense form *began* instead of the past participle *begun*. (Even if the present perfect verb had been formed properly, it still wouldn't work in this context because the past perfect is needed to indicate that producing the movie occurred before interplanetary explorations had taken place.)

Original Passage

[5]

The company's name reflects this African American focus as well. *Glory* is meant to evoke
$\underline{\text{to evoke}}$
41
both the exultant spirit of gospel churches and the movie $\underline{\text{during the Civil War}}$ of the same name, which
42
tells the story of a black regiment. [43]

[6]

With twenty full-time employees in its administrative offices, Glory Foods has come a long way from its beginnings. America's dinner tables $\underline{\text{were}}$ the beneficiaries of Bill Williams's drive,
44
determination, and culinary expertise.

Revised Passage

The company's name **reflects** this African American focus as well. *Glory* **is** meant to evoke both the exultant spirit of gospel churches and the movie of the same name, which **tells** the story of a black regiment during the Civil War.

With twenty full-time employees in its administrative offices, Glory Foods **has** come a long way from its beginnings. America's dinner tables $\underline{\text{were}}$ the beneficiaries of Bill Williams's drive,
44
determination, and culinary expertise.

---

44. F. NO CHANGE

   G. had been

   H. would have been

   J. are

The best answer is J because it maintains the present tense (*are*). Notice that present tense is used throughout the essay. A tense shift here would be illogical.

The best answer is NOT:

   F because it makes an illogical and confusing shift from present tense to past tense.

   G because it makes an illogical and confusing shift from present tense to past perfect tense.

   H because it makes an illogical and confusing shift from the present tense to the past conditional mood.

I thought the Nancy Drew mystery series had <u>went out</u> of style. ₄₆	**46. F.** NO CHANGE **G.** gone out of **H.** went from **J.** gone from

The best answer is G because the past perfect verb *had gone* is made up of the past tense form *had* and the past participle *gone*. Past perfect is called for here because if the Nancy Drew mystery series had gone out of style, it would have occurred prior to the events narrated here in past tense ("I thought …"). Furthermore, "gone out of style" is a conventional, idiomatic expression indicating that something has become unfashionable.

The best answer is NOT:

    F because *had went* is an improperly formed past perfect verb that uses the past tense form *went* instead of the past participle *gone*.

    H because *had went* is an improperly formed past perfect verb that uses the past tense form *went* instead of the past participle *gone* and because "went from style" isn't a conventional, idiomatic expression in standard English.

    J because "gone from style" isn't a conventional, idiomatic expression in standard English.

Doesn't anyone play pinball anymore? I was disappointed the other day when I took my kids to a game arcade. <u>Afterwards, I went to the movies.</u> ₄₆ Not one of the many colorful machines with flashing lights <u>were a</u> pinball machine. Video games filled ₄₇ the room.	**47. A.** NO CHANGE **B.** was a **C.** were an actual **D.** would have been an actual

The best answer is B because the past tense (*was*) is consistent with the rest of the paragraph. In addition, the singular verb *was* is in agreement with the singular subject *one*.

The best answer is NOT:

> **A** because the subject and verb do not agree in number. The subject *one* is singular and therefore requires a singular verb. The verb *were* is plural.

> **C** because, again, the subject and verb do not agree. The subject *one* is singular, and the verb *were* is plural and therefore incorrect.

> **D** because the past conditional mood (*would have been*) is inappropriate and confusing. In addition, adding the adjective *actual* would make the sentence unnecessarily wordy.

Original Passage	**18. A.** NO CHANGE
During the early morning hours of October 28, 1965, engineers stationed 630 feet above the ground made careful measurements for the days work. The results indicated a problem that threatened to postpone and delay the topping-out ceremony marking the placement of the final section between the two freestanding legs of the St. Louis Gateway Arch. 20	**B.** had been threatened
	C. will have threatened
	D. threatens
Revised Passage	
During the early morning hours of October 28, 1965, engineers **stationed** 630 feet above the ground **made** careful measurements for the day's work. The results **indicated** a problem that threatened to postpone the topping-out ceremony marking the placement of the final section between the two freestanding legs of the St. Louis Gateway Arch.	

To answer this question, look at the other verbs within the paragraph, which have been highlighted here in bold. Typically, the verb for a question like this will have the same tense as other verbs within the paragraph.

The best answer is A because this story of the last step in the construction of the Gateway Arch is told in the past tense. The past tense verb threatened is consistent with the other predicate verbs used in this paragraph—*stationed, made, indicated*.

The best answer is NOT:

> **B** because the passive voice of the verb *had been threatened* doesn't make sense in this sentence. Typically, *had been* would only be used if one past tense event in a sentence needed to be situated as occurring before another past tense event. For example, "By the time the train arrived, we <u>had been</u> waiting for over an hour." It is rare for *had been* to be correct on the ACT English test.

C because the future perfect tense verb *will have threatened* creates an awkward and confusing shift from the past tense used elsewhere in this essay.

D because the present tense verb *threatens* creates a similarly awkward and confusing shift in tense.

[1] I can understand why video games might seem more attractive than pinball. [2] Video screens <u>which have been</u> populated by movie stars, ₄₈ monsters, and heroes. [3] You can blow up cities, escape from dungeons, and battle all sorts of villains. [4] Pinball machines, on the other hand, are essentially all the same.	**48. F.** NO CHANGE **G.** that are **H.** are **J.** OMIT the underlined portion.

The best answer is H because it provides the predicate *are,* which produces a complete sentence. A statement that has no predicate is a sentence fragment (an incomplete sentence).

The best answer is NOT:

F because placing the relative pronoun *which* between the subject ("Video screens") and predicate ("have been populated") creates a sentence fragment.

G because it creates a sentence fragment. In this case, the relative pronoun *that* is placed between the subject and predicate.

J because it fails to provide a predicate, which creates another incomplete sentence.

My grandfather is not known for embracing technological <u>change. He still drives</u> his '59 Chevy ₁ Impala. (He <u>says,</u> he can't imagine needing frivolous ₂ options like automatic transmission or power steering.) So, when he <u>has went</u> to buy a new color ₃ television—<u>owing to the knowledge that</u> his old ₄ black-and-white model had finally quit—and the salesperson tried to talk him into buying a model with a remote control, he resisted. He said that he had two good legs and was perfectly capable of getting out of his chair. [5]	**3. A.** NO CHANGE **B.** had went **C.** went **D.** goes

The best answer is C because it provides the correct past tense form of the irregular verb *go.*

The best answer is NOT:

A because the verb *has went* is grammatically incorrect. It should be *has gone* (which would still be incorrect here because it would create an awkward tense shift).

B because the verb *had went* is grammatically incorrect. It should be had *gone.*

D because it is in the present tense, creating a shift in verb tense in this sentence. The three verbs that follow this one in the sentence are all in the past tense: *had quit, tried,* and *resisted.*

The United States has competed with other
₆₃
countries to explore space. By 2003, the National Aeronautics and Space Administration (NASA) would of sent thirty spacecraft to the red planet,
₆₄
speculation has been prompted that a human
₆₅
voyage may no longer be the stuff of fiction.
	64. F. NO CHANGE
	
	   G. had sent
	
	   H. send
	
	   J. have sent

The best answer is G because the past perfect tense verb had sent is made up of the past tense form had and the past participle sent. Past perfect is called for here to indicate that one event in the past (NASA sending its thirtieth spacecraft to Mars) took place before another past event ("By 2003").

The best answer is NOT:

F because "would of sent" is an improperly formed verb that uses the word of instead of have.

H because the simple past tense verb send is inappropriate given that a past perfect verb is needed to make clear that NASA had already sent its thirtieth spacecraft to Mars "By 2003."

J because the present perfect tense verb "have sent" is inappropriate given that a past perfect verb is needed to make clear that NASA had already sent its thirtieth spacecraft to Mars "By 2003."

5

Chapter 5: Conventions of Standard English and Sample Questions: Punctuation

This chapter reviews proper use of commas and common errors such as comma splices. This chapter also covers subordinating conjunctions and introductory phrases, which you can use to add variety to your own sentence structures as you write. Punctuation marks including colons, semicolons, parentheses, dashes, apostrophes, and quotation marks will also be discussed.

Commas

Most students know that a comma signifies where one would naturally pause when speaking. For written English, commas do not always represent a pause in speaking. Rather, they set off different elements of a sentence to make the structure and ideas clearer. Studying some comma rules will help you realize when and where to use a comma and also how to identify when no comma is needed.

1. You should *not* separate the subject of a sentence from its verb with just one comma.

   WRONG The gray cat, is irritable around new people.

   CORRECT The gray cat is irritable around new people.

2. You can separate a subject from its verb with a nonessential clause that is **framed by commas.** Correct answers often include no commas or two framing commas. Notice that the nonessential phrase "which is hypoallergenic" can be cut out of the sentence, and the sentence still makes sense.

   WRONG The Russian blue cat, which is hypoallergenic does not trigger my allergies.

   CORRECT The Russian blue cat, which is hypoallergenic, does not trigger my allergies.

   This rule also applies when two adjectives are synonyms. In these cases, typically the first word used will be less common and the second word will give a more commonly known word.

   WRONG Alpha, or dominant wolves assert their dominance by standing tall rather than lowering their bodies as submissive wolves do.

   WRONG Alpha, or dominant wolves, assert their dominance by standing tall rather than lowering their bodies as submissive wolves do.

   CORRECT Alpha, or dominant, wolves assert their dominance by standing tall rather than lowering their bodies as submissive wolves do.

   Explanation: The word *alpha* is a synonym for *dominant*. Therefore, it is not necessary to say "or dominant," and therefore that phrase should be framed by commas because it can be cut out of the sentence. You can't cut out the whole phrase "or dominant wolves," because you need to retain the word *wolves* for the sentence to make sense.

   EXCEPTION The word *both* can be interpreted as a synonym for *lacrosse and volleyball* in the following sentence, but there should not be a comma before *both* and *lacrosse and volleyball*. In this context, the word *both* functions like a pronoun.

Both lacrosse and volleyball are signature sports for female athletes at our school.

3.   You should not separate an adjective from the noun it modifies with a comma. You can see more information on this concept in the section on adjectives.

WRONG The gray, cat is irritable around new people.

CORRECT The gray cat is irritable around new people.

Appositives and Commas

An appositive is a phrase that describes a noun. It renames or explains the phrase that it follows or precedes. An appositive functions like an adjective, and it is made up of nouns, pronouns, and prepositions. Most appositive phrases are set off by commas or dashes unless they are essential to the meaning of the sentence. Let's take a look at the underlined appositive in the following sentence. The appositive phrase "one of several Hindu festivals" describes the proper noun it follows.

Example

Diwali, one of several Hindu festivals, is celebrated through gift giving, fireworks, and lighting lamps.

The following is an example of a real ACT question that offers an appositive phrase as one of the answer choices.

Architect Eero Saarinen, who created the design
           ₈
that symbolized the memorial's theme of St. Louis as the "Gateway to the West."
	8. F. NO CHANGE
	
	   G. Saarinen, creator of
	
	   H. Saarinen created
	
	   J. Saarinen creating

The best answer is H because it is the only choice that makes this a complete sentence.

The best answer is NOT:

F because it creates a sentence fragment—a noun phrase ("Architect Eero Saarinen") and a dependent clause that modifies the noun phrase ("who created the design that symbolized the memorial's theme").

G because it creates a sentence fragment—a noun phrase ("Architect Eero Saarinen") and an appositive phrase that renames the noun phrase ("creator of the design that symbolized the memorial's theme").

J because it creates a sentence fragment—a noun phrase ("Architect Eero Saarinen") and a participial phrase modifying the noun phrase ("creating the design that symbolized the memorial's theme").

Let's look at a variety of real ACT questions about commas.

Thirty-two years of planning and effort resulted in this moment. In 1933, <u>attorney and civic leader</u>
                ₂₁
Luther Ely Smith envisioned a memorial that would recognize St. Louis's major role in the westward expansion of the United States.
	21. F. NO CHANGE
	
	  G. attorney, and civic leader
	
	  H. attorney and civic leader,
	
	  J. attorney, and civic leader,

The best answer is F because the phrase "Luther Ely Smith" is an appositive for (renames or explains) the phrase it follows, "attorney and civic leader." Most appositive phrases are set off by commas, but this one should not be, because it is essential to the meaning of the sentence. Try reading the sentence without "Luther Ely Smith"—doesn't it sound strange or clunky?

The best answer is NOT:

    G because the comma between the nouns *attorney* and *civic leader* is unnecessary and distracting. The word *and* is linking up these two nouns; the comma just gets in the way of that.

    H because there should not be a comma separating the noun phrase "attorney and civic leader" and the noun phrase that defines and specifies it, "Luther Ely Smith."

    J because it is incorrect for the reasons given for **G** and **H**, and because the proliferation of commas just totally confuses things: "In 1933, attorney, and civic leader" starts looking like it might be a series of three items.

But in pinball, you have three factors to consider: you, the machine, and chance, which is sometimes your <u>enemy</u> sometimes your ally.
     ₅₇
	57. A. NO CHANGE
	
	  B. enemy,
	
	  C. enemy;
	
	  D. enemy, and,

The best answer is B because the comma between these two noun phrases ("sometimes your enemy" and "sometimes your ally") provides clarity for this sentence.

The best answer is NOT:

    A because without the comma there, the statement becomes ambiguous and confusing. It's hard to tell whether the second *sometimes* is modifying your enemy or your ally.

    C because it improperly uses a semicolon between these two noun phrases. By the way, those phrases are called "predicate nouns" because they follow the linking verb is.

    D because even though the conjunction and could be used between these two sentence elements, setting off the conjunction with commas is inappropriate and confusing.

When she was doing something she loved, whether it was <u>making freezer jam or researching tribal history</u>, she refused to be <u>rushed in a hurry</u>. "I'm on Miami time today," she would say. Conversely, if we were running late for an <u>appointment. She would</u> chide us by saying, "Get a move on. We're not running on Miami time today, you know."	4. **F.** NO CHANGE **G.** appointment; she **H.** appointment and she **J.** appointment, she

The best answer is J because a comma is appropriate between the long introductory adverbial clause "if we were running late for an appointment" and the sentence's main clause, which begins with *she*.

The best answer is NOT:

  F because placing a period after the word *appointment* makes the introductory adverbial clause (subordinated by the conjunction *if*) into a sentence fragment and because doing so obscures how the ideas are related.

  G because placing a semicolon after the word *appointment* makes the introductory adverbial clause into a sentence fragment and obscures how the ideas are related.

  H because the coordinating conjunction *and* should not be used to join two unequal sentence elements, such as a subordinate clause and a main clause, as would be the case here.

The two "little brothers" of Ligia's host family, who had <u>volunteered to move, to those bedrooms for a year</u>, had to be moved upstairs to the room Ligia was using.	7. **A.** NO CHANGE **B.** volunteered to move to those bedrooms for a year **C.** volunteered to move to those bedrooms for a year, **D.** volunteered, to move to those bedrooms for a year,

The best answer is C because it correctly inserts a comma after the word *year*. Notice that this comma is necessary to set off the nonessential clause "who had volunteered to move." A nonessential clause adds information that is not necessary to the main idea. Nonessential clauses are set off with commas on both ends.

The best answer is NOT:

  A because it inserts an unnecessary and confusing comma after *move*.

  B because it fails to insert the required comma after *year*. This comma is necessary to set off the nonessential clause that begins with "who had volunteered …."

  D because it inserts an unnecessary and confusing comma after *volunteered*.

And Fannie Lou Hamer, Ella Baker, and Rosa Parks showed leadership and strength during the civil rights <u>movement, it happened in</u> the 1950s 29 and 1960s.	**29. A.** NO CHANGE **B.** movement, it took place in **C.** movement, that happened in **D.** movement of

The best answer is D because the phrase "movement of " creates a clear, complete sentence, with the preposition *of* heading the phrase of the 1950s and 1960s.

The best answer is NOT:

A because "movement, it happened in" forms a second independent clause in the sentence joined to the original independent clause by only a comma, creating a comma splice.

B because "movement, it took place in" forms a second independent clause in the sentence joined to the original independent clause by only a comma, creating a comma splice.

C because "movement, that happened in" forms a second independent clause in the sentence joined to the original independent clause by only a comma, creating a comma splice.

By 1895, he was working with the new invention. [5] He found <u>out, however,</u> that the public preferred 34 live magic acts to filmed versions. [35]	**34. F.** NO CHANGE **G.** out, however; **H.** out, however **J.** out however,

The best answer is F because when a conjunctive adverb such as *however* is used in the middle of a sentence, it needs to be set off by commas.

The best answer is NOT:

G because the semicolon after the word *however* creates an abbreviated main clause ("he found out, however;") followed by an inappropriate sentence fragment ("that the public preferred live magic acts to filmed versions").

H because the phrase "out, however" lacks the comma after the word *however* needed to set off the conjunctive adverb from the rest of the sentence.

J because the phrase "out however," lacks the comma after the word *out* needed to set off the conjunctive adverb from the rest of the sentence.

Glory Foods' <u>president, and founder Bill Williams,</u> ³² explains the unusual slogan by admitting that while he knows that his foods can't beat the taste of real home cooking, <u>it does</u> come very close. ³³	**32. F.** NO CHANGE **G.** president, and founder Bill Williams **H.** president and founder Bill Williams, **J.** president and founder, Bill Williams,

The best answer is J because it provides the best punctuation to set off the appositive "Bill Williams." An appositive is a noun or pronoun that identifies and follows another noun or pronoun. In this sentence, "Bill Williams" identifies "Glory Foods' president and founder." Appositives are set off by commas (except when the apposition is restrictive, such as in the phrase "my sister Sue" when I have three sisters).

The best answer is NOT:

F because it inserts an unnecessary and confusing comma between *president* and *and*. In addition, it fails to set off the appositive with a necessary comma between *founder* and *Bill*.

G because it inserts an unnecessary and confusing comma between *president* and *and*.

H because it fails to set off the appositive by adding the necessary comma between *founder* and *Bill*.

Nancy Drew, the teenaged heroine of <u>heaps</u> of ⁴⁹ young adult mystery <u>novels, is alive</u> and well and ⁵⁰ still on the job.	**50. F.** NO CHANGE **G.** novels, is alive, **H.** novels is alive, **J.** novels is alive

The best answer is F because the comma after the word *novels* is needed to finish setting off the nonrestrictive appositive "the teenaged heroine of hundreds of young adult mystery novels" from Nancy Drew, the noun the appositive describes.

The best answer is NOT:

G because the comma after the word *alive* is unnecessary because the list of adjectives "alive and well and still on the job" is already linked by the coordinating conjunction *and*.

H because a comma is needed after the word *novels* to finish setting off the nonrestrictive appositive "the teenaged heroine of hundreds of young adult mystery novels" from Nancy Drew, the noun the appositive describes, and because the comma after the word *alive* is unnecessary because the list of adjectives "alive and well and still on the job" is already linked by the coordinating conjunction *and*.

J because a comma is needed after the word *novels* to finish setting off the nonrestrictive appositive "the teenaged heroine of hundreds of young adult mystery novels" from Nancy Drew, the noun the appositive describes.

[1] On a familiar trail near our house, I was pushing Jeremy in his stroller and <u>were thinking</u>
          9
of the day ahead and the tasks I had to complete. [2] Suddenly, he squealed with pure delight and pointed toward a clearing. [3] There, two <u>does and</u>
<u>three fawns</u> stood watching us.
          10
	10. F. NO CHANGE
	
	G. does, and three fawns
	
	H. does and three fawns,
	
	J. does and, three fawns

The best answer is F because no punctuation should interrupt the compound subject "two does and three fawns" or separate it from the rest of the sentence.

The best answer is NOT:

G because it places an unnecessary comma between parts of the compound subject.

H because it places an unnecessary comma between the compound subject and the verb *stood*.

J because it places an unnecessary comma between parts of the compound subject.

This is a startling number, especially in light of the fact that the International Space Station, the most ambitious NASA project <u>yet,</u> carried a projected 67 price tag of "only" 17 billion dollars.	**67. A.** NO CHANGE **B.** yet **C.** yet: **D.** yet—

The best answer is A because the nonrestrictive appositive "the most ambitious NASA project yet" is nonessential explanatory information that needs to be set off by commas from the rest of the sentence.

The best answer is NOT:

B because a comma is needed after the word *yet* to finish setting off the nonrestrictive appositive "the most ambitious NASA project yet" from the rest of the sentence.

C because a comma, not a colon, is needed after the word *yet* to finish setting off the nonrestrictive appositive "the most ambitious NASA project yet" from the rest of the sentence.

D because a comma, not a dash, is needed after the word *yet* to finish setting off the nonrestrictive appositive "the most ambitious NASA project yet" from the rest of the sentence. Although a pair of dashes could have been used to set off the nonrestrictive appositive, the writer uses a comma after the word *Station,* so parallelism requires that a second comma follow the word *yet*.

These eight <u>women the story explains,</u> strove in their various ways to support the cause of justice in the world.	**20. F.** NO CHANGE **G.** women, the story explains— **H.** women the story explains— **J.** women, the story explains,

The best answer is J because the interposed explanatory phrase "the story explains" is properly set off from the rest of the sentence by two commas, indicating that the phrase could be omitted without changing the basic meaning of the sentence.

The best answer is NOT:

    F because the interposed explanatory phrase "the story explains" is not preceded by a comma, which would be needed to set the phrase off properly from the rest of the sentence.

    G because the interposed explanatory phrase "the story explains" is improperly set off from the rest of the sentence by a comma before the phrase and a dash after the phrase. Either two commas or two dashes would be appropriate, but not one of each.

    H because the interposed explanatory phrase "the story explains" is not preceded by a dash, which would be needed to set the phrase off properly from the rest of the sentence.

Eventually, the letters reorder themselves on the screen. Not all <u>viruses however,</u> straighten themselves out.	**63. A.** NO CHANGE **B.** viruses; however, **C.** viruses, however **D.** viruses, however,

The best answer is D because it appropriately sets off the conjunctive adverb *however* with commas. When a conjunctive adverb or transitional expression interrupts a clause, as *however* does in this sentence, it should usually be set off with commas.

The best answer is NOT:

    A because it places a comma after *however* but omits the corresponding comma before the word.

    B because it inappropriately uses a semicolon instead of a comma before the adverb *however*.

    C because it is incorrect because it places a comma before *however* but omits the corresponding comma after the word.

Grandpa's favorite feature on the remote is the sleep function. This option automatically turns the TV off after a preset amount of time, which is very <u>convenient when</u> he falls asleep while watching a
10
show. For him, Grandpa says what he wants his TV doing, <u>even when he sleeps, is to know a source of both pleasure and power.</u>
11

10. F. NO CHANGE

   G. convenient, when

   H. convenient. When

   J. convenient; when

The best answer is F because it appropriately punctuates this complex sentence. A complex sentence, by definition, contains an independent clause ("This option automatically turns the TV off after a preset amount of time") and one or more dependent clauses ("which is very convenient" and "when he falls asleep while watching a show").

The best answer is NOT:

G because by inserting a comma before the clause "when he falls asleep while watching a show" and setting it off from the rest of the sentence, the writer is signaling that the clause is not essential to the meaning of the rest of the sentence. But that is not so. Try reading the sentence without that final clause. The option of automatically turning off the TV is not always convenient, but it's sure handy when Grandpa falls asleep in the middle of a show.

H because it creates a sentence fragment. "When he falls asleep while watching a show" cannot stand alone. It's not a complete thought. Readers want to know more.

J because it creates a sentence fragment. As it is used here, the semicolon is signaling that the statements on either side of the semicolon should be independent clauses (complete thoughts).

Coordinating Conjunctions

The coordinating conjunctions, which are also known as the FANBOYS conjunctions, are as follows: *for, and, nor, but, or, yet, so.* **And** is the most commonly tested FANBOYS conjunction. These conjunctions follow a certain set of rules.

Rule 1 If a conjunction comes <u>before</u> a subject and a verb, it must have a comma before it.

Rule 2 If a conjunction is *not* followed by a subject and a verb, then it *cannot* have a comma before it.

Correct Examples

1.   I want to buy organic food, **but** it is too expensive.

2.   Organic food is delicious **but** expensive.

3.   I like to buy fresh **and** local ingredients.

4.   I like to buy fresh **and** local ingredients, **and** it is easy to do so because there is a farmers' market in my town each week.

The computer is probably sick, <u>unless</u> the ₆₂ diagnosis may be that the computer has a virus.	**62. F.** NO CHANGE **G.** except **H.** and **J.** as if

The best answer is H because it effectively and logically uses the coordinating conjunction (linking word) *and* to connect the two independent clauses in this sentence.

The best answer is NOT:

F because the use of the conjunction *unless* here creates an illogical statement. It makes no sense to say, "The computer is probably sick, unless … [it] has a virus."

G because the use of the conjunction *except* also creates an illogical statement. A computer with a virus is not an exception to a computer being sick.

J because the use of the conjunction *as if* creates a confusing and ambiguous sentence.

However, my grandpa could punch in the <u>time, and</u> ₆ the <u>channel</u> of his favorite daily news program, and ₇ the TV would turn on that program at the proper time.	**7. A.** NO CHANGE **B.** time and, the channel, **C.** time and the channel **D.** time and the channel,

The best answer is C because the absence of commas here creates the clearest and most understandable sentence. This is another case where less is more.

The best answer is NOT:

A because it inserts a comma that confounds your ability to understand the sentence. The comma after the word *time* makes you think that Grandpa punched in the time and then he punched in the channel of his favorite news program, when actually he punched in the time that the program came on and the channel it was on.

B because it also inserts an unnecessary and confusing comma, this time after the conjunction *and* rather than just before it.

D because the comma after the word *channel* indicates that the phrase "of his favorite daily news program" is not essential. It's set off from the rest of the sentence with commas, as if it were parenthetical—a nice piece of information but not necessary to the meaning of the sentence. But if you try reading the sentence without this phrase, the meaning of the sentence is no longer clear.

Comma Splices

Typically, if a comma is followed directly by a subject and a verb, it creates what is called a comma splice. A comma splice occurs when a comma is used where a period or semicolon would be more appropriate. Technically a colon or a dash can separate two independent clauses as well, but this is not as frequently tested on standardized tests. The following question tests this concept.

Every year my high school hosts international exchange <u>students, those teenagers</u> join our senior class. 1	1. **A.** NO CHANGE **B.** students, he or she is invited to **C.** students who **D.** students they

The best answer is C because it appropriately uses the relative pronoun *who* to introduce the clause that modifies students —"who join our senior class." Besides introducing that clause, the pronoun *who* also functions as the subject of the clause.

The best answer is NOT:

   A because it creates a comma splice (two or more complete sentences separated only by a comma). The phrase "those teenagers" is the subject of the second complete sentence.

   B because it produces a comma splice. In addition, it creates grammatical disagreement between the plural *students* and the singular *he or she*.

   D because it creates a run-on, or fused, sentence. There is no punctuation or conjunction (connecting word) between the two statements.

Subordinating Conjunctions

Subordinating conjunctions join a dependent and an independent clause. They show cause and effect, timing, and spatial relationships. Some subordinating conjunctions such as *although* and *while* signal contrast. Review the following list of several common subordinating conjunctions.

after	even though
although	if
as long as	in order that
because	lest
before	now
even if	once

provided that	when
rather than	whenever
since	where
so that	whereas
than	wherever
that	whether
though	whether or not
unless	while
until	why

Notice that an independent clause comes after an introductory phrase that begins with a subordinating conjunction, which has been identified in bold.

Example 1

CORRECT Although it was raining, the parade was not canceled.

Example 2

WRONG Because it was <u>raining;</u> we went to the movies.

1

CORRECT Because it was <u>raining,</u> we went to the movies.

1

Explanation: The original incorrect sentence begins with a subordinating conjunction *because*. This must be followed by a comma. It cannot be followed by a semicolon because "Because it was raining …" is not a complete thought. This is a common pattern on the ACT. A subordinating conjunction will *begin* what would otherwise be an independent clause. Notice that on its own "It was raining" is an independent clause. It contains a subject and a verb. "We went to the movies" is also an independent clause. Adding *because* to the introductory phrase "Because it was raining" leads this clause to be dependent on the clause "we went to the movies."

When a sentence *begins* with a subordinating conjunction, what comes first is a dependent clause, which is also sometimes called a subordinate clause. You can hear this when you read the sentence up until the comma: "Although it was raining" is clearly an incomplete thought.

By contrast, when a subordinating conjunction appears in the *middle* of a sentence, no commas are needed. In this case, the subordinating conjunction is joining two independent clauses.

Example 3

CORRECT

Beginning	**Although** it was raining, we went hiking.
Middle	We went hiking **although** it was raining.

Example 4

CORRECT

Beginning	**Because** the movie scared me to death, I did not sleep.
Middle	I did not sleep **because** the movie scared me to death.

Introductory Phrases

An introductory clause begins a sentence and provides information typically about location, time, or position. These clauses are dependent because they cannot stand on their own as a sentence. Often introductory clauses begin with subordinating conjunctions such as *although, while, because,* or *until*. Notice that most of these introductory clauses begin with prepositions and are followed immediately by a comma and an independent clause.

Examples

1. <u>In the 1690s</u>, it was not uncommon for people to be imprisoned if they were suspected of being witches.

2. <u>Down the road from my house</u>, there is a beautiful waterfall.

3. <u>During the first few years of life</u>, the brain develops rapidly.

4. <u>At the university's infant cognition center</u>, studies are finding that human beings seem to be altruistic from birth.

The following questions involve introductory clauses.

Down the street from the <u>college, I attend,</u> the
                                    16
Save-U Laundromat is always open, and someone is always there.
	16. F. NO CHANGE
	   G. college, I attend
	   H. college I attend,
	   J. college I attend

The best answer is H because it uses a comma after *attend* to appropriately set off the introductory phrase from the main clause. Without this comma, the reader might be confused and think that the narrator attended the laundromat.

The best answer is NOT:

F because it adds an unnecessary and confusing comma between *college* and *I.*

G because it adds an unnecessary and confusing comma between *college* and *I.* In addition, it fails to add the appropriate comma after *attend.*

J because it omits the comma after *attend,* producing a potentially confusing statement for readers.

During the early morning hours of October 28, 1965, engineers stationed 630 feet above the 61 ground made careful measurements for the day's work.	**61. A.** NO CHANGE **B.** 1965, and engineers **C.** 1965. Engineers **D.** 1965; engineers

The best answer is A because it provides the punctuation (a comma) that best indicates the relationship between the introductory prepositional phrases ("During the early morning hours of October 28, 1965") and the main clause ("engineers stationed 630 feet above the ground made careful measurements").

The best answer is NOT:

B because the connecting word *and* creates confusion here. A word such as *and* usually connects similar kinds of grammatical units: nouns (Tom and Mary), verbs (wander and search), adverbs (high and low), and so on. Here, the word tries to connect an introductory phrase and a main clause.

C because placing a period here creates a sentence fragment: "During the early morning hours of October 28, 1965."

D because placing a semicolon here creates a sentence fragment. A semicolon is usually used to connect two independent clauses (that is, clauses that could each stand alone as complete sentences).

The Oxford Comma

If you have three or more items in a list, you should include a comma before *and* like so: A, B, and C.

Example

I like biking, skiing, and playing basketball.

If you only have two items in a list, you should not use a comma to separate the items in the list.

Example

I like biking and skiing.

No Comma

Students are often uncomfortable choosing an answer that contains no commas, but often choosing such an answer is the correct choice. As we saw previously, a comma should not separate a subject from its verb. Often commas are avoided immediately before or after prepositions as well.

Commas and Prepositions

It is rare for a comma to come immediately before or after a preposition. This makes sense because the purpose of a preposition is to join two words. In the rare case of a preposition appropriately having a comma right before or after it, the prepositional phrase is likely part of a nonessential clause that can be cut out of the sentence without affecting the meaning of the sentence.

Example

Electus parrots, in both sexes, are brilliantly colorful.

It was on a corner, across the street; from a drugstore on one side and a big park on the other.	**18. F.** NO CHANGE **G.** street from, **H.** street, from **J.** street from

The best answer is J because no punctuation is needed here. The absence of punctuation creates the clearest and most understandable sentence.

The best answer is NOT:

F because it places a semicolon between two descriptive phrases, which is a misuse of the semicolon.

G because it inserts an unnecessary and confusing comma between a preposition and its object.

H because it places an unnecessary comma between the two descriptive phrases. There is no pause or separation between the phrases "across the street" and "from a drugstore." They belong together as one description.

It was a difficult concept for me to grasp. My
    5
grandmother tried to explain that "Miami time"
referred to those <u>moments, when</u> time seemed
                6
to slow down or stand still. Recently, the meaning
of her <u>words</u> started to sink in. One morning, my
        7
son and I <u>will inadvertently slip</u> out of the world
                8
measured in seconds, minutes, and hours, and into
one measured by curiosity and sensation.
	6. **F.** NO CHANGE
	
	   G. moments when
	
	   H. moments, as if
	
	   J. moments, because

The best answer is G because the dependent clause "when time seemed to slow down or stand still" is necessary information to explain which moments are being referred to and thus should not be set off from the rest of the sentence by a comma.

The best answer is NOT:

F because the comma between the words *moments* and *when* identifies the information in the dependent clause "when time seemed to slow down or stand still" as unnecessary information when, in fact, the clause is vital to defining the moments of Miami time.

H because the comma between the words *moments* and *as if* identifies the information in the dependent clause "as if time seemed to slow down or stand still" as unnecessary information and because the conjunction *as if* does not appropriately link the ideas in this sentence.

J because the comma between the words *moments* and *because* identifies the information in the dependent clause "because time seemed to slow down or stand still" as unnecessary information and because the conjunction *because* does not appropriately link the ideas in this sentence.

Among the schools that benefited from this
<u>generosity, were</u> those that Mary McLeod Bethune
        28
opened and ran in order to provide a better
education for Black students.
	28. **F.** NO CHANGE
	
	   G. generosity; were
	
	   H. generosity were
	
	   J. generosity were:

The best answer is H because no punctuation is warranted in this underlined portion. "Among the schools that benefited from this generosity" is an introductory adverbial phrase that, because it immediately precedes the verb it modifies, should not be set off by a comma. Had the sentence elements been arranged in the more typical subject-verb-object order ("Those [schools] that Mary McLeod Bethune opened and ran in order to provide a better education for Black students were among the schools that benefited from this generosity"), it would've been more obvious that no internal punctuation is required.

The best answer is NOT:

F because the comma after the word *generosity* is an unwarranted break between the prepositional phrase and the verb it modifies.

G because the semicolon after the word *generosity* creates two inappropriate sentence fragments, as neither what precedes nor what follows the semicolon is an independent clause.

J because the colon after the word *were* is unwarranted; what follows the colon is not a series, a list, an explanation, or a clarification. What comes before a colon must be a complete sentence, and, in this case, it is not.

Our technologically advanced times <u>has allowed</u> 31 filmmakers to create spectacular science fiction films to intrigue us with worlds beyond our experience. Imagine the excitement in <u>1902 when</u> 32 audiences first saw *Le Voyage dans la lune (A Trip to the Moon)*, a groundbreaking movie produced by Georges Méliès.	**32. F.** NO CHANGE **G.** 1902, and when **H.** 1902, which **J.** 1902, where

The best answer is F because the relative adverb *when* is appropriately used to follow a time expression ("in 1902"); no punctuation is needed.

The best answer is NOT:

G because the coordinating conjunction *and* treats a dependent clause ("when audiences first saw …") as a second independent clause, creating a nonsensical sentence.

H because the relative pronoun *which* logically refers to 1902, both implying that audiences first saw the year 1902 (rather than first seeing a groundbreaking movie) and creating a garbled sentence.

J because the relative adverb *where* doesn't fit logically into this context, since 1902 refers to time rather than place

The firm also employs African American <u>professional advisers</u> and subcontractors whenever 39 possible and contracts African American farmers to grow much of the produce that goes into Glory Foods	**39. A.** NO CHANGE **B.** professional, advisers, **C.** professional advisers, **D.** professional advisers;

The best answer is A because no punctuation is needed here. The absence of commas makes this the clearest sentence.

The best answer is NOT:

   B because it adds unnecessary commas and incorrectly treats "professional, advisers, and subcontractors" as if they were items in a series, but *professional* functions as an adjective modifying the noun *advisers*.

   C because the unnecessary comma between the two parts of the compound direct object "advisers and subcontractors" adds confusion to the sentence.

   D because it inserts an inappropriate and confusing semicolon between *advisers* and *subcontractors*.

Then again, you can sometimes get lucky, and a ball you thought was <u>lost, will</u> inexplicably bounce
　　　　　　　　　₅₃
back into play.
	53. A. NO CHANGE
	   B. lost will
	   C. lost, will,
	   D. lost will,

The best answer is B because the absence of a comma here creates the clearest and most understandable sentence.

The best answer is NOT:

   A because it places an unnecessary and distracting comma between the subject clause ("a ball you thought was lost") and the predicate ("will … bounce").

   C because it sets off the auxiliary (*helping*) verb will for no logical reason.

   D because it places an unnecessary and distracting comma between the auxiliary verb *will* from the main verb bounce.

Suddenly, without warning, each of the <u>letters, in</u>
<u>front of you tumbles</u> to the bottom of the screen.
  ₆₁
	61. A. NO CHANGE
	   B. letters in front of you tumbles,
	   C. letters in front of you, tumbles
	   D. letters in front of you tumbles

The best answer is D because the absence of commas here creates the clearest and most understandable sentence.

The best answer is NOT:

A because it inserts an unnecessary and confusing comma between the noun *letters* and the preposition *in*. The phrase "in front of you" modifies letters, and these elements should not be separated by any punctuation.

B because it inappropriately and confusingly inserts a comma between the verb *tumbles* and the preposition *to*.

C because it inserts an unnecessary and confusing comma between the complete subject phrase ("each of the letters in front of you") and the verb *tumbles*.

By the time Liana went back to <u>school and had</u> ₅₂ followed Nancy Drew on a safari to <u>solve</u> *The* ₅₃ *Spider Sapphire Mystery* and had explored Incan ruins for clues to *The Secret of the Crossword Cipher.* With Nancy's help, <u>Liana had read about different places and various cultures all over the world.</u> ₅₄	**53. A.** NO CHANGE **B.** solve: **C.** solve; **D.** solve,

The best answer is A because no punctuation is warranted between the verb solve and its direct object, *The Spider Sapphire Mystery*.

The best answer is NOT:

B because the colon between the verb *solve* and its direct object, *The Spider Sapphire Mystery*, is unnecessary and confusing.

C because the semicolon between the verb *solve* and its direct object, *The Spider Sapphire Mystery*, is unnecessary and confusing.

D because the comma between the verb *solve* and its direct object, *The Spider Sapphire Mystery*, is unnecessary and confusing.

My grandfather is not known for embracing technological <u>change. He still drives</u> his '59 Chevy ₁ Impala. (He <u>says,</u> he can't imagine needing ₂ frivolous options like automatic transmission or power steering.)	**2. F.** NO CHANGE **G.** says **H.** says, that **J.** says, that,

The best answer is G because it correctly punctuates this sentence, which is actually a fairly simple subject-verb-direct object sentence except that the direct object is a noun clause. The sentence could also be written with the word *that* introducing the clause.

The best answer is NOT:

F because it inserts an unnecessary comma between the verb *says* and the direct object, which is what he says ("he can't imagine needing frivolous options like automatic transmission or power steering"). It's worth pointing out that the comma would be correct if what followed the verb were a direct quotation, as in speech: He says, "I can't imagine needing frivolous options."

H because it inserts an unnecessary comma between the verb and the direct object clause.

J because it adds an unnecessary comma, plus it places an unnecessary comma between the pronoun *that* and the clause it introduces

Commas and Quotation Marks

Recently the ACT English test has asked when a comma should come before a quotation. Most students are accustomed to properly introducing quotes into literary analysis.

Examples

1.   She says, "I'm Rochelle Satterwhite."

2.   She says, "I'm Rochelle Satterwhite" (30).

   Note: The number 30 refers to the page number on which the quote appears in the original text.

      In fiction, you likely have seen dialogue written as follows:

3.   "I'm Rochelle Satterwhite," she said, holding out her hand.

4.   "Do you need this?" she said.

5.   "Do you need this?" she said (30).

      When the quotation marks are highlighting a specialized term, such as one that was recently coined, there should not be a comma before the quotation, as follows:

6.   Charles Darwin termed this process "natural selection."

7.   In Augustus's reign, public baths—part of the "bread and circus" largesse with which the imperial city contented the masses—included libraries among their amenities.

Source: This excerpt is adapted from *Library: An Unquiet History by Matthew Battles* (©2003 by Matthew Battles).

Dashes

Dashes serve a variety of functions. Here is a brief summary of the main ways in which dashes are used.

1. To set aside nonessential information the same way framing commas or parentheses can in the middle of a sentence

Examples

A.   Students will be asked to write creative assignments—poems, dramas, and short stories—that mimic the literature we're studying.

B.   Joe set a world record by eating the most hot dogs—74 of them—that anyone had ever eaten in under ten minutes.

These **framing dashes** could be replaced by parentheses also, as follows.

C.   Students will be asked to write creative assignments (poems, dramas, and short stories) that mimic the literature we're studying.

D.   Joe set a world record by eating the most hot dogs (74 of them) that anyone had ever eaten in under ten minutes.

2. To highlight nonessential information at the end of a sentence after an independent clause in the same way a comma or colon can

Examples

E.   The pronghorn ran 56 miles per hour—the fastest speed ever recorded for an American land mammal.

F.   You will generate an artist's statement—a reflection on your artistic choices.

Note: When the nonessential information is a number, a dash is considered better than a comma or colon because these numbers are typically used for dramatic emphasis and a dash creates greater emphasis than a colon or a comma or commas.

3. To separate two independent clauses the same way that a period, semicolon, or colon can; students tend to dislike that so many different punctuation marks can be appropriately placed between two independent clauses

Example

G.   I am lactose intolerant—I cannot eat cheese.

In contrast, the two Mars Rovers—robotic spacecraft launched in 2003—carried a combined
70
price tag of less than one billion dollars.

70. Given that all the choices are true, which one most effectively describes what the Mars Rovers are?

F. NO CHANGE

G. which captured the imagination of the general public—

H. the products described at length in the media—

J. familiar to many who watched the news coverage at the time—

The best answer is F because "robotic spacecraft launched in 2003" offers an effective description of the Mars Rovers.

The best answer is NOT:

G because "which captured the imagination of the general public" doesn't offer any specific description of the Mars Rovers.

H because "the products described at length in the media" doesn't offer any specific description of the Mars Rovers.

J because "familiar to many who watched the news coverage at the time" doesn't offer any specific description of the Mars Rovers.

Parentheses

Parentheses set off nonessential information. Whatever is framed by parentheses, also known as a parenthetical, should be able to be cut out of the sentence without compromising the grammatical integrity of the sentence. Parentheticals can be framed by parenthesis, dashes, or commas. The sentence should still function without the parenthetical. Often parentheticals are used to introduce an acronym as seen in the following example.

CORRECT Example 1

The National Aeronautics and Space Administration **(NASA)** provides a wealth of valuable information that benefits people around the world.

Parentheses also set aside information that is not essential to the meaning of the sentence. Often this information is essentially a synonym for another word in the sentence.

CORRECT Example 2

Mary Shelley was named after her mother (Mary Wollstonecraft).

CORRECT Example 3

The bichon frise Flynn (last year's winner) is back at the dog show this year to compete again.

CORRECT Example 4

After Caesar's death, his supporter Asinius Pollio and the writer Varro (whose treatise on library administration, the *De bibliothecis,* does not survive) took up the cause, building Rome's first public library in the Forum around 39 BC.

Source: This excerpt is adapted from *Library: An Unquiet History by Matthew Battles* (©2003 by Matthew Battles).

CORRECT Example 5

As the classicist Elizabeth Rawson has pointed out, Rome lacked schools and universities (many Roman elite went to Greece for schooling); no formal competitions existed for writers and artists, as they had in Greece.

Source: This excerpt is adapted from *Library: An Unquiet History by Matthew Battles* (©2003 by Matthew Battles).

CORRECT Example 6

Though it is less popular than other parks (Great Smoky Mountains National Park, for example, drew over 11 million visitors in 2018), Grand Teton National Park is stunning.

Notice, for example, that the following parenthetical could be cut out of the following sentence.

"(Great Smoky Mountains National Park, for example, drew over 11 million visitors in 2018),"

Cutting out the parenthetical would leave simply:

"Though it is less popular than other parks, Grand Teton National Park is stunning."

Including both parentheses and framing commas is considered redundant. The introductory clause, "**Though** it is less popular than other parks," requires a comma after it because *though* is a subordinating conjunction, meaning that "Though it is less popular than other parks," is a dependent clause that must be followed by an independent clause. You may recall the following general structure of sentences that begin with a subordinating conjunction.

Subordinating conjunction + *dependent clause* + comma + <u>independent clause.</u>

Though *it is less popular than other parks*, <u>Grand Teton National Park is stunning.</u>

Here are several examples of incorrect comma usage coupled with the parenthetical.

WRONG Though it is less popular than other parks (Great Smoky Mountains National Park, for example, drew over 11 million visitors in 2018) Grand Teton National Park is stunning.

WRONG Though it is less popular than other parks, (Great Smoky Mountains National Park for example, drew over 11 million visitors in 2018), Grand Teton National Park is stunning.

WRONG Though it is less popular than other parks, (Great Smoky Mountains National Park, for example, drew over 11 million visitors in 2018), Grand Teton National Park is stunning.

Here are several examples of questions that offer parentheses as an answer choice.

Doesn't anyone play pinball anymore? I was disappointed the other day when I took my kids to a game arcade. <u>Afterwards, I went to the movies.</u> 46 Not one of the many colorful machines with flashing lights was a pinball machine. Video games filled the room.	**46. F.** NO CHANGE **G.** I made my way to the movie theater after that. **H.** (The movie theater was my next stop.) **J.** OMIT the underlined portion.

The best answer is J because the paragraph is more focused when the underlined portion is omitted. Mentioning the writer's trip to the movies diverts the reader's attention from the focus of the paragraph, which is a description of the game arcade.

The best answer is NOT:

F because adding information about the writer's trip to the movies is irrelevant to this paragraph and should be omitted. If you read the entire paragraph, you will see that this information does not belong.

G because it adds information that distracts the reader from the main focus of this introductory paragraph.

H because it adds information that distracts the reader from the main focus of this introductory paragraph. Even though this information is set off by parentheses, it still distracts the reader and is irrelevant.

The two "little brothers" of Ligia's host family, who had volunteered to move to those bedrooms for a year, had to be moved <u>upstairs to the room Ligia was using.</u> 8	**8. F.** NO CHANGE **G.** upstairs to the room Ligia was using, which had been freshly painted just that year. **H.** upstairs (it was a two-story house) to Ligia's room. **J.** OMIT the underlined portion and end the sentence with a period.

The best answer is F because it provides the best explanation of the host family's situation and why Ligia needed a place to stay. This choice provides relevant information to show that after the storm, the two brothers needed their upstairs room back—the same room that Ligia had been using.

The best answer is NOT:

G because it adds irrelevant information. The detail that the upstairs room "had been freshly painted" distracts the reader from the main point of the sentence, which is to show why Ligia needed another place to live.

H because the statement in parentheses, "it was a two-story house," is also irrelevant to the writer's purpose here.

J because if the sentence simply ended with "had to be moved," it would not clearly explain why Ligia needed a new place to live.

Colons

Colons serve many functions. A colon must have a complete sentence before it. Just because what follows a colon is a list does not mean that a colon is the appropriate punctuation mark. First, you must check that the sentence before the colon is a complete sentence. Here are some examples of the various functions of a colon.

1. Colons introduce lists that have a complete sentence before them.

Example 1

WRONG I like winter sports <u>such as:</u> skiing, snowboarding, and ice hockey.
                                      19

CORRECT I like the following winter sports: skiing, snowboarding, and ice hockey.

Note: "such as: " is *always* incorrect because the phrase "such as" makes what comes before the colon not a complete sentence. Most students can develop their ear to hear that "I like winter sports such as …" is not a complete sentence. You may need to simply memorize this rule if you struggle to develop an ear for what is and is not a complete sentence.

Strategy: Replace the punctuation mark with the word *specifically*. If it fits logically, then a colon is a good choice of punctuation mark. If these words do not fit into the context, that does not necessarily mean that a colon is not the correct punctuation mark. A colon suits a variety of purposes, which makes it challenging to evaluate whether or not a colon is the best punctuation mark to resolve an error. Let's test this strategy with the following sentence.

2. A colon works perfectly if you are trying to essentially say *specifically* or *in particular*.

Example 2

WRONG Rob thought that another factor contributed to the <u>miscommunication; texting.</u>
                                                                        11

CORRECT Rob thought that another factor contributed to the miscommunication: texting.

Strategy: Rob thought that another factor contributed to the miscommunication, **specifically** texting.

Because the word *specifically* functions well within the context of this sentence, you can feel confident selecting the colon as the correct punctuation mark to properly revise the original sentence.

3. **A colon** can also separate two independent clauses. This tends to be confusing to students because they think of a period as being the only correct punctuation mark to separate two independent clauses. A colon, semicolon, or dash can also separate two independent clauses, however. A colon is the best choice if the sentence that comes after the colon is essentially restating what comes before the colon. Often the second sentence will be a more specific version of the other sentence, often giving a concrete example. Notice that a lowercase letter follows the colon in this scenario.

Example 3

CORRECT Traffic is terrible around Thanksgiving: over forty-eight million drivers hit the roads for this holiday.

CORRECT Traffic is terrible around Thanksgiving; over forty-eight million drivers hit the roads for this holiday.

CORRECT Traffic is terrible around Thanksgiving. Over forty-eight million drivers hit the roads for this holiday.

CORRECT Traffic is terrible around Thanksgiving—over forty-eight million drivers hit the roads for this holiday.

CORRECT Everyone knows that traffic is terrible around Thanksgiving, but over forty-eight million drivers still hit the roads for this holiday.

Example 4

In this light, the flourishing libraries of Rome are unique: they are the nearest thing Rome had to incorporated, official cultural institutions as we know them today.

Source: This excerpt is adapted from *Library: An Unquiet History by Matthew Battles* (©2003 by Matthew Battles).

As you can see, a colon, semicolon, period, and dash can all separate two independent clauses. A comma followed by a coordinating conjunction can also separate two independent clauses. See the section on commas for more information.

Let's look at a real ACT English test question that offers a dash and a colon in the answer choices.

This is a startling number, especially in light of the fact that the International Space Station, the most ambitious NASA project <u>yet</u>, carried a projected price tag of "only" 17 billion dollars.	**67. A.** NO CHANGE **B.** yet **C.** yet: **D.** yet—

The best answer is A because the nonrestrictive appositive "the most ambitious NASA project yet" is nonessential explanatory information that needs to be set off by commas from the rest of the sentence.

The best answer is NOT:

B because a comma is needed after the word *yet* to finish setting off the nonrestrictive appositive "the most ambitious NASA project yet" from the rest of the sentence.

C because a comma, not a colon, is needed after the word *yet* to finish setting off the nonrestrictive appositive "the most ambitious NASA project yet" from the rest of the sentence.

D because a comma, not a dash, is needed after the word *yet* to finish setting off the nonrestrictive appositive "the most ambitious NASA project yet" from the rest of the sentence. Although a pair of dashes could have been used to set off the nonrestrictive appositive, the writer uses a comma after the word *Station,* so parallelism requires that a second comma follow the word *yet.*

Semicolons

For the purposes of the ACT English test, you can treat a semicolon essentially as though it were a period. A semicolon separates two independent clauses. Remember that an independent clause contains a subject and a verb. Identifying a subject and a verb in what comes before and after a semicolon can help you determine if the semicolon is surrounded by two independent clauses. A semicolon is preferable to a period if the two independent clauses are closely related to one another but also sufficiently different from one another. A colon, by contrast, serves many functions, one of which is to separate two independent clauses that are saying the same idea in different terms. There are several situations in which a subject and verb may be present in a dependent clause, and this can make it more difficult to determine if what comes before and after the semicolon is, in fact, an independent clause. A semicolon can also be used to separate phrases in a list.

Semicolons can be used before **conjunctive adverbs** such as the following: *accordingly, furthermore, moreover, similarly, also, hence, namely, still, anyway, however, nevertheless, then, besides, incidentally, next, thereafter, certainly, indeed, nonetheless, therefore, consequently, instead, now, thus, finally, likewise, otherwise, undoubtedly, further,* and *meanwhile.*

Here are some questions that explore this concept.

They don't need to be reminded that girls can be <u>successful they know</u> that. ₅₉	**59. A.** NO CHANGE **B.** successful they already know **C.** successful; they know **D.** successful, knowing

The best answer is C because the semicolon after the word *successful* is appropriately used to divide this sentence into two closely related independent clauses.

Correction: They don't need to be reminded that girls can be successful; they know that.

The best answer is NOT:

A because the lack of appropriate punctuation and/or a conjunction between the words *successful* and *they* creates a fused sentence.

B because the lack of appropriate punctuation and/or a conjunction between the words *successful* and *they* creates a fused sentence.

D because "successful, knowing" creates a confusing, possibly redundant sentence, as it's not clear who knows what.

Evidence that some software writers have played up the medical analogy is found in the names of their <u>programs:</u> Vaccine, Checkup, Antitoxin, and ₆₉ Disinfectant.	**69. A.** NO CHANGE **B.** programs; **C.** programs **D.** programs,

The best answer is A because it appropriately uses a colon to introduce the list of names of the programs. Introducing a list is one function of the colon.

The best answer is NOT:

B because it improperly uses the semicolon, which is generally used to separate two independent clauses.

C because it omits the necessary punctuation. The colon is needed here to signal to readers that a list of "the names of their programs" will follow.

D because the comma is not a strong-enough punctuation mark here. Is this comma the same as or part of the series of commas that follow in this sentence?

Apostrophes and Possession

Apostrophes are used to create contractions such as *can't, won't, should've* or *shouldn't*. This use of an apostrophe is not commonly tested on the ACT English test. Apostrophes can also be used to demonstrate possession. When an apostrophe is followed by a noun or by an adjective and a noun, the apostrophe signals possession. The surrounding context and the sentence itself should help you determine if the possessor is singular or plural.

For example, in the first sentence, the word *they* makes it clear that this is referring to *students* plural. The teacher figuratively belongs to the students. Therefore, using an apostrophe to signify possession is appropriate. Notice that it does not matter what is being possessed. For example, in Sentence 1, one teacher is missed by multiple students. Ending students with *s'* is appropriate because the word *students* is plural. In Example 2, multiple students miss multiple teachers. Still, the reason *students* ends in *s'* is that the word *students* is plural. This is clear because the second half of the sentence reiterates the idea that multiple students are wondering if their teachers will return.

1. The **students'** teacher has been absent for four weeks, and **they** miss her because the substitute is not as knowledgeable.

2. The **students'** teachers have been on strike for four weeks, and **the students** are beginning to wonder when the teachers will return.

3. The **student's** tutors all quit because **the student** was not doing **her** homework.

4. The **countries'** flags are prominently displayed.

5. The **students'** tutor quit when she took a full-time job as a children's book author. Her **students** understood this decision.

Note: In the last example, the word *children* is plural but does not end in *s*. In this case, it is appropriate to have the apostrophe come before the letter *s* to signify possession.

Sometimes adjectives are placed before the noun being possessed. It can also be difficult to identify that apostrophes should be used to show possession when the noun being possessed is intangible. Abstract nouns such as *justice, progress,* and *compassion* can be possessed. In the following examples, what is being possessed has been underlined. The clues that signal whether the possessor is singular or plural have been identified in bold.

Examples

1. **The students'** yellow <u>pencils</u> are sharpened before **their** exam.

2. **The yearbook's** <u>issues</u> improve each year.

3. The **citizens'** <u>freedom of expression</u> was restricted by the new government regulations imposed on **them.**

4. The **school's** educational philosophy emphasizes critical thinking and hands-on learning in **its** classrooms.

5. The **students'** imaginations ran wild when they saw **their** teacher talking to a police officer.

Strategy: To test if you should use an apostrophe to indicate possession, replace the word *students'* with the possessive pronoun *their*. For example, Example 3 would read "Their freedom of expression was restricted by the new government regulations imposed on **them.**" This makes sense. Therefore, *citizens'* is a good choice.

Often questions asking about apostrophes will also include an answer choice with no apostrophes. When a word is followed by a verb, the word is typically the subject of the sentence. It should *not* have an apostrophe.

Examples

1. The **students** are studying.

2. The **students** study all night long.

3. The **stores** are open on Thanksgiving.

By contrast, when a word is followed by a noun or an adjective and a noun, then an apostrophe is typically used to signal possession.

Examples

4. The **students'** study session was effective. **They** felt prepared for their test.

5. The **student's** study session was effective. **She** felt prepared for her test.

6. The **store's** grand opening was postponed.

Its versus It's versus Its'

Its indicates possession but does not include an apostrophe. This is because the contraction *it's* means "it is." Some ACT English test questions offer *its'* as an answer choice. This is always wrong! *Its'* does not make sense because *it* is singular and *s'* is used to signify possession when the possessor is plural. Table 5.1 summarizes how to navigate these choices.

Table 5.1 Its versus It's versus Its'

It's	Contraction = It is
Its	Singular possessive
Its'	Always wrong

Examples

1. **Allison's** dog Dulce loves playing with **its** toy hedgehog.

2. The company takes pride in **its** reputation for excellence.

3. Betsy just announced that she is pregnant, and **it's** a girl!

4. **It's** a shame that we do not have composting on campus.

Their, They're, and There

Their is the possessive form of *they*. Think of it as being similar to *its*. *They're* is the contraction "They are." Think of it as being similar to "It is." *There* refers to places. Think of it as being similar to the word *here,* which also refers to location. Table 5.2 demonstrates these points.

Table 5.2 Their, They're, and There

Similar to	Word	Meaning	Example
Its	Their	Possessive form of *they,* followed by a noun	Teenagers love **their** phones.
It's	They're	They are	**They're** always texting on their phones.
Here	There	Identifies a location	A. I left my phone right **there.** B. I went to school **there.** C. **There** is an app that can track how many hours you spend on your phone each day.

About halfway through the school year, I learned that the exchange program was looking for a new home for Ligia. After a severe storm, the basement of <u>her hosts</u> house had flooded, leaving two ₆ bedrooms unusable.	**6. F.** NO CHANGE **G.** her hosts' **H.** Ligia's hosts **J.** Ligias hosts'

The best answer is G because the plural possessive form *hosts'* is the correct punctuation here. The phrase "her hosts' house" shows possession and requires an apostrophe.

The best answer is NOT:

F because it fails to use the required apostrophe to show possession.

H because it fails to use an apostrophe after the plural *hosts*.

J because although it does use the required apostrophe after *hosts*, it fails to use the required apostrophe to show possession in Ligia's.

You have to admire the honesty of a company who's slogan is "Just About the Best."
 <u>   </u>
 31
	31. A. NO CHANGE
	
	    B. whose
	
	    C. that's
	
	    D. that the

The best answer is B because it correctly uses the relative pronoun *whose* to introduce the clause that describes the company that the narrator admires. The pronoun whose indicates possession and is appropriate here.

The best answer is NOT:

A because it uses a contraction (*who's*) instead of the required pronoun (*whose*). The contraction *who's* means "who is" and does not indicate possession.

C because it incorrectly uses the contraction *that's*, which means "that is."

D because it is creates an unclear statement, and it fails to use the proper relative pronoun *whose* to indicate possession.

Undaunted, Méliès honed his photographic skills to tell fantasy stories instead. [2] Méliès, a French magician, was fascinated by the workings of the new motion picture camera. [3] Specializing in stage illusions, he thought the camera offered potential to expand <u>its</u> spectacular magic productions. ₃₃	**33. A.** NO CHANGE
	
	    B. their
	
	    C. his
	
	    D. it's

The best answer is C because *his* is the appropriate masculine singular pronoun to refer to the male magician Méliès.

The best answer is NOT:

A because the singular pronoun *its* refers to things, not people, and in the sentence would illogically refer to the camera rather than Méliès.

B because the plural pronoun *their* has no logical antecedent in the sentence.

D because *it's* is a contraction meaning "it is," which makes no sense in the sentence.

During the early morning hours of October 28, 1965, engineers stationed 630 feet above the ground made careful measurements for the <u>days</u> work. 62	**62. F.** NO CHANGE **G.** days' **H.** day's **J.** days's

The best answer is H because it shows the correct use of the apostrophe in expressions of time. You're probably more familiar with the uses of the apostrophe to express possession or ownership or to indicate a contraction (letters left out when words are combined). But you've probably seen phrases such as "yesterday's news" and "tomorrow's headlines" and "an hour's delay"—they all follow the same punctuation rule as "the day's work."

The best answer is NOT:

> **F** because it leaves out that necessary apostrophe. Without the apostrophe, a reader might misread *the days* as a subject and *work* as a predicate.

> **G** because it places the apostrophe in the wrong location. The rest of this sentence makes it clear that this is one day's work.

> **J** because one would never use an apostrophe like this—by adding *'s* to the end of a plural noun.

The firefighters, using 700 feet of hose, were able to reach as high as 550 feet on the south leg in <u>they're attempt to reduce its</u> expansion. 71	**71. A.** NO CHANGE **B.** they're attempt to reduce it's **C.** their attempt to reduce its **D.** their attempt to reduce it's

The best answer is C because this phrasing uses the correct forms of the possessive pronouns *their* and *its*: "in their attempt to reduce its expansion." Notice that an apostrophe is not used in *its* because *it's* is a contraction for "it is."

The best answer is NOT:

> **A** because it uses the contraction *they're* (meaning "they are") where the possessive pronoun *their* is called for.

> **B** because it uses the contraction *they're* and the contraction *it's* (meaning "it is") where the possessive pronouns *their* and *its* are called for.

> **D** because it uses the contraction *it's* where the possessive pronoun *its* is called for.

The well empties into Beaver Creek, which can dwindle to a trickle in a drought, then quickly spill out of <u>its banks</u> when the rains come. 49	**49. A.** NO CHANGE **B.** it's banks' **C.** it's banks **D.** its bank's

The best answer is A because the possessive pronoun *its* is called for. This demonstrates that the banks belong to Beaver Creek.

The best answer in NOT:

> **B** because it uses the contraction *it's* (meaning "it is") where the possessive pronoun *its* is called for. It also uses the possessive *bank's* when there is nothing being possessed by the banks. Notice that the word *banks* is not followed directly by a noun.

> **C** because it uses the contraction *it's* (meaning "it is") where the possessive pronoun *its* is called for.

> **D** because it uses the possessive *bank's* when there is nothing being possessed by the banks. Notice that the word *banks* is not followed directly by a noun.

Chapter 6: Production of Writing

This chapter reviews transition between sentences and paragraphs. Using transition words effectively is an important means of connecting your ideas. This chapter also reviews logical paragraph placement and the conventions of introductory and concluding paragraphs.

Topic Development

Some questions in the ACT English test assess your ability to consider the cohesion of one paragraph or the way the paragraphs function together to support the main idea of the whole passage. Sometimes these kinds of questions will include a sentence that is entirely underlined, meaning that this entire sentence will be kept or replaced by a more appropriate answer that fully replaces the underlined sentence. Sometimes these questions will ask about the writer's "goal," which means their purpose in writing or how a certain portion of the text supports the central claim of the passage as a whole.

To answer these questions correctly, you may wish to skim the introduction and the topic sentences of each body paragraph, which should give you a general framework for the content of the full passage. If the underlined sentence is the first sentence of that paragraph, then the question is essentially asking what the topic sentence of the paragraph should be. In other words, what is the main idea of the paragraph as it connects to the main idea of the passage as a whole? You cannot just look at this one paragraph in isolation. If you did, you may incorrectly choose the NO CHANGE answer, which says that the underlined sentence does seem to capture the essence of the paragraph, but it might not fit into the context of the passage as a whole.

Transitions between Sentences

Including transitions between sentences helps writing flow. Transition words also demonstrate the relationships between sentences. The following sentences demonstrate how different types of transition words function in context.

Elaboration Words

1. A capsule wardrobe is a small collection of high-quality clothing items that serves as the foundation for one's wardrobe. **For example,** a capsule wardrobe may include classic pieces such as a navy blazer, a solid blouse, or a pencil skirt.

2. A tiny house can be a good investment for a recent college graduate who does not wish to become burdened with a 30-year mortgage. **For instance,** my older sister lived in a tiny house for five years after college, and then sold it once she had saved enough money for a more traditional home.

3. Some students believe that cheating is justified because of the importance grades play in the college admissions process. **In other words**, students are sacrificing learning opportunities simply in order to earn higher grades.

4. High school students have a great deal to accomplish over the summer. They often complete internships, travel, and learn to drive. **Furthermore,** some students study for their standardized tests over the summer.

Contrast Words

5. Snowy owls sometimes travel as far south as Florida in the winter, **but** they are rarely seen below Canada in the summer.

6. Usually crocuses appear as early as February; **however**, this year they bloomed in late April.

7. **Although** my aunt was sick of her dull wooden kitchen cabinets, she was not ready to commit to the vibrant red paint she had picked up at the hardware store.

Cause-and-Effect Words

8. Vijay was training for a marathon. **Therefore,** he increased his caloric intake to fuel his training regimen.

9. Stella was passionate about art. **Accordingly,** she studied abroad in Italy where she was able to take classes with a professor who helped restore the Sistine Chapel.

10. If you do not pay your monthly credit card balance, you will need to pay an interest fee. **Consequently,** you should pay your bill ahead of schedule to avoid incurring additional expenses.

Emphasis Words

11. Proper handwashing is important for your overall health, **especially** during flu season.

12. While most individuals think that the name Frankenstein refers to the creature in Mary Shelley's novel, the name, **in fact**, belongs to the scientist who created the monster.

13. It is widely believed that chameleons change their color in order to camouflage themselves. Their color changes due to shifts in their emotions and physiological state, **though**.

Table 6.1 shows some transition words broken down by their function.

Table 6.1 Transition Words

Elaboration	Contrast	Cause and Effect
additionally	alternatively	as a result
also	alternately	as such
as well as	despite	because
as illustrated by	even though	for
as shown by	in spite of	thus
essentially	on the other hand	therefore
furthermore	otherwise	since
for instance	rather	so
in other words	surprisingly	
such as	though	**Emphasis**
moreover	whereas	clearly
Comparison	yet	in particular
likewise		notably
in the same way		regardless
similarly		
		Sequence
		then
		meanwhile
		next
		subsequently
		ultimately
		in the end

The following strategies should help you answer questions about transition word questions.

1.   Be skeptical about choosing NO CHANGE as an answer for questions asking about transitions between sentences. Often when students read the NO CHANGE answer choice, they think they are simply evaluating if the sentence itself is grammatically correct, but transition word questions are actually asking if the meaning of the sentence fits the context of the paragraph.

2.   If the answer choices offer a word from the contrast section of the table, look at the sentence before the transition word and think about what would be the opposite of whatever adjective comes before the transition word. Read the first sentence, and then imagine, "What would be the opposite of this?"

Contrast Examples

Herbal remedies can treat numerous ailments.

What idea could contrast with the previous sentence? The opposite of herbal remedies might be traditional medicine; therefore, the sentence above may be followed by a sentence about traditional medicine as follows:

Herbal remedies can treat numerous ailments; however, one should consult a doctor before taking these natural alternative medicines.

The meal was beautifully presented.

What idea could contrast with the previous sentence? The opposite of beautiful should be a negative word like ugly. Because this sentence is describing a meal, the sentence that follows should address a negative quality of the dish such as its taste or smell.

The meal was beautifully presented, but it tasted terrible.

3.   For questions that offer transition words in the cause-and-effect category, look at the first sentence. Read it, and then imagine, "What could this cause?" Completing this process before rereading the next sentence will help you think about what cause-and-effect relationships are plausible.

Cause-and-Effect Examples

I accidentally did not charge my phone last night.

What could the result be?

I accidentally did not charge my phone last night. Therefore, my alarm did not go off, and I slept through my first period class.

The road flooded.

What could the cause be?

There was a torrential downpour last night. Consequently, the road flooded.

4. If you are offered two words that come from the same general category of transition word, it is likely that both answers are wrong. If you are offered the following choices for example, you know that answer D is correct without even reading the passage. *However,* is the only word that is sufficiently different from the rest, and, therefore, it must be the correct answer.

    A. As a result

    B. Consequently

    C. Accordingly

    D. However

Last year, one of our school's exchange students being Ligia Antolinez, <u>who came</u> ₃ from Bucaramanga, Colombia. I was a <u>junior then.</u> ₄ I wasn't in any of Ligia's classes and didn't know her, but I saw her at school events, which are sometimes supported financially by local businesses.	**4. F.** NO CHANGE
	
	   G. junior, therefore, so
	
	   H. junior because
	
	   J. junior, since

The best answer is F because this short sentence expresses a complete thought and is clear, concise, and grammatically sound. It also logically fits between the preceding sentence and the sentence that follows.

The best answer is NOT:

G because it creates a statement that is not logical. The conjunction (connecting word) therefore suggests a cause-effect relationship that makes no sense. The fact that the narrator "was a junior then" was not the cause of her not being in classes with Ligia.

H because it makes no sense. It illogically suggests that the narrator was a junior because she "wasn't in any of Ligia's classes."

J because it illogically suggests that the narrator was a junior because she "wasn't in any of Ligia's classes."

Thus, the answers to these questions can be
<u>Thus,</u> the answers to these questions can be
17
found in the artwork itself. Ringgold has told <u>the story</u>
<u>of this gathering on two horizontal panels of text.</u>
18
One panel is sewn into the piece's top border,
the other into <u>it's</u> bottom border. These eight
19
<u>women the story explains, strove in their various</u>
20   21
<u>ways</u> to support the cause of justice in the world.

In <u>reality,</u> these women never met to piece
22
together a quilt. The scene comes out of the
<u>artists imagination</u> as a statement of the unity of
23
purpose that she perceives in their lives.

22. **F.** NO CHANGE

   G. summary,

   H. addition,

   J. contrast,

The best answer is F because the rest of the paragraph explains that the women depicted in the artwork lived at different times and so couldn't have sat together and made a quilt.

The best answer is NOT:

   G because the phrase "in summary" illogically suggests that the sentence summarizes the preceding text, which it does not do.

   H because the phrase "in addition" illogically suggests that the sentence directly adds to the preceding text, which it does not do.

   J because the phrase "in contrast" illogically suggests that the sentence provides a direct contrast to the preceding text, which it does not do.

When I was a girl in the 1960s, my friends and I loved Nancy Drew. [55] We loved her loyal companions, her bravado, and <u>there was a love for her freedom to do what she wanted.</u>
56
We <u>also</u> loved how smart she was and how pretty,
57
how confident and successful.

57. Which of the following alternatives to the underlined portion would be LEAST acceptable?

   A. furthermore

   B. therefore

   C. likewise

   D. DELETE the underlined portion.

The best answer is B because the word *therefore* is the only one of the four alternatives that, in the context of the sentence, can't reasonably be used as a substitute for the underlined portion (*also*). *Therefore* introduces something that is a result of something else but also signals the addition of one or more things. Thus, *therefore* is the LEAST acceptable alternative to *also*.

The best answer is NOT:

A because the word *furthermore,* meaning "in addition," is an acceptable alternative to the word *also,* because the two mean essentially the same thing in this context.

C because the word *likewise,* meaning "in a similar manner," is an acceptable alternative to the word *also,* because the two mean essentially the same thing in this context.

D because deleting the underlined portion doesn't change the meaning of the sentence much if at all. Even without the word *also,* the sentence is clearly adding to the list of qualities that the narrator and her friends loved about Nancy Drew.

Sending machines unaccompanied by humans to Mars does drain some of the romance out of aging or older visions of space travel. In other words, we need to keep in mind that the right equipment can accomplish as much as any crew of scientists, if not more—such as a fraction of the cost. Before any astronaut boards a spacecraft for that distant planet, the staggering expense of such a mission should be carefully considered. 75

72 73 74

73. A. NO CHANGE

   B. For that reason alone,

   C. In that time frame,

   D. Even so,

The best answer is D because the phrase "Even so," meaning "despite that," effectively signals the contrast between the preceding sentence, which says that using only machines to explore Mars may take some of the romance out of space travel, and this sentence, which says that we nevertheless need to remember that the right machines can do as much as if not more than humans can and at a fraction of the cost.

The best answer is NOT:

A because the phrase "In other words" incorrectly indicates that this sentence restates or summarizes the preceding sentence. Instead, this sentence offers a contrast to the preceding one.

B because the phrase "For that reason alone" incorrectly indicates that this sentence offers a consequence following from a circumstance identified in the preceding sentence. Instead, this sentence offers a contrast to the preceding one.

C because the phrase "In that time frame" makes no sense in context, because no time frame is indicated in the preceding sentence. Instead, this sentence offers a contrast to the preceding one.

Sending machines unaccompanied by humans to Mars does drain some of the romance out of <u>aging or older</u> visions of space travel.
72

<u>In other words,</u> we need to keep in mind that
73

the right equipment can accomplish as much as any crew of scientists, if not more—<u>such as a</u>
74

fraction of the cost. Before any astronaut boards a spacecraft for that distant planet, the staggering expense of such a mission should be carefully considered. [75]

74. F. NO CHANGE

G. at

H. but only

J. DELETE the underlined portion.

The best answer is G because the word *at* creates a conventional, idiomatic expression ("at a fraction of the cost") that makes sense in the context of the writer identifying an additional consideration (machines doing as much as if not more than humans and at a much lower cost).

The best answer is NOT:

F because the phrase "such as" creates a nonsensical expression ("such as a fraction of the cost").

H because the phrase "but only" is missing the word *at,* which would make it a conventional, idiomatic expression ("but only at a fraction of the cost"), and because *but* suggests a contrast with what precedes it in the sentence when what follows is an additional consideration (machines doing as much as if not more than humans and at a much lower cost). (The writer here might have used "at only," for example, but not "but only.")

J because deleting the underlined portion creates a nonsensical expression. "A fraction of the cost" suggests that what precedes it in the sentence identifies a cost (e.g., "… less than one billion dollars—a fraction of the cost [of a human mission]"), but this isn't the case.

Grandpa is intrigued by the various uses for that remote. He has confided in me that the volume control is perfect for turning up the sound whenever Grandma asks him to take out the garbage. <u>For example,</u> he says, the button
8

that mutes the sound lets him cut <u>them</u> off in
9

midsentence.

8. F. NO CHANGE

G. To illustrate,

H. On the one hand,

J. On the other hand,

Strategy: For transition word question, try to eliminate words that are similar to each other. "For example" and "to illustrate" both introduce specific examples. It is unlikely that one of these answer choices would be superior to the other. Therefore, they are both likely wrong.

The best answer is J because the phrase "On the other hand" signals that this sentence is going to provide a contrasting point or a different perspective. Grandpa's logic goes like this: The remote control's volume button is great for drowning out someone he doesn't want to hear; on the other hand (from another perspective), the mute button is great for silencing the television when he doesn't want to hear it.

The best answer is NOT:

F because the phrase "For example" indicates that this sentence will offer an example of the statement expressed in the sentence before it. This sentence does not provide that payoff.

G because the phrase "To illustrate" is fairly close in meaning to "For example."

H because the phrase "On the one hand" suggests that the writer is going to make a point here and then make another point. But the other point never gets made here; this is the last sentence in this paragraph. "On the one hand" should be followed by "on the other hand" or some equivalent.

Architect Eero <u>Saarinen, who created</u> the design
              23
 that symbolized the memorial's theme of St. Louis as the "Gateway to the West." <u>Meanwhile, the</u> arch
                       24
 would have a stainless steel exterior and interior structural supports made of concrete. Both legs of the arch would be built simultaneously using triangular sections. Those at the base of each arch leg would be the largest, with the higher sections progressively smaller.
	24. A. NO CHANGE
	
	 B. Therefore, the
	
	 C. However, the
	
	 D. The

The best answer is D because this question asks you to decide which word would provide the most logical and effective transition from one sentence to another. The best decision here is to use no transitional adverb at all. The preceding sentence states that Saarinen designed the Gateway Arch. This sentence is the first of three that describe the details of that design.

The best answer is NOT:

A because the sense of *Meanwhile* is that this event takes place at the same time that the preceding event takes place. That sense doesn't work logically here.

B because the sense of *Therefore* is that this condition exists or event takes place as a result of the preceding condition or event. That sense would work here only if we'd already been told that Saarinen's designs always look like the description that follows.

C because the sense of *However* is that this condition exists or event takes place in contrast to the preceding condition or event. That sense would work only if we'd already been told that Saarinen's designs never look like the description that follows.

We spent the rest of the morning veering from the trail to investigate small snatches of life. Lizards lazing in the sun and quail <u>rustled</u> through grasses
               12
 surprised us. Wild blackberries melted on our tongues. <u>For example, the</u> aroma of crushed
           13
 eucalyptus leaves tingled in our noses.
	13. A. NO CHANGE
	
	    B. On the other hand, the
	
	    C. Just in case, the
	
	    D. The

The best answer is D because no transition word or phrase is necessary here to make the sentence part of a list of sensory experiences the narrator and son had: seeing lizards and quail, eating wild blackberries, and smelling crushed eucalyptus leaves.

The best answer is NOT:

A because the phrase "For example" illogically suggests that the aroma of crushed eucalyptus leaves is an example of the taste of wild blackberries rather than being the third item in a list of sensory experiences.

B because the phrase "On the other hand" illogically suggests that the aroma of crushed eucalyptus leaves is somehow in opposition to the taste of wild blackberries rather than being the third item in a list of sensory experiences.

C because the phrase "Just in case" makes no sense in this context; it is unclear what smelling the aroma of crushed eucalyptus leaves would be designed to prevent.

Transitions between Paragraphs

Questions about transitions between paragraphs can be completed using a process similar to the approach taken for transitions between sentences. With transitions between paragraphs, you should always reread the paragraph directly before the topic sentence that you are specifically being asked about. Often this requires flipping the page back-and-forth, which sometimes is enough to make a student just wildly guess on this type of question. Remember that the end of one paragraph and the beginning of the next should have a logical bridge. This is a good piece of information to keep in mind when you are writing your own essays. **Reminder:** Brackets identify the number of the paragraph.

[3]

The attractions of video games, however, are superficial and short-lived. As you guide your character through the game's challenges, you come to know exactly how the machine that's built to last <u>machine that's built to last</u> will respond to your every move. <u>He or she learns</u> where the hazards lurk and the special weapons are hidden. Pinball, <u>though,</u> can't be predicted with such accuracy. You never know when the ball will drain straight down the middle, out of reach of both flippers, Then again, you can sometimes get lucky, and a ball you thought was <u>lost, will</u> inexplicably bounce back into play.

[4]

<u>It is the element of chance that makes pinball</u> more interesting than video games. Most video games are designed so that your main opponent <u>in these video games</u> is a predictable computer program. Once you have mastered a game, the challenge is gone, and <u>you must look</u> for a new game to conquer. After you learn the new game, you get bored again. The cycle keeps repeating. But in pinball, you have three factors to consider: you, the machine, and chance, which is sometimes your <u>enemy</u> sometimes your ally. No matter how many games you play on any pinball machine, <u>the various times of each</u> game is different. That's what makes pinball a <u>continually</u> challenge.

54. Which choice would most effectively and appropriately lead the reader from the topic of Paragraph 3 to that of Paragraph 4?

F. NO CHANGE

G. Pinball does share certain similarities with video games.

H. Pinball, although less challenging than video games, can still be fun to play.

J. Video games do generally evolve into subsequent editions or enhanced versions.

Strategy: Review the content of the paragraph that follows and try to develop two key ideas that should be captured in the topic sentence. Also consider if the topic sentence serves as a logical transition from the previous paragraph.

The best answer is F because it most effectively links the topic of Paragraph 3 (pinball is less predictable than video games) and the topic of Paragraph 4 (the element of chance makes pinball more interesting than video games).

The best answer is NOT:

   G because it fails to provide an effective link between the topics of the two paragraphs. This choice undermines the writer's argument by saying that pinball games are similar to video games.

H because it fails to provide an effective transition from Paragraph 3 to Paragraph 4. It also contradicts the writer's previously stated point that pinball is challenging.

J because it provides an ineffective transition between the ideas presented in the two paragraphs. In addition, if you inserted this sentence at the beginning of Paragraph 4, the next sentence would not logically follow.

[1]

Imagine sitting in front of a computer monitor, filling the screen with your mind's jumbled thoughts. Tomorrow's assignment is slowly materializing before your eyes. Suddenly, without warning, each of the letters, in front of you tumbles to the bottom
                                     61
of the screen. Is this a bad dream? Not exactly. The computer is probably sick, unless the diagnosis
                                        62
may be that the computer has a virus.

[2]

Analogous to a biological virus that takes over a living cell, a computer virus is a program, or set of instructions, that invades a computer either to create mischief or do real damage. The type of computer virus mentioned above is more mischievous than harmful. Eventually, the letters reorder themselves on the screen. Not all viruses however, straighten themselves out.
63

[3]

Computer viruses range from being temporary
                                        64
annoyances to permanently destroying data. Computer vandals rig these viruses to go off at a preset time. These bombs can permanently destroy data, and that can be disastrous to the
operation of a computer.   65

64. Which choice is the most effective first sentence of Paragraph 3?

F. NO CHANGE

G. Among the more serious viruses are those referred to as "bombs."

H. Most people would agree that they'd rather have a computer virus than a virus that puts them in bed for a week.

J. Despite technological advances, computers are still fragile devices in many ways.

Strategy: Look for demonstrative adjectives such as *this, that, these,* and *those.* Make sure that these pronouns have a clear referent. In other words, make sure that they refer back to a concrete noun earlier in the passage. This paragraph contains the phrases "these viruses" and "these bombs," which should help you realize that the previous sentences should include nouns that could be referred back to as "these viruses" and "these bombs."

The best answer is G because it provides the most effective introductory sentence for Paragraph 3. The topic of the paragraph is the serious computer viruses known as "bombs." Notice that the second sentence in this paragraph logically follows and further defines these "bombs." That sentence is as follows: "Computer vandals rig these viruses to go off at a preset time." Bombs are among the most serious computer viruses. Note that this question is asking you to completely replace the underlined sentence. Noting that the first answer choice is NO CHANGE helps make this clear.

The corrections to the passage read as follows:

Not all viruses, however, straighten themselves out.

Among the more serious viruses are those referred to as "**bombs.**" Computer vandals rig **these viruses** to go off at a preset time. **These bombs** can permanently destroy data.

The best answer is NOT:

F because the information is too broad. The topic of the paragraph is not all computer viruses; rather, it is the much narrower topic of viruses called "bombs." In addition, if this sentence opened the paragraph, the reader would not understand, later in the paragraph, what "these bombs" referred to.

H because it introduces a topic other than the "bombs." If you read the paragraph with this sentence as the introduction, the paragraph makes no sense.

J because it, too, strays from the main topic of the paragraph, which is the computer viruses referred to as "bombs."

With its distinctive red tint and its polar ice caps, the planet Mars has fascinated humans for thousands of years. There were ancient Babylonian
                                                                61
astronomers who associated Mars with their war god Negral, to twentieth-century science fiction writers whose works become best-sellers, this
                                                62
planet has often been a symbol of ill will and danger.

The United States has competed with other countries to explore space. By 2003, the National
                                   63
Aeronautics and Space Administration (NASA) would of sent thirty spacecraft to the red planet,
            64
speculation has been prompted that a human
                            65
voyage may no longer be the stuff of fiction.

63. Given that all the choices are true, which one best leads from the preceding paragraph to the subject of this paragraph?

A. NO CHANGE

B. Today, such negative associations seem to be dissipating.

C. In 1958, the United States founded an agency to run its space program.

D. Earth and Mars are both planets in the inner solar system.

The best answer is B because this sentence effectively ties together the bad reputation Mars has often had ("such negative associations"), described in the preceding paragraph, and the more recent interest in robotic and human missions to Mars, discussed in this paragraph.

The best answer is NOT:

A because this sentence about the United States competing with other countries to explore space is at best only loosely relevant to the topic of this paragraph, which is recent interest in robotic and human missions to Mars, and is unconnected to the topic of the preceding paragraph, which is Mars's impact on thought and culture.

C because this sentence about which year the United States founded its space agency is loosely relevant to the topic of this paragraph, which is recent interest in robotic and human missions to Mars, but is unconnected to the topic of the preceding paragraph, which is Mars's impact on thought and culture.

D because this sentence about Earth and Mars being planets in the inner solar system offers encyclopedia- or textbook-style information that is only loosely related to the topic of this paragraph, which is recent interest in robotic and human missions to Mars, and the topic of the preceding paragraph, which is Mars's impact on thought and culture.

Few would deny that the idea of a human mission ‾‾‾ 66 to Mars is exciting, who is ready to pay for such an expedition?	**66. F.** NO CHANGE **G.** Maybe a few **H.** Although few **J.** Few, if any,

The best answer is H because the phrase "Although few" begins a subordinate introductory clause that is set off from the sentence's main clause with a comma, resulting in a complete and logical sentence.

The best answer is NOT:

F because the lack of a subordinating conjunction in front of the word *Few* turns the introductory clause into an independent clause joined to the sentence's main clause by only the comma after the word *exciting*. The result is a comma splice.

G because the lack of a subordinating conjunction in front of the words "Maybe a few" turns the introductory clause into an independent clause joined to the sentence's main clause by only the comma after the word *exciting*. The result is a comma splice.

J because the lack of a subordinating conjunction in front of the words "Few, if any," turns the introductory clause into an independent clause joined to the sentence's main clause by only the comma after the word *exciting*. The result is a comma splice.

In contrast, the two Mars Rovers—robotic spacecraft launched in 2003—carried a combined ‾‾‾ 70 price tag of less than one billion dollars.	**70.** Given that all the choices are true, which one most effectively describes what the Mars Rovers are? **F.** NO CHANGE **G.** which captured the imagination of the general public— **H.** the products described at length in the media— **J.** familiar to many who watched the news coverage at the time—

The best answer is F because "robotic spacecraft launched in 2003" offers an effective description of the Mars Rovers.

The best answer is NOT:

G because "which captured the imagination of the general public" doesn't offer any specific description of the Mars Rovers.

H because "the products described at length in the media" doesn't offer any specific description of the Mars Rovers.

J because "familiar to many who watched the news coverage at the time" doesn't offer any specific description of the Mars Rovers.

However, the salesperson was persistent and, appealing to Grandpa's TV-viewing habits, described the various functions on the remote. However, my grandpa could punch in the time, and ₆ the channel of his favorite daily news program, and ₇ the TV would turn on that program at the proper time.	**6. F.** NO CHANGE **G.** Additionally, Grandpa **H.** Conversely, my grandpa **J.** Grandpa

The best answer is J because, here, no adverb or phrase is needed to make a connection between these two sentences. The essay works fine here without that kind of help.

The best answer is NOT:

F because the adverb *however,* as it is used here, indicates that this sentence is going to contradict or contrast with the statement in the preceding sentence. This sentence does not do that.

G because the adverb *additionally* indicates that this sentence is going to add a point that builds on the statement in the preceding sentence. This sentence does not do that.

H because the adverb *conversely* expresses the same general idea that *however* does. This sentence does not provide a contrast to the statement in the preceding sentence.

Paragraph Placement

Some questions will ask you where one paragraph should be placed within a passage. Knowing the typical structure of a passage can help you determine where a paragraph should be placed. The initial paragraphs of a passage typically define the key terms of the passage. For example, the passage "Bill Williams Brings America Home to Dinner" begins by introducing Bill Williams's line of food products, which is designed to replicate home cooking. Then it narrows to focus on how Williams brought his products into the mainstream by selling them at grocery stores. The body paragraphs describe the evolution of Williams's company. The conclusion emphasizes how far the company has come in such a short time.

Original Passage

[1]

You have to admire the honesty of a company who's slogan is "Just About the Best." Glory Foods'
<u>who's slogan is "Just About the Best." Glory Foods'</u>
31
<u>president, and founder Bill Williams,</u> explains the
32
unusual slogan by admitting that while he knows that his foods can't beat the taste of real home cooking, <u>it does</u> come very close.
33

[2]

Even as a child, Williams loved to prepare food, and as a young adult, <u>he refined his cooking skills</u>
34
at the <u>prestigiously acclaimed</u> Culinary Institute of
35
America. <u>In 1989, he came up with his idea for a</u>
<u>line of Southern-inspired cuisine,</u> a time when there
36
were no convenience foods designed for African American consumers. Over the next three years, he developed a line of products that included canned greens, sweet potatoes, beans, and okra, as well as bottled hot sauce and cornbread mixes.

[3]

Eventually, Williams was ready to launch his products in grocery stores. <u>Initially, Glory Foods</u>
37
were first offered for sale in Ohio in 1992 and soon became available in neighboring states. Within a year, sales were twice the original projections. 38

[4]

The company's African American focus is evident in all aspects of Glory Foods. The firm's headquarters are located in the same black neighborhood where Williams grew up, and the company helps to support several local community projects. The firm also employs African American <u>professional advisers</u> and subcontractors whenever
39
possible and contracts African American farmers to grow much of the produce that goes into Glory Foods. 40

The following paragraphs may or may not be in the most logical order. Each paragraph is numbered in brackets, and Question 45 will ask you to choose where Paragraph 1 should most logically be placed.

45. For the sake of logic and coherence, Paragraph 1 should be placed:

A. where it is now.

B. after Paragraph 2.

C. after Paragraph 3.

D. after Paragraph 6.

[5]

The company's name reflects this African American focus as well. Glory is meant <u>to evoke</u>
₄₁
both the exultant spirit of gospel churches and the movie <u>during the Civil War</u> of the same name,
₄₂
which tells the story of a black regiment. [43]

[6]

With twenty full-time employees in its administrative offices, Glory Foods has come a long way from its beginnings. America's dinner tables <u>were</u> the beneficiaries of Bill Williams's drive,
₄₄
determination, and culinary expertise. [45]

Revised Passage

[1]

You have to admire the honesty of a company whose slogan is "Just About the Best." Glory Foods' president and founder, Bill Williams, explains the unusual slogan by admitting that while he knows that his foods can't beat the taste of real home cooking, they do come very close.

[2]

Even as a child, Williams loved to prepare food, and as a young adult, he refined his cooking skills at the prestigious Culinary Institute of America. He came up with his idea for a line of Southern-inspired cuisine in 1989, a time when there were no convenience foods designed for African American consumers. Over the next three years, he developed a line of products that included canned greens, sweet potatoes, beans, and okra, as well as bottled hot sauce and cornbread mixes.

[3]

Eventually, Williams was ready to launch his products in grocery stores. Glory Foods were first offered for sale in Ohio in 1992 and soon became available in neighboring states. Within a year, sales were twice the original projections.

(continued)

Revised Passage (*continued*)

[4]

The company's African American focus is evident in all aspects of Glory Foods. The firm's headquarters are located in the same black neighborhood where Williams grew up, and the company helps to support several local community projects. The firm also employs African American professional advisers and subcontractors whenever possible and contracts African American farmers to grow much of the produce that goes into Glory Foods.

[5]

The company's name reflects this African American focus as well. *Glory* is meant to evoke both the exultant spirit of gospel churches and the movie of the same name, which tells the story of a black regiment during the Civil War.

[6]

With twenty full-time employees in its administrative offices, Glory Foods has come a long way from its beginnings. America's dinner tables are the beneficiaries of Bill Williams's drive, determination, and culinary expertise.

The best answer is A because it provides the most effective introductory paragraph. This is the best opening for the essay because it introduces the main topic, which is Bill Williams and his company, Glory Foods.

The best answer is NOT:

    B because Paragraph 2 would be an ineffective and confusing opening for this essay. Look at its first sentence: "Even as a child, Williams loved to prepare food." The clue that this is not a good opening sentence is that most essays would not begin this abruptly. The reader would not know who this Williams person was.

    C because placing Paragraph 1 after Paragraph 3 makes Paragraph 2 the opening paragraph, but that paragraph begins too abruptly to provide an effective introduction.

    D because Paragraph 2 is not an effective introduction, any move of Paragraph 1 results in the wrong answer choice.

Conclusion Questions

Some questions will ask you to add a concluding sentence to the passage or paragraph. Knowing the typical structure of a passage can help you determine what content should appear in the conclusion. The initial paragraphs of a passage typically define the key terms of the passage. For example, the passage "My 'Sister' Ligia" begins by introducing the general concept of exchange students. Then it narrows the focus to one particular exchange student: Ligia. The body paragraphs describe Ligia's experience living with a host family from the perspective of a member of the host family. The conclusion reflects all that the family has gained through the experience. It essentially recaps the main ideas of the passage, which is typical of a concluding paragraph. Sometimes important ideas can be found beyond the first sentence of each paragraph. Some of the important ideas have been highlighted in **bold** in this next passage in order to help you think about the content and tone of the concluding sentence.

PASSAGE I: My "Sister" Ligia	
Every year my high school hosts international exchange <u>students, those teenagers</u> join our senior ₁ class. Each student usually lives with the family of one of the seniors. I can recall students from Costa Rica, Italy, Norway, and Nigeria. Last year, **one of our school's exchange <u>students being</u> Ligia** ₂ **Antolinez, <u>who</u> came from Bucaramanga,** ₃ **Colombia**. I was a <u>junior then</u>. I wasn't in any of ₄ Ligia's classes and didn't know her, but I <u>saw her</u> at school events, which are sometimes supported financially by local businesses. ₅	

(continued)

PASSAGE I: My "Sister" Ligia (continued)

About halfway through the school year, **I learned that the exchange program was looking for a new home for Ligia.** After a severe storm, the basement of her hosts house had flooded, leaving
6
two bedrooms unusable. The two "little brothers" of Ligia's host family, who had volunteered to move, to those bedrooms for a year, had to be moved
7
upstairs to the room Ligia was using.
8

I told my parents about Ligia's problem, which needed to be solved. We agreed that it
9   10
would be fun to host a student from another country. My older sister had gotten married the summer before, so not only did we have a room for Ligia, and we all admitted that the
11
house had seemed too quiet lately.

The second half of my junior year was anything but quiet. **Introduced by me to my favorite music, at top volume, I started being taught by Ligia the most popular Colombian dance steps.**
12
My father spoke fondly of the days before two

teenagers taken over the phone, the stereo, the
13
kitchen—well, most of the house, really. My mother helped Ligia with her math homework, and **Ligia taught Mom beginning Spanish.** Both Ligia and I were studying French that year, and we practiced it at home. When we planned a surprise anniversary party for my mom and dad, we did it all right under their noses, in French.

At the end of the year, Ligia had gone home to
14
Colombia. This year I'm busy with senior activities and with a part-time job. I'm trying to save enough to go see my new sister next year. [15]

15. Which of the following true sentences, if inserted here, would best conclude the essay as well as maintain the positive tone established earlier in the essay?

A. I'm afraid of flying, but I think I'll be OK.

B. I'm eager to eventually join the workforce full time.

C. I've been practicing my Spanish—and my dance steps.

D. Senior activities are a lot of fun.

The best answer is C because it concludes the essay by referring back to topics that were previously mentioned: that Ligia spoke Spanish and that she taught the narrator Colombian dance steps. In addition, it logically follows the preceding sentence by explaining how the narrator continues to make plans for a visit to Ligia.

The best answer is NOT:

    A because although it does somewhat follow the preceding sentence, it does not refer back to any of the ideas mentioned in the essay. It is therefore a poor conclusion when compared with C. The passage does not address the narrator's fear of flying. The tone is also too negative.

    B because this is a poor conclusion for the essay because it introduces an entirely new topic: joining the workforce.

    D because although the essay does refer previously to "senior activities," this is also a weak conclusion because it is a vague generalization. In addition, it does not logically follow the statement that the narrator is "trying to save enough to go see my new sister next year."

The Save-U has a neon sign out front that says "Friendly 24-Hour Service," but as far as I can tell, no one really works there. The washers and dryers are lime green, and the paneling on the walls <u>has been</u> painted to match, although it was later
22
varnished with some kind of artificial wood grain finish. [23] I often stare at that paneling when I don't have a magazine or newspaper to read and don't want to do my schoolwork. Deep in thought, I contemplate the competence of the laundromat's interior designer.

    <u>Some machines even provide a certain amount of sustenance and entertainment.</u> This laundromat
24
has three soda machines, two candy machines, two pinball machines, five video machines, and a machine that eats dollar bills and spits out too <u>much or too few</u> quarters.
25

    There are many regular customers whose faces have become familiar—mostly older people from around the neighborhood. [26]
Usually a crowd of thirteen-year-old <u>kids that is</u>
27
gathered around the video machines, regardless of the time of day.

24. Which choice most effectively guides the reader from the preceding paragraph into this new paragraph?

    F. NO CHANGE

    G. The Save-U has to have friendly service because it is across the street from a park.

    H. Maybe what the Save-U means by friendly service is an abundance of machines.

    J. Washing machines are the Save-U's version of 24-hour service.

The best answer is H because it effectively links the new paragraph to the question implied by the preceding paragraph: why does the neon sign promise friendly service? **H** also provides the most effective introduction to the information in the new paragraph.

The best answer is NOT:

    F because it does not link the theme of friendly service that is questioned in the preceding paragraph to the description of the machines in this new paragraph. In addition, it shifts to a more formal tone.

G because it makes no sense. Being "across the street from a park" has nothing to do with friendly service. Besides, in the first paragraph, the writer states that "the park isn't really a park at all."

J because it misleads the reader into thinking that the topic of the new paragraph will be "washing machines."

For this question, the surrounding paragraphs have been reproduced because the question asks about a sentence that comes between paragraphs.

[1]

You have to admire the honesty of a company who's slogan is "Just About the Best." Glory Foods'
31
president, and founder Bill Williams, explains the
32
unusual slogan by admitting that while he knows that his foods can't beat the taste of real home cooking, it does come very close.
33

[2]

Even as a child, Williams loved to prepare food, and as a young adult, he refined his cooking skills
34
at the prestigiously acclaimed Culinary Institute
35
of America. In 1989, he came up with his idea for a line of Southern-inspired cuisine, a time
36
when there were no convenience foods designed for African American consumers. Over the next three years, he developed a line of products that included canned greens, sweet potatoes, beans, and okra, as well as bottled hot sauce and cornbread mixes.

[3]

Eventually, Williams was ready to launch his products in grocery stores. Initially, Glory Foods were
37
first offered for sale in Ohio in 1992 and soon became available in neighboring states. Within a year, sales were twice the original projections. [38]

[4]

The company's African American focus is evident in all aspects of Glory Foods. The firm's headquarters are located in the same black neighborhood where Williams grew up, and the

38. Given that all of the following sentences are true, which one would most effectively conclude this paragraph?

F. Bill Williams's company continues to refine the recipes of its products.

G. By 1995, Glory Foods were being distributed in twenty-two states.

H. Today, there are several other companies that target their products to African American consumers.

J. Bill Williams, however, sought the advice of food marketing experts.

company helps to support several local community projects. The firm also employs African American professional advisers and subcontractors whenever
39
possible and contracts African American farmers to grow much of the produce that goes into Glory Foods. 40

The best answer is G because it most effectively concludes this paragraph by continuing the theme of Glory Foods' business success. That Glory Foods "were being distributed in twenty-two states" logically follows the information that "sales were twice the original projections."

The best answer is NOT:

F because it changes the topic by discussing recipes instead of the company's success.

H because it shifts to an entirely new topic, that of "several other companies."

J because the use of the word *however* makes this statement illogical. As it is used here, *however* indicates that this sentence is going to contradict the statement in the preceding sentence, but this sentence does not do that.

Méliès's magician's eye led him to discover the basics of special effects. 36 He experimented with effects such as speeding up and slowing down the action, reversing it for backward movement, and superimposing images of fantastic creatures over real people. Using overhead pulleys and trapdoors, he was able to do interesting things.
37

37. Given that all the choices are true, which one would best conclude this sentence so that it illustrates Méliès's skill and inventiveness?

A. NO CHANGE

B. he used effects commonly seen in his stage productions.

C. his actors could enter and leave the scene.

D. he perfected eerie film entrances and exits.

The best answer is D because perfecting "eerie film entrances and exits" is a specific example of Méliès's skill and inventiveness.

The best answer is NOT:

A because the clause "he was able to do interesting things" is vague and doesn't give any specific illustration of Méliès's skill and inventiveness.

B because the clause "he used effects commonly seen in his stage productions" doesn't suggest that Méliès was particularly skillful or inventive; on the contrary, it suggests that the best Méliès could do as a filmmaker was to copy himself.

C because "his actors could enter and leave the scene" shifts the focus away from Méliès to his actors, which doesn't effectively highlight Méliès's skill and inventiveness and because relative to D, C is imprecise.

Our technologically advanced times has allowed
<u>has allowed</u>
31
filmmakers to create spectacular science fiction films to intrigue us with worlds beyond our experience. Imagine the excitement in <u>1902 when</u>
32
audiences first saw *Le Voyage dans la lune (A Trip to the Moon)*, a groundbreaking movie produced by Georges Méliès.

[1] Undaunted, Méliès honed his photographic skills to tell fantasy stories instead. [2] Méliès, a French magician, was fascinated by the workings of the new motion picture camera. [3] Specializing in stage illusions, he thought the camera offered potential to expand <u>its</u> spectacular magic
33
productions. [4] By 1895, he was working with the new invention. [5] He found <u>out, however,</u> that the
34
public preferred live magic acts to filmed versions. 35

Méliès's magician's eye led him to discover the basics of special effects. 36 He experimented with effects such as speeding up and slowing down the action, reversing it for backward movement, and superimposing images of fantastic creatures over real people. Using overhead pulleys and trapdoors, <u>he was able to do interesting things.</u>
37
Aware of the popularity of Jules Verne's science fiction novels, Méliès saw exciting possibilities in filming a space odyssey. The interplanetary travel film that he created, *A Trip to the Moon*, had production costs of $4,000, <u>highly excessively</u>
38
for its time. In this film, a space capsule <u>that is fired and thereby launched and projected</u> from a
39
cannon lands in the eye of the Man in the Moon.

In a strange terrain filled with hostile <u>creatures,</u> the
40
space travelers experience many adventures. They escape back to Earth in the capsule by falling off the edge of the <u>moon, landing</u> in the ocean, they
41
bob around until a passing ship finally rescues them.

Producing the film long before interplanetary explorations <u>had began,</u> Méliès could <u>arouse</u> his
42   43
audience's curiosity with unconstrained fantasy. <u>People are still going to theaters to see science fiction film.</u>
44

44. Given that all the choices are true, which one would most effectively express the writer's viewpoint about Méliès's role in science fiction filmmaking?

F. NO CHANGE

G. This first space odyssey provided the genesis for a film genre that still packs theaters.

H. Méliès made an important contribution to filmmaking many years ago.

J. In Méliès's production even the film crew knew a lot about space.

The best answer is G because the writer's assertion that *A Trip to the Moon* "provided the genesis for a film genre"—science fiction—"that still packs theaters" is both specific and consistent with the writer's point, made throughout the essay, that Méliès produced a landmark movie.

The best answer is NOT:

F because the assertion that "People are still going to theaters to see science fiction films" has no clear tie to Méliès's role in science fiction filmmaking.

H because the assertion that "Méliès made an important contribution to filmmaking many years ago" is vague and doesn't clearly express the writer's viewpoint about Méliès's role in science fiction filmmaking.

J because the assertion that "In Méliès's production even the film crew knew a lot about space" shifts the focus away from Méliès's own role in science fiction filmmaking.

PASSAGE IV: Pinball and Chance

[1]

Doesn't anyone play pinball anymore? I was disappointed the other day when I took my kids to a game arcade. Afterwards, I went to the
46
movies. Not one of the many colorful machines with flashing lights were a pinball machine. Video
47
games filled the room.

[2]

[1] I can understand why video games might seem more attractive than pinball. [2] Video screens which have been populated by movie
48
stars, monsters, and heroes. [3] You can blow up cities, escape from dungeons, and battle all sorts of villains. [4] Pinball machines, on the other hand, are essentially all the same. [5] Some machines are bigger and fancier than others, but the object of pinball never changes: you have to keep a steel ball in play long enough to rack up a high score and win a free game. 49

(continued)

PASSAGE IV: Pinball and Chance (*continued*)

[3]

The attractions of video games, however, are superficial and short-lived. As you guide your character through the game's challenges, you come to know exactly how the <u>machine that's built to last</u>
50
will respond to your every move. <u>He or she learns</u>
51
where the hazards lurk and the special weapons are hidden. Pinball, <u>though,</u> can't be predicted with
52
such accuracy. You never know when the ball will drain straight down the middle, out of reach of both flippers, Then again, you can sometimes get lucky, and a ball you thought was <u>lost, will</u> inexplicably
53
bounce back into play.

[4]

It is <u>the element of chance that makes pinball</u>
<u>more interesting than video games.</u> Most video
54
games are designed so that your main opponent
<u>in these video games</u> is a predictable computer
55
program. Once you have mastered a game, the challenge is gone, and <u>you must look</u> for a new
56
game to conquer. After you learn the new game, you get bored again. The cycle keeps repeating. But in pinball, you have three factors to consider: you, the machine, and chance, which is sometimes your <u>enemy</u> sometimes your ally. No matter how
57
many games you play on any pinball machine, <u>the</u>
<u>various times of each</u> game is different. That's what
58
makes pinball a <u>continually</u> challenge. [60]
59

60. Suppose the writer had chosen to write an essay that indicates that pinball is superior to video games. Would this essay fulfill the writer's goal?

F. No, because the writer admits that video games have become more popular than pinball machines.

G. No, because the writer states that video games are designed to challenge the skills of the player.

H. Yes, because the writer claims that pinball games require luck and are more visually attractive than video games.

J. Yes, because the writer suggests that it is more difficult to become skilled at a pinball machine than at a video game.

Strategy: Before looking at the answer choices, imagine what you would see in a passage meant to indicate that pinball is superior to video games. You would likely see an emphasis on the positive attributes of pinball. Such an excerpt may also highlight the downside of video games. In general, you would expect to see words and phrases that emphasize comparison like *better, newer,* or *more entertaining.*

The best answer is J because throughout the essay, the writer suggests that "pinball is superior" by making the argument that pinball requires more skill and is more challenging than video games. It is reasonable to conclude, then, that this essay fulfilled the writer's goal.

The best answer is NOT:

F because the writer does suggest in this essay that video games "might seem more attractive than pinball," but this has nothing to do with the writer's goal of writing an essay that shows pinball as being superior to video games.

G because this choice can be ruled out for two reasons: first, the essay does fulfill the writer's goal, and second, the writer does not say that video games challenge the skills of the player.

H because this answer states that the essay does fulfill the writer's goal, but the reason given is not accurate. The writer never states that pinball games "are more visually attractive than video games."

PASSAGE V: Visiting Mars on a Budget

With its distinctive red tint and its polar ice caps, the planet Mars has fascinated humans for thousands of years. There were ancient Babylonian
<u>61</u>
astronomers who associated Mars with their war god Negral, to twentieth-century science fiction writers <u>whose works become best-sellers, this</u>
<u>62</u>
planet has often been a symbol of ill will and danger.

<u>The United States has competed with other countries to explore space.</u> By 2003, the National
<u>63</u>
Aeronautics and Space Administration (NASA) <u>would of sent</u> thirty spacecraft to the red planet,
<u>64</u>
<u>speculation has been prompted</u> that a human
<u>65</u>
voyage may no longer be the stuff of fiction. <u>Few</u>
<u>66</u>
would deny that the idea of a human mission to Mars is exciting, who is ready to pay for such an expedition?

Recent reports suggest that the cost of a human voyage to Mars could run as high as 100 billion dollars. This is a startling number, especially in light of the fact that the International Space Station, the most ambitious NASA project <u>yet,</u> carried a
<u>67</u>
projected price tag of "only" 17 billion dollars. In the end, NASA overspent on the International Space Station. [68] One can only imagine <u>if</u> the final price
<u>69</u>
of a human voyage to Mars would be.

(continued)

PASSAGE V: Visiting Mars on a Budget (*continued*)

In contrast, the two Mars Rovers—robotic spacecraft launched in 2003— carried a combined <u>70</u> price tag of less than one billion dollars. These Rovers are sophisticated pieces of technology, with the <u>capacity and ability</u> to examine soil and rocks. <u>71</u> Their equipment may answer questions that have long been posed about the presence of water and life on Mars.

Sending machines unaccompanied by humans to Mars does drain some of the romance out of <u>aging or older</u> visions of space travel. <u>In other words,</u> we <u>72</u> <u>73</u> need to keep in mind that the right equipment can accomplish as much as any crew of scientists, if not more—<u>such as</u> a fraction of the cost. Before <u>74</u> any astronaut boards a spacecraft for that distant planet, the staggering expense of such a mission should be carefully considered. [75]

75. The writer is considering ending the essay with the following statement:

With the passage of time, humans will continue to gaze in awe toward the heavenly skies as a source of inspiration and mystery.

Should the writer add this sentence here?

A. Yes, because it captures the emotion that is the basis for the space exploration described in the essay.

B. Yes, because it invites the reader to reflect on the insignificance of money in relation to the mystery of space.

C. No, because it does not logically follow the essay's chronological history of people who traveled in space.

D. No, because it strays too far from the essay's focus on Mars and the cost of sending humans there.

The best answer is D because concluding the essay with the proposed sentence would blur the essay's focus on Mars and the cost of sending humans there.

The best answer is NOT:

A because although the proposed sentence may capture the emotion that is the basis for the space exploration described in the essay, the sentence is out of place as a conclusion to an essay focused mainly on the expense of a human mission to Mars.

B because although the proposed sentence may invite the reader to reflect on the insignificance of money in relation to the mystery of space, the sentence is out of place as a conclusion to a paragraph and essay on the expense of a human mission to Mars.

C because the proposed sentence shouldn't be added at this point; the essay doesn't contain a chronological history of people who traveled in space.

PASSAGE V: When a Computer Gets Sick

[1]

Imagine sitting in front of a computer monitor, filling the screen with your mind's jumbled thoughts. Tomorrow's assignment is slowly materializing before your eyes. Suddenly, without warning, each of the <u>letters, in front of you tumbles</u> to the bottom <u>61</u> of the screen. Is this a bad dream? Not exactly. The computer is probably sick, <u>unless</u> the diagnosis <u>62</u> may be that the computer has a virus.

[2]

Analogous to a biological virus that takes over a living cell, a computer virus is a program, or set of instructions, that invades a computer either to create mischief or do real damage. The type of computer virus mentioned above is more mischievous than harmful. Eventually, the letters reorder themselves on the screen. Not all viruses however, straighten themselves out.

_____
63

[3]

Computer viruses range from being temporary annoyances to permanently destroying data.

_____
64

Computer vandals rig these viruses to go off at a preset time. These bombs can permanently destroy data, and that can be disastrous to the operation of

_____
65

a computer.

[4]

Detection programs are available that searches

_____
66

for and then destroys computer viruses. Evidence

_____
67

that some software writers have played up the medical analogy being found in the names of

_____
68

their programs: Vaccine, Checkup, Antitoxin, and

_____
69

Disinfectant.

[5]

As with all diseases, the best cure is prevention.

_____
70

Experts suggest that you avoid borrowing flash drives because they might contain viruses. They warn that many of these viruses are quite sophisticated in their programming. They also say

_____
71

that you should make copies of your computer files, so that if a virus does strike and you must delete your infected files, you will at least have backup copies. Experts also point out that using the Internet and World Wide Web has led to new risks of infection in the form of viruses hidden in programs downloaded from these resources.

[6]

If there is a virus in your system, you had hope that it better responds to the appropriate treatment

_____
72

and therapy. Otherwise, you could be in for a long night at the computer.

The following question asks about the passage as a whole.

75. Suppose the writer had decided to write an essay discussing the moral and ethical consequences of programming a computer virus to tamper with a computer system. Would this essay successfully fulfill the writer's goal?

A. Yes, because the essay explains the moral and ethical consequences when a virus enters a computer system.

B. Yes, because the essay details the process of ridding a computer system of viruses, which helps the reader understand the consequences of programming computer viruses.

C. No, because the essay does not explain how to program a virus, so the reader has no basis for making a moral or ethical judgment.

D. No, because the essay limits itself to describing computer viruses and the basic precautions to be taken against them.

Strategy: First think about what the purpose of the passage seems to be. Imagine what a passage would look like if it were "discussing the moral and ethical consequences of programming a computer virus to tamper with a computer system." Compare your summary of the purpose of the passage to the passage described in the question.

The best answer is D because the essay does limit itself "to describing computer viruses and the basic precautions to be taken against them." The essay does not discuss the ethics of tampering with a computer system, so it would not meet the writer's goal as described in this question.

The best answer is NOT:

A because the essay does not explain any moral or ethical consequences resulting from computer viruses.

B because the process of ridding a computer system of viruses is not explained in detail.

C because a reader would not necessarily have to know how a virus is programmed in order to make a judgment about the morality or ethics of programming a virus.

Grandpa's favorite feature on the remote is the sleep function. This option automatically turns the TV off after a preset amount of time, which is very <u>convenient when</u> he falls asleep while watching a
10
show. <u>For him, Grandpa says what he wants his TV doing, even when he sleeps, is to know a source of both pleasure and power.</u>
11

11. A. NO CHANGE

B. Even when he sleeps, Grandpa says that to know his TV is doing what he wants is a source of both pleasure and power for him.

C. Doing what he wants, even when he sleeps, is to know his TV is a source of both pleasure and power for him, Grandpa says.

D. Grandpa says that to know his TV is doing what he wants, even when he sleeps, is a source of both pleasure and power for him.

The best answer is D. Think of this sentence as a jigsaw puzzle. Each puzzle piece is a phrase or clause. In this version, all the pieces of this sentence fit together well. And the "picture" that results looks like something that we can understand.

The best answer is NOT:

A because the parts of this complex sentence are poorly arranged—to the point of nonsense. Perhaps the best way of answering this question is to listen carefully to each wording as you read it out loud to yourself. The clause "what he wants his TV doing … is to know a source of both pleasure and power" is pretty funny, but it's probably not what the writer meant to say here.

B because of a flawed arrangement of the elements of this sentence. Placing the introductory clause "Even when he sleeps" directly before the statement "Grandpa says" gives readers the wrong impression that Grandpa is talking in his sleep.

C because of its clumsiness. The following makes little or no sense at all: "Doing what he wants … is to know his TV is a source of both pleasure and power for him."

PASSAGE VI: Grandpa's Remote Control

[1]

My grandfather is not known for embracing technological <u>change. He still drives</u> his '59 Chevy
₁
Impala. (He <u>says,</u> he can't imagine needing
₂
frivolous options like automatic transmission or power steering.) So, when he <u>has went</u> to buy a
₃
new color television—<u>owing to the knowledge that</u>
₄
his old black-and-white model had finally quit— and the salesperson tried to talk him into buying a model with a remote control, he resisted. He said that he had two good legs and was perfectly capable of getting out of his chair. [5]

[2]

However, the salesperson was persistent and, appealing to Grandpa's TV-viewing habits, described the various functions on the remote. <u>However, my grandpa</u> could punch in the <u>time, and</u>
₆
<u>the channel</u> of his favorite daily news program, and
₇
the TV would turn on that program at the proper time. In the end, Grandpa did buy the remote, and it has since become something he uses all the time.

[3]

Grandpa is intrigued by the various uses for that remote. He has confided in me that the volume control is perfect for turning up the sound whenever Grandma asks him to take out the garbage. <u>For example,</u> he says, the button
₈
that mutes the sound lets him cut <u>them</u> off in
₉
midsentence.

(continued)

PASSAGE VI: Grandpa's Remote Control (*continued*)

[4]

Grandpa's favorite feature on the remote is the sleep function. This option automatically turns the TV off after a preset amount of time, which is very convenient when he falls asleep while watching a
10
show. For him, Grandpa says what he wants his TV doing, even when he sleeps, is to know a source of both pleasure and power.
11

[5]

[1] As for the programming function, Grandpa not only uses it for the news but also for playing jokes on his youngest grandchildren. [2] Explaining to the unsuspecting child that he has a remote control implanted in his little finger, Grandpa points his
12
finger at the TV and, to the child's amazement, seemingly turns it on. [3] I suppose Grandpa hasn't learned all the possible uses of the remote control, but I don't doubt he will continue to discover new and creative ways of using it.
13

13. Which of the choices would provide an ending most consistent with the essay as a whole?

A. NO CHANGE

B. and he probably won't bother learning them either.

C. so the salesperson should explain how to interpret the 200-page manual.

D. and Grandma gratefully acknowledges this.

The best answer is A because it provides a fitting ending for this personal essay because it refers to Grandpa's continuing discovery of creative ways of using his new television remote control.

The best answer is NOT:

B because it provides a description of Grandpa as uninterested in learning how to use his remote control. That's inconsistent with the rest of the essay's portrayal of him as embracing this new technology.

C because it introduces elements that are insignificant in terms of the rest of the essay. The 200-page manual had not been mentioned elsewhere in the story, and the salesperson had only a minor role early in the story.

D because it suggests that the grandmother's feelings or thoughts are central to the essay, but the rest of the essay has focused on the actions and opinions of the grandfather.

PASSAGE VII: "Topping Out" the Gateway Arch

During the early morning hours of October 28, 1965, engineers stationed 630 feet above the

ground made careful measurements for the days work. The results indicated a problem that
<u>16</u>
<u>17</u>

threatened to postpone and delay the topping-
<u>18</u>   <u>19</u>

out ceremony marking the placement of the final section between the two freestanding legs of the St. Louis Gateway Arch. [20]

Thirty-two years of planning and effort resulted in this moment. In 1933, attorney and civic leader
<u>21</u>

Luther Ely Smith envisioned a memorial that would recognize St. Louis's major role in the westward expansion of the United States. [22] Architect Eero Saarinen, who created the design that symbolized
<u>23</u>

the memorial's theme of St. Louis as the "Gateway to the West." Meanwhile, the arch would have a
<u>24</u>

stainless steel exterior and interior structural supports made of concrete. Both legs of the arch would be built simultaneously using triangular sections. Those at the base of each arch leg would be the largest, with the higher sections progressively smaller.

After nearly three years of construction, the day had come to place the final section at the top of the arch and finish the project. But a problem had arisen. The engineers confirmed that the heat of the sun had caused the south leg of the arch to expand five inches. This small but critical deviation caused concern that the two legs and the final section might not connect properly. The engineers called in local firefighters in the hope that spraying the leg with water to cool it would make it contract.
<u>25</u>

The firefighters, using 700 feet of hose, were able to reach as high as 550 feet on the south leg in they're
<u>26</u>

attempt to reduce its expansion.

The plan worked. By late morning, the crowd cheered as, welded to the two legs of the arch, the final section was hoisted up. Over three decades
<u>27</u>

and more than thirty years of planning and building
<u>28</u>

had come to a conclusion, and the tallest monument
<u>29</u>

in the United States was now complete. [30]

The following question asks about the passage as a whole.

30. Suppose the writer had intended to write a brief essay that describes the entire process of designing and building the St. Louis Gateway Arch. Would this essay successfully fulfill the writer's goal?

A. Yes, because it offers such details as the materials used to make the exterior and the interior structural supports.

B. Yes, because it explains in detail each step in the design and construction of the arch.

C. No, because it focuses primarily on one point in the development of the arch rather than on the entire process.

D. No, because it is primarily a historical essay about the early stages in the development of the arch.

The best answer is C because the title of this essay—"'Topping Out' the Gateway Arch"—is a fairly good summary of the piece and actually helps us to arrive at the answer. The essay does not do a good job of describing the entire process of designing and building the Gateway Arch because it focuses instead on telling the story of this one step in the process.

The best answer is NOT:

   A because this essay does mention the materials used to make the exterior and interior structural supports, but that doesn't mean it has described the entire design and construction process.

   B simply because it presents an inaccurate description of this essay. An essay that does what **B** claims to do would indeed fulfill the intended goal.

   D because it inaccurately describes this essay. This essay devotes just a few sentences to the early stages in the development of the arch.

PASSAGE I: Miami Time

My family is part of the Miami <u>tribe a Native American people,</u> with strong ties to territory in
₁
present-day Ohio, Indiana, and Illinois. Growing up in the Midwest, I often heard my grandmother talk about "Miami time." When she was doing something she loved, whether it was <u>making freezer jam or researching tribal history,</u> she
₂
refused to be <u>rushed in a hurry.</u> I'm on Miami
₃
time today," she would say. Conversely, if we were running late for an <u>appointment. She</u> would chide
₄
us by saying, "Get a move on. We're not running on Miami time today, you know."

   <u>It was a difficult concept for me to grasp.</u> My
₅
grandmother tried to explain that "Miami time" referred to those <u>moments, when</u> time seemed
₆
to slow down or stand still. Recently, the meaning of her <u>words</u> started to sink in. One morning, my
₇
son and I <u>will inadvertently slip</u> out of the world
₈
measured in seconds, minutes, and hours, and into one measured by curiosity and sensation.

[1] On a familiar trail near our house, I was pushing Jeremy in his stroller and <u>were thinking</u>
₉
of the day ahead and the tasks I had to complete. [2] Suddenly, he squealed with pure delight and pointed toward a clearing. [3] There, two <u>does and three fawns</u> stood watching us. [4] Five pairs
₁₀
of ears flicked like antennae seeking a signal. [5] After a few moments, the deer lowered their heads and began to eat, as if they had decided we were harmless. [6] By then, my son's face was full of wonder. [11]

We spent the rest of the morning veering from the trail to investigate small snatches of life. Lizards lazing in the sun and quail <u>rustled</u> through
₁₂
grasses surprised us. Wild blackberries melted on our tongues. <u>For example,</u> the aroma of crushed
₁₃
eucalyptus leaves tingled in our noses.

By the time we found our way back to the car, the sun was high in the sky. We had taken three hours to complete a hike we usually finished in forty-five minutes. Yet the hike felt <u>shorter then</u> ever.
₁₄
As we drove off, I remembered something else my grandmother used to say: "Miami time passes all too quickly."

Question 15 asks about the preceding passage as a whole.

15. Suppose the writer's goal had been to write a brief essay conveying a personal experience with "Miami time." Would this essay successfully fulfill that goal?

   A. Yes, because it presents the narrator's firsthand experience of a morning spent in Miami time.

   B. Yes, because it reveals that after a conversation with the grandmother, the narrator decided to live in Miami time.

   C. No, because it shares the views of more than one person with regard to the meaning of Miami time.

   D. No, because the term "Miami time" belonged to the grandmother, not to the narrator.

The best answer is A because most of the essay narrates a hike that took a long time but seemed short, the rhetorical aim being to illustrate one of the narrator's personal experiences with Miami time because that concept is defined in the early part of the essay.

The best answer is NOT:

B because although the essay has met the goal specified in the question, which was to convey a personal experience with Miami time, the reason given here is inaccurate. The essay doesn't reveal whether the narrator decided to live in Miami time, nor is it clear that one can actually choose to live always in Miami time.

C because the essay has met the goal specified in the question, which was to convey a personal experience with Miami time. That the grandmother's view of Miami time is represented doesn't detract from the fact that the essay still relates the narrator's personal experience.

D because the essay has met the goal specified in the question, which was to convey a personal experience with Miami time. It is unclear what it would mean for the term "Miami time" to belong to the grandmother; in any case, the essay indicates that the narrator and the grandmother came to share a similar sense of Miami time.

Chapter 7: Knowledge of Language

This chapter reviews the concept of redundancy, which means the needless repetition of ideas. It also examines questions about wordiness, meaning the inclusion of needless words. Students often write in a wordy style in an effort to impress readers, but clarity is the primary goal of writing. Accordingly, writing should express ideas in as few words as possible. Finally, this chapter reviews collocations, which are combinations of words designed to create a certain meaning.

Redundancy

Writing should be clear and concise. Accordingly, unnecessary words should be omitted. *To omit* means "to leave out or delete." If you see a set of answers in which three of the answers are lengthy while the last is short, this should prompt you to think about whether or not the other answers are redundant. When reviewing the answer choices for a redundancy question, you may think to yourself that the answers are all essentially the same and that none of the answers contains a grammar error. Typically, an answer choice of "OMIT the underlined portion" is a clue that a question may be addressing redundancy. Likewise, one short answer, sometimes just a single-word answer, should prompt you to consider if the other answer choices are needlessly wordy. Sometimes you need to review the introduction and the body paragraphs that appear prior to this particular question in order to identify redundancies. Often the redundancies are not contained just within the sentence itself.

Signs are posted all over the lawn threatening every sort of drastic action against <u>trespassers who wrongfully enter the property.</u> 20	**20. F.** NO CHANGE **G.** those who trespass by walking on private property. **H.** trespassers who ignore the signs and walk on the grass. **J.** trespassers.

The best answer is J because it states the idea most clearly and concisely. It does not repeat the same idea twice, and it does not add unnecessary words to the sentence.

The best answer is NOT:

F because it is redundant (repeats the same idea) and wordy (adds unnecessary words). The descriptive phrase "who wrongfully enter the property" is really a repetition of the same idea expressed by the use of the word *trespassers*. In other words, the descriptive phrase restates the obvious.

G because the phrase "who trespass by walking on private property" adds wordiness and redundancy.

H because it is wordy. It is not necessary to state the obvious. It is already clear to readers that people "who ignore the signs and walk on the grass" are trespassers.

Even as a child, Williams loved to prepare food, and as a young adult, he refined his cooking skills at the <u>prestigiously acclaimed</u> Culinary Institute 35 of America	**35. A.** NO CHANGE **B.** famed, renowned, and notable **C.** luscious **D.** prestigious

The best answer is D because it is the clearest and most concise statement. The writer logically describes the Culinary Institute of America as "prestigious."

The best answer is NOT:

A because it is redundant. That is, it repeats the same idea twice: *prestigious* and *acclaimed* mean the same thing.

B because it, too, is redundant. It repeats the same idea three times: *famed, renowned,* and *notable* all have similar meanings.

C because the adjective *luscious* makes no sense in this context. Food might be "luscious," but an institute would not be.

Eventually, Williams was ready to launch his products in grocery stores. <u>Initially, Glory Foods were</u> ⁣⁣⁣⁣37 first offered for sale in Ohio in 1992 and soon became available in neighboring states.	**37. A.** NO CHANGE **B.** Glory Foods were **C.** They were originally **D.** At the outset, the earliest Glory Foods were

The best answer is B because it creates the clearest, most logical, and most concise statement. This is another case where the least wordy choice is best.

The best answer is NOT:

A because it is redundant. It states the same idea twice. The introductory word *Initially* is redundant because the sentence later states that "Glory Foods were first offered for sale in Ohio in 1992."

C because it is redundant. In this case, the words *originally* and *first* mean the same thing.

D because it is both wordy and redundant. The phrases "At the outset" and "the earliest" both imply the same thing.

The interplanetary travel film that he created, *A Trip to the Moon,* had production costs of $4,000, <u>highly excessively</u> for its time. In this film, a space ⁣⁣⁣⁣38 capsule <u>that is fired and thereby launched and</u> ⁣⁣⁣⁣39 <u>projected</u> from a cannon lands in the eye of the Man in the Moon.	**39. A.** NO CHANGE **B.** fired **C.** fired from and consequently projected **D.** fired and thereby propelled

The best answer is B because the verb *fired* is sufficient to indicate the action clearly.

The best answer is NOT:

A because the words *fired, launched,* and *projected* mean essentially the same thing in this context, making the phrasing redundant.

C because the words *fired* and *projected* mean essentially the same thing in this context, making the phrasing redundant.

D because the words *fired* and *propelled* mean essentially the same thing in this context, making the phrasing redundant.

The attractions of video games, however, are superficial and short-lived. As you guide your character through the game's challenges, you come to know exactly how the <u>machine that's built to last</u> ⁣⁣⁣⁣50 will respond to your every move.	**50. F.** NO CHANGE **G.** machine, which is constructed durably, **H.** machine, which is built to last, **J.** machine

The best answer is J because information about the durability of video games is not relevant to the writer's argument in this paragraph. The main point of the paragraph is that video games are more predictable than pinball machines. Adding information about how video games are "built to last" or are "constructed durably" distracts the reader.

The best answer is NOT:

> **F** because information about how the machines have been "built to last" diverts the reader from the main focus of the paragraph.

> **G** because it is incorrect. Adding the irrelevant information that the machine "is constructed durably" is distracting to the reader.

> **H** because it is incorrect. Adding the irrelevant information that the machine "is built to last" is distracting to the reader.

Most video games are designed so that your main opponent <u>in these video games</u> is a predictable computer program. 55	**55. A.** NO CHANGE **B.** during these video games **C.** in video games **D.** OMIT the underlined portion.

The best answer is D because it results in the clearest and most concise response. In other words, it avoids redundancy (repeating the same idea) and wordiness.

The best answer is NOT:

> **A** because it is redundant. At this point in the sentence, it is already clear that the writer is referring to "these video games."

> **B** because it is redundant.

> **C** because it is redundant.

No matter how many games you play on any pinball machine, <u>the various times of each</u> game is different. 58	**58. F.** NO CHANGE **G.** each **H.** each single unique **J.** every single time, each

The best answer is G because it provides the most concise way to make the writer's point.

The best answer is NOT:

> **F** because it is vague and unnecessarily wordy. In addition, it creates a clause that lacks subject-verb agreement. The subject *times* is plural and requires a plural verb, not the singular verb is.

H because it is redundant (it repeats the same idea). In this sentence, *each, single,* and *unique* all mean the same thing.

J because the phrase "every single time" and the word *each* make this sentence wordy and repetitive.

These bombs can permanently destroy data, and that can be <u>disastrous to the operation</u> of a computer. ₆₅	**65. A.** NO CHANGE **B.** a devastative disaster to the operation **C.** devastation to the operating **D.** possibly disastrous to operating

The best answer is A because it most clearly and concisely expresses the point being made in this sentence.

The best answer is NOT:

B because the phrase "devastative disaster" is redundant (repeating information). In this case, the use of the adjective *devastative* is redundant because the noun *disaster* expresses the same thought.

C because this phrasing is confusing if not nonsensical. How can something be "devastation to the operating of a computer"?

D because it is redundant and unclear. The redundancy occurs in the phrase "can be possibly." Also, the phrase "operating of a computer" is not idiomatic English; that is, it's not the way English speakers would usually say or write the phrase.

<u>Detection programs</u> are available that ₆₆ <u>searches for and then destroys</u> computer viruses. ₆₇	**66. F.** NO CHANGE **G.** Detection programs that detect computer viruses **H.** Computer viruses can be found by detection programs that **J.** Detection programs that find computer viruses

The best answer is F because it is the clearest and most concise of the four choices given.

The best answer is NOT:

G because the phrase "that detect computer viruses" is redundant. The phrase is not necessary because the reader already knows that detection programs, by definition, "detect computer viruses." In addition, the phrase "computer viruses" appears a second time at the end of the sentence.

H because it is also unnecessarily wordy and redundant. The phrase "computer viruses" appears twice in this short sentence.

J because it, too, unnecessarily repeats the phrase "computer viruses."

During the early morning hours of October 28, 1965, <u>engineers</u> stationed 630 feet above the
₁₆
ground made careful measurements for the <u>days</u> work. The results indicated a problem that
₁₇
<u>threatened</u> to postpone <u>and delay</u> the topping-
₁₈   ₁₉
out ceremony marking the placement of the final section between the two freestanding legs of the St. Louis Gateway Arch.

19. F. NO CHANGE

    G. to a later time

    H. by delaying

    J. OMIT the underlined portion.

The best answer is J because it provides the most concise wording for this sentence and avoids the pointless repetition of the other choices.

The best answer is NOT:

    F because it is pointlessly repetitive. The word *delay* doesn't add any information here that's not already clearly expressed by the word *postpone*.

    G because the phrase "postpone to a later time" is pointlessly wordy. Can you postpone something to an earlier time? The information "to a later time" is already clearly expressed by the word *postpone*.

    H because it is pointlessly repetitive. The phrase "postpone by delaying" is another example of verbal overkill. Readers can sometimes feel disrespected when an essay tells them the same thing over and over.

The plan worked. By late morning, <u>the crowd cheered as, welded to the two legs of the arch, the final section was hoisted up.</u> Over three
₂₇
<u>decades and more than thirty years</u> of planning and
₂₈
building had <u>come to a conclusion,</u> and the tallest
₂₉
monument in the United States was now complete.

28. A. NO CHANGE

    B. decades amounting to more than thirty years

    C. decades—over thirty years—

    D. decades

The best answer is D because it offers the most concise wording and avoids the redundancy of the other choices. (Have you ever heard of the Department of Redundancy Department? That might be a handy way to remember what the word *redundant* means.) This answer choice is the most concise.

The best answer is NOT:

    A because a decade is ten years, and three decades are thirty years, the phrase "Over three decades and more than thirty years" is redundant.

    B because its phrasing is redundant and pointless. "Over three decades" do amount to "more than thirty years," but there's no reason to inform readers of that here.

C because the parenthetical phrase "over thirty years" merely repeats the time span just reported in a different measure of time (decades).

When she was doing something she loved, whether it was <u>making freezer jam or researching tribal history,</u> 2 she refused to be <u>rushed in a hurry.</u> "I'm on Miami 3 time today," she would say.	**3. A.** NO CHANGE **B.** hurried or rushed. **C.** made to go faster or rushed. **D.** rushed.

The best answer is D because the word rushed by itself is sufficient to express the idea "urged to hasten."

The best answer is NOT:

A because the word *rushed* and the phrase "in a hurry" are redundant.

B because the words *hurried* and *rushed* are redundant.

C because the phrase "made to go faster" and the word *rushed* are redundant.

Recently, the ACT has included redundancy questions that require you to consider information that was already introduced earlier in the passage. For example, the next question cannot be answered correctly if you are focusing only on the sentence itself. The redundancies occur in the first paragraph of the passage. Those redundancies have been bolded in the passage.

PASSAGE V: Will Allen, Urban Farmer

Will Allen transformed an empty lot in a deteriorating **Milwaukee neighborhood** into Growing Power, a two-acre, **nonprofit urban farm** that provides affordable food to an area with no grocery stores. Using <u>techniques employed by</u> 61 <u>farmers</u> in sustainable agriculture, Allen also found a way to enrich a neighborhood. Recognizing the importance of nutrient-rich soil in maximizing plant growth on his farm, <u>a unique composting system</u> was devised by 62 Allen. Each week the <u>farm, which is nonprofit,</u> 63 recycles 80,000 pounds of food waste from city markets and wholesalers by letting it partially decompose into compost.	**63. A.** NO CHANGE **B.** farm, which is located in a Milwaukee neighborhood, **C.** farm, a nonprofit urban farm located in Milwaukee, **D.** farm

The best answer is D because answers **A, B,** and **C** include information that has already been stated previously in the passage.

The best answer is NOT:

    A because the introduction already made it clear that the farm is a nonprofit.

    B because the introduction already made it clear that the farm is located in a Milwaukee neighborhood.

    C because the introduction already made it clear that the farm is a nonprofit and that it is located in a Milwaukee neighborhood.

Here is a list of redundancies that have appeared on past ACTs.

    1.   sloping hill

    2.   annually each year

    3.   lunar moon

    4.   initially, originally, at the outset, and first

    5.   recently, as of late, and lately

    6.   Wooded, pine covered

    7.   Repeated again

It is redundant to use *while* and *and* in the same sentence.

Example

    WRONG While I did my homework, and I watched tv.

    CORRECT While I did my homework, I watched tv.

    CORRECT I did my homework, and I watched tv.

Wordiness

Wordiness is not quite the same as redundancy. Wordiness means more words are used than needed. These needless words may not necessarily repeat ideas expressed elsewhere in the passage. A sentence can lack redundancies but still not be concise. If a sentence shares a simple idea in a convoluted way, then a question may be asked to assess your ability to determine when there is a more concise way to express an idea. The following ACT English test questions will help you practice identifying ways to make your writing clearer and more concise.

I told my parents about Ligia's <u>problem, which needed to be solved.</u>
 ₉
	9. A. NO CHANGE
	
	   B. problem, which was a dilemma.
	
	   C. problem that needed a solution.
	
	   D. problem.

The best answer is D because, of the four choices, **D** makes the point in the clearest, most concise way.

The best answer is NOT:

A because it is redundant; that is, it repeats an idea that has already been stated. The sentence states that the narrator was aware of "Ligia's problem." Adding that this problem "needed to be solved" is overstating the obvious. It is better to end the sentence with the word *problem.*

B because it is unnecessarily wordy. The word *problem* already implies a dilemma.

C because it is unnecessarily wordy. That Ligia's problem "needed a solution" overstates the obvious and lacks conciseness.

It was a difficult concept for me to grasp. My grandmother tried to explain that "Miami time" referred to those moments, when time seemed to slow down or stand still. Recently, the meaning of her words started to sink in. One morning, my son and I will inadvertently slip out of the world measured in seconds, minutes, and hours, and into one measured by curiosity and sensation.	**7. A.** NO CHANGE **B.** spoken statements to my ears **C.** expressed opinions on the matter **D.** verbal remarks in conversation

The best answer is A because the word *words* by itself is a sufficient, clear, and appropriate way to refer to what the grandmother had said.

The best answer is NOT:

B because the phrase "spoken statements to my ears" is clumsy, wordy, and overly formal for the tone of the essay.

C because the phrase "expressed opinions on the matter" is wordy and overly formal for the tone of the essay.

D because the phrase "verbal remarks in conversation" is wordy, redundant, and overly formal for the tone of the essay

In a strange terrain filled with hostile creatures, the space travelers experience many adventures.	**40. F.** NO CHANGE **G.** creatures, who they now realize live there, **H.** creatures, whom they are encountering, **J.** creatures who are found there,

The best answer is F because the noun *creatures* is sufficient to indicate clearly what the terrain was filled with.

The best answer is NOT:

G because the clause "who they now realize live there" adds only wordiness to the sentence, which already strongly implies that the space travelers realize that the hostile creatures they encounter live in the strange terrain.

H because the clause "whom they are encountering" adds only wordiness to the sentence, which already clearly indicates that the space travelers encounter hostile creatures in the strange terrain.

J because the clause "who are found there" adds only wordiness to the sentence, which already clearly indicates that hostile creatures are found in the strange terrain.

My grandfather is not known for embracing technological change. He still drives his '59 Chevy Impala. (He says, he can't imagine needing frivolous options like automatic transmission or power steering.) So, when he has went to buy a new color television—owing to the knowledge that his old black-and-white model had finally quit—and the salesperson tried to talk him into buying a model with a remote control, he resisted. He said that he had two good legs and was perfectly capable of getting out of his chair. [5]	**4. F.** NO CHANGE
	
	    G. due to the understandable fact that
	
	    H. because
	
	    J. so

(Underlines in passage: "change. He still drives"[1], "says,"[2], "went"[3], "owing to the knowledge that"[4])

The best answer is H because the coordinating word because clearly and concisely links this parenthetical clause ("because his old black-and-white model had finally quit") to the preceding clause ("he went to buy a new color television").

The best answer is NOT:

F because it is excessively wordy and clunky. The phrase "owing to the knowledge that his old black-and-white model had finally quit" doesn't express anything that the clause "because his old black-and-white model had finally quit" doesn't express more clearly and more precisely.

G because it is unnecessarily wordy. The clause "due to the understandable fact that his old black-and-white model had finally quit" seems, on first glance, impressive. But it is empty, pretentious language, and not consistent with the style of the rest of this essay.

J because the coordinating word *so* does not logically link this parenthetical clause to the preceding clause.

Word Choice

Questions asking you to evaluate word choice are *not* simply asking you for a synonym for a word or phrase in the passage. Often the wrong answers to these questions are synonyms to the original word. These questions ask you to consider how context affects the meaning of a word. Sometimes these questions are asking you to choose a word that is in keeping with the tone of the passage as a whole. To successfully answer these types of questions, follow these steps.

1. Return to the passage and read the sentence, saying the word *blank* in place of the word.

2. Then predict a word that would fit well in context. You need to look at the context in order to get this type of question right. You cannot just rely on your preexisting knowledge about the meaning of the word. Sometimes refreshing your memory about the content of the paragraph that the sentence is within can be helpful.

3. Look at the answer choices and determine which one is most similar to your prediction.

4. Plug that answer choice into the original sentence. If it sounds logical, choose that answer. If it does not, plug in another answer choice.

5. Check for redundancy.

6. Ask yourself what ideas are lost in the shortest answer choice. What is gained in the lengthier answers?

These Rovers are sophisticated pieces of technology, with the capacity and ability to examine soil and rocks. 71	**71. A.** NO CHANGE **B.** genuine capacity **C.** potential capacity **D.** capacity

The best answer is D because the word *capacity* is sufficient to refer to the capability of the Mars Rovers to examine soil and rocks.

The best answer is NOT:

A because the words *capacity* and *ability* are redundant; they mean basically the same thing in this context.

B because the adjective *genuine* in the phrase "genuine capacity" creates a confusing expression; *genuine* suggests there might be some doubt about the Rovers' capability, but no doubts have been raised.

C because the phrase "potential capacity" is a confusing expression; *potential* suggests there might be some conditions or limits on the Rovers' capability, but no conditions or limits have been mentioned.

Nancy Drew, the teenaged heroine of <u>heaps of</u>
49
young adult mystery <u>novels, is alive</u> and well and
50
still on the job.

49. Which choice provides the most specific information?

A. NO CHANGE

B. a high number

C. hundreds

D. plenty

The best answer is C because of the four choices, the word *hundreds* provides the most specific information about the number of Nancy Drew novels in existence.

The best answer is NOT:

  A because the word *heaps* is vague and too informal for the style and tone of the essay.

  B because the phrase "a high number" is vague.

  D because the word *plenty* is vague.

With its distinctive red tint and its polar ice caps, the planet Mars has fascinated humans for thousands of years. <u>There were</u> ancient Babylonian
61
astronomers who associated Mars with their war god Nergal, to twentieth-century science fiction writers <u>whose works become best-sellers,</u>
62
this planet has often been a symbol of ill will and danger.

61. A. NO CHANGE

B. When

C. From

D. Those

The best answer is C because the preposition *from* effectively sets up the long introductory phrase "From ancient Babylonian astronomers … to twentieth-century science fiction writers" that begins the sentence.

The best answer is NOT:

  A because the words "there were" introduce another independent clause into the sentence, resulting in ungrammatical and confusing sentence structure.

  B because the subordinating conjunction *when* creates a nonsensical introductory phrase and an ungrammatical sentence.

  D because the adjective *those* creates a nonsensical introductory phrase and an ungrammatical sentence.

Recent reports suggest that the cost of a human voyage to Mars could run as high as 100 billion dollars. This is a startling number, especially in light of the fact that the International Space Station, the most ambitious NASA project yet, carried a
$$\underline{}_{67}$$
projected price tag of "only" 17 billion dollars. In the end, NASA overspent on the International Space Station. 49 One can only imagine if the final price of
$$\underline{}_{69}$$
a human voyage to Mars would be.

69. A. NO CHANGE

B. what

C. how

D. DELETE the underlined portion.

The best answer is B because *what* is the logical introductory word in the noun clause functioning as the direct object of the verb *imagine,* resulting in "what the final price of a human voyage to Mars would be." Turning this clause around reinforces the idea that *what* is the best answer: "The final price of a human voyage to Mars would be what?"

The best answer is NOT:

A because *if* is an illogical introductory word in the noun clause functioning as the direct object of the verb *imagine.* Turning the clause around makes this clear: "The final price of a human voyage to Mars would be if?"

C because *how* is an illogical introductory word in the noun clause functioning as the direct object of the verb *imagine.* Turning the clause around makes this clear: "The final price of a human voyage to Mars would be how?"

D because deleting the underlined portion results in an illogical, incomplete-sounding sentence: "One can only imagine the final price of a human voyage to Mars would be."

If there is a virus in your system, you had hope that it better responds to the appropriate treatment and
$$\underline{}_{72}$$
therapy. Otherwise, you could be in for a long night at the computer.

72. The best placement for the underlined portion would be:

F. where it is now.

G. after the word *your.*

H. after the word *had.*

J. after the word *responds.*

The best answer is H because placing the word *better* into the phrasing "you had better hope" provides the clearest statement and best clarifies the meaning of the sentence.

The best answer is NOT:

F because here, *better* inappropriately modifies responds, which confuses the meaning of the sentence. Also, the resultant phrase "you had hope" sounds wrong in this sentence along with its two present tense verbs (*is* and *responds*).

G because in this arrangement, *better* modifies system and implies a comparison that does not exist. "If there is a virus in your better system" wrongly suggests that there are two systems.

J because here *better* inappropriately modifies responds, which confuses the meaning of the sentence. Also, the resultant phrase "you had hope" sounds wrong in this sentence along with its two present tense verbs (*is* and *responds*).

After nearly three years of construction, the day had come to place the final section at the top of the arch and finish the project. But a problem had arisen. The engineers confirmed that the heat of the sun had caused the south leg of the arch to expand five inches. This small but critical deviation caused concern that the two legs and the final section might not connect properly. The engineers called in local firefighters in the hope that spraying the leg with water to cool it would make it contract.
25

The firefighters, using 700 feet of hose, were able to reach as high as 550 feet on the south leg in they're attempt to reduce its expansion.
26

25. F. NO CHANGE

G. reduce.

H. decrease.

J. compress.

The best answer is F. All of these word choices are similar in meaning, having something to do with "decreasing or reducing in size," but they are not interchangeable synonyms. The context of this sentence helps us to decide the best choice: "spraying the [metal and concrete] leg [of the Gateway Arch] with water to cool it would make it contract." Contract means a reduction in volume, which could be a logical outcome of cooling.

The best answer is NOT:

G because *reduce* has more of a sense of "bringing down or lowering in size or degree or intensity," which is not exactly the action being described in this sentence. It's a much less precise word choice than *contract* is.

H because *decrease* has more of a sense of "declining in size or number or amount," which is not exactly the action being described here. It's a much less precise word choice than *contract* is.

J because *compress* primarily means "to reduce in size by pressing or squeezing," which is not the action being described here.

Developing an Ear for Collocations

You likely read daily—text messages, school assignments, and news articles—and through this process, you have developed an ear for proper grammar and word choice. Watching sophisticated television programming or listening to intellectual podcasts can also play a role in developing your ear for stylistic and grammatical correctness. The ACT English test often asks between one and three questions per test that assess your knowledge of collocations: word combinations that create a certain meaning. Collocations often involve prepositions. Using a different preposition can affect the connotation of the words near it. ACT's explanations for these questions typically state that the correct answer choice is "idiomatically correct." While you may think of idioms as expressions like "It's raining cats and dogs," this terminology can also describe proper collocations.

The following are examples of expressions that have appeared on past ACT English tests. Students often have difficulty recognizing these phrases as correct because the phrases often do not sound right. You can improve your success on these questions by looking for these phrases on your own in your daily reading, conversations, and viewing of television shows. If a phrase sounds unusual to you, write it down. Look it up on a web browser, and see if you can find additional uses of this phrase. These phrases might sound off to you upon first encountering them, but they are all correct.

Examples

- The president asked her administrative assistant to read back the speech she had <u>dictated to</u> him.

- Where you get accepted for college will be <u>dictated by</u> your GPA, standardized test scores, recommendations, college essay, and extracurricular activities.

- The delicious and thoughtfully decorated cupcakes helped Shaila's campaign for class president <u>as did the fact</u> that she had done a wonderful job in that position <u>the year prior.</u>

- We are selling this bookcase <u>at a fraction of the cost</u> because we have to move this week.

- You <u>need not be concerned</u> about your phone being damaged by the rain because your phone is waterproof.

Note: The word *need,* in its most common usage, is a regular verb. For example, the word *need* in this sentence is used in its common form: I need to eat before I go to the concert.

- Average standardized test scores <u>need not</u> mean that the student is average.

- <u>Having worked as a professor</u> of physics at the University of California, Sally Ride was well suited for the task of operating robots on a space shuttle trip.

- She is typical of most Americans <u>in that</u> she drinks coffee each morning.

- What some call strategy others <u>might call</u> luck.

- The phenomenon of increased prices for goods marketed to women <u>might be called</u> the pink tax though it is not actually a tax.

Here are two examples of these types of question from a real ACT English test.

Sending machines unaccompanied by humans to Mars does drain some of the romance out of <u>aging or older</u> visions of space travel.
₇₂

72. F. NO CHANGE

G. old age

H. aging old

J. age-old

The best answer is J because *age-old*, which means having been around for a long time, is a conventional, idiomatic expression that makes sense in this context.

The best answer is NOT

F because the words *aging* and *older* are redundant; they mean basically the same thing in this context. "Aging or older visions" is also not likely what the writer intends to say here, because the writer suggests in the essay that there's a timeless appeal to the notion of human spaceflight.

G because "old age" creates a silly expression ("old age visions") that implies that visions of human space travel are held only by old people.

H because "aging old" creates a nonsensical expression ("aging old visions").

Evidence that some software writers have played up the medical analogy is found in the names of their programs: Vaccine, Checkup, Antitoxin, and Disinfectant. <u>As with</u> all diseases, the best cure is prevention.   ₇₀

70. F. NO CHANGE

G. Similarly to

H. In the same way as

J. According with

The best answer is F because it is the clearest and most logical of the four choices. It also provides a proper idiom of Standard written English. The phrase "As with all diseases" indicates that the best cure for computer viruses is that same as that for all diseases: prevention.

The best answer is NOT:

G because it results in an ambiguous and illogical statement. It states that "the best cure" is "similarly to all diseases," which is illogical and ungrammatical.

H because it is unclear. The use of the phrase "In the same way as" suggests that the writer is trying to compare apples ("all diseases") and oranges ("the best cure").

J because "According with" is not an idiom of Standard written English. Even if the sentence began "According to all diseases," which is idiomatic, the sentence still wouldn't make sense.

Chapter 8:
An Overview of the
ACT Writing Test

Innovation

As a society, we invest a lot of time, effort, and money into creating new ideas, products, and methods. We believe that through innovation, we can solve problems and improve our lives. But even our best attempts to innovate can have unexpected consequences. In our pursuit of constant change and improvement, we sometimes cause new problems or replace things that already work well. Given these complications, does our society place too much value on innovation?

Read and carefully consider these perspectives. Each suggests a particular way of thinking about the question above.

Perspective One	Perspective Two	Perspective Three
Our emphasis on innovation leads to waste. In our constant attempts to create the next new thing, we devote our limited resources to a process that often ends in failure.	Keeping up with the demands of the modern world comes with risks. Even flawed new ideas teach us valuable lessons, and it is better to make new mistakes than to keep repeating old ones.	Most so-called innovations are just the same old things in shiny new packaging. Our obsession with innovation leads us to spend our hard-earned money on slightly different versions of what we already have.

Essay Task

Write a unified, coherent essay in which you address the question of whether our society places too much value on innovation. In your essay, be sure to:

- clearly state your own perspective and analyze the relationship between your perspective and at least one other perspective
- develop and support your ideas with reasoning and examples
- organize your ideas clearly and logically
- communicate your ideas effectively in standard written English

Your perspective may be in full agreement with any of those given, in partial agreement, or completely different.

Subject Matter

The ACT writing test prompts center on complex, real-world issues. These prompts reflect current and enduring political, social, and cultural conversations and concerns. Test developers strive to present students with content they can engage with critically by drawing on their knowledge, experience, and personal interests.

The prompt on innovation meets these content criteria. Whether in education, business, or commerce, the call for innovative solutions to modern problems is constant. Individuals and companies alike often turn to technology for such solutions, which has contributed to the rapid evolution in everything from personal devices to cloud computing to artificial intelligence.

But with these novel solutions have come novel problems. Cloud computing has introduced new security challenges for businesses that store valuable intellectual property digitally. Social media platforms have facilitated the spread of faulty information and raised data protection and privacy concerns. Artificial intelligence threatens to render humans obsolete in many industries. And our beloved smartphones and other devices cause environmental harm when disposed of improperly, a problem that is exacerbated by the rapid replacement of our devices with newer versions.

You have likely noticed that the "Innovation" prompt itself has not supplied any of these examples, and perhaps none of them came to mind when you thought about the topic of innovation. Rest assured that there are many productive ways of contextualizing the concept of innovation and illustrating your ideas. Perhaps your sports team tried a new strategy one season. Maybe your teacher implemented a new instructional method or your parents replaced a family tradition. Maybe you felt as though these attempts at progress were effective; maybe you felt as though they failed. And maybe you felt as though they were entirely unnecessary to begin with. Our personal experiences can be powerful means of supporting an argument and can help us contextualize and analyze an issue in just the same way we might by invoking a well-known real-world example.

Of course, you may not have personal experience with the subject of any given prompt. Again, there is no requirement that you support your ideas with a relevant personal anecdote. After all, there are many productive ways to develop an argument. Consider the topic of students and sleep. You may not personally feel as though you suffer from too little sleep, so you may not have a personal example at hand. A sound approach here would be to reason through the ideas in the prompt and perspectives. What do you believe would result from starting the school day later? Who would benefit from that change? What negative consequences can you imagine? Many of the prompt's perspectives are answering one or more of these larger questions. Do their arguments seem to be well founded? Is it possible that multiple viewpoints on the issue might be valid? If so, how should we proceed?

There are still more ways to ground and bolster an argument. Does a given prompt's issue fit into a larger historical context? Does a perspective's main idea reflect a larger philosophy? Do the stakes of the prompt's issue extend beyond the circumstances described in the prompt? Big ideas, examples from literature, specialized knowledge, personal experience, logic, and reasoning—all these are useful tools for framing your argument, and, when employed effectively, for engaging critically with the writing task.

Scoring

The ACT writing test (the essay) is not factored into the English score nor does it have weighted percentages. The 40-minute writing test is composed of a total of five scores: a single subject-level writing score reported on a scale of 2–12 and four domain scores based on an analytic scoring rubric. The four domain scores are Ideas and Analysis, Development and Support, Organization, and Language Use. The subject-level score will be the rounded average of the four domain scores. An image of your essay will be available to your high school and the colleges to which you have ACT report your scores from that test date.

Your perspective on the issue presented in the writing prompt does not affect the score. In other words, if you argue that the school day should begin at 9 a.m., and the grader personally disagrees with your argument, the grader's personal stance does not affect the score given to you. The grader may think that the school day should begin at 7 a.m., but if the grader thinks your evidence is persuasive, the grader will reward your essay with an appropriate score. Your essay will be scored in each of the domains by two trained graders. Each domain score represents the sum of the two readers' scores. If their overall scores differ by more than one point, a third reader will evaluate your essay.

The Scoring Rubric

Your essay will be scored with a rubric. You likely have familiarity with rubrics through feedback you have received from your English teachers. A rubric outlines the expectations for different elements of your response. The ACT writing test essay is evaluated with an analytic rubric, meaning that the different categories of the rubric are assessed separately rather than holistically. The rubric describes different levels of success with various dimensions of the essay task: Ideas and Analysis, Development and Support, Organization, and Language Use.

The ACT Writing Test Analytic Rubric

	Ideas and Analysis	*Development and Support*	*Organization*	*Language Use and Conventions*
Score 6: **Responses at this scorepoint demonstrate effective skill in writing an argumentative essay.**	The writer generates an argument that critically engages with multiple perspectives on the given issue. The argument's thesis reflects nuance and precision in thought and purpose. The argument establishes and employs an insightful context for analysis of the issue and its perspectives. The analysis examines implications, complexities and tensions, and/or underlying values and assumptions.	Development of ideas and support for claims deepen insight and broaden context. An integrated line of skillful reasoning and illustration effectively conveys the significance of the argument. Qualifications and complications enrich and bolster ideas and analysis.	The response exhibits a skillful organizational strategy. The response is unified by a controlling idea or purpose, and a logical progression of ideas increases the effectiveness of the writer's argument. Transitions between and within paragraphs strengthen the relationships among ideas.	The use of language enhances the argument. Word choice is skillful and precise. Sentence structures are consistently varied and clear. Stylistic and register choices, including voice and tone, are strategic and effective. While a few minor errors in grammar, usage, and mechanics may be present, they do not impede understanding.
Score 5: **Responses at this scorepoint demonstrate well-developed skill in writing an argumentative essay.**	The writer generates an argument that productively engages with multiple perspectives on the given issue. The argument's thesis reflects precision in thought and purpose. The argument establishes and employs a thoughtful context for analysis of the issue and its perspectives. The analysis addresses implications, complexities and tensions, and/or underlying values and assumptions.	Development of ideas and support for claims deepen understanding. A mostly integrated line of purposeful reasoning and illustration capably conveys the significance of the argument. Qualifications and complications enrich ideas and analysis.	The response exhibits a productive organizational strategy. The response is mostly unified by a controlling idea or purpose, and a logical sequencing of ideas contributes to the effectiveness of the argument. Transitions between and within paragraphs consistently clarify the relationships among ideas.	The use of language works in service of the argument. Word choice is precise. Sentence structures are clear and varied often. Stylistic and register choices, including voice and tone, are purposeful and productive. While minor errors in grammar, usage, and mechanics may be present, they do not impede understanding.
Score 4: **Responses at this scorepoint demonstrate adequate skill in writing an argumentative essay.**	The writer generates an argument that engages with multiple perspectives on the given issue. The argument's thesis reflects clarity in thought and purpose. The argument establishes and employs a relevant context for analysis of the issue and its perspectives. The analysis recognizes implications, complexities and tensions, and/or underlying values and assumptions.	Development of ideas and support for claims clarify meaning and purpose. Lines of clear reasoning and illustration adequately convey the significance of the argument. Qualifications and complications extend ideas and analysis.	The response exhibits a clear organizational strategy. The overall shape of the response reflects an emergent controlling idea or purpose. Ideas are logically grouped and sequenced. Transitions between and within paragraphs clarify the relationships among ideas.	The use of language conveys the argument with clarity. Word choice is adequate and sometimes precise. Sentence structures are clear and demonstrate some variety. Stylistic and register choices, including voice and tone, are appropriate for the rhetorical purpose. While errors in grammar, usage, and mechanics are present, they rarely impede understanding.
Score 3: **Responses at this scorepoint demonstrate some developing skill in writing an argumentative essay.**	The writer generates an argument that responds to multiple perspectives on the given issue. The argument's thesis reflects some clarity in thought and purpose. The argument establishes a limited or tangential context for analysis of the issue and its perspectives. Analysis is simplistic or somewhat unclear.	Development of ideas and support for claims are mostly relevant but are overly general or simplistic. Reasoning and illustration largely clarify the argument but may be somewhat repetitive or imprecise.	The response exhibits a basic organizational structure. The response largely coheres, with most ideas logically grouped. Transitions between and within paragraphs sometimes clarify the relationships among ideas.	The use of language is basic and only somewhat clear. Word choice is general and occasionally imprecise. Sentence structures are usually clear but show little variety. Stylistic and register choices, including voice and tone, are not always appropriate for the rhetorical purpose. Distracting errors in grammar, usage, and mechanics may be present, but they generally do not impede understanding.

	Ideas and Analysis	*Development and Support*	*Organization*	*Language Use and Conventions*
Score 2: **Responses at this scorepoint demonstrate weak or inconsistent skill in writing an argumentative essay.**	The writer generates an argument that weakly responds to multiple perspectives on the given issue. The argument's thesis, if evident, reflects little clarity in thought and purpose. Attempts at analysis are incomplete, largely irrelevant, or consist primarily of restatement of the issue and its perspectives.	Development of ideas and support for claims are weak, confused, or disjointed. Reasoning and illustration are inadequate, illogical, or circular, and fail to fully clarify the argument.	The response exhibits a rudimentary organizational structure. Grouping of ideas is inconsistent and often unclear. Transitions between and within paragraphs are misleading or poorly formed.	The use of language is inconsistent and often unclear. Word choice is rudimentary and frequently imprecise. Sentence structures are sometimes unclear. Stylistic and register choices, including voice and tone, are inconsistent and are not always appropriate for the rhetorical purpose. Distracting errors in grammar, usage, and mechanics are present, and they sometimes impede understanding.
Score 1: **Responses at this scorepoint demonstrate little or no skill in writing an argumentative essay.**	The writer fails to generate an argument that responds intelligibly to the task. The writer's intentions are difficult to discern. Attempts at analysis are unclear or irrelevant.	Ideas lack development, and claims lack support. Reasoning and illustration are unclear, incoherent, or largely absent.	The response does not exhibit an organizational structure. There is little grouping of ideas. When present, transitional devices fail to connect ideas.	The use of language fails to demonstrate skill in responding to the task. Word choice is imprecise and often difficult to comprehend. Sentence structures are often unclear. Stylistic and register choices are difficult to identify. Errors in grammar, usage, and mechanics are pervasive and often impede understanding.

*   *   *

The chapters in the rest of the guide will review several strategies for quickly writing persuasive prose for the ACT writing test. They will explore the nature of the prompts and the rubrics used to evaluate these essays and also provide exemplar essays for two of the prompts. These prompts, entitled "Innovation" and "Students and Sleep" (found in chapter 13), model the essential features of all ACT writing test prompts. The following pages will present brief summaries of core prompt elements. Chapter 11 will also detail the process of analyzing a prompt, developing support, outlining, and writing an essay. The art of cogent argument is a learnable skill that will serve you well in a variety of situations you will face in school, the workplace, and everyday life.

Chapter 9:
The Setup of the Writing Test

This chapter will give an overview of the format of the writing test prompt. Every test follows this same format, so familiarizing yourself with the standard content within the prompt should help you navigate the information more effectively on the day of your test.

Students and Sleep

Research suggests that the natural sleep cycle of adolescents differs in important ways from the cycles of adults and young children. For the average teenager, a natural sleep pattern involves going to bed late at night and sleeping in until late morning. But many middle and high schools begin early in the morning. This means it is difficult for teenage students to follow their natural sleep patterns. If the adolescent sleep cycle entails staying up and sleeping in, should the school day begin later?

Read and carefully consider these perspectives. Each suggests a particular way of thinking about the question above.

Perspective One	Perspective Two	Perspective Three
Students will be expected to wake up early as they pursue their college and career goals after high school. Starting the school day early helps train teens for their futures.	When we're tired, our levels of energy and attention suffer. An early start time prevents students from learning as much as they would if they were well rested.	If the day started later, it would end later as well. This would make it harder for schools to schedule extracurricular activities and would pose a major problem for students who have jobs.

Essay Task

Write a unified, coherent essay in which you address the question of whether the school day should begin later. In your essay, be sure to:

- clearly state your own perspective and analyze the relationship between your perspective and at least one other perspective
- develop and support your ideas with reasoning and examples
- organize your ideas clearly and logically
- communicate your ideas effectively in standard written English

Your perspective may be in full agreement with any of those given, in partial agreement, or completely different.

Introductory Paragraph in the Prompt

Each prompt begins with a paragraph that introduces the prompt's central issue and question. These paragraphs usually consist of five sentences, each serving a particular function toward this end. The first four sentences establish the issue. They do so by presenting an apparent tension or problem involving two factors—common beliefs, behaviors, tendencies, or phenomena, for example. The first two sentences present the first of these factors, and then sentences three to four present the second. The fifth sentence poses a question that directly engages the issue. This question becomes the focal point of the writing task.

The prompts in this guide reflect this structure. The first two sentences of "Innovation" describe a prominent belief in the power of continual progress, and sentences three and four offer considerations that complicate this belief. The final sentence sums up the issue and guides argumentation: considering its possible downsides, do we place too much value on innovation?

"Students and Sleep," the second sample prompt, depicts an apparent conflict between early morning school start times and teenagers' biological preference for sleeping in. In the introductory paragraph, sentences one and two establish the latter notion, and three and four are devoted to the former. The central question brings the tension into focus: if teens' natural sleep patterns involve sleeping in, should the school day start later?

Perspectives in the Prompt

Each prompt presents three points of view on the central question. Each of these viewpoints expresses a reasonable position that represents a way of thinking likely shared by many people. Underneath these ways of thinking lie worldviews, beliefs, and values. In terms of their stances on the given issue, the perspectives depart from one another to some extent. In some cases, they are in direct conflict. Each perspective approaches the central question from a different angle, reflective of different motives, mind-sets, and assumptions. Taken as a whole, they depict a dynamic conversation about the issue at hand.

We find such a conversation in "Innovation." Perspective One identifies a potential consequence of failed innovation: waste. Perspective Two also notes the risk of failure but argues that failing can bring benefits along with costs. Perspective Three finds a new angle into the discussion, claiming that most innovation is driven by capital interests and not the desire for meaningful progress. These viewpoints consider implications of the issue—benefits and costs of prioritizing innovation and how this priority fits into society at large.

The perspectives in "Students and Sleep" center on competing priorities. Perspective One considers implications for life after high school, and Perspective Two is concerned with more immediate consequences for learning. Perspective Three raises practical considerations for extracurricular activities and work hours for students with jobs. Each of these viewpoints is grounded in larger ideas about the purpose of education and the needs of students inside and outside of school, and, in this way, each perspective has situated the question about school start times in a critical context.

As a writer, part of your task involves contextualizing the central question and multiple responses to it. By understanding the ways in which the perspectives model these critical behaviors, you will be better prepared to perform them yourselves, and your analysis of the issue and perspectives will benefit.

Essay Task Box

At the bottom of each prompt, the essay task box restates the central question and establishes the writing purpose. Four bullet points describe an effective argument and signal the criteria by which essays will be evaluated. Aside from the first sentence, the language in this box is identical for every prompt.

The writing task is to compose "a unified, coherent essay" in response to the central question. In doing so, you are to establish your own perspective on the question and relate it to at least one other point of view, making sure to develop and support your ideas, organize them logically, and convey them with clarity.

The final sentence of the box notes that your own perspective on the question "may be in full agreement with any of those given, in partial agreement, or completely different." This is an important point. You will be neither rewarded nor punished for adopting or departing from the views promoted by the perspectives. The perspectives are intended to aid you in understanding the issue and question and generating your own ideas in response, and also to serve as viewpoints for you to analyze as you relate your own perspective to at least one more. The perspectives are not intended to limit the range of positions you might take. It is also important to understand that, for our purposes, prompt questions do not have correct answers. Scorers do not assign or subtract points depending on your stance on the question of whether society overvalues innovation, or whether the school day should begin later, or on any other question a prompt may pose.

Planning Page

Each test booklet includes two pages of space for you to employ planning and prewriting strategies. To support this process, the test booklet also includes targeted questions intended to help you engage the issue, analyze multiple perspectives, and formulate you own point of view. These questions are included in every test booklet and do not change according to the prompt.

Planning Your Essay

Your work on these prewriting pages will not be scored.

Use the space below and on the back cover to generate ideas and plan your essay. You may wish to consider the following as you think critically about the task:

Strengths and weaknesses of different perspectives on the issue
- What insights do they offer, and what do they fail to consider?
- Why might they be persuasive to others, or why might they fail to persuade?

Your own knowledge, experience, and values
- What is your perspective on this issue, and what are its strengths and weaknesses?
- How will you support your perspective in your essay?

If you need more space to plan, please continue on the back of this page.

Planning Your Essay

Use this page to continue planning your essay. Your work on this page will not be scored.

Directions

Within 40 minutes, you are expected to read the directions and read the prompt: a set of three brief positions on a common topic. The positions will differ to some extent, but they may also overlap. The directions will always be the same, so you can familiarize yourself with them now to save time on test day.

These are the directions you are given for each essay prompt before you open your test booklet.

Directions

This is a test of your writing skills. You will have **forty** (40) minutes to read the prompt, plan your response, and write an essay in English. Before you begin working, read all material in this test booklet carefully to understand exactly what you are being asked to do.

You will write your essay on the lined pages in the **answer document** provided. Your writing on those pages will be scored. You may use the unlined pages in this test booklet to plan your essay. Your work on these pages will not be scored.

Your essay will be evaluated based on the evidence it provides of your ability to:

- clearly state your own perspective on a complex issue and analyze the relationship between your perspective and at least one other perspective
- develop and support your ideas with reasoning and examples
- organize your ideas clearly and logically
- communicate your ideas effectively in standard written English

Lay your pencil down immediately when time is called.

DO NOT OPEN THIS BOOKLET UNTIL TOLD TO DO SO.

You are then given four (4) blank pages to respond to the prompt.

You may wish to photocopy these sample answer document pages to respond to the practice ACT Writing Test.

Please enter the information at the right before beginning the writing test.

Use a soft lead No. 2 pencil only. Do NOT use a mechanical pencil, ink, ballpoint, or felt-tip pen.

WRITING TEST BOOKLET NUMBER

Print your 6-digit **Booklet Number** in the boxes at the right.

WRITING TEST FORM

Print your 5-character **Test Form** in the boxes above and fill in the corresponding oval at the right.

- ○ 16W1A
- ○ 16W2A
- ○ 16W3A
- ○ 18W4A
- ○ 19WT5

Begin WRITING TEST here.

_____

_____

_____

_____

_____

_____

_____

_____

_____

_____

_____

_____

_____

_____

_____

_____

_____

_____

_____

_____

If you need more space, please continue on the next page.

WRITING TEST

_____

_____

_____

_____

_____

_____

_____

_____

_____

_____

_____

_____

_____

_____

_____

_____

_____

_____

_____

_____

_____

_____

_____

_____

_____

If you need more space, please continue on the back of this page.

WRITING TEST

If you need more space, please continue on the next page.

WRITING TEST

_____

_____

_____

_____

_____

_____

_____

_____

_____

_____

_____

_____

_____

_____

_____

_____

_____

_____

_____

_____

_____

_____

_____

_____

_____

_____

STOP here with the writing test.

10 Chapter 10: The Essay Structure

This chapter covers the ideal content and form for your essay. It also includes advice about how to avoid common pitfalls. Understanding the expectations for your response will help you write an essay that scores well when assessed with the ACT writing test rubric.

Organization

Having an organized essay means including the traditional structure of a thesis-driven essay. The conventions for the introduction, thesis statement, body paragraphs, and conclusion of an argumentative essay have been described in the following sections to give you an idea of what you should try to achieve in your own essay.

The Introduction

Common wisdom tells us that an introduction should warm a reader up and prepare the reader for what is to come. It should neither oversell nor undersell the product that follows. It should make the essay's purpose clear. Many writing manuals teach you to envision the introduction as a funnel that begins broadly and narrows its focus, previewing the essay to come with topic sentences that lay out the content of the essay, and ending with the thesis.

An ACT writing test essay should follow a shortened version of this approach. The introduction can be as short as four sentences. The graders care most about the quality of the support in the body paragraphs of the essay. Graders want to see that you have incorporated an introduction and conclusion, and that they align with the well-established guidelines for their content and form. An essay lacking an introduction or a conclusion cannot earn a top score. A single sentence conclusion is better than none at all. Aim for four to five sentences each for your introduction and conclusion so that you can focus on the body paragraphs for the majority of the time. Leaving out the introduction or conclusion suggests poor planning and a weak understanding of the conventions of essay writing.

The Hook

The essay should open with a broad lead in statement, which is sometimes called the hook. This is intended to grab the reader's attention and to give the reader an idea of what the essay will be about. Here are several examples of strategies for the hook

- A startling statistic

   Example: One third of music listeners are still illegally downloading music.

- An analogy

   Example: Stealing music off the Internet is no different from stealing a CD (compact disc) from a store.

- A rhetorical question

   Example: Why would anyone want to work for free?

- A quote

   Example: Oscar Wilde once said, "In your soul are infinitely precious things that cannot be taken from you."

   Note: Some teachers do not like this last approach because they think it is unwise to begin an essay by quoting someone else because the essay should showcase your ability to engage the reader.

Avoid overdone words and phrases in your hook. Test prep companies often give students bad advice to use awkward and contrived transition statements such as first, second, and third. The following are some additional words and phrases to strive to avoid:

Nowadays   In the modern world   In the modern era

Rather than saying "in the modern world," you can simply say "now." This will sound more natural. For example, you might write, "Much of the media we consume is **now** supplied at low cost or no cost to the consumer." Alternately, you may write, "Much of the media we consume **today** is supplied at low cost or no cost to the consumer."

You should then narrow your focus, aiming to hint at the thesis that is to come. You should ideally preview the **topic sentences** for the body paragraphs that will follow. Your thesis should be clearly articulated as one sentence. Typically, this is the last sentence of the paragraph. Try to not use the exact language as the prompt. Make sure that you have not misinterpreted any key terms in the prompt. For example, make sure that you understand the meaning of terms and phrases such as "artificial intelligence" or "immigration."

The Thesis Statement

Your thesis statement should clearly articulate your stance, and it should not merely state, "I agree with Perspective One the most." Instead, state your view, which can borrow language from the perspectives. It is perfectly acceptable to take a stance that blends two of the given perspectives or that integrates one perspective with a new idea. You can also address one of the perspectives by asserting a claim that disagrees with it.

The Body Paragraphs

The body paragraphs are the heart of your essay. The ideas that you brainstorm for your essay will ultimately dictate your thesis. Develop a thesis that enables you to easily support your argument with sufficient content even if you do not personally agree with your stance. Remember that your essay does not need to agree with any of the prompts; it just needs to *address* at least one of the perspectives. Addressing one of the perspectives can mean agreeing with it, disagreeing with it, or qualifying one of the statements. You do not need to agree with the viewpoint you articulate. In some cases, you may need to argue a position that you do not fully agree with because it is the position that you are best able to support.

Avoid repeating the exact ideas that are within the prompt itself. Try to develop examples that sufficiently differ from the given content. This will help you come across as creative and insightful. For example, if a prompt about vocational education mentions "classes in auto repair, office skills, and woodworking," you could respond with different examples, such as classes in cosmetology, culinary arts, or heating, cooling and ventilation (HVAC). Each body paragraph could simply examine an example to back up your claim. Your evidence can come from history, literature, science, or even your personal experience.

The Conclusion

The conclusion ties the essay together. Your goal is to contextualize your paper in a broader discourse about the topic. Avoid adding entirely *new* ideas that have not been hinted at in the essay thus far. The ACT essay conclusion should summarize the key points made in the essay.

If you are aiming for a top score, ideally avoid artificial lead-in statements such as "As this essay has shown …" or "In conclusion." Instead, you can begin your conclusion with the word "Clearly," which is subtler than the phrase "in conclusion." You should restate your thesis, but you should use different language than the language used to articulate your thesis in the introduction. Your goal is to offer an answer to the question "so what?" Why does your essay matter? What insights does it offer about the human experience?

The final sentence should be especially powerful so that it leaves a good impression on readers. Try to be particularly articulate, clever, or insightful. One strategy is to express an idea that gives a sense of circularity to the paper. Return to an idea you discussed in the introduction. Another strategy is to end with a famous quote if you know one for the topic. Again, some teachers do not like this, so be aware of that when writing essays in your regular English class. Because of the speed at which the essays are graded, conclusions should be written in a direct style that reiterates the thesis and the key pieces of support without many distractions.

Example of a strong concluding sentence:

> In the end, innovation gives us chance for life, and a better one, but it must be pursued responsibly.

Clear Transitions

You should strive to have clear transitions between sentences and paragraphs. To further familiarize yourself with these words, you may wish to review chapter 6.

Addressing the Counterargument

One strategy for expanding the content of your essay is to describe the apparent merits of the opposition's view, and then unravel the premises that are foundational to the opposition's argument. Here are some sentence stems and vocabulary terms that may help you address the counterargument.

Example

> Some argue that preventing new fast food restaurants from establishing stores in the town will diminish unhealthy eating. This is not logical because there are many ways for citizens to access unhealthy foods. It does not follow that preventing fast food businesses from opening in a town would prevent people from consuming burgers, fries, and other unhealthy foods.

Here is some vocabulary that you may wish to use while addressing the counterargument.

Myopic: shortsighted, not taking into account the broader picture

Example

Some argue ____; however, this is a <u>myopic</u> stance that does not take into account the long-term effects of implementing this rule.

Reductive: when you make an argument too simple and don't acknowledge the various facets of the problem that make the problem complicated

Example

Some argue ____; however, this is an excessively <u>reductive</u> way of looking at the issue.

Spurious: flawed, full of holes, false

Example

Some argue ____; however, this logic is <u>spurious</u>.

Tenuous at best: flimsy, full of holes

Example

Some argue ____; however, this logic is <u>tenuous at best</u>.

Deleterious: harmful, negative

Example

This could have <u>deleterious</u> effects.

Dubious: suspect, doubtful

Example

Some argue ____; however, this logic is <u>dubious</u> at best.

Supposed: means so-called; implies that the definition is not suitable

Example

The <u>supposed</u> progress achieved through industrialization has actually led human beings to regress in many ways.

Knowing What Is Expected for the Rubric Categories

Below you will find analysis of different elements found in the rubric. This section aims to paraphrase the content of the rubric in order to enhance your understanding of what graders are looking for in top-scoring essays.

Ideas and Analysis

The Ideas and Analysis category of the rubric will be negatively affected if your thesis lacks robust support. The highest score for the Ideas and Analysis category of the rubric states that high-scoring essays will demonstrate the following:

> The writer generates an argument that critically engages with multiple perspectives on the given issue. The argument's thesis reflects nuance and precision in thought and purpose. The argument establishes and employs an insightful context for analysis of the issue and its perspectives. The analysis examines implications, complexities and tensions, and/or underlying values and assumptions.

Further information about how to score well in this category can be found in the section "Avoiding Simplistic Thinking" in chapter 12.

Though it is not explicitly stated in the directions, it is clear from this rubric that top-scoring essays must address at least *two* stances on the topic because the rubric says essays must engage with "**multiple** perspectives on the given issue." This does not mean that you have to address two of the given perspectives. You could address one of the perspectives and develop your own response that does not perfectly align with one of the given perspectives. As you process the positions, try to determine where they overlap and where they diverge.

Development and Support

Aim to write at least three handwritten pages. That is equivalent to about one page single-spaced when typed, which may be helpful to know if you wish to begin your practice by typing out your essays. You will type your essay if you are taking the computer-based test. Your score in this category is impacted by the degree to which your response meets the outlined expectations. Your score will suffer if your essay does not include sufficient evidence to support its claims.

The rubric for Development and Support states that high-scoring essays will demonstrate the following:

> Development of ideas and support for claims deepen insight and broaden context. An integrated line of skillful reasoning and illustration effectively conveys the significance of the argument. Qualifications and complications enrich and bolster ideas and analysis.

Organization

The essay should be organized. A classic five-paragraph essay structure works well for the essay, though you should let the logic of your ideas dictate the number of body paragraphs included in your essay. Ideally, you will be able to write three substantial body paragraphs or more. Your essay should include an introduction and conclusion. These can be brief. Aim to write four sentences at least, but if your introduction or conclusion is on the shorter side, this does not dramatically affect your overall score. The persuasiveness and clarity of the body paragraphs will have the greatest impact on your score.

Make sure that your stance is clear. This stance should be articulated in your thesis toward the end of your introduction paragraph. Your topic sentences and the content of the body paragraphs should reinforce your thesis, and your conclusion should reiterate your stance and your best points. This most likely will mean that you cannot agree with each of the perspectives because doing so would result in a chaotic essay.

The highest score for the Organization category of the rubric states that high-scoring essays will demonstrate the following:

> The response exhibits a skillful organizational strategy. The response is unified by a controlling idea or purpose, and a logical progression of ideas increases the effectiveness of the writer's argument. Transitions between and within paragraphs strengthen the relationships among ideas.

See the discussion in chapter 6 for further information about transition words.

Language Use

Your language use will also be evaluated as part of your essay score. The highest score for the Language Use category of the rubric states that high-scoring essays will demonstrate the following:

> The use of language enhances the argument. Word choice is skillful and precise. Sentence structures are consistently varied and clear. Stylistic and register choices, including voice and tone, are strategic and effective. Although a few minor errors in grammar, usage, and mechanics may be present, they do not impede understanding.

This means that when you use sophisticated vocabulary, you do so effortlessly. Your word choices should not feel forced. Do not use esoteric (i.e., obscure) words in an effort to impress the reader if you are not confident that you are using words properly. Notice that this description still allows some room for error. The graders acknowledge the difficulty of writing a polished essay under timed conditions.

Chapter 11:
Writing
Your Essay

Vocational Education

For many years, public high schools in the United States emphasized vocational skills—the skills students would need to learn a trade and get a job. Classes in auto repair, office skills, and woodworking, for example, were common. The last few decades have seen career and technical training fall out of favor in public education, replaced gradually by additional academic courses. While many schools maintain a vocational program, these programs are often threatened with elimination when school budgets are strained. Given its uncertain status in many schools, it is worth considering what value vocational training adds to education.

Read and carefully consider these perspectives. Each suggests a particular way of thinking about the value of vocational training in education.

Perspective One	Perspective Two	Perspective Three
Schools must seek to prepare all students for their futures. Career training provides focus for many students and helps schools reach those who don't excel in academic subjects.	In every field, the skills workers need today are based on knowledge and communication. As such, schools should focus on academic subjects only.	No one knows what jobs will be available in the future, so it is not wise to train today's students for any specific career.

Essay Task

Write a unified, coherent essay about the value of vocational training in education. In your essay, be sure to:

- clearly state your own perspective on the issue and analyze the relationship between your perspective and at least one other perspective
- develop and support your ideas with reasoning and examples
- organize your ideas clearly and logically
- communicate your ideas effectively in standard written English

Your perspective may be in full agreement with any of those given, in partial agreement, or completely different.

Let's take a look at the key components that a strong essay writing process will include. Keep the "Vocational Education" prompt in mind as we review the steps for completing an essay.

Purpose and Point of View

The purpose of the essay is to persuade. Developing a clear and supportable thesis is essential to writing a persuasive essay. The point of view that should be emphasized is your own as articulated in your thesis.

Avoid Personal Pronouns

Though the prompt says to "clearly state **your own perspective** on the issue," you should try to avoid using personal pronouns such as *I, me,* and *my* unless you are using a personal anecdote to support your reasoning. For example, you should try to avoid writing, "**I think** vocational education is important." It would be more emphatic and persuasive to simply say "Vocational education is important." Do not say "I think …" or "I believe …" or "In my opinion …." It is implied that the ideas in the essay are your own, and prefacing your assertions with "I think" makes your thoughts come across as less authoritative.

You can, of course, use personal pronouns if you are relating a personal anecdote in order to support your argument. For example, you might say, "<u>My</u> high school decided to move the start of the school day to 8:30 a.m., and the effects have been positive." Anecdotes are considered valid evidence for your reasoning. Remember you only have 40 minutes to write your essay on the ACT writing test, so you may need to use personal anecdotes if you cannot think of other types of support for your essay.

Personal anecdotes can help humanize a writer or orator and serve as valid support for an argument if the source is credible. This is why politicians frequently allude to everyday people in their campaign speeches. Doing so can help persuade the audience through emotional appeals. Incorporating personal anecdotes is an effective strategy for expanding your reasoning by elaborating with real-world anecdotal evidence. Many questions ask about human nature, so it is only natural to write about your knowledge of the world through your own experience. When you are offering a personal anecdote about someone other than yourself, give the person a first name even if you cannot actually remember the person's name. This makes it easier to refer to the person throughout the paragraph.

The following excerpt comes from a real student's essay in response to the prompt on "Innovation." The student's thesis is "Our obsession with innovation leads us to spend our hard-earned money on slightly different versions of what we already have. Some examples of this include the latest iPhones, house appliances, or most recently I've seen, holiday decorations."

The following supporting anecdote is vague and therefore does not contribute to support the thesis in the same way a clearer and more specific anecdote could:

The latest thing I've seen is holiday decorations. They have recently come out with a new thing that you can set in your yard and it will shine. Different pictures on your house for each holiday. As you can imagine. It's not cheap. But instead of spending a few dollars on lights and hanging them up, people would rather spend a ton of money for this new gadget.

The following excerpt from another student essay is a personal anecdote used to bolster the argument that students should all read the same text in an English class rather than reading different texts. It provides a clearer piece of support than the previous example.

When my class studied Lord of the Flies, my classmates and I engaged in a robust debate about whether or not human beings are inherently evil. The conversation was so interesting that my friends and I continued talking about it at lunch following the conclusion of class. This class discussion also helped me retain facts about the story because I engaged with those facts during our in class discussion. Had we not all read Lord of the Flies, we would not have all had a common text from which we could draw support for our claims. This would have made it nearly impossible to have the rich kind of discussion we were able to have because we all read a common text.

The following example was developed by a student in another essay about the place of sports in schools.

There is a student athlete at my school, Jacob, who devotes over twelve hours a week to Varsity basketball, but he is not the star player on the team. He is constantly exhausted and struggles to find time to prepare for his AP courses. In fact, last year he earned a 2 on his AP US History test because he could not find the time to adequately prepare. Had Jacob played JV basketball, which meets only six hours a week, or had he not participated in basketball at all, he would have had sufficient time to focus on academics. Instead, his inability to strike an appropriate balance between athletics and academics limited his academic potential.

Avoid Saying, "Perspective 1 ..."

Do not try to address each perspective. Some students try to structure their three body paragraphs on the three perspectives. Doing so is not necessary and will likely yield an incoherent essay that does not have a clear central argument. Remember that your primary goal is to write a coherent, thesis-driven essay. Ideally, do not say. "As Perspective 1 states ...." Writing out Perspective 1 highlights the artificiality of the essay task. Your goal is to write an essay that sounds like it is contributing to an ongoing scholarly debate about a topic that is of concern to humanity as a whole. Instead, it would be better to simply write, "**Some individuals** argue that artificial intelligence is superior to human beings when it comes to simple repetitive task. **Others** believe that artificial intelligence threatens our sense of what it means to be a human being."

Intended Audience and Tone

The intended audience is an academic one. Accordingly, casual language should be avoided.

The tone of your writing should be scholarly even if you are incorporating personal anecdotes. Table 11.1 shows words to avoid and words you can use to create an intellectual tone.

Table 11.1   Suitable Words to Use in Your Essay

Instead of This	Say This
stuff or things	elements, phenomena, factors,
kind of	to some extent, partially, somewhat, incompletely, fairly, moderately, relatively
a lot	a great deal of, many, the majority, numerous, untold numbers of, untold amounts, innumerable, countless, endless, unlimited, vast
bad	detrimental, harmful, deleterious, damaging, adverse, destructive
huge	major, astronomical, immense, monumental, important, tremendous, colossal
stupid	foolish, unwise, baffled, obtuse, vacuous, unintelligent, misguided, senseless, ignorant

Consider how these sentences come across differently.

Examples

Bad: Kids will do <u>things</u> to get good grades.

Better: Kids will stop at nothing to get good grades.

Best: Kids will manipulate the system in order to earn high grades.

Bad: It would be <u>very bad</u> to not get enough sleep and to then be <u>stupid</u> in class.

Better: It would be detrimental to not get enough sleep and then to be cognitively challenged during the school day.

Best: Sleep deprivation has negative consequences in the classroom.

Note: The "best" example is strong because it is clear and succinct.

Prewriting

Spend time analyzing the prompt, developing your stance, and establishing supporting evidence. Briefly try to develop your own reaction after reading the introductory paragraph and before reading the three perspectives. This should help expand your thinking so that your essay does not sound too heavily influenced by the given perspectives.

Another strategy is to begin by brainstorming your concrete examples before drawing a conclusion from your examples. This may help expand your thinking before limiting it by attempting to find a pattern in the data and opinions you can generate.

Outline your essay so that you have a general structure to guide your thinking as you write. Be sure to address at least one perspective in your essay. You could disagree with it. Make sure that your thesis is clear and that each paragraph supports your thesis. In this stage, it can also be helpful to jot down vocabulary that you will try to weave into the essay.

Prewriting for an essay on vocational education, for example, might look like this:

- What is the purpose of education?
- Horticulture growing plants in adverse conditions
- Welding
- Textile manufacturing

Vocabulary

pragmatic   aesthetic   obsolete   indispensable   lucrative   fulfilling

Outline Structure Organized by Profession

Paragraph 1: Horticulture

- Vegetables and herbs will always be in demand for their nutritional value.
- Fertile land is in short supply.
- Plants bring beauty into our lives.

Paragraph 2: Textile Manufacturing

- Textiles are a major part of our lives:
  - Carpets
  - Drapes
  - Bedding
- Human beings place a high value on the perceived beauty of the objects they surround themselves with.

Paragraph 3: Welding

- Welding is a sophisticated skill that binds pieces of metal together.
- Welding is an essential step in manufacturing structures like bridges.
- Welding is critical in aerospace engineering.

You could develop the essay by either beginning or ending with a focus on the purpose of education. You could question if high school should simply prepare students for the kind of academic learning they may find at a traditional college, if it should prepare them to enter the workforce, or if it should suit a different purpose. Ideally your examples should differ from those given in the prompt itself. Based on this brainstorm you could devote one paragraph to each of the three career paths you thought of. Here are definitions for the example vocabulary in case those terms are not familiar to you:

aesthetic	having to do with beauty or appearance
indispensable	useful, important, necessary
fulfilling	encouraging, gratifying, rewarding, heartwarming
lucrative	profitable, favorable, likely to generate money
obsolete	unnecessary, outdated, useless, antiquated
pragmatic	practical, useful

You may not use all of the vocabulary terms you brainstorm, but here are some ideas for sentences you might develop based on this vocabulary about the "Vocational Education" prompt.

1. Millennials, a key demographic for the textile industry, are quite concerned with cultivating a beautiful environment in their homes. Accordingly, the production of **aesthetically** pleasing carpets, drapes, and furniture will be in demand for years to come.

2. It is **fulfilling** to create beautiful textiles that then bring joy to others for years to come.

3. The skill of welding will always be marketable. Therefore, becoming trained in this skill is both **pragmatic** and **lucrative.**

4. Welding is an **indispensable** means of solidly joining two pieces of metal.

5. A traditional education—one rooted in book learning—is becoming **obsolete.**

Timing During the Actual Test

Below are two approaches to the timing of writing the essay. You will need to experiment to determine what works best for you. For example, some students prefer to invest more time up front in the brainstorming process. This then tends to lead the students to generate the content of their body paragraphs more quickly because they have thought about it more deeply at the beginning. Other students prefer to do that thinking as they write the body paragraphs.

Of course, each prompt is different, so you should practice the full process of writing the essay in response to several prompts. Be sure to include the process of seeing the prompt for the first time and brainstorming within the allotted 40 minutes.

Timing with Three Body Paragraphs

3 minutes	Read the prompt and develop an outline for your own essay.
5 minutes	Write the introduction.
8 minutes	Write body paragraph 1.
8 minutes	Write body paragraph 2.
8 minutes	Write body paragraph 3.
5 minutes	Write the conclusion.
3 minutes	Proofread your essay.

Timing with Four Body Paragraphs

2 minutes	Read the prompt and develop an outline for your own essay.
2 minutes	Write the introduction.
8 minutes	Write body paragraph 1.
8 minutes	Write body paragraph 2.
8 minutes	Write body paragraph 3.
8 minutes	Write body paragraph 4.
2 minutes	Write the conclusion.
2 minutes	Proofread your essay.

Revising

You should ideally leave about two to three minutes at the end of your essay to reread your work, checking for glaring errors. Look for errors that detract from the reader's ability to understand your intended meaning. If you forget an idea and wish to add it in, you can use an asterisk (*) to indicate this. You place an asterisk where you wish to insert the new idea. Then at the bottom of the page, include another asterisk (*). Then write the new idea. If you need to do this more than once, simply use two asterisks (**). You should not do this more than twice because doing so will make your essay seem poorly thought out. Ideally, cross out your errors with a single line. This will show graders that you thoughtfully revised your work. If you prefer, you can erase your error and replace it.

Basic Strategies for Improving Your Writing

Writing essays in response to different prompts is good practice, but to ensure a higher score on the ACT writing test, incorporate these strategies as you practice:

1. Read prompts and practice developing your thesis and supporting information.

2. Read high-scoring model essays. Several are provided in chapter 13. Also look at the analysis of why these essays scored as they did.

3. Attempt to write your own essay within the allotted time. If you are beginning your test preparation early, you may wish to type your essays in order to facilitate the revision process. If you only have a month or so to prepare for the exam, you should practice handwriting your essays from the start because this is what is expected on the exam at most test centers. Additionally, most students think differently when writing by hand. You will want to gain practice with this aspect of the test. For example, when writing an essay by hand, you do not have the capability to copy and paste information in order to restructure an essay. Thus, it is important to outline your essay in the prewriting stage. This will help your ideas flow logically.

4. Take a little time after completing your essay to read it and then grade it with the rubric. You may wish to have a teacher, friend, parent, or guardian grade the essay as well.

5. Revise your essay. By revising your essay, you will learn more about how to write your essay well the first time.

6. Finally, you should practice writing essays by hand in one complete draft without revising.

7. Keep a notebook with sentences you have read that you think are well written. Perhaps try to mimic them as practice.

8. Work on developing a list of historical anecdotes, current events, and personal anecdotes that you can draw from for your essay. This can be as simple as reflecting on the personal anecdotes you often share in your everyday life. Think about the messages those stories convey. You can also think of any studying you are doing in your history class as a method of building your fund of knowledge for the ACT writing test essay. You are encouraged to weave current events into your essays as well. More advice about this can be found in the section "Building Your Fund of Knowledge" in chapter 12.

Revising Your First Drafts

Although you have little time to revise your work within the constraints of the actual test, you can still benefit from revising the essays you have written as practice prior to the actual test. Here are some questions you can ask yourself when analyzing your essay to see how you could have improved it:

1. Do you maintain a focus on your thesis? Remember that this is your primary goal.

2. Does the essay demonstrate a clear understanding of the key terms in the prompt?

3. Is your argument too broad in scope?

4. Is your argument too narrow in scope?

5. Does your introduction say your essay will address topics that your body paragraphs failed to address?

6. Is your supporting evidence sufficiently different from the examples given in the prompt itself?

7. Did you use vocabulary correctly? Did you try to use sophisticated vocabulary that you do not fully understand?

8. Is the sentence structure varied? For example, do you have short sentences and more complex sentences?

9. Does it seem like you tried to force an argument? When others read your essay, what is their response when you ask them, "What argument did the essay make? What was the support? Was it persuasive?"

12

Chapter 12: Strengthen Your Essay with Vocabulary, Writing Mechanics, and Other Strategies

Vocabulary

When you develop your vocabulary, you can make skillful, precise word choices to express your ideas. Learning new words even helps you form more complex thoughts and insightful arguments. Many wonderful apps can help you easily study vocabulary on your phone or tablet during your free time. It can also be helpful to keep a vocabulary journal where you write down new words as you learn them. Writing down a synonym, definition, or a sentence that properly uses the word can help you retain its meaning. Physical or digital flashcards can also help you retain the meanings of these words.

Varied Sentence Structures and Punctuation

Review chapter 5, which covers colons, semicolons, dashes, and commas. Practice using these punctuation marks in the written work you do for school. Reviewing transition words and subordinating conjunctions can also help you create complex sentence structures. Knowledge of these words and sentence structures can also help emphasize the relationships between ideas.

Proper use of punctuation can add a nice rhetorical flourish to a piece. For example, an essay in response to the prompt on the topic of innovation may focus on examples of controversial scientific advancements such as the development of gene editing. That essay could end with the following rhetorical question: "Where do we draw the line when it comes to our pursuit of scientific knowledge?"

Rhetorical Questions

One feature of many strong sample essays is effective use of rhetorical questioning. Here are several examples of rhetorical questions:

- How is a teacher supposed to create hundreds of different quizzes?

- Are we really prepared for the possibilities that science can make available to us?

- Where would be today if we had ignored the Holocaust because it happened at a distance?

- Where do we draw the line?

A well-timed rhetorical question can be just the stylistic flourish needed to push an essay score one point higher. The distinctions between the categories on the rubric are subtle and arguably subjective. One high-scoring ACT writing test essay opened by posing this thought-provoking question, "Have you ever wondered what it would be like to live in a country where all of your choices are made for you by the government?" The writer essentially made his position clear through his skillful use of rhetorical questioning. Who, after all, would want to live in such a country? Rhetorical questioning is an effective strategy for leading readers to draw the same conclusion you are asserting through your essay.

Avoiding Simplistic Thinking

The graders reward students who demonstrate an in-depth understanding of the complexity of the problem presented. Accordingly, simplistic and reductive thinking should be avoided. Your essay should demonstrate a nuanced understanding of the situation. Good academic writing acknowledges the subtle layers of meaning. One should be wary of absolutes within academic writing because speaking in absolutes tends to neglect the complexities of an issue. Avoid extreme words such as the following:

Absolute Words

never	no	certainly	undeniably	constantly
always	all	obviously	undoubtedly	continually
entirely	every	definitely	incontrovertibly	
none	proves	unquestionably	indisputably	

It is better to include nuanced, qualified language such as the following:

often	in most cases	not necessarily	most likely
some of the time	in many cases	not mutually exclusive	might
in some cases	in rare cases	in certain situations	frequently

Brainstorming about Your Values

Typically, the essay question is broad and philosophical in nature. For example, past prompts have addressed topics such as artificial intelligence, health care, and free music. These topics all connect to a broader underlying issue. Thinking about your stance on some broader social subjects may help you process a given prompt. Try to develop some ideas in response to the following questions. This should help you come up with support more easily when it comes time to take the ACT writing test essay.

- Should limits be placed on technology?

- Are there drawbacks to our focus on having a highly efficient, fast-paced society?

- What are the important parts of the human experience? What does it mean to be human?

- How can we curb the negative aspects of human nature?

- Do we need an authority figure to guide us to act properly and in accordance with what is best for the majority?

- How do human beings react to rules and regulations?

- Should the government have sweeping power to control the everyday lives of citizens?

- What is the value of art?

- What would a fair society look like?

- Do citizens from one country have any responsibility to citizens from another country?

- What is the role of the individual within society?

- What is the purpose of education?

- What would the ideal school look like?

- What is the role of sports in society?

- What do people deserve to be compensated for?

- How should we treat the environment?

- How do we create the greatest good for the greatest number of people?

- Is it best to make decisions that resolve problems in the short term or the long term?

Building Your Fund of Knowledge

One commonly recommended strategy for success on the ACT writing test essay is to go into the test with several historical and literary anecdotes fresh in mind. This is a strategy taught by most test prep companies. Some companies even go so far as to supply students with dossiers on a wide range of figures from Rosalind Franklin, who first x-rayed DNA's double-helix structure, to Elon Musk, a successful electric vehicle entrepreneur. This gives students a source of information from which to draw. Work on developing your own list of historical events and figures to use in your ACT writing test essay.

Try to be mindful that some historical figures may be regarded as controversial. For example, most high school students now have a fuller picture of Christopher Columbus, and accordingly you may wish to avoid writing about him in a purely positive light. Likewise, some figures have been overdone in these types of essays, perhaps due to the test prep industry's approach of providing students with ready-made content about figures like Thomas Edison and Steve Jobs. Modern political figures should also be avoided in order to avoid inadvertently tapping into the subconscious bias of the essay scorers.

In addition to building a fund of knowledge from which to draw, you can also improve your ACT writing test essays by analyzing model argumentative essays and your own past essay attempts. After writing your first draft of an essay, it could be helpful to revise your essay in order to learn how to improve on the weaknesses of your initial draft. Try to find a peer, a parent or guardian, a tutor, or a teacher to grade your essay with the ACT writing test rubric in order to provide objective feedback on your writing. Because you know the intended meaning of your written words, it would be difficult to objectively score your own essay. Of course, when you take the official ACT writing test essay, there will be no opportunity for revision, but there are benefits to going through a revision process as you practice.

The ultimate goal should be to plan and write a coherent essay within the allotted time, but the road to getting there does not need to involve immediately jumping to this stage. Growing as a writer is not always a linear process. Some prompts may prove more challenging than others. Building your fund of knowledge should help you swiftly develop support for your answer. Writing practice essays and revising them should help you become aware of your own personal pitfalls when it comes to the ACT writing test essay. You can also practice analyzing the prompts themselves and brainstorming support for your argument.

Avoid What You Don't Know

Try to avoid calling attention to any gaps in your knowledge. For example, if you wish to refer to the psychological concept of the hierarchy of needs but cannot recall that the psychologist who developed that notion was Abraham Maslow, you can simply say "A prominent humanist psychologist …." If your recollection of a personal anecdote is fuzzy, it is not necessary to indicate this in your essay. No one is going to call your grandmother and fact check your personal anecdote.

13

Chapter 13: Sample Prompts and Essays with Analysis

This chapter includes two real ACT writing test essay prompts and several real student essays. The weaker essays come first and the stronger essays come after. If you are short on time, we recommend focusing on reading the higher-scoring essays. Please take the time to read the analysis that explains why the essays received the subscores they received. The rubric has also been reproduced. With practice, you will surely improve your ability to manage the demands of the ACT writing test essay, and you may even improve your writing overall through the process.

Practice with the following prompt, and then read several real student essays that responded to this prompt.

Writing Test: Innovation

Innovation

As a society, we invest a lot of time, effort, and money into creating new ideas, products, and methods. We believe that through innovation, we can solve problems and improve our lives. But even our best attempts to innovate can have unexpected consequences. In our pursuit of constant change and improvement, we sometimes cause new problems or replace things that already work well. Given these complications, does our society place too much value on innovation?

Read and carefully consider these perspectives. Each suggests a particular way of thinking about the question above.

Perspective One	Perspective Two	Perspective Three
Our emphasis on innovation leads to waste. In our constant attempts to create the next new thing, we devote our limited resources to a process that often ends in failure.	Keeping up with the demands of the modern world comes with risks. Even flawed new ideas teach us valuable lessons, and it is better to make new mistakes than to keep repeating old ones.	Most so-called innovations are just the same old things in shiny new packaging. Our obsession with innovation leads us to spend our hard-earned money on slightly different versions of what we already have.

Essay Task

Write a unified, coherent essay in which you address the question of whether our society places too much value on innovation. In your essay, be sure to:

- clearly state your own perspective and analyze the relationship between your perspective and at least one other perspective
- develop and support your ideas with reasoning and examples
- organize your ideas clearly and logically
- communicate your ideas effectively in standard written English

Your perspective may be in full agreement with any of those given, in partial agreement, or completely different.

Innovation Essay 1 (Score: 4445)

As the knowledge of the world expands, new ideas and items become more prominent. It's as if the world is changing every second because of these innovations being thought of. The society of today's world does not place too much value on innovations because it often leads to new perspectives or ideas. Even with its benefits, sometimes it becomes unnecessary. But without innovations, the world would not have advanced the way it has.

The value given to innovations in society is not overdone, because even if the intentional purpose does not work out, other benefits may arise. For example, in an attempt to reduse the waste/litter across the world, recycling plants opened up everywhere. Even though this worked it still wasn't doing enough to prevent landfills from overflowing, and from this scientists were able to develop more biodegradable products. This innovation would help keep nature clean. If innovations weren't given as much value, there wouldn't be as rapid of an expansion of knowledge or products. Another example of a beneficial innovation was the creation of Coca-Cola. Originally the product was created as a medicine, but when determined to be a soft drink rather than its design, it would become a part of a very profitable industry. This would bring more jobs to society

(continued)

Innovation Essay 1 (Score: 4445) *(continued)*

to produce enough of the wanted drink. Though sometimes innovations may not turn out as planned, they can bring great benefits to the world and society.

Even with the beneficial compounds of innovations, sometimes it can be valued even when unnecessary. In today's society, most people value having a smartphone. They begin to anticipate the next version of their current phone even though nothing much has been improved. People begin to place unnecessary values on so-called "innovations" when in truth, it's just "the same old things in shiny new packaging" (P3). The new design of a product isn't anything to be valued, because it is just the old product in disguise. Though this may be the case for certain products, it does not mean the same for others that could be beneficial.

In the society that currently resides across the globe today, much value is placed on the innovation of ideas and products. It is valid for one to do so because with it comes the benefits of a different perspective on ideas as well as an accidental creation, such as unintended uses. But even though this may be considered a positive, occasionally these values can become unnecessary. Sometimes, it may be the same product with a different case, and being falsely considered an "innovation."

Analysis

Ideas and Analysis score point: 4: The writer generates an argument that engages with multiple perspectives on the issue of innovation. The thesis—society's high regard for innovation stems from the perception that all innovations are capable of conferring benefits—reflects clarity in thought and purpose. The essay establishes and employs a context for analysis by discussing how even initially unsuccessful innovations can still help society progress. Analysis recognizes the practical implications of public enthusiasm for innovation ("If innovations weren't given as much value, there wouldn't be as rapid an expansion of knowledge and products; ... even if the intentional purpose does not work out, other benefits may arise.").

Development and Support score point: 4: Development of ideas and support for claims clarify meaning and purpose. Lines of clear reasoning and illustration adequately convey the significance of the argument that innovation is beneficial overall by demonstrating that even failed innovations can spark later, successful innovations ("... in an attempt to reduse the waste/litter across the world, recycling plants opened up everywhere."). Qualifications and complications include the concession that some innovations are just "the old product in disguise" and the example of multiple versions of smartphones extends the idea that innovation is so valued that people embrace it even when there is little real change.

Organization score point: 4: The response exhibits a clear organizational strategy. The overall shape of the essay reflects the emergent controlling purpose of demonstrating that innovations are so valued because one innovation might lead to others. Logical sequencing is evident. The response provides examples of innovations that spurred or necessitated further innovations, along with the societal benefits conferred by them. The argument then turns to the idea that some innovations may be valued even when unnecessary because of the need to foster the spirit of discovery and creation before summarizing the argument in the conclusion. Transitions aid in clarifying relationships among ideas ("For example, in an attempt to ..."; "Though sometimes innovations may not turn out as planned, they can ..."; Even with the beneficial compounds of ...").

Language Use score point: 5: The use of language in this response works in service of the argument. Word choice is precise ("Even though this worked it still wasn't enough to prevent landfills from overflowing, and from this scientists were able to develop more biodegradable products."). Sentence structures are clear and varied often ("The value given to innovations in society is not overdone, because even if the intentional purpose does not work out, other benefits may arise."). Stylistic choices, such as statements of concession before making a persuasive point, are purposeful and productive ("Though sometimes innovations may not turn out as planned, they can bring great benefits to the world and society."). Minor errors in mechanics do not impede understanding.

Innovation Essay 2 (Score: 5555)

There is no doubt that endless amounts of people create ideas, products and methods daily. Wheter or not each inovation is successful, shouldn't matter. As humans, each of us will fail at some point in life. Our society today is based upon the principle of developing, changing and becoming more advanced. By not appreciating the value of Innovation, I do not believe our society would be able to advance. You cannot have success without failure, valuable lessons can be learnt through different struggles, and advancements throughout our world wouldn't be as drastic if it weren't for innovations.

Innovations are people's ways of thinking outside the box, being creative. Saying too much time is spent on innovations is kind of like saying there's too much time spent on creativity. It is healthy for the human mind to be creative. If people weren't creative, we wouldn't have the innovations we have now. Being able to express, and put thoughts into real life is a great way people can innovate. I don't believe that valuing innovation is a bad thing.

Another reason a problem is seen in innovation is due to the fact many innovators fail. However, failing teaches valuable lessons, and teaches people lots. Innovating comes with risks, you can't expect for everything to work out exactally as planned all the time. Along with failure also comes success. You cannot be successful unless you try, and by trying, you are always exposing yourself to failure. People know that, and if people would have stopped trying after they had failed, there would be no innovations. There is a demand in the world to always be developing always trying to advance. If we didn't focus so much time and value on innovation then the advancements that are necessary in our world wouldn't be achieved.

In perspective three, it is stated

(continued)

Innovation Essay 2 (Score: 5555) (*continued*)

that innovations, "are just the same old things in shiny new package." That may be true, but little do we realize that that "shiny new package" could be answers, cures, and so much more. Everyday new ideas are brought to life, and just because it may be similar to something already existing, doesn't mean it isn't better. In the society live in, there is a constant need for change, and development. Without new advancements we wouldn't be growing as a society. So many helpful, live-changing innovations have been created. It takes money to develop an idea. Yes, some money goes to failure. but some money also goes to success. In the world of innovations there needs to be more focus on success and how it's helped society today, and less on failure. Innovations can be old things in a "shiny new package," but whos to say that package isn't life changing.

The creation of ideas, products, and methods should truly be valued. Without the value of innovations remaining consistently high, our society would never be where it is today. The practice of people being able to create and work to better the society we live in is a great thing. Innovations can change lives and though there are problems, and downfalls, the reward is defiantly worth it. Innovation should always be valued due to the society we live in.

Analysis

Ideas and Analysis score point: 5: The writer generates an argument that productively engages with multiple perspectives on innovation. The thesis—it is essential to progress that innovation is highly valued—reflects precision in thought and purpose. The argument establishes respect for the innovative process and its outcomes as a thoughtful context for analysis. The argument addresses underlying values of the issue by addressing the traits that compel humans toward innovation (creativity, the desire to develop and advance). Analysis counters the underlying assumption of perspective 1—that a failed innovation is also a failed experience—by addressing the positive implications of failure on the road to innovation ("… failing teaches valuable lessons and teaches people lots of innovating comes with risks").

Development and Support score point: 5: Development of ideas and support for claims deepen understanding. A mostly integrated line of purposeful reasoning and illustration capably conveys the significance of the argument that, regardless of the individual outcome, valuing the innovative process is essential for human advancement ("You cannot be successful unless you try, and by trying, you are always exposing yourself to failure. People know that, and if people would have stopped trying after they failed, there would be no innovations."). Analysis of perspective 3's idea that much so-called innovation is merely repackaging is enriched by qualifications and complications that recast small innovations as important to society ("… just because it is similar to something already existing doesn't mean it isn't better"; "Innovations can be old things in a shiny new package, but whos to say that package isn't life changing.").

Organization score point: 5: The response exhibits a productive organizational strategy, mostly unified by the controlling idea that we owe so much to innovation that it cannot be overvalued. A logical sequencing of ideas contributes to the effectiveness of the argument. The response begins by arguing that creativity is essential for innovation, and then proceeds to argue in favor of things that foster innovation and creativity—welcoming risk and encouraging even small innovations— before concluding on a prescriptive note. Transitions between and within paragraphs consistently clarify the relationships among ideas ("Another reason a problem is seen in innovation is due to the fact that … "; "That may be true, but little do we realize …").

Language Use score point: 5: The use of language works in service of the argument. Word choice is precise ("Our society is based upon the principle of developing, changing, and becoming more advanced."). Sentences are clear and varied often ("Saying too much time is spent on innovations is kind of like saying there's too much time spent on creativity. It is healthy for the human mind to be creative."). Stylistic and register choices, including an optimistic tone, are purposeful and productive in the advocacy of casting aside reservations about innovation ("Yes, some money goes to failure, but some money also goes to success. In the world of innovations there needs to be more focus on success today, and less on failure."). Minor errors do not impede understanding.

Innovation Essay 3 (Score: 6666)

Editor's note: *This is a real student essay written under timed conditions. It has been typed because the handwriting of the original essay was difficult to read. Spelling, grammar, and style errors have been reproduced as they were originally written.*

* * *

Innovation has been the key to our modern society. Before the Industrial Revolution, technology had been slowly developing until it exploded around 1750. Since then, our societies have been growing larger, more efficient, and more prosperous due to insistent innovation. In order to manage the consequences of the past and to ensure a safe and sustainable world, innovation must continue.

Innovation keeps the singular goal of improving the good while reducing the harm and waste. This pattern has its basis in both economic theory—producing the highest quality goods and continuing to do so to improve the market—and in the Enlightenment concept of self-improvement. While the Enlightenment was primarily a societal and individual reform movement, it inspired many to believe in the endless ability of human progress in any field they wished. This idea of progress lives through innovation and must be applied to our current problems. With an expanding population, and an increased need for resources, current technologies and resource levels will not satisfy the demand. Through improvements in agriculture (such as disease and predator resistant seeds), housing (such as LEED certification guidelines), infrastructure, and clean energy (wind, solar, geothermal) and transportation, problems of hunger, housing, and pollution will at least be helped. Although numerous risks naturally accompany any innovation, good judgment and persistence will aid in reducing these risks. In our world, innovation is not overvalued; its abilities to solve some of our most pressing global problems is perhaps under-valued.

One reason innovation is undervalued is that some argue that innovation too often leads to failure as well as to wasted resources while rushing forward. This perspective applies most often in the realms of medical research and technology. While these projects do fail more often than those in other areas, their importance cannot be denied.

Medical procedures, sadly, require endless testing, but a failed test is still a step to something that will work, as scientists wisely study others' work. Cures for polio and smallpox are testaments to the importance of incremental innovation that eventually overcame early research failures. Moreover, technological advances also require this kind of effort. When Microsoft introduced its Vista operating system, it was widely considered to be a disaster. But that "failure" led to the development of other, much more successful, operating systems. Beyond failure, innovation is also said to lead to wasted resources. But how can this be the case? The institutions and companies involved in these innovations often receive money from the government or from investors for the sole purpose of innovating. Otherwise that money would be spent on producing the same flawed objects or procedures.

Ultimately, innovation should be highly valued if only because of the global health and welfare. Of course, some innovation is not necessary, such as some smart phones and gaming systems, but innovation creates endless opportunities and choices. The key is good judgment and ensuring that innovation truly benefits us and is not yet another needless upgrade of an advanced technology. We are, collectively and individually, responsible for making the world a better place, and innovation will allow us to do just that. The harm produced from socially beneficial innovation is slight, really, and all innovation should not be discontinued because of failures along the way. In the end, innovation gives us a chance for life, and a better one, but it must be pursued responsibly.

Analysis

Ideas and Analysis score point: 6: The writer generates an argument that critically engages with multiple perspectives on the issue of whether society places too much value on innovation. The argument's thesis—true innovation, distinct from "needless upgrades," is necessary and worth any risks incurred because it can "solve some of our most pressing global problems"—reflects nuance and precision in thought and purpose. The argument establishes and employs an insightful context that focuses on the broad question of innovation and its implications for "global health and welfare" and questions whether innovation is truly the issue. The analysis examines tensions and complexities ("With an expanding population, and an increased need for resources, current technologies and resource levels will not satisfy the demand. Through improvements in agriculture [such as disease and predator resistant seeds], housing [such as LEED certification guidelines], infrastructure, and clean energy [wind, solar, geothermal] and transportation problems of hunger, housing, and population will at least be helped."). Underlying assumptions ("Innovation keeps the singular goal of improving the good while reducing harm and waste.") and underlying values ("… to ensure a safe and sustainable world, innovation must continue.") are also examined.

Development and Support score point: 6: Development of ideas and support for claims deepen insight and broaden context. An integrated line of skillful reasoning and illustration effectively conveys the significance of the argument that innovation, when it is truly needed, should not be perceived as wasteful ("Medical procedures, sadly, require endless testing, but a failed test is still a step to something that will work; technological advances also require this kind of effort …"; "Of course, some innovation is not necessary, such as some smart phones and gaming systems, but innovation creates endless opportunities and choices. The key is good judgment and ensuring that innovation truly benefits us and is not yet another needless upgrade of an advanced technology. We are, collectively and individually, responsible for making the world a better place, and innovation will allow us to do just that."). Qualifications ("In our world, innovation is not overvalued; its abilities to solve some of our most pressing global problems is perhaps under-valued,"; "The harm produced from socially beneficial innovation is slight, really, and all innovation should not be discontinued because of failures along the way.") and complications ("This idea of progress lives through innovation and must be applied to our current problems. With an expanding population, and an increased need for resources, current technologies and resource levels will not satisfy the demand.") enrich and bolster ideas and analysis.

Organization score point: 6: The response exhibits a skillful organizational strategy. The essay is unified by the controlling purpose of analyzing each perspective through the lens of the carefully established introduction ("… our societies have been growing larger, more efficient, and more prosperous due to insistent innovation."). A logical progression of ideas increases the effectiveness of the argument as the writer first explores the purpose of innovation and whether society places too much value on it by discussing its cons and pros, leading logically to a conclusion that explains that innovation gives us a better life, "but it must be pursued responsibly." Transitions between and within paragraphs strengthen the relationships among ideas ("Since then, our societies have been growing …"; "Innovation keeps the singular goal of improving …"; "This pattern has its basis …"; "This idea of progress …"; "Although numerous risks…"; "While these projects do fail …" ; "Moreover, technological advances also require this kind of effort …"; "… of course, some innovation is not necessary…"; "In the end …").

Language Use score point: 6: The use of language enhances the argument. Word choice is skillful and precise ("keeps the singular goal of improving"; "expanding population"; "numerous risks naturally accompany any innovation"; "persistence"; "our most pressing global problems"; "needless upgrade"; "in the realms of medical research"; "reform movement"; "the endless ability of human progress") and sentence structures are consistently varied and clear ("Before the Industrial Revolution, technology had been slowly developing until it exploded around 1750. Since then, our societies have been growing larger, more efficient, and more prosperous due to insistent innovation."; "This perspective applies most often in the realms of medical research and technology. While these projects do fail more often than those in other areas, their importance cannot be denied."). Voice and tone are persuasive, strategic, and effective ("While the Enlightenment was primarily a social and individual reform movement, it inspired many to believe in the endless ability of human progress in any field they wished."). Minor language errors do not impede understanding.

Writing Test: Students and Sleep

Students and Sleep

Research suggests that the natural sleep cycle of adolescents differs in important ways from the cycles of adults and young children. For the average teenager, a natural sleep pattern involves going to bed late at night and sleeping in until late morning. But many middle and high schools begin early in the morning. This means it is difficult for teenage students to follow their natural sleep patterns. If the adolescent sleep cycle entails staying up and sleeping in, should the school day begin later?

Read and carefully consider these perspectives. Each suggests a particular way of thinking about the question above.

Perspective One	Perspective Two	Perspective Three
Students will be expected to wake up early as they pursue their college and career goals after high school. Starting the school day early helps train teens for their futures.	When we're tired, our levels of energy and attention suffer. An early start time prevents students from learning as much as they would if they were well rested.	If the day started later, it would end later as well. This would make it harder for schools to schedule extracurricular activities and would pose a major problem for students who have jobs.

Essay Task

Write a unified, coherent essay in which you address the question of whether the school day should begin later. In your essay, be sure to:

- clearly state your own perspective and analyze the relationship between your perspective and at least one other perspective
- develop and support your ideas with reasoning and examples
- organize your ideas clearly and logically
- communicate your ideas effectively in standard written English

Your perspective may be in full agreement with any of those given, in partial agreement, or completely different.

Students and Sleep Essay 1 (Score: 2222)

As a teenager being a high school student some days its sucks getting up early in the moring and coming to school. I belive they should keep stncol the same time it is now. If we didnt start a seven ih the morning and the cnaned it to start till like ten or elevien we would bein school all day once we got home it would be too late to do anything.

First of all I belive it would be a bad idea for school to start latter we wouldnt get home till late in the day. Depending on what time of year it is we would only have a few hours of daylight left once we got home

Another reason its a good idea to leave it now it is and start eurly in the morning. It dose prepare us to be ready to go into the working felid. I know from expeince me and my dud get up. At the same time during school but when summer comes and i start to sleepin when erevi need to get up early its really hard and im super tired.

A reason why it would be a good idea is we would be a lot more awake and focused. We wouldn't be so tired getting up in the morning and we wold wake ot ot easier.

Analysis

Ideas and Analysis score point: 2: The writer generates an argument that weakly responds to multiple perspectives on the issue of schools starting later to accommodate students' sleep cycles. Attempts at analysis are incomplete ("…we wouldn't get home till late in the day. Depending on what time of year it is we would only have a few hours of daylight left once we got home.") and sometimes amount to little more than restatement of the prompt's perspectives ("It dose prepare us to be ready to go into the working felid.").

Development and Support score point: 2: Development of ideas and support for claims are weak and confused. For instance, the attempt to support the claim that waking up early prepares one for life in the workforce fails to clarify the rationale behind this idea ("I know from experince me and my dad get up at the same time during school but when summer comes and i start to sleep in when ever i need to get up early it is really hard and im super tired"). On the whole, reasoning and illustration are inadequate.

Organization score point: 2: The response exhibits a rudimentary organizational structure. Grouping of ideas is inconsistent; the first paragraph, for example, consists of contradictory ideas that are not connected by transitions. Although ideas elsewhere are mostly collected in paragraphs according to their basic topic, organization of the response as a whole does not display the level of control required at higher score points.

Language Use score point: 2: The use of language is inconsistent and often unclear. Word choice is rudimentary and frequently imprecise ("the same time it is now"; "bad idea"; "super tired"). Sentence structures are sometimes unclear ("If we didnt start a seven in the morning and the chaned it to start till like ten or eleven we would be in school all day once we got home it would be too late to do anything."). Stylistic and register choices, including a casual tone, are inconsistent and are not always appropriate for the rhetorical purpose ("some days it sucks…"). Distracting errors in grammar, usage, and mechanics are present, and they sometimes impede understanding.

Students and Sleep Essay 2 (Score: 3233)

Due to the Sleeping Patterns of high school and middle school Students, Schools should start later in the day. Because when Schools Start early in the morning it does not give the Students the amount of Sleep they need to get through their classes. Middle School and high School Students usually go to sleep late at night and wake up in the late morning. So, for that reason, Schools would need to begin later in the morning so that those student will be more focused. But what would happen to those high School Students who have Jobs or extracurricular activities?

Well, for those students, they would either have to take night Shifts, or have to leave early during the School day to get to those Jobs. Then there are the Students with extracurricular activities. For those who Play Sports, they would have to again, either leave early or have an excused abscense for their Practices. So, there can be issues that Can come about with Schools Starting later in the day, but we can always find a way to fix those issues. Can there be Positives for Starting early in the future.

If schools continue to start early in the morning, then it can be a plus for students who have to go into their job early in the morning when they are adults. Most buisnesses start early in the morning, so they will need people to come in early to start working. So the schools are kind of helping prepair students for their future jobs. But for a lot of students, they would prefer to start school later in the day.

Analysis

Ideas and Analysis score point: 3: The writer generates an argument that responds to multiple perspectives on whether the school day should begin later. The argument's thesis (Starting the school day later may cause issues, and an early start has some advantages, but most students would prefer a later start to get enough sleep.) reflects some clarity in thought and purpose as argued. The argument establishes a limited context for analysis by acknowledging the conflict between early school start times and teenage students' sleep patterns. Analysis is simplistic in its dismissal of potential complexities of the issue ("So, there can be issues that can come about with schools starting later in the day, but we can always find a way to fix those issues.").

Development and Support score point: 2: Development of ideas and support for claims are weak in that little development is offered. Reasoning and illustration are inadequate and fail to clarify the argument. For instance, although there is a little reasoning as to how students with jobs or extracurricular activities would be affected by a later start ("… they would have to again, either leave early or have an excused abscense"), further development to clarify the "issues" that might arise is lacking, as the argument abandons this discussion and moves to the next point ("Can there be positives for starting early …").

Organization score point: 3: The response exhibits a basic organizational structure. Most ideas are logically grouped within paragraphs, leading to a response that largely coheres: the first paragraph introduces the issue, the second discusses effects of a later start time on students with after-school activities, and the third discusses early start times in relation to future jobs. Although transitions between and within paragraphs are at times awkward (e.g., the transitional sentence at the end of the second paragraph), they sometimes clarify the relationships among ideas ("So, for that reason …"; "But what would happen …"; "Well for those students …"; "Then there are the students …"; "So, there can be …"; "But for a lot of students …").

Language Use score point: 3: The use of language is basic and only somewhat clear. Word choice is general, repetitious, and occasionally imprecise ("there can be issues that can come about"; "a way to fix those issues"; "it can be a plus"; "can there be positives"). Sentence structures are usually clear, but sentence variety is limited, in part by the relative brevity of the response. Stylistic and register choices, including voice and tone, are hindered by general language and are not always appropriate ("So the schools are kind of helping …").

Students and Sleep Essay 3 (Score: 3333)

If schools were to begin later then they do now students would not have time for their extracurricular activities, homework would keep them up even later because they'd get home late, and they'd have even less time to themselves or to spend with their family and friend. If you agree with me then keep reading, if not then keep reading and maybe you'll change your mind.

First of all, if school started later their would be no time for extracurricular activities. Students are always told to participate but if they're getting home late then they'd have no time. They're also told to get their excersize and the right amount of it, but most kids excersize comes from their after school activities so if they lose that they also lose their excersize. So if you're involved in after school activities that you'd hate to lose, maybe you should just deal with school early in the morning.

Secondly, homework would keep students up even later then it does when school starts early. Homework takes up a good amount of students nights so they tend to not be able to have the time they need to do what they have to do at night such as shower, eat, chores, etc. So if school started later they'd get home later and have even less time to do what they need to do. Also some homework takes longer than other homework, for example writing an essay or doing a project takes longer than a couple math problems. If you want more time to yourself at night, a later start to your day is not the answer you're looking for because homework will keep you up.

Last but not least, if school started later you'd have even less time to yourself or to your family and friends. If you like to read at night or anything else you're not gonna have a lot of time to, you'll still have time, just not the amount you need. Also if you and your family like to go out and have dinner on Tuesday nights you might not be able to because you'd get home later and most restraunts close a little early on week days. Then say you and your friends like hanging out on weekdays, well you wouldn't have a lot of time together because you'd need to get home and do what you have to do.

In conclusion, schools starting later is not a good idea because you'd have less time for extracurricular activities, less time to finish homework, and less time

(continued)

Students and Sleep Essay 3 (Score: 3333) *(continued)*

to yourself, family, and friends. So if you like time to do these things I suggest just getting over it and going to school early.

Analysis

Ideas and Analysis score point: 3: The writer generates an argument that responds to multiple perspectives on the issue of students and sleep. The thesis (if students want enough time for activities other than school, they should not support later starting times) shows some clarity in thought and purpose. The argument looks at the time demanded for several activities outside of school, providing a limited context for analysis. Analysis of the argument that delaying school start times would cause scheduling problems later in the day is relevant but simplistic ("Students are always told to participate but if they're getting home late then they'd have no time"; "Homework takes up a good amount of students night so they tend to not be able to have the time the need to do what they have to do at night …").

Development and Support score point: 3: Development of ideas and support for claims are mostly relevant, but simplistic. Reasoning and illustration give examples of a few ways late start times would inconvenience students ("Also some homework takes longer than other homework, for example writing an essay or doing a project takes longer than a couple math problems …"). Though somewhat repetitious about the effect of school start times on after-school schedules, these examples largely clarify the argument that getting out of school later would have a negative impact on after-school activities ("Also if you and your family like to go out and have dinner on Tuesday nights you might not be able to because you'd get home later and most restaurants close a little early on week days.").

Organization score point: 3: The response exhibits a basic organizational structure with an introduction, body, and conclusion. Most ideas are logically grouped, and the response largely coheres around the three main points presented in the argument. Transitions within and between paragraphs sometimes clarify relationships among ideas ("Secondly, homework would keep students up even later …"; "Also if you and your family like to go out and have dinner…"; "Last but not least, if school started earlier …").

Language Use score point: 3: The use of language is basic and only somewhat clear. Word choice is general and occasionally imprecise ("Then say you and your friends like hanging out on weekdays, well you wouldn't have a lot of time together because you'd need to get home and do what you have to do."). Sentence structures are mostly clear but show little variety ("So if school started later they'd get home later and have even less time to do what they need to do."). Stylistic and register choices, including voice and tone, are not always appropriate for the rhetorical purpose of convincing students that later start times are a bad idea ("So if you're involved in after school activities that you'd hate to lose, maybe you should just deal with school early in the morning."). Errors in grammar, usage, and mechanics are distracting, but they generally do not impede understanding ("… even less time to themselves or to spend with their family and friends.").

Students and Sleep Essay 4 (Score: 4444)

There are many different things that teenagers are in need of in today's society; one of these things being more sleep. Many teenagers would say that the school day should start later so that we can sleep in more. However, I tend to disagree with this popular opinion. If the school day were to start later, it also would end late. This would make it incredibly difficult for students to be apart of after school clubs, sports, or even keep their job.

As a teen myself, I feel as though it is expected of me to want to sleep in more, therefore wanting school to start late. I do enjoy sleeping in, but not enough to give up my youth group or my sports or my job. It is also incredibly important for a student to be active in things other than just school. Research has shown that it is important for teens to have physical activity and create and maintain relationships. If school started late, scheduling for these events becomes a lot more difficult and we are left depend.

Some would argue that just because scheduling these events may become harder, but scheduling them wouldn't be impossible. However, even if those events were to be scheduled on a late school, clubs, work or practice run the threat of being shortened. This is also a downside because students wouldn't have as long in the evenings to do homework, eat or shower to keep themselves clean.

(continued)

Students and Sleep Essay 4 (Score: 4444) (*continued*)

Another reason to keep the school day starting early is because of routine. High schoolers will not stay high schoolers forever. They will eventually have to get a job that may require them to wake up early, or maybe even college classes that demand that they wake up early to make it to class on time. Most jobs do not accept tardiness daily, there are repercussions. It's important that we as teens understand that sleep is not the most important thing in the world!

Opposing teenagers may argue that not all jobs require their employees to wake up early, and they would be right. However, it is still important to get into a routine. Also, a lot of jobs do require their employees to wake early in the morning, why not get prepared now?

I think that it is very important that we keep the school day starting early. I have a job and am a part of different clubs. I already feel as if the school day is late enough, sometimes I still run out of time to do everything required of me. I find it hard to hang out with my friends, do all my homework, stay active, maintain a healthy diet and stay steadily involved in all of my clubs and in my workplace. We need to consider all points of view before jumping to conclusions automatically and switching up the schedule for many of today's teenagers.

The school day should be kept the way it
is now, starting early, ending early. If we keep it this way,
it makes it easier for teenagers to stay involved
in sports, clubs and extracurricular activities. It would also
help teens start a routine for their career later in life.
It is important to start school early.

Analysis

Ideas and Analysis score point: 4: The writer generates an argument that engages with multiple perspectives on the issue of students and sleep. The argument's thesis—that the school day should start early and end early so it's easier for teenagers to stay involved in extracurricular activities—reflects clarity in thought and purpose. The argument establishes and employs a relevant context that acknowledges teenagers are sleep deprived and focuses analysis on the drawbacks of implementing a later school start time as a solution to this problem. Analysis recognizes complexities, tensions, and implications (e.g., that starting school early helps students establish a routine that will benefit them in the future).

Development and Support score point: 4: Development of ideas and support for claims clarify meaning and purpose. Lines of clear reasoning and illustration adequately convey the significance of the argument that a later start to the school day would be detrimental for students because it would make it difficult to stay involved in activities outside of school ("I do enjoy sleeping in, but not enough to give up my youth group or my sports or my job. It is incredibly important for a student to be active in things other than just school. Research has shown that it is important for teens to have physical activity and create and maintain relationships. If schools started later, scheduling for these events becomes a lot more difficult and we are left deprived."). In anticipating and addressing a counterargument, the writer also acknowledges complications ("Opposing teenagers may argue that not all jobs require their employees to wake up early, and they would be right. However, it is still important to get into a routine).

Organization score point: 4: The response exhibits a clear organizational strategy. The overall shape of the response reflects an emergent controlling purpose of exploring the drawbacks of school's starting later. Ideas are logically grouped and sequenced. The piece begins by discussing the importance of teenagers being involved in extracurricular activities, then discusses the benefits of establishing a routine, and finally elaborates on how a later start time complicates a student's involvement in clubs. Transitions between and within these paragraphs clarify the relationships among ideas ("However, I tend to disagree …"; "Another reason …"; "Also, a lot of jobs …") and connect the discussions to the thesis.

Language Use score point: 4: The use of language conveys the argument with clarity. Word choice is adequate and sometimes precise ("popular opinion"; "repercussions"; "jumping to conclusions"). Sentence structures are clear and demonstrate some variety ("If the school day were to start later, it also would end later. This would make it incredibly difficult for students to be a part of after school club."). Stylistic and register choices are appropriate for the rhetorical purpose ("Opposing teenagers may argue. . ".; "Also, a lot of jobs do require their employees to wake early in the morning, why not get prepared now?"; "We need to consider all points of view …"). Errors in grammar, usage, and mechanics are present, but they rarely impede understanding.

Students and Sleep Essay 5 (Score: 5455)

As teenagers grow & develop, their brains undergo radical changes. Among these changes is a fundamental change to levels of melatonin, the sleep hormone, in the brain. As a result of these shifts, teenagers wake up later & go to sleep later; they are more awake later in the morning. However, most schools ignore this fact. Schools commonly start at 8:00 am, before teenagers are naturally awake. This early start time can pose myriad issues. Schools should consider whether later start & end times would be best for their students.

Teenagers have very specific sleep needs individual to their age group. Therefore, the early times that work for adults do not work for them. Furthermore, as teens develop into adults, their sleep schedules will shift to make early mornings easier. Therefore, it is unnecessary to "train" students for college & jobs by forcing them to wake up earlier. As their brains develop, earlier bed times & wake ups will happen naturally. Forcing teens to wake up early is unnecessary & pointless.

Even beyond that, however, early mornings could be dangerous, both physically & mentally. Early start times force teens to drive to school before they are fully awake. This state of unalertness can lead to increased traffic accidents. Students also cannot benefit fully from their education if they are still half-asleep. With later start times, teens would be able to fully understand & immerse themselves in the material, rather than dozing through their morning classes. Starting the school day later would result in safer, better educated teenagers.

Later start times are not without drawbacks, though. Later start times will require later end times, as well. With school extending later in the afternoon, there would be reduced time for extracurriculars. It would also restrict those with after-school jobs. For these reasons, school officials need to consider their individual school & their students when considering later start times. A school with many working students & a huge percentage of students who use public transportation, for example, may decide that the traditional early start works for them. A school where many people drive, with few people in extracurriculars, may choose a later start. Other schools may choose to start late & end early, but extend the school year further into the summer. It is up to each school to weigh the risks & benefits for themselves.

The answer may not lie in allowing students to wake up later, but go to bed earlier. Students are often so busy that they get only a few hours of sleep, exacerbating the problem. Reducing homework & standardized tests would allow students more sleep. Schools should also look at extracurriculars to determine whether they are too intense & demand too much time. A multifaceted approach may be the best way to help students.

Schools need to look critically at their schedules & policies in order to help students the most. Currently, students are dangerously tired & barely alert in the morning. Without also hurting students involved in after-school activities & jobs, schools have a responsibility to do all they can to insure well-rested students. Schools must consider the natural biology of the teenage brain, as well as the additional stresses placed on students by modern society. Failure to do so is a failure to truly see students for what they are: the future.

Analysis

Ideas and Analysis score point: 5: The writer generates an argument that productively engages with multiple perspectives on the issue of students and sleep. The argument's thesis (schools have a responsibility to ensure well-rested students, so each school should consider whether later start times would be best for their particular students) reflects precision in thought and purpose. The argument establishes a thoughtful context by setting out the conflict between adolescent development and the common school schedule. This context is employed in analysis by exploring both the argument for starting school later as well as the argument against a late start. Analysis addresses these complexities by discussing how the best answer may be different depending on the school and refutes the claim of Perspective One that starting school earlier will train teens for the future ("…as teens develop into adults, their sleep schedule will shift to make early mornings easier. Therefore, it is unnecessary to "train" students for college + jobs by forcing them to wake earlier.").

Development and Support score point: 4: Development of ideas and support for claims clarify meaning and purpose. Lines of clear reasoning and illustration adequately convey the significance of the argument that later start times may work for some students but not for others ("For these reasons, school officials need to consider their individual school + their students when considering later start times. A school with many working students + a large percentage of students who use public transportation, for example, may decide that the traditional early start works for them. A school where many people drive, with few people in extracurriculars, may choose a later start. Other schools …"). Qualifications and complications extend ideas and analysis by beginning to explore the challenges of a one-size fits all solution ("It is up to each school to weigh the risks + benefits for themselves"; "The answer may not lie in allowing students to wake up later, but go to bed earlier"; "A multifaceted approach may be the best way to help students").

Organization score point: 5: The response exhibits a productive organizational strategy that is mostly unified by the controlling idea that a later start time may work well for some schools but not others. After introducing the main idea, the writer discusses the drawbacks of early and late start times in turn. Having established the potential limitations of either approach, the argument urges schools to consider the circumstances of their particular students when deciding start times. This logical sequencing contributes to the effectiveness of the argument. Along the way, transitions consistently clarify the relationships among ideas ("Even beyond that, however, early mornings …"; "This state of unalertness …"; "With later start times …"; "Later start times are not without drawbacks, though").

Language Use score point: 5: The use of language works in service of the argument. Word choice and phrasing is precise, and sentence structures are clear and varied. This precision and variety aids in conveying well-developed argumentative skill. Stylistic choices are purposeful and productive, including momentary shifts in tone ("Failure to do so is a failure to truly see students for what they are: the future"). Minor errors do not impede understanding.

Students and Sleep Essay 6 (Score: 5555)

Everyone has no doubt felt the terrible grogginess of an early-morning routine, or the groans in the morning amidst a large group of teenagers. It's not easy to bring oneself to get out of bed after a long night of a mix of homework and, mostly, socialization and video games. As a teenager, it only makes sense that he or she should not have to wake up early—school should just start later! Many students have argued for school to begin at later hours of the morning in favor of a "sleep late, wake late" schedule. The problem with this, though, is that there is a reason why school starts around 8:00AM and not noon. In fact, there are several reasons, all of which have been brushed aside in the students' arguments.

One very important issue with scheduling school later is that if a school were to start later would it not end later, too? For students in athletics and other extracurricular activities, this would pose a huge setback. There would be less time to practice, less motivation to meet, and ultimately the clubs would grow weak in

(continued)

Students and Sleep Essay 6 (Score: 5555) (continued)

merit if no progress is being made. Along with clubs, students who work part-time would likely not be able to make decent hours, if they're even hired in the first place. Most businesses close around 10:00 PM, so there would be little time to clock in and work. On the off chance that a student gets a job with later hours, it could prove to be unhealthy or even dangerous. Imagine a child working at a gas station until 2:00 AM. It's an unsettling sight.

Even knowing this, though, students still argue for later starting hours. The most common argument is that teenagers, in particular, have a natural sleep cycle of staying up late, followed by waking up late. Honestly, this is about the weakest argument that has ever been presented in such a big debate. Adults would sleep late if they were able to; however, they have responsibilities to tend to and do not have a say in it. Sleep cycles are not the problem here. In order to function well, an adolescent needs around 8 hours of sleep. There's no mention of late or early. They only need the proper amount of hours. In order to fix this, students would simply just have to go to sleep earlier — the easiest solution that anybody can do!

Finally, though, there is one more important reason as to why school starts early in the morning: accessibility. Assuming the child is under 16 years old, and therefore unable to drive, the only way for students to reach the school campus is with the aid of their parents or guardians, or through the use of a schoolbus. By choosing to start school later in the day, one mode of transportation is immediately eliminated. Most to all parents or guardians of children work for a living in order to support their child. Normally, work starts early in the morning. If the student is left at home after the parent leaves for work, how are they supposed to get to school? School buses cannot pick up everybody, and most schools would not enjoy having to fund more transportation methods for the student population.

All in all, it is not a good idea to change the school schedule. The consequences outweigh the advantages by a ton. The idea to start school later has likely already been attempted at this point in time, and they went back to the early mornings for a reason. If the system works in society, why change it for just a few hours of sleep when the simple solution is to just go to bed early and don't stay up late playing games? That's the question that should be asked here.

Analysis

Ideas and Analysis score point: 5: The writer generates an argument that productively engages with multiple perspectives on whether the school day should begin later. The argument's thesis (because starting school later than is typical would have many consequences that are difficult to resolve, and since students could be better rested if they simply went to sleep earlier, school start times should not be changed) reflects precision in thought and purpose. The argument establishes and employs a thoughtful context that focuses analysis on the reasons why school start times are what they are. The analysis addresses the implications of later start times for students who pursue extracurricular activities and/or jobs, implications for school transportation systems, and underlying assumptions of the issue (e.g., the assumption that the timing of teens' sleep cycles is more important than simply getting a sufficient amount of sleep).

Development and Support score point: 5: Development of ideas and support for claims deepen understanding. A mostly integrated line of purposeful reasoning and illustration capably conveys the significance of the argument that later start times would create insurmountable problems related to work and transportation ("Assuming the child is under 16 years old, and therefore unable to drive … ."; "If the student is left at home after the parent leaves for work, how are they supposed to get to school? School buses cannot pick up everybody, and most schools would not enjoy having to fund more transportation methods for the student population."). Qualifications and complications enrich the analysis of negative consequences for students with jobs ("Most businesses close around 10:00 PM, so there would be little time to clock in and work. On the off chance that a student gets a job with later hours, it could prove to be unhealthy or even dangerous. Imagine a child working at a gas station until 2:00 AM.").

Organization score point: 5: The response exhibits a productive organizational strategy. It is mostly unified by the controlling purpose of explaining why it is both impractical and unnecessary to change school start times. A logical sequencing of ideas contributes to the effectiveness of the argument as it first explores negative outcomes for students with jobs, then criticizes the supposed need for a later start time as being based on flawed assumptions about sleep cycles, and finally rejects any proposed change as impossible due to transportation logistics. All this builds toward the conclusion ("If the system works in society, why change it."). Transitions between and within paragraphs consistently clarify the relationships among ideas ("The problem with this …"; "Even knowing this, students still argue …"; "In order to fix this …"; "Finally, though, there is one more important reason …").

Language Use score point: 5: The use of language works in service of the argument. Word choice is precise ("the terrible grogginess of an early-morning routine"; "socialization and video games"; "brushed aside"; "clock in"; "responsibilities to tend to"; "accessibility"; "transportation methods"). Sentence structures are clear and varied often, contributing to the writer's lively, conversational tone ("As a teenager, it only makes sense that he or she should not have to wake up early—school should just start later!"). Stylistic and register choices, including a voice that distances the writer from teenagers as a whole by criticizing their habits and perspective, are purposeful and productive ("The most common argument is that teenagers, in particular, have a natural sleep cycle… ." If the system works in society, why change it … when the simple solution is just to go to bed early and don't stay up playing games?"). Although minor errors are present, they do not impede understanding.

Students and Sleep Essay 7 (Score: 6556)

Editor's note: *This is a real student essay written under timed conditions. It has been typed because the handwriting of the original essay was difficult to read. Spelling, grammar, and style errors have been reproduced as they were originally written.*

* * *

Sleep is essential for the growth, development, and functionability of any adolescent mind. While most teenagers are well-aware of this fact, the hard truth is that sleep deprivation runs rampant in high schoolers. The answer to this issue is like a single incriminating piece of evidence, lost under a pile of overanalyzed information. School should not start any later in the day; teenagers simply need to learn the responsible time to fall asleep.

The adult world runs on a tight schedule. To succeed in any corporate or business environment, one must play by the rules. What better cultural norm to follow than the proper sleep schedule? When your livelihood depends on a person's salary to survive, they can't stay up till 2 A.M. watching Netflix, as many teenagers do, because the responsibility far outweighs the reward. College schedules are incredibly similar. If a student decides to stay up late, it is not the proffesor's job to go easier on them. Changing the way a tight schedule runs would be pointless, even destructive, for a learning environment as it would teach students to not follow the well-established rules of productivity.

Sustainable energy and clean energy are often remarked as loft goals set to be accomplished by the human race. Natural lighting is becoming ever more popular in the modern world as a result. Changing the school schedule to start later would only increase the amount of artificial lighting usage. Imagine keeping huge spotlights on multiple practice fields as students begin football or soccer practice. It would end up forcing many impracticalities and inefficient habits for extracurricular activities.

While many students optimistically believe that setting the start of school back would help them sleep better, this simply cannot be proven. If a high school's changed from 8-3:30 to 11-6:30, for example, students would simply go to bed even later than before, therefore nullifying the effects of starting late. Being well-rested can greatly affect a student's comprehensive ability, but the real issue lies in student behavior, not time slots. Focusing in on individual behaviors, for instance, the average amount of screen time a student has per day, would have a greater overall impact on fixing sleep deprivation issues in school.

The responsibility of sleep is a mighty one. No person would be able to function without it. In order to most efficiently obtain enough sleep per night, sleep schedules must be strictly followed. Setting back the time when school starts would simply be redundant in terms of trying to get students more sleep time. It might also cause major issues such as wasting more energy and making it hard to do extracurriculars at night. School schedules were designed to fit perfectly into the adult world's schedule. Fixing something that isn't broken can often lead to more issues than positive results.

Analysis

Ideas and Analysis score point: 6: The writer generates an argument that critically engages with multiple perspectives on the issue of whether school start times should accommodate teenagers' sleep cycles. The argument's thesis (while teenagers need adequate sleep for optimal well-being, it is their own responsibility to see that they get it) reflects nuance and precision in thought and purpose. The argument establishes and employs an insightful context that centers on the negative impacts of changing the school start time. The analysis examines implications, such as the increased energy usage needed to provide outdoor lighting for extracurricular sports held later due to the longer school day. The analysis also examines complexities of other likely causes of students' loss of sleep ("Being well-rested can greatly affect a student's comprehensive ability, but the real issue lies in student behavior, not time slots. Focusing in on individual behaviors, for instance, the average amount of screen time a student has per day, would have a greater overall impact on fixing sleep deprivation issues in school."), implications for fitting into the "adult" world ("If a student decides to stay up late, it is not the proffessor's job to go easier on them."), and underlying values such as personal responsibility.

Development and Support score point: 5: Development of ideas and support for claims deepen understanding. A mostly integrated line of purposeful reasoning and illustration capably conveys the significance of the argument that school start times should not be adjusted, as the writer begins to draw out the larger impact of the consequences the argument anticipates ("Sustainable energy and clean energy [are important goals] …"; "Changing the school schedule [would require more artificial light] … forcing many impracticalities & inefficient habits for extracurricular activities."). Qualifications and complications enrich ideas and analysis ("While many students optimistically believe that setting the start of school back will help them sleep better, this simply cannot be proven. If a high school's schedule changed from 8-3:30 to 11-6:30, for example, students would simply go to bed even later than before, therefore nullifying the effects of starting late.").

Organization score point: 5: The response exhibits a purposeful organizational strategy. The response is mostly unified by a controlling idea that adjusting school start times will not solve the problem of teenager's sleep deprivation. A logical sequencing of ideas contributes to the effectiveness of the argument. The piece begins by emphasizing personal responsibility of teens to adapt to adult schedules, examines the problems associated with changing start times, and finally arrives at a conclusion that reaffirms the thesis. Transitions between and within paragraphs consistently clarify the relationships among ideas ("Sleep is essential …"; "The answer to this issue …"; "The adult world runs …"; "If a student decides …"; "Changing the school schedule …"; "Imagine …"; "While many students …"; "Focusing in on …"; "In order to …"; "It might also cause …").

Language Use score point: 6: The use of language enhances the argument. Word choice is skillful and precise ("runs rampant"; "single incriminating piece of evidence"; "cultural norm"; "livelihood"; "well-established rules of productivity"; "Sustainable energy"; "lofty goals"; "artificial lighting usage"; "impracticalities & inefficient habits"; "optimistically believe"; "nullifying the effects"; "comprehensive ability"; "mighty one"; "redundant"). Sentence structures are consistently varied and clear ("When a livelihood depends on a person's salary to survive, they can't stay up till 2 A.M. watching Netflix, as many teenagers do, because the responsibility far outweighs the reward."). Stylistic and register choices are strategic and effective. Although a few minor errors are present, they do not impede understanding.

Chapter 14: Practice Questions

This chapter contains a wide variety of sample ACT English test questions. These are all official ACT questions so be sure to look over them in detail.

Some of these questions are ones that you have seen throughout the rest of the guide. Don't skip them just because you've seen them once. The more you practice, the better off you will be on the test.

Finally, this item bank is not set up like a practice test so don't feel as though you need to go through each set of questions in sequential order or on a timed basis. Simply answer the questions to the best of your ability. Be sure to look at the answer key, which provides a detailed explanation to each question.

PASSAGE I

Miami Time

My family is part of the Miami

tribe a Native American people, with strong
_____
1

ties to territory in present-day Ohio, Indiana,

and Illinois. Growing up in the Midwest, I often

heard my grandmother talk about "Miami time."

When she was doing something she loved, whether

it was making freezer jam or researching tribal history,
_____
2

she refused to be rushed in a hurry. "I'm on Miami time
_____
3

today," she would say. Conversely, if we were running

late for an appointment. She would chide us by saying,
_____
4

"Get a move on. We're not running on Miami time today,

you know."

1. **A.** NO CHANGE
    B. tribe, a Native American, people
    C. tribe, a Native American people
    D. tribe; a Native American people

2. At this point, the writer would like to provide a glimpse into the grandmother's interests. Given that all the choices are true, which one best accomplishes this purpose?
    F. NO CHANGE
    G. being actively involved in her pursuits,
    H. things I really hope she'll teach me one day,
    J. historical research as well as domestic projects,

3. **A.** NO CHANGE
    B. hurried or rushed.
    C. made to go faster or rushed.
    D. rushed.

4. **F.** NO CHANGE
    G. appointment; she
    H. appointment and she
    J. appointment, she

It was a difficult concept for me to grasp. My
                    5
grandmother tried to explain that "Miami time" referred to

those moments, when time seemed to slow down or stand
          6

still. Recently, the meaning of her words started to sink in.
                                        7

One morning, my son and I will inadvertently slip out of
                              8
the world measured in seconds, minutes, and hours, and

into one measured by curiosity and sensation.

[1] On a familiar trail near our house, I was pushing

Jeremy in his stroller and were thinking of the day ahead
                              9
and the tasks I had to complete. [2] Suddenly, he squealed

with pure delight and pointed toward a clearing. [3] There,

two does and three fawns stood watching us. [4] Five pairs
        10
of ears flicked like antennae seeking a signal. [5] After a

few moments, the deer lowered their heads and began to

eat, as if they had decided we were harmless. [6] By then,

my son's face was full of wonder. [11]

We spent the rest of the morning veering from the

trail to investigate small snatches of life. Lizards lazing

in the sun and quail rustled through grasses surprised us.
                      12

Wild blackberries melted on our tongues. For example, the
                                          13
aroma of crushed eucalyptus leaves tingled in our noses.

5. Given that all the choices are true, which one provides
   the best opening to this paragraph?
   A. NO CHANGE
   B. I remember being late for a doctor's appointment
      one day.
   C. My grandmother lived with us, and as a result she
      and I became close over the years.
   D. My son asks me about my grandmother, whom he
      never met.

6. F. NO CHANGE
   G. moments when
   H. moments, as if
   J. moments, because

7. A. NO CHANGE
   B. spoken statements to my ears
   C. expressed opinions on the matter
   D. verbal remarks in conversation

8. F. NO CHANGE
   G. inadvertently slip
   H. are inadvertently slipping
   J. inadvertently slipped

9. A. NO CHANGE
   B. were having thoughts
   C. thinking
   D. DELETE the underlined portion.

10. F. NO CHANGE
    G. does, and three fawns
    H. does and three fawns,
    J. does and, three fawns

11. For the sake of the logic and coherence of this para-
    graph, Sentence 3 should be placed:
    A. where it is now.
    B. before Sentence 1.
    C. after Sentence 1.
    D. after Sentence 4.

12. F. NO CHANGE
    G. rustling
    H. were rustling
    J. DELETE the underlined portion.

13. A. NO CHANGE
    B. On the other hand, the
    C. Just in case, the
    D. The

By the time we found our way back to the car, the sun was high in the sky. We had taken three hours to complete a hike we usually finished in forty-five minutes. Yet the hike felt <u>shorter then</u> ever. As we drove off, I remembered

14
something else my grandmother used to say: "Miami time passes all too quickly."

14. **F.** NO CHANGE
G. more shorter then
H. the shortest than
J. shorter than

> Question 15 asks about the preceding passage as a whole.

15. Suppose the writer's goal had been to write a brief essay conveying a personal experience with "Miami time." Would this essay successfully fulfill that goal?

A. Yes, because it presents the narrator's firsthand experience of a morning spent in Miami time.
B. Yes, because it reveals that after a conversation with the grandmother, the narrator decided to live in Miami time.
C. No, because it shares the views of more than one person with regard to the meaning of Miami time.
D. No, because the term "Miami time" belonged to the grandmother, not to the narrator.

PASSAGE II

Faith Ringgold's Quilting Bee

The artist Faith Ringgold has made a name for herself with her "story quilts," lively combinations of painting, quilting, and storytelling. Each artwork consists of a painting framed by quilted squares of fabric and story panels. One of these artworks, *The Sunflowers Quilting Bee at Arles*, depicts a scene of women at work on a quilt in a field of towering yellow <u>flowers that eight</u> African

16
American women sit around the quilt that covers their laps. Who are these people stitching among the flowers? What brings them so close that their shoulders touch?

16. **F.** NO CHANGE
G. flowers and eight
H. flowers. Eight
J. flowers, eight

Thus, the answers to these questions can
<u>   </u>
17
be found in the artwork itself. Ringgold has told

<u>the story of this gathering on two horizontal panels of text.</u>
18
One panel is sewn into the piece's top border,

the other into <u>it's</u> bottom border. These eight
19

<u>women the story explains, strove</u>
20

<u>in their various ways</u> to support
21
the cause of justice in the world.

In <u>reality,</u> these women never met to piece together
22

a quilt. The scene comes out of the <u>artists imagination</u> as
23
a statement of the unity of purpose that she perceives in

their lives. Sojourner Truth and Harriet Tubman fought

to abolish slavery and, later, <u>was active in the crusade</u>
24
for suffrage. Newspaper journalist Ida B. Wells

<u>courageously spoke out for social and racial justice</u>
25
in the late nineteenth and early twentieth centuries.
25

17. **A.** NO CHANGE
  B. Instead, the
  C. Furthermore, the
  D. The

18. **F.** NO CHANGE
  G. of this gathering the story on two horizontal panels of text.
  H. on two horizontal panels the story of this gathering of text.
  J. the story on two horizontal panels of text of this gathering.

19. **A.** NO CHANGE
  B. its'
  C. its
  D. their

20. **F.** NO CHANGE
  G. women, the story explains—
  H. women the story explains—
  J. women, the story explains,

21. The underlined phrase could be placed in all the following locations EXCEPT:
  A. where it is now.
  B. after the word *support*.
  C. after the word *cause*.
  D. after the word *world* (ending the sentence with a period).

22. **F.** NO CHANGE
  G. summary,
  H. addition,
  J. contrast,

23. **A.** NO CHANGE
  B. artist's imagination
  C. artists' imagination
  D. artists imagination,

24. **F.** NO CHANGE
  G. was actively engaged
  H. was engaged
  J. were active

25. Given that all the choices are true, which one provides the most relevant information at this point in the essay?
  A. NO CHANGE
  B. married Ferdinand Barnett, editor of the first Black newspaper in Chicago, the *Chicago Conservator*.
  C. wrote for newspapers in Memphis, New York City, and finally, Chicago.
  D. was born in Holly Springs, Mississippi, in 1862, the eldest of eight children.

Establishing her own hair products <u>business, herself</u>
₂₆
in the first decade of the twentieth century,

<u>millions of dollars were later bequeathed by Madam</u>
₂₇
<u>C. J. Walker to charities and educational institutions.</u>
₂₇
Among the schools that benefited from this

<u>generosity, were</u> those that Mary McLeod Bethune
₂₈
opened and ran in order to provide a better education

for Black students. And Fannie Lou Hamer, Ella Baker,

and Rosa Parks showed leadership and strength during the

civil rights <u>movement, it happened in</u> the 1950s and 1960s.
₂₉
   In the artwork, Ringgold has surrounded these women

with bright sunflowers. The flowers seem to celebrate the

women's accomplishments and the beauty of their shared

vision. [30]

26. **F.** NO CHANGE
    G. business belonging to her
    H. business, herself,
    J. business

27. **A.** NO CHANGE
    B. Madam C. J. Walker later bequeathed millions of dollars to charities and educational institutions.
    C. charities and educational institutions later received millions of dollars from Madam C. J. Walker.
    D. millions of dollars were later bequeathed to charities and educational institutions by Madam C. J. Walker.

28. **F.** NO CHANGE
    G. generosity; were
    H. generosity were
    J. generosity were:

29. **A.** NO CHANGE
    B. movement, it took place in
    C. movement, that happened in
    D. movement of

30. If the writer were to delete the preceding sentence, the essay would primarily lose:

    F. an interpretation of the artwork that serves to summarize the essay.
    G. a reflection on the women depicted in the artwork that compares them to Ringgold.
    H. a description of a brushwork technique that refers back to the essay's opening.
    J. an evaluation of Ringgold's artistic talent that places her in a historical context.

PASSAGE III

1902: A Space Odyssey

   Our technologically advanced times <u>has allowed</u>
₃₁
filmmakers to create spectacular science fiction films to

intrigue us with worlds beyond our experience. Imagine

the excitement in <u>1902 when</u> audiences first saw *Le Voyage*
₃₂
dans la lune (A Trip to the Moon), a groundbreaking movie

produced by Georges Méliès.

31. **A.** NO CHANGE
    B. have allowed
    C. allows
    D. was allowing

32. **F.** NO CHANGE
    G. 1902, and when
    H. 1902, which
    J. 1902, where

[1] Undaunted, Méliès honed his photographic skills to tell fantasy stories instead. [2] Méliès, a French magician, was fascinated by the workings of the new motion picture camera. [3] Specializing in stage illusions, he thought the camera offered potential to expand its spectacular magic productions. [4] By 1895, he
33
was working with the new invention. [5] He found

out, however, that the public preferred live magic
34

acts to filmed versions. 35

Méliès's magician's eye led him to discover the basics of special effects. 36 He experimented with effects such as speeding up and slowing down the action, reversing it for backward movement, and superimposing images of fantastic creatures over real people. Using overhead

pulleys and trapdoors, he was able to do interesting things.
37
Aware of the popularity of Jules Verne's science fiction novels, Méliès saw exciting possibilities in filming a space odyssey. The interplanetary travel film that he created, *A Trip to the Moon*, had production costs of $4,000, highly excessively for its time. In this film, a space
38

capsule that is fired and thereby launched and projected
39
from a cannon lands in the eye of the Man in the Moon.

33. **A.** NO CHANGE
    B. their
    C. his
    D. it's

34. **F.** NO CHANGE
    G. out, however;
    H. out, however
    J. out however,

35. For the sake of the logic and coherence of this paragraph, Sentence 1 should be placed:

    A. where it is now.
    B. after Sentence 2.
    C. after Sentence 3.
    D. after Sentence 5.

36. The writer is considering deleting the preceding sentence from the essay. The sentence should NOT be deleted because it:

    F. describes Méliès's ability as a magician, which is important to understanding the essay.
    G. begins to explain the techniques of trick photography that Méliès eventually learned.
    H. creates a transition that provides a further connection between Méliès the magician and Méliès the filmmaker.
    J. indicates that Méliès's interest in learning about trick photography existed before his interest in magic.

37. Given that all the choices are true, which one would best conclude this sentence so that it illustrates Méliès's skill and inventiveness?

    A. NO CHANGE
    B. he used effects commonly seen in his stage productions.
    C. his actors could enter and leave the scene.
    D. he perfected eerie film entrances and exits.

38. **F.** NO CHANGE
    G. exceeding highly
    H. high excessively
    J. exceedingly high

39. **A.** NO CHANGE
    B. fired
    C. fired from and consequently projected
    D. fired and thereby propelled

In a strange terrain filled with hostile creatures, the
_____
      40
space travelers experience many adventures. They

escape back to Earth in the capsule by falling off the

edge of the moon, landing in the ocean, they bob
          _____
               41
around until a passing ship finally rescues them.

   Producing the film long before

interplanetary explorations had began,
                      _____
                           42

Méliès could arouse his audience's
          _____
            43
curiosity with unconstrained fantasy.

People are still going to theaters to see
_____
              44
science fiction films.
_____
      44

40. F. NO CHANGE
   G. creatures, who they now realize live there,
   H. creatures, whom they are encountering,
   J. creatures who are found there,

41. A. NO CHANGE
   B. moon after landing
   C. moon. Landing
   D. moon, after landing

42. F. NO CHANGE
   G. would of begun,
   H. have began,
   J. had begun,

43. Which of the following alternatives to the underlined word would be LEAST acceptable?
   A. whet
   B. stimulate
   C. awaken
   D. disturb

44. Given that all the choices are true, which one would most effectively express the writer's viewpoint about Méliès's role in science fiction filmmaking?
   F. NO CHANGE
   G. This first space odyssey provided the genesis for a film genre that still packs theaters.
   H. Méliès made an important contribution to film-making many years ago.
   J. In Méliès's production even the film crew knew a lot about space.

┌───┐
│ Question 45 asks about the preceding passage │
│ as a whole.   │
└───┘

45. Suppose the writer's goal had been to write a brief essay highlighting the contributions a single artist can make to a particular art form. Would this essay fulfill that goal?
   A. Yes, because the essay asserts that Méliès's work as a magician never would have succeeded without the contributions of the artists in the film industry.
   B. Yes, because the essay presents Méliès as a magician who used his talents and curiosity to explore and excel in the film world.
   C. No, because the essay focuses on the process of making science fiction films, not on a single artist's work.
   D. No, because the essay suggests that it took many artists working together to create the success that Méliès enjoyed.

PASSAGE IV

Nancy Drew in the Twenty-First Century

I thought the Nancy Drew mystery series had

went out of style. I was sure that girls growing up
‾‾‾‾‾‾‾‾‾‾‾‾
46

today would have more up-to-date role models and my

generation's favorite sleuth would of been retired to the
‾‾‾‾‾‾‾‾‾‾‾‾‾‾‾‾‾
47

library's dusty, back rooms. I was wrong.
‾‾‾‾‾‾‾‾‾‾‾‾‾
48

Nancy Drew, the teenaged heroine of heaps of young
‾‾‾‾‾
49

adult mystery novels, is alive and well and still on the job.
‾‾‾‾‾‾‾‾‾‾‾‾‾‾
50
I know because my niece, Liana, and her friends were

reading that all summer long. By the time Liana went back
‾‾‾‾
51

to school and had followed Nancy Drew on a safari to
‾‾‾‾‾‾‾‾‾‾‾‾‾
52

solve *The Spider Sapphire Mystery* and had explored Incan
‾‾‾‾‾
53
ruins for clues to *The Secret of the Crossword Cipher.*

With Nancy's help, Liana had read about different
‾‾‾‾‾‾‾‾‾‾‾‾‾‾‾‾‾
54
places and various cultures all over the world.
‾‾‾‾‾‾‾‾‾‾‾‾‾‾‾‾‾
54

46. F. NO CHANGE
G. gone out of
H. went from
J. gone from

47. A. NO CHANGE
B. would have been
C. would of
D. DELETE the underlined portion.

48. F. NO CHANGE
G. libraries dusty,
H. libraries dusty
J. library's dusty

49. Which choice provides the most specific information?
A. NO CHANGE
B. a high number
C. hundreds
D. plenty

50. F. NO CHANGE
G. novels, is alive,
H. novels is alive,
J. novels is alive

51. A. NO CHANGE
B. the mysteries
C. up on that
D. it over

52. F. NO CHANGE
G. school, she had
H. school, having
J. school, she

53. A. NO CHANGE
B. solve:
C. solve;
D. solve,

54. Given that all the choices are true, which one best illustrates the variety of settings for the Nancy Drew mysteries and also expresses Liana's interest in these books?
F. NO CHANGE
G. Along with Nancy, Liana had many breathtaking adventures involving all sorts of colorful characters.
H. With Nancy in the lead, Liana had chased suspects from Arizona to Argentina, from Nairobi to New York.
J. Through her exposure to Nancy, Liana learned about many new places around the world.

When I was a girl in the 1960s, my friends and I loved Nancy Drew. 55

We loved her loyal companions, her bravado, and there was a love for her freedom to do what she wanted. 56

We also loved how smart she was and how pretty, how 57 confident and successful. We were surprised and delighted that eighteen-year-old Nancy was so accomplished at so many things. She was able to solve crimes, win golf 58 tournaments, kick bad guys in the shins, and impress her father's distinguished clients. She did it all—and without scuffing her shoes or losing her supportive boyfriend, Ned.

Liana and her friends don't seem to care that Nancy is pretty or popular. They laugh, mockingly I think, at Nancy's friend Bess, who squeals at spiders. They prefer her other girlfriend George, the judo expert and computer whiz. They skip over the long descriptions of outfits and fashion accessories. According to Liana, they just want to get on with the story.

55. At this point, the writer is thinking about adding the following true statement:

> One of a number of series that have featured the young female detective, the Nancy Drew Mystery Story series was begun in 1930 and now totals 173 books.

Should the writer make this addition here?

- **A.** Yes, because it supports statements about the longevity and popularity of this series.
- **B.** Yes, because it helps to explain why the narrator "loved Nancy Drew."
- **C.** No, because it distracts the reader from the main focus of this paragraph.
- **D.** No, because it fails to include relevant information about the author of the series.

56. F. NO CHANGE
  G. a love for her freedom to do what she wanted.
  H. her freedom to do what she wanted.
  J. the freedom to do as one wants.

57. Which of the following alternatives to the underlined portion would be LEAST acceptable?
  A. furthermore
  B. therefore
  C. likewise
  D. DELETE the underlined portion.

58. F. NO CHANGE
  G. was capable of solving crimes,
  H. was good at crime solving,
  J. solved crimes,

Perhaps I am overly optimistic, but I'd like to believe
that Liana's generation doesn't love Nancy Drew because
she's a successful girl detective. They don't need to be
reminded that girls can be <u>successful they know that.</u>
₅₉
What these girls need and love are the stories themselves:

<u>those exciting adventure tales spiced with mystery.</u>
₆₀

59. **A.** NO CHANGE
    B. successful they already know
    C. successful; they know
    D. successful, knowing

60. Which choice most effectively supports the point being
    made in the first part of this sentence?
    F. NO CHANGE
    G. the answers to the mysteries of their lives.
    H. a strong role model for their generation.
    J. the ability to overcome obstacles.

PASSAGE V

Visiting Mars on a Budget

With its distinctive red tint and its polar ice caps,
the planet Mars has fascinated humans for thousands
of years. <u>There were</u> ancient Babylonian astronomers
₆₁
who associated Mars with their war god Negral, to
twentieth-century science fiction writers
<u>whose works become best-sellers,</u> this planet
₆₂
has often been a symbol of ill will and danger.

<u>The United States has competed with other countries</u>
₆₃
<u>to explore space.</u> By 2003, the National Aeronautics and
₆₃

Space Administration (NASA) <u>would of sent</u> thirty
₆₄

spacecraft to the red planet, <u>speculation has been prompted</u>
₆₅
that a human voyage may no longer be the stuff of fiction.

61. **A.** NO CHANGE
    B. When
    C. From
    D. Those

62. Given that all the choices are true, which one is most
    relevant to the statement that follows in this sentence?
    F. NO CHANGE
    G. with their wild imaginations about outer space,
    H. who penned spine-tingling stories of "little green
        men from Mars,"
    J. who created images of Mars in literature,

63. Given that all the choices are true, which one best
    leads from the preceding paragraph to the subject of
    this paragraph?
    A. NO CHANGE
    B. Today, such negative associations seem to be
        dissipating.
    C. In 1958, the United States founded an agency to
        run its space program.
    D. Earth and Mars are both planets in the inner solar
        system.

64. **F.** NO CHANGE
    G. had sent
    H. send
    J. have sent

65. **A.** NO CHANGE
    B. to which speculation has prompted
    C. prompting speculation
    D. which is speculation

Few would deny that the idea of a human mission to Mars
<u> </u>
 66

is exciting, who is ready to pay for such an expedition?

    Recent reports suggest that the cost of a human

voyage to Mars could run as high as 100 billion dollars.

This is a startling number, especially in light of the fact

that the International Space Station, the most ambitious

NASA project <u>yet,</u> carried a projected price tag of "only"
              67

17 billion dollars. In the end, NASA overspent on the

International Space Station. ⬚68 One can only imagine

if the final price of a human voyage to Mars would be.
 69

    In contrast, the two Mars Rovers—

<u>robotic spacecraft launched in 2003—</u>carried
                                    70

a combined price tag of less than one billion

dollars. These Rovers are sophisticated pieces of

technology, with the <u>capacity and ability</u> to examine soil
                               71

and rocks. Their equipment may answer questions that

have long been posed about the presence of water and life

on Mars.

66. **F.** NO CHANGE
    G. Maybe a few
    H. Although few
    J. Few, if any,

67. **A.** NO CHANGE
    B. yet
    C. yet:
    D. yet—

68. The writer is considering adding the following true information to the end of the preceding sentence (placing a comma after the word *Station*):

    > with a final construction cost of almost 30 billion dollars.

    Should the writer make this addition?

    F. Yes, because it strengthens the assertion made in this sentence by adding explicit detail.
    G. Yes, because it proves space flight will be more affordable in the future.
    H. No, because it weakens the point made in the paragraph about the cost of human flight to Mars.
    J. No, because it detracts from the essay's focus on the human experience in travel to Mars.

69. **A.** NO CHANGE
    B. what
    C. how
    D. DELETE the underlined portion.

70. Given that all the choices are true, which one most effectively describes what the Mars Rovers are?

    F. NO CHANGE
    G. which captured the imagination of the general public—
    H. the products described at length in the media—
    J. familiar to many who watched the news coverage at the time—

71. **A.** NO CHANGE
    B. genuine capacity
    C. potential capacity
    D. capacity

Sending machines unaccompanied by humans to

Mars does drain some of the romance out of aging or older
                                                    ——————————
                                                         72

visions of space travel. In other words, we need to keep in
                          ————————————
                                73

mind that the right equipment can accomplish as much as

any crew of scientists, if not more—such as a fraction of
                                        —————
                                          74

the cost. Before any astronaut boards a spacecraft for that

distant planet, the staggering expense of such a mission

should be carefully considered. ☐75

72. **F.** NO CHANGE
    G. old age
    H. aging old
    J. age-old

73. **A.** NO CHANGE
    B. For that reason alone,
    C. In that time frame,
    D. Even so,

74. **F.** NO CHANGE
    G. at
    H. but only
    J. DELETE the underlined portion.

75. The writer is considering ending the essay with the fol-
    lowing statement:

    > With the passage of time, humans will con-
    > tinue to gaze in awe toward the heavenly skies
    > as a source of inspiration and mystery.

    Should the writer add this sentence here?

    A. Yes, because it captures the emotion that is the
        basis for the space exploration described in the
        essay.
    B. Yes, because it invites the reader to reflect on the
        insignificance of money in relation to the mystery
        of space.
    C. No, because it does not logically follow the
        essay's chronological history of people who trav-
        eled in space.
    D. No, because it strays too far from the essay's focus
        on Mars and the cost of sending humans there.

PASSAGE I

My "Sister" Ligia

Every year my high school hosts international exchange students, those teenagers join our senior class. Each student

usually lives with the family of one of the seniors. I can recall students from Costa Rica, Italy, Norway, and Nigeria. Last year, one of our school's exchange students being

Ligia Antolinez, who came from Bucaramanga, Colombia.

I was a junior then. I wasn't in any of Ligia's classes and didn't

know her, but I saw her at school events, which are sometimes supported financially by local businesses.

About halfway through the school year, I learned that the exchange program was looking for a new home for Ligia. After a severe storm, the basement of her hosts house had flooded,

leaving two bedrooms unusable. The two "little brothers" of Ligia's host family, who had volunteered to move, to those bedrooms for a year, had to be moved

upstairs to the room Ligia was using.

76. Refer to the underlined portion of the passage at number 1, and choose the alternative you consider best.
    A. NO CHANGE
    B. students, he or she is invited to
    C. students who
    D. students they

77. Refer to the underlined portion of the passage at number 2, and choose the alternative you consider best.
    F. NO CHANGE
    G. students was
    H. students, named
    J. students,

78. Refer to the underlined portion of the passage at number 3, and choose the alternative you consider best.
    A. NO CHANGE
    B. whom
    C. which
    D. she who

79. Refer to the underlined portion of the passage at number 4, and choose the alternative you consider best.
    F. NO CHANGE
    G. junior, therefore, so
    H. junior because
    J. junior, since

80. Given that all of the choices are true, which one provides the most relevant information with regard to the narrator's familiarity with Ligia?
    A. NO CHANGE
    B. had read a story about her in our school paper, which is written by students interested in journalism.
    C. saw her at school events and had read a story about her in our school paper.
    D. had read a story about her when I was checking our school paper for local movie listings.

81. Refer to the underlined portion of the passage at number 6, and choose the alternative you consider best.
    F. NO CHANGE
    G. her hosts'
    H. Ligia's hosts
    J. Ligias hosts'

82. Refer to the underlined portion of the passage at number 7, and choose the alternative you consider best.
    A. NO CHANGE
    B. volunteered to move to those bedrooms for a year
    C. volunteered to move to those bedrooms for a year,
    D. volunteered, to move to those bedrooms for a year,

83. Refer to the underlined portion of the passage at number 8, and choose the alternative you consider best.
    F. NO CHANGE
    G. upstairs to the room Ligia was using, which had been freshly painted just that year.
    H. upstairs (it was a two-story house) to Ligia's room.
    J. OMIT the underlined portion and end the sentence with a period.

I told my parents about Ligia's <u>problem, which needed to be solved.</u>
₉

We <u>agreed</u> that it would be fun to host a student from another
₁₀
country. My older sister had gotten married the summer before, so not only did we have a room for Ligia,

and we all <u>admitted</u> that the house had seemed too quiet lately.
₁₁

The second half of my junior year was anything but quiet. <u>Introduced by me to my favorite music, at top volume, I started being taught by Ligia the most popular Colombian dance steps.</u>
₁₂

My father spoke fondly of the days before two teenagers <u>taken</u>
₁₃
over the phone, the stereo, the kitchen—well, most of the house, really. My mother helped Ligia with her math homework, and Ligia taught Mom beginning Spanish. Both Ligia and I were studying French that year, and we practiced it at home. When we planned a surprise anniversary party for my mom and dad, we did it all right under their noses, in French.

At the end of the year, Ligia <u>had gone</u> home to Colombia.
₁₄
This year I'm busy with senior activities and with a part-time

job. I'm trying to save enough to go see my new sister next year. [15]

84. Refer to the underlined portion of the passage at number 9, and choose the alternative you consider best.
   A. NO CHANGE
   B. problem, which was a dilemma.
   C. problem that needed a solution.
   D. problem.

85. Three of these choices indicate that the family felt confident about inviting Ligia to live in their home. Which choice does NOT do so?
   F. NO CHANGE
   G. decided
   H. knew
   J. supposed

86. Refer to the underlined portion of the passage at number 11, and choose the alternative you consider best.
   A. NO CHANGE
   B. but
   C. while
   D. yet

87. Refer to the underlined portion of the passage at number 12, and choose the alternative you consider best.
   F. NO CHANGE
   G. Introducing Ligia to my favorite music, at top volume, she started teaching me the most popular Colombian dance steps.
   H. Teaching me the most popular Colombian dance steps, Ligia was introduced by me to my favorite music, at top volume.
   J. I introduced Ligia to my favorite music, at top volume, and she started teaching me the most popular Colombian dance steps.

88. Refer to the underlined portion of the passage at number 13, and choose the alternative you consider best.
   A. NO CHANGE
   B. took
   C. had took
   D. begun to take

89. Refer to the underlined portion of the passage at number 14, and choose the alternative you consider best.
   F. NO CHANGE
   G. will have gone
   H. went
   J. goes

90. Which of the following true sentences, if inserted here, would best conclude the essay as well as maintain the positive tone established earlier in the essay?
   A. I'm afraid of flying, but I think I'll be OK.
   B. I'm eager to eventually join the workforce full time.
   C. I've been practicing my Spanish—and my dance steps.
   D. Senior activities are a lot of fun.

PASSAGE II

Down at the Laundromat

[1] Down the street from the college, I attend, the Save-U
                                    ─────────────────
                                          16
Laundromat is always open, and someone is always there. [2]

It was on a corner, across the
   ──
   17

street; from a drugstore on one side and a big park on the other.
──────────
    18

[3] The park isn't really a park at all but part of the grounds
of a private boarding school. [4] But no one is ever around to
enforce the threats, and in the summer everyone enjoys the
benches, the grass, and the coolly magnificence of the shade
                              ─────────────────
                                     19

trees. [5] Signs are posted all over the lawn threatening every

sort of drastic action against trespassers who wrongfully enter
                               ───────────────────────────────
                                            20

the property. ⬚21

---

91. Refer to the underlined portion of the passage at number
    16, and choose the alternative you consider best.
    F. NO CHANGE
    G. college, I attend
    H. college I attend,
    J. college I attend

92. Refer to the underlined portion of the passage at number
    17, and choose the alternative you consider best.
    A. NO CHANGE
    B. is
    C. had been
    D. was located

93. Refer to the underlined portion of the passage at number
    18, and choose the alternative you consider best.
    F. NO CHANGE
    G. street from,
    H. street, from
    J. street from

94. Refer to the underlined portion of the passage at number
    19, and choose the alternative you consider best.
    A. NO CHANGE
    B. cool magnificence
    C. magnificently cool
    D. cool magnificent

95. Refer to the underlined portion of the passage at number
    20, and choose the alternative you consider best.
    F. NO CHANGE
    G. those who trespass by walking on private property.
    H. trespassers who ignore the signs and walk on the grass.
    J. trespassers.

96. For the sake of logic and coherence, Sentence 5 should
    be placed:
    A. where it is now.
    B. before Sentence 1.
    C. after Sentence 1.
    D. after Sentence 3.

The Save-U has a neon sign out front that says "Friendly 24-Hour Service," but as far as I can tell, no one really works there. The washers and dryers are lime green, and the paneling on the walls has been painted to match, although it was later varnished
22

with some kind of artificial wood grain finish. 23 I often stare at that paneling when I don't have a magazine or newspaper to read and don't want to do my schoolwork. Deep in thought, I contemplate the competence of the laundromat's interior designer.

Some machines even provide a certain amount of sustenance and
24
entertainment. This laundromat has three soda machines, two candy machines, two pinball machines, five video machines, and a machine that eats dollar bills and spits out too

much or too few quarters.
25

There are many regular customers whose faces have become familiar—mostly older people from around the neighborhood. 26

Usually a crowd of thirteen-year-old kids that is gathered around
27
the video machines, regardless of the time of day.

97. Refer to the underlined portion of the passage at number 22, and choose the alternative you consider best.
   F. NO CHANGE
   G. have been
   H. were
   J. are

98. At this point, the writer wants to add a sentence that would further describe the laundromat's paneling. Which of the following sentences would best accomplish this?
   A. I guess the brush strokes are intended to resemble wood grain, but they don't.
   B. I know that the varnish provides some protection for the wood paneling.
   C. To me, it seems that lime green was a bizarre choice for an interior wall paint.
   D. I imagine that the person who chose that color scheme must be a unique individual.

99. Which choice most effectively guides the reader from the preceding paragraph into this new paragraph?
   F. NO CHANGE
   G. The Save-U has to have friendly service because it is across the street from a park.
   H. Maybe what the Save-U means by friendly service is an abundance of machines.
   J. Washing machines are the Save-U's version of 24-hour service.

100. Refer to the underlined portion of the passage at number 25, and choose the alternative you consider best.
   A. NO CHANGE
   B. many or too fewer
   C. many or too few
   D. much or few

101. The writer is considering deleting the following phrase from the preceding sentence: "mostly older people from around the neighborhood." If the writer were to make this deletion, the essay would primarily lose:
   F. specific descriptive material.
   G. detail providing a logical transition.
   H. foreshadowing of the conclusion.
   J. an understatement of important information.

102. Refer to the underlined portion of the passage at number 27, and choose the alternative you consider best.
   A. NO CHANGE
   B. kids who
   C. kids, and they
   D. kids

Imagining all these people, it is that I know they remain
                                              28
there even after I have left. I know that I could go in there
anytime, and someone would look up from playing pinball or

folding clothes and nods and smiles at me. It is comforting to
                                   29

know that the Save-U Laundromat. And its people are always
                                          30
nearby.

103. Refer to the underlined portion of the passage at number
     28, and choose the alternative you consider best.

     F.   NO CHANGE
     G.   It being that I imagine all these people, they
     H.   Imagining all these people, they
     J.   I imagine that all these people

104. Refer to the underlined portion of the passage at number
     29, and choose the alternative you consider best.

     A.   NO CHANGE
     B.   nod and smile
     C.   nodding and smiling
     D.   nods to smile

105. Refer to the underlined portion of the passage at number
     30, and choose the alternative you consider best.

     F.   NO CHANGE
     G.   Laundromat. Its
     H.   Laundromat and that its
     J.   Laundromat and its

PASSAGE III

Bill Williams Brings America Home to Dinner

*The following paragraphs may or may not be in the most
logical order. Each paragraph is numbered in brackets, and
Question 120 will ask you to choose where Paragraph 1 should
most logically be placed.*

[1]

You have to admire the honesty of a company who's slogan
                                                    31

is "Just About the Best." Glory Foods' president, and founder
                                            32
Bill Williams, explains the unusual slogan by admitting that

while he knows that his foods can't beat the taste of real home
cooking, it does come very close.
         33

[2]

Even as a child, Williams loved to prepare food, and as a
young adult, he refined his cooking skills at the
                    34

106. Refer to the underlined portion of the passage at number
     31, and choose the alternative you consider best.

     A.   NO CHANGE
     B.   whose
     C.   that's
     D.   that the

107. Refer to the underlined portion of the passage at number
     32, and choose the alternative you consider best.

     F.   NO CHANGE
     G.   president, and founder Bill Williams
     H.   president and founder Bill Williams,
     J.   president and founder, Bill Williams,

108. Refer to the underlined portion of the passage at number
     33, and choose the alternative you consider best.

     A.   NO CHANGE
     B.   it has
     C.   they do
     D.   and that they

109. Refer to the underlined portion of the passage at number
     34, and choose the alternative you consider best.

     F.   NO CHANGE
     G.   his cooking skills were refined
     H.   his skill in cooking was refined
     J.   the refinement of his cooking skills occurred

prestigiously acclaimed Culinary Institute of America.
35

In 1989, he came up with his idea for a line of Southern-
36
inspired cuisine, a time when there were no convenience foods designed for African American consumers. Over the next three years, he developed a line of products that included canned greens, sweet potatoes, beans, and okra, as well as bottled hot sauce and cornbread mixes.

[3]

Eventually, Williams was ready to launch his products in grocery stores. Initially, Glory Foods were first offered for sale
37

in Ohio in 1992 and soon became available in neighboring states. Within a year, sales were twice the original projections. 38

[4]

The company's African American focus is evident in all aspects of Glory Foods. The firm's headquarters are located in the same black neighborhood where Williams grew up, and the company helps to support several local community projects. The firm also employs African American professional advisers
39

and subcontractors whenever possible and contracts African American farmers to grow much of the produce that goes into Glory Foods. 40

110. Refer to the underlined portion of the passage at number 35, and choose the alternative you consider best.
   A. NO CHANGE
   B. famed, renowned, and notable
   C. luscious
   D. prestigious

111. Refer to the underlined portion of the passage at number 36, and choose the alternative you consider best.
   F. NO CHANGE
   G. He came up with his idea for a line of Southern-inspired cuisine in 1989,
   H. He came up in 1989, with his idea for a line of Southern-inspired cuisine,
   J. The idea came to him in 1989, that a line of Southern-inspired cuisine should be marketed,

112. Refer to the underlined portion of the passage at number 37, and choose the alternative you consider best.
   A. NO CHANGE
   B. Glory Foods were
   C. They were originally
   D. At the outset, the earliest Glory Foods were

113. Given that all of the following sentences are true, which one would most effectively conclude this paragraph?
   F. Bill Williams's company continues to refine the recipes of its products.
   G. By 1995, Glory Foods were being distributed in twenty-two states.
   H. Today, there are several other companies that target their products to African American consumers.
   J. Bill Williams, however, sought the advice of food marketing experts.

114. Refer to the underlined portion of the passage at number 39, and choose the alternative you consider best.
   A. NO CHANGE
   B. professional, advisers,
   C. professional advisers,
   D. professional advisers;

115. The writer is considering deleting the phrases "whenever possible" and "much of" from the preceding sentence. If the writer were to delete these phrases, would the meaning of the sentence change?
   F. Yes, because without these phrases, the reader would think that all of the subcontractors and farmers were African Americans.
   G. Yes, because without these phrases, the reader would not know that the company made an attempt to employ African American contractors in the production of its goods.
   H. No, because these phrases are examples of wordiness, and they can easily be eliminated from the sentence.
   J. No, because although these phrases describe the subcontractors and the farmers and provide interesting detail, they are not essential to the meaning of the sentence.

[5]

The company's name reflects this African American focus as well. *Glory* is meant to evoke both the exultant spirit of

gospel churches and the movie during the Civil War of the same
42

name, which tells the story of a black regiment. [43]

[6]

With twenty full-time employees in its administrative offices, Glory Foods has come a long way from its beginnings. America's dinner tables were the beneficiaries of Bill Williams's
44

drive, determination, and culinary expertise.

---

116. Refer to the underlined portion of the passage at number 41, and choose the alternative you consider best.
   - **A.** NO CHANGE
   - **B.** at evoking
   - **C.** in evoking of
   - **D.** OMIT the underlined portion.

117. The best placement for the underlined portion would be:
   - **F.** where it is now.
   - **G.** after the word *name* (but before the comma).
   - **H.** after the word *story*.
   - **J.** after the word *regiment* (ending the sentence with a period).

118. At this point, the writer is considering adding the following sentence: The actor Denzel Washington starred in the film, which earned several awards. Should the writer make this addition?
   - **A.** Yes, because the additional detail explains why the film *Glory* was so inspiring.
   - **B.** Yes, because if readers understand that the film *Glory* earned awards, they will also understand why the company was named "Glory Foods."
   - **C.** No, because the information distracts the reader from the focus of the essay.
   - **D.** No, because the essay does not say if Bill Williams had ever met the actor Denzel Washington.

119. Refer to the underlined portion of the passage at number 44, and choose the alternative you consider best.
   - **F.** NO CHANGE
   - **G.** had been
   - **H.** would have been
   - **J.** are

Question 120 asks about the passage as a whole.

---

120. For the sake of logic and coherence, Paragraph 1 should be placed:
   - **A.** where it is now.
   - **B.** after Paragraph 2.
   - **C.** after Paragraph 3.
   - **D.** after Paragraph 6.

PASSAGE IV

Pinball and Chance

[1]

Doesn't anyone play pinball anymore? I was disappointed the other day when I took my kids to a game arcade. Afterwards, I went to the movies. Not one of the many colorful machines
46

121. Refer to the underlined portion of the passage at number 46, and choose the alternative you consider best.
   - **F.** NO CHANGE
   - **G.** I made my way to the movie theater after that.
   - **H.** (The movie theater was my next stop.)
   - **J.** OMIT the underlined portion.

with flashing lights <u>were a</u> pinball machine. Video games filled
the room. ₄₇

[2]

[1] I can understand why video games might seem more
attractive than pinball. [2] Video screens <u>which have been</u>
₄₈
populated by movie stars, monsters, and heroes. [3] You can
blow up cities, escape from dungeons, and battle all sorts of
villains. [4] Pinball machines, on the other hand, are essentially
all the same. [5] Some machines are bigger and fancier than
others, but the object of pinball never changes: you have to keep
a steel ball in play long enough to rack up a high score and win
a free game. [49]

[3]

The attractions of video games, however, are superficial and
short-lived. As you guide your character through the game's

challenges, you come to know exactly how the <u>machine that's</u>
₅₀

<u>built to last</u> will respond to your every move. <u>He or she learns</u>
₅₁
where the hazards lurk and the special weapons are hidden.

Pinball, <u>though,</u> can't be predicted with such accuracy. You
₅₂
never know when the ball will drain straight down the middle,
out of reach of both flippers, Then again, you can sometimes get

lucky, and a ball you thought was <u>lost, will</u> inexplicably bounce
back into play. ₅₃

122. Refer to the underlined portion of the passage at number
47, and choose the alternative you consider best.
   A.   NO CHANGE
   B.   was a
   C.   were an actual
   D.   would have been an actual

123. Refer to the underlined portion of the passage at number
48, and choose the alternative you consider best.
   F.   NO CHANGE
   G.   that are
   H.   are
   J.   OMIT the underlined portion.

124. For the sake of the logic and coherence of Paragraph 2,
Sentence 4 should be:
   A.   placed where it is now.
   B.   placed after Sentence 1.
   C.   placed after Sentence 5.
   D.   OMITTED, because the paragraph focuses only on
        video games.

125. Refer to the underlined portion of the passage at number
50, and choose the alternative you consider best.
   F.   NO CHANGE
   G.   machine, which is constructed durably,
   H.   machine, which is built to last,
   J.   machine

126. Refer to the underlined portion of the passage at number
51, and choose the alternative you consider best.
   A.   NO CHANGE
   B.   We learn
   C.   You learn
   D.   People learned

127. Which of the following alternatives to the underlined
portion would be LEAST acceptable?
   F.   therefore,
   G.   however,
   H.   by contrast,
   J.   on the contrary,

128. Refer to the underlined portion of the passage at number
53, and choose the alternative you consider best.
   A.   NO CHANGE
   B.   lost will
   C.   lost, will,
   D.   lost will,

[4]

It is the element of chance that makes pinball more interesting
54

than video games. Most video games are designed so that your

main opponent in these video games is a predictable computer
55

program. Once you have mastered a game, the challenge is

gone, and you must look for a new game to conquer. After
56

you learn the new game, you get bored again. The cycle keeps
repeating. But in pinball, you have three factors to consider:
you, the machine, and chance, which is sometimes your enemy
57

sometimes your ally. No matter how many games you play on
any pinball machine, the various times of each game is different.
58

That's what makes pinball a continually challenge.
59

129. Which choice would most effectively and appropriately lead the reader from the topic of Paragraph 3 to that of Paragraph 4?
   F. NO CHANGE
   G. Pinball does share certain similarities with video games.
   H. Pinball, although less challenging than video games, can still be fun to play.
   J. Video games do generally evolve into subsequent editions or enhanced versions.

130. Refer to the underlined portion of the passage at number 55, and choose the alternative you consider best.
   A. NO CHANGE
   B. during these video games
   C. in video games
   D. OMIT the underlined portion.

131. Refer to the underlined portion of the passage at number 56, and choose the alternative you consider best.
   F. NO CHANGE
   G. you then looked
   H. one then looks
   J. one must look

132. Refer to the underlined portion of the passage at number 57, and choose the alternative you consider best.
   A. NO CHANGE
   B. enemy,
   C. enemy;
   D. enemy, and,

133. Refer to the underlined portion of the passage at number 58, and choose the alternative you consider best.
   F. NO CHANGE
   G. each
   H. each single unique
   J. every single time, each

134. Refer to the underlined portion of the passage at number 59, and choose the alternative you consider best.
   A. NO CHANGE
   B. continuously
   C. continual
   D. continue

135. The following question asks about the passage as a whole.

Suppose the writer had chosen to write an essay that indicates that pinball is superior to video games. Would this essay fulfill the writer's goal?
   F. No, because the writer admits that video games have become more popular than pinball machines.
   G. No, because the writer states that video games are designed to challenge the skills of the player.
   H. Yes, because the writer claims that pinball games require luck and are more visually attractive than video games.
   J. Yes, because the writer suggests that it is more difficult to become skilled at a pinball machine than at a video game.

PASSAGE V

When a Computer Gets Sick

[1]

Imagine sitting in front of a computer monitor, filling the screen with your mind's jumbled thoughts. Tomorrow's assignment is slowly materializing before your eyes. Suddenly, without warning, each of the <u>letters, in front of you tumbles</u> to
<u>61</u>

the bottom of the screen. Is this a bad dream? Not exactly. The computer is probably sick, <u>unless</u> the diagnosis may be that the
<u>62</u>

computer has a virus.

[2]

Analogous to a biological virus that takes over a living cell, a computer virus is a program, or set of instructions, that invades a computer either to create mischief or do real damage. The type of computer virus mentioned above is more mischievous than harmful. Eventually, the letters reorder themselves on the screen. Not all <u>viruses however,</u> straighten themselves out.
<u>63</u>

[3]

<u>Computer viruses range from being temporary annoyances
to permanently destroying data.</u> Computer vandals rig these
<u>64</u>

viruses to go off at a preset time. These bombs can permanently destroy data, and that can be <u>disastrous to the operation</u> of a computer.
<u>65</u>

136. Refer to the underlined portion of the passage at number 61, and choose the alternative you consider best.

  A. NO CHANGE
  B. letters in front of you tumbles,
  C. letters in front of you, tumbles
  D. letters in front of you tumbles

137. Refer to the underlined portion of the passage at number 62, and choose the alternative you consider best.

  F. NO CHANGE
  G. except
  H. and
  J. as if

138. Refer to the underlined portion of the passage at number 63, and choose the alternative you consider best.

  A. NO CHANGE
  B. viruses; however,
  C. viruses, however
  D. viruses, however,

139. Which choice is the most effective first sentence of Paragraph 3?

  F. NO CHANGE
  G. Among the more serious viruses are those referred to as "bombs."
  H. Most people would agree that they'd rather have a computer virus than a virus that puts them in bed for a week.
  J. Despite technological advances, computers are still fragile devices in many ways.

140. Refer to the underlined portion of the passage at number 65, and choose the alternative you consider best.

  A. NO CHANGE
  B. a devastative disaster to the operation
  C. devastation to the operating
  D. possibly disastrous to operating

[4]

Detection programs are available that
66

searches for and then destroys computer viruses. Evidence that
67

some software writers have played up the medical analogy being
68

found in the names of their programs: Vaccine, Checkup,
69

Antitoxin, and Disinfectant.

[5]

As with all diseases, the best cure is prevention. Experts
70

suggest that you avoid borrowing flash drives because they might contain viruses. They warn that many of these viruses are quite sophisticated in their programming. They also say that
71
you should make copies of your computer files, so that if a virus does strike and you must delete your infected files, you will at least have backup copies. Experts also point out that using the Internet and World Wide Web has led to new risks of infection in the form of viruses hidden in programs downloaded from these resources.

141. Refer to the underlined portion of the passage at number 66, and choose the alternative you consider best.
   F. NO CHANGE
   G. Detection programs that detect computer viruses
   H. Computer viruses can be found by detection programs that
   J. Detection programs that find computer viruses

142. Refer to the underlined portion of the passage at number 67, and choose the alternative you consider best.
   A. NO CHANGE
   B. searches for and destroys
   C. search for and destroys
   D. search for and destroy

143. Refer to the underlined portion of the passage at number 68, and choose the alternative you consider best.
   F. NO CHANGE
   G. analogy is
   H. analogy, having been
   J. analogy,

144. Refer to the underlined portion of the passage at number 69, and choose the alternative you consider best.
   A. NO CHANGE
   B. programs;
   C. programs
   D. programs,

145. Refer to the underlined portion of the passage at number 70, and choose the alternative you consider best.
   F. NO CHANGE
   G. Similarly to
   H. In the same way as
   J. According with

146. In this paragraph, the writer intends to recommend a number of specific ways to protect computer data against viruses. This is to be the second recommendation. Given that all of the choices are true, which one would best accomplish the writer's intention?
   A. NO CHANGE
   B. propose adding software that checks the spelling in the papers you write on your computer.
   C. advise you to give your system frequent checkups with antivirus programs.
   D. suggest that in order to protect your computer, you must be aware of the various ways to prevent viruses.

[6]

If there is a virus in your system, you had hope that it <u>better</u>

72

responds to the appropriate treatment and therapy. Otherwise, you could be in for a long night at the computer.

147. The best placement for the underlined portion would be:

- **F.** where it is now.
- **G.** after the word *your*.
- **H.** after the word *had*.
- **J.** after the word *responds*.

148. The following question asks about the passage as a whole.

Upon reviewing this essay and realizing that some information has been left out, the writer composes the following sentence, incorporating that information: Names like these suggest that the problem is serious. The most logical and effective place to add this sentence would be after the last sentence of Paragraph:

- **A.** 2.
- **B.** 3.
- **C.** 4.
- **D.** 5.

149. The following question asks about the passage as a whole.

Paragraphs 1, 5, and 6 of this essay are written in the second person (*you, your*). If these paragraphs were revised so that the second-person pronouns were replaced with the pronouns *one* and *one's*, the essay would primarily:

- **F.** gain a more polite and formal tone appropriate to the purpose of the essay.
- **G.** gain accessibility by speaking to a broader and more inclusive audience.
- **H.** lose the sense of directly addressing and advising the reader.
- **J.** lose the immediacy of its setting in terms of time and place.

150. The following question asks about the passage as a whole.

Suppose the writer had decided to write an essay discussing the moral and ethical consequences of programming a computer virus to tamper with a computer system. Would this essay successfully fulfill the writer's goal?

- **A.** Yes, because the essay explains the moral and ethical consequences when a virus enters a computer system.
- **B.** Yes, because the essay details the process of ridding a computer system of viruses, which helps the reader understand the consequences of programming computer viruses.
- **C.** No, because the essay does not explain how to program a virus, so the reader has no basis for making a moral or ethical judgment.
- **D.** No, because the essay limits itself to describing computer viruses and the basic precautions to be taken against them.

PASSAGE VI

Grandpa's Remote Control

[1]

My grandfather is not known for embracing technological change. He still drives his '59 Chevy Impala.
                                          76

(He says, he can't imagine needing frivolous options like
        77

automatic transmission or power steering.) So, when he has went
                                                            78

to buy a new color television—owing to the knowledge that his
                                              79
old black-and-white model had finally quit—and the salesperson

tried to talk him into buying a model with a remote control, he resisted. He said that he had two good legs and was perfectly capable of getting out of his chair. [80]

[2]

However, the salesperson was persistent and, appealing to Grandpa's TV-viewing habits, described the various functions

on the remote. However,my grandpa could punch in the time,
                      81

and the channel of his favorite daily news program, and the
    82
TV would turn on that program at the proper time. In the end, Grandpa did buy the remote, and it has since become something he uses all the time.

151. Refer to the underlined portion of the passage at number 76, and choose the alternative you consider best.

   A. NO CHANGE
   B. change he still drives
   C. change still driving,
   D. change, and still driving

152. Refer to the underlined portion of the passage at number 77, and choose the alternative you consider best.

   F. NO CHANGE
   G. says
   H. says, that
   J. says, that,

153. Refer to the underlined portion of the passage at number 78, and choose the alternative you consider best.

   A. NO CHANGE
   B. had went
   C. went
   D. goes

154. Refer to the underlined portion of the passage at number 79, and choose the alternative you consider best.

   F. NO CHANGE
   G. due to the understandable fact that
   H. because
   J. so

155. Given that all are true, which of the following additions to the preceding sentence (replacing "chair.") would be most relevant?

   A. chair that was made of black leather.
   B. chair when he wanted to change the channel.
   C. chair by the south window in the family room.
   D. chair where he liked to sit.

156. Refer to the underlined portion of the passage at number 81, and choose the alternative you consider best.

   F. NO CHANGE
   G. Additionally, Grandpa
   H. Conversely, my grandpa
   J. Grandpa

157. Refer to the underlined portion of the passage at number 82, and choose the alternative you consider best.

   A. NO CHANGE
   B. time and, the channel,
   C. time and the channel
   D. time and the channel,

[3]

Grandpa is intrigued by the various uses for that remote. He has confided in me that the volume control is perfect for turning up the sound whenever Grandma asks him to take out

the garbage. <u>For example,</u> he says, the button that mutes the
83

sound lets him cut <u>them</u> off in midsentence.
84

[4]

Grandpa's favorite feature on the remote is the sleep function. This option automatically turns the TV off after a preset amount of time, which is very <u>convenient when</u> he falls
85

asleep while watching a show. <u>For him, Grandpa says what he
wants his TV doing, even when he sleeps, is to know a source
of both pleasure and power.</u>
86

[5]

[1] As for the programming function, Grandpa not only uses it for the news but also for playing jokes on his youngest grandchildren. [2] Explaining to the unsuspecting child that

he has a remote control implanted in his little finger, <u>Grandpa
points</u> his finger at the TV and, to the child's amazement,
87

seemingly turns it on. [3] I suppose Grandpa hasn't learned all the possible uses of the remote control, <u>but I don't doubt he will
continue to discover new and creative ways of using it.</u> 89
88

158. Refer to the underlined portion of the passage at number 83, and choose the alternative you consider best.
   F. NO CHANGE
   G. To illustrate,
   H. On the one hand,
   J. On the other hand,

159. Refer to the underlined portion of the passage at number 84, and choose the alternative you consider best.
   A. NO CHANGE
   B. advertisers
   C. it
   D. its function

160. Refer to the underlined portion of the passage at number 85, and choose the alternative you consider best.
   F. NO CHANGE
   G. convenient, when
   H. convenient. When
   J. convenient; when

161. Refer to the underlined portion of the passage at number 86, and choose the alternative you consider best.
   A. NO CHANGE
   B. Even when he sleeps, Grandpa says that to know his TV is doing what he wants is a source of both pleasure and power for him.
   C. Doing what he wants, even when he sleeps, is to know his TV is a source of both pleasure and power for him, Grandpa says.
   D. Grandpa says that to know his TV is doing what he wants, even when he sleeps, is a source of both pleasure and power for him.

162. Refer to the underlined portion of the passage at number 87, and choose the alternative you consider best.
   F. NO CHANGE
   G. pointing
   H. having pointed
   J. Grandpa has pointed

163. Which of the choices would provide an ending most consistent with the essay as a whole?
   A. NO CHANGE
   B. and he probably won't bother learning them either.
   C. so the salesperson should explain how to interpret the 200-page manual.
   D. and Grandma gratefully acknowledges this.

164. Upon reviewing Paragraph 5 and realizing that some information has been left out, the writer composes the following sentence:

He programs the TV to turn on at a time when a grandchild will be visiting. The most logical placement for this sentence would be:

   F. before Sentence 1.
   G. after Sentence 1.
   H. after Sentence 2.
   J. after Sentence 3.

165. This question asks about the passage as a whole.

The writer is considering deleting the first sentence from Paragraph 3. If the writer removed this sentence, the essay would primarily lose:

   A. information about the intriguing uses of the remote.
   B. details supporting the fact that Grandpa liked using the remote.
   C. a humorous blend of descriptive details and relevant information.
   D. a transition from the first two paragraphs to the rest of the essay.

PASSAGE VII

"Topping Out" the Gateway Arch

During the early morning hours of October 28, <u>1965, engineers</u> stationed 630 feet above the ground made careful
₉₁

measurements for the <u>days</u> work. The results indicated a
₉₂

problem that <u>threatened</u> to postpone
₉₃

<u>and delay</u> the topping-out
₉₄

166. Refer to the underlined portion of the passage at number 91, and choose the alternative you consider best.

   A. NO CHANGE
   B. 1965, and engineers
   C. 1965. Engineers
   D. 1965; engineers

167. Refer to the underlined portion of the passage at number 92, and choose the alternative you consider best.

   F. NO CHANGE
   G. days'
   H. day's
   J. days's

168. Refer to the underlined portion of the passage at number 93, and choose the alternative you consider best.

   A. NO CHANGE
   B. had been threatened
   C. will have threatened
   D. threatens

169. Refer to the underlined portion of the passage at number 94, and choose the alternative you consider best.

   F. NO CHANGE
   G. to a later time
   H. by delaying
   J. OMIT the underlined portion.

ceremony marking the placement of the final section between the two freestanding legs of the St. Louis Gateway Arch. ⬚95

Thirty-two years of planning and effort resulted in this moment. In 1933, <u>attorney and civic leader</u> Luther Ely Smith
96

envisioned a memorial that would recognize St. Louis's major role in the westward expansion of the United States. ⬚97
Architect Eero

<u>Saarinen, who created</u> the design that symbolized the
98
memorial's theme of St. Louis as the "Gateway to the West."

<u>Meanwhile, the</u> arch would have a stainless steel exterior and
99
interior structural supports made of concrete. Both legs of the arch would be built simultaneously using triangular sections. Those at the base of each arch leg would be the largest, with the higher sections progressively smaller.

   After nearly three years of construction, the day had come to place the final section at the top of the arch and finish the project. But a problem had arisen. The engineers confirmed that the heat of the sun had caused the south leg of the arch to expand five inches. This small 'but critical deviation caused concern that the two legs and the final section might not connect properly. The engineers called in local firefighters in the hope that spraying the leg with water to cool it would make it <u>contract.</u> The firefighters, using 700 feet of hose, were able to
100

170. The writer is considering deleting the following from the preceding sentence:

marking the placement of the final section between the two freestanding legs of the St. Louis Gateway Arch

If the writer were to delete this phrase, the essay would primarily lose:

  A. a minor detail in the essay's opening paragraph.
  B. an explanation of the term "topping-out ceremony."
  C. the writer's opinion about the significance of the topping-out ceremony.
  D. an indication of the topping-out ceremony's importance to the people of St. Louis.

171. Refer to the underlined portion of the passage at number 96, and choose the alternative you consider best.

  F. NO CHANGE
  G. attorney, and civic leader
  H. attorney and civic leader,
  J. attorney, and civic leader,

172. If the writer were to delete the preceding sentence, the paragraph would primarily lose:

  A. an explanation of why St. Louis had a major role in the westward expansion of the United States.
  B. details about what Luther Ely Smith thought the memorial he envisioned should look like.
  C. background information about the history leading to the Gateway Arch.
  D. biographical information about Luther Ely Smith.

173. Refer to the underlined portion of the passage at number 98, and choose the alternative you consider best.

  F. NO CHANGE
  G. Saarinen, creator of
  H. Saarinen created
  J. Saarinen creating

174. Refer to the underlined portion of the passage at number 99, and choose the alternative you consider best.

  A. NO CHANGE
  B. Therefore, the
  C. However, the
  D. The

175. Refer to the underlined portion of the passage at number 100, and choose the alternative you consider best.

  F. NO CHANGE
  G. reduce.
  H. decrease.
  J. compress.

reach as high as 550 feet on the south leg in <u>they're attempt to</u>
<u>reduce its</u> expansion.
                            ₁₀₁

The plan worked. By late morning, <u>the crowd cheered as,</u>

<u>welded to the two legs of the arch, the final section was hoisted</u>
                            ₁₀₂

<u>up.</u>

Over three <u>decades and more than thirty years</u> of planning and
                            ₁₀₃

building had <u>come to a conclusion,</u> and the tallest monument in
                            ₁₀₄
the United States was now complete.

176. Refer to the underlined portion of the passage at number 101, and choose the alternative you consider best.

   A. NO CHANGE
   B. they're attempt to reduce it's
   C. their attempt to reduce its
   D. their attempt to reduce it's

177. Refer to the underlined portion of the passage at number 102, and choose the alternative you consider best.

   F. NO CHANGE
   G. as the crowd cheered, the final section was hoisted up and welded to the two legs of the arch.
   H. as the crowd cheered, welded to the two legs of the arch, the final section was hoisted up.
   J. the final section was hoisted up as the crowd cheered and welded to the two legs of the arch.

178. Refer to the underlined portion of the passage at number 103, and choose the alternative you consider best.

   A. NO CHANGE
   B. decades amounting to more than thirty years
   C. decades—over thirty year—
   D. decades

179. Which of the following alternatives to the underlined portion would be LEAST acceptable in terms of the context of this sentence?

   F. reached completion,
   G. come to a halt,
   H. come to an end,
   J. ended,

180. The following question asks about the passage as a whole.
Suppose the writer had intended to write a brief essay that describes the entire process of designing and building the St. Louis Gateway Arch. Would this essay successfully fulfill the writer's goal?

   A. Yes, because it offers such details as the materials used to make the exterior and the interior structural supports.
   B. Yes, because it explains in detail each step in the design and construction of the arch.
   C. No, because it focuses primarily on one point in the development of the arch rather than on the entire process.
   D. No, because it is primarily a historical essay about the early stages in the development of the arch.

PASSAGE XIII

Amalia Hernxez's Ballet Folklórico de México

Amalia Hernández bowed gracefully before the

crowd, many viewers stood and applauded, showing their
<u>   </u>
181

appreciation for the performance they had just witnessed.

Hernández didn't know it yet, but she and her Ballet

Folklórico dancers had just won first prize at the 1961

Paris Festival of Nations. 182

Growing up, in Mexico in the 1920s Hernández
    <u>   </u>
             183

believed she was born to dance. Her father, a prominent

rancher and politician, did not approve of his daughter

exhibiting herself in such a manner. But Amalia was

persistent. Despite this, her father acquiesced,
           <u>   </u>
           184

181. A. NO CHANGE
    B. crowd many
    C. crowd. Many
    D. crowd. While many

182. At this point the writer is considering adding the following true statement:

> Many of Mexico's most famous dancers began their careers with the Ballet Folklórico.

Should the writer make this addition here?

    F. Yes, because it maintains the essay's focus on the many famous ballet dancers of Mexico.
    G. Yes, because it shows how difficult it is to become a professional dancer.
    H. No, because it interrupts the introduction of Amalia Hernández.
    J. No, because it contradicts information offered elsewhere in the essay.

183. A. NO CHANGE
    B. up in Mexico in the 1920s,
    C. up, in Mexico in the 1920s,
    D. up in Mexico, in the 1920s

184. F. NO CHANGE
    G. Finally,
    H. In fact,
    J. On the other hand,

when he thought about it and gave in, allowing,
—————————————————
               185
even helping, her to pursue her dream.

   Senator Hernández built a dance studio and hired

Europe's finest teachers to instruct Amalia in: classical
                                            ——————
                                               186
and modern ballet. The young woman relished the

experience and excelled in her studies, but something

wasn't right. 187

   So Amalia began studying under Mexican folklorist

Luis Felipe Obregón. She learned that her countrys
                                          ————————
                                             188

folklore was a fusion of Aztec, Mayan, Spanish,
              —————
               189
French, Dutch, and African influences. The songs

and dances she cherished chronicled life, death, and

to have a rebirth; they celebrated creation and revolution;
—————————————
     190

they celebrated the seasons and the harvest. However,
                                              ————————
                                                 191
Hernández decided to translate this lore into a new

kind of ballet.

185. **A.** NO CHANGE
     B. in that he gave in,
     C. by finally agreeing,
     D. OMIT the underlined portion.

186. **F.** NO CHANGE
     G. in, classical
     H. in classical
     J. in classical,

187. Which of the following sentences, if added here, would most effectively conclude this paragraph and introduce the topic of the next?
     A. The music did not make her feel alive, as the folk music and dances of Mexico did.
     B. She did not like the music well enough to want to continue to dance.
     C. However, she had to admit that she deeply appreciated the dance studio where she studied.
     D. Even though Amalia valued her teacher's skills, she truly wanted to focus on modern ballet.

188. **F.** NO CHANGE
     G. countrys'
     H. country's
     J. countries

189. Which of the following alternatives to the underlined portion is LEAST acceptable?
     A. grouping
     B. combination
     C. blend
     D. mixture

190. **F.** NO CHANGE
     G. rebirth;
     H. to be reborn;
     J. to have rebirth;

191. **A.** NO CHANGE
     B. Nevertheless,
     C. Instead,
     D. OMIT the underlined portion.

In 1952, she left a prestigious job at Mexico's Institute of Fine Arts to start her own dance company, the Ballet Folklórico de México. She immediately began to develop a program for her small troupe of dancers. [192]

In 1954, Mexico's Department of Tourism made the Ballet Folklórico an official cultural ambassador. It has won hundreds of awards and toured over eighty countries, performing in a range of venues from the Greek Parthenon to New York's Radio City Music Hall.

Though Hernández died in 2000, her legacy: the Ballet Folklórico—lives on,
193

as an outstanding dance company.
194

192. The writer is considering adding the following clause to the end of the preceding sentence (changing the period after the word *dancers* to a comma):

> eventually choreographing over forty ballets for the company.

Should the writer make this addition there?

  F. Yes, because it further describes the scope of Hernández's contributions to her dance company.
  G. Yes, because it helps the reader gain a sense of what Hernández's ballets were like.
  H. No, because it fails to maintain the paragraph's focus on Hernández's job at Mexico's Institute of Fine Arts.
  J. No, because it disrupts the description of Hernández's role in the Ballet Folklórico.

193. A. NO CHANGE
  B. legacy,
  C. legacy—
  D. legacy

194. Which choice would most effectively guide readers to understand the valuable contributions made by the Ballet Folklórico?

  F. NO CHANGE
  G. sharing Mexico's cultural heritage with the world.
  H. as a well-known performing group.
  J. showing that the group will continue into the future.

Question 195 asks about the preceding passage as a whole.

---

195. Suppose the author intended to write an essay that illustrates how the traditions and customs of an artist's culture can be the foundation for his or her art. Would this essay successfully fulfill that goal?

  A. Yes, because the essay describes the many awards and honors Hernández's dance company received.
  B. Yes, because the essay explains that Hernández drew upon the folklore of Mexico as a basis for her ballets.
  C. No, because the author focuses on Hernández and her dance company rather than on artists in general.
  D. No, because the essay states that Hernández was educated in a variety of dance forms.

PASSAGE XIV

A Propensity for Pens

"You have plenty of pens," my friend said gently.

"Give me mine back."

I often find myself in this situation—sheepishly

handing back someone else's pen. I'm the type who
                        196
inadvertently attempts to walk away with the pen at the

bank, even though it's chained to the counter. This is not

a deliberate act, which I just unconsciously assume
              197

that all pens belong to me. [198]

Perhaps this is because being a writer and I never
                          199
really feel comfortable without a pen in my possession.

I usually carry a good solid fistful of pens in my backpack.
                      200

I simply feel better to know a pen is handy. Who knows
                    201

when they will run dry?
      202
Maybe I'm afraid an important thought will come

to me and I'll have no way to record it. You can always

capture an idea by scribbling a sentence on a napkin,

a bit of newspaper, or even your hand. As long as

you have a pen, paper is a secondary concern.

196. **F.** NO CHANGE
     G. elses'
     H. elses
     J. else

197. **A.** NO CHANGE
     B. act that
     C. act.
     D. act

198. If the writer were to delete the words *sheepishly*, *inadvertently*, and *unconsciously* from this paragraph, the paragraph would primarily lose:
     F. clarification that the narrator doesn't mean to take others' pens.
     G. description that outlines the narrator's method of deception.
     H. evidence that the narrator feels threatened.
     J. an indication that the narrator is indecisive.

199. **A.** NO CHANGE
     B. being that I'm
     C. my being
     D. I'm

200. Which of the following alternatives to the underlined portion would NOT be acceptable?
     F. a large number
     G. a handful
     H. many
     J. a lot

201. **A.** NO CHANGE
     B. to know that
     C. known that
     D. knowing

202. **F.** NO CHANGE
     G. the one I'm using
     H. something
     J. either one

Pens are also featured prominently at my bedside. Small piles of uncapped ballpoints <u>gather</u> as if of their own
₂₀₃

accord, on my night table. [204] Although I can't think of a time when I have actually woken up in the middle of the night with a brilliant thought, the pens' presence indicates my continuing belief that someday I might.

My pen habit, like most habits, is not without <u>it's</u>
₂₀₅
negative consequences. I'm not just referring to the embarrassment of being caught walking off with someone else's property. There's <u>still</u> the fact that
₂₀₆

most of my clothes <u>have been decorating</u> with ink stains
₂₀₇
from leaking pens or scrawls from moments of unconscious doodling.

[1] <u>After a recent mishap involving</u> half of my travel
₂₀₈
wardrobe, my father convinced me not to pack pens in my suitcase. [2] And to me, that feels like traveling light. [3] The low air pressure in the plane's cargo hold is bound to make them leak and ruin my clothes. [4] Despite such calamities, I still travel with at least five pens, capped but ready in my pocket. [209]

203. **A.** NO CHANGE
   B. gather;
   C. gather,
   D. gather:

204. At this point, the writer is considering adding the following true statement:

   I'll even find one under my pillow occasionally.

   Should the writer make this addition here?

   F. Yes, because it provides a detail that is relevant to this paragraph.
   G. Yes, because it helps explain the statement made in the preceding sentence.
   H. No, because it distracts readers from the main focus of this paragraph.
   J. No, because the information it provides is vague and pointless.

205. **A.** NO CHANGE
   B. there
   C. their
   D. its

206. **F.** NO CHANGE
   G. consequently
   H. instead
   J. also

207. **A.** NO CHANGE
   B. had been decorated
   C. are decorating
   D. are decorated

208. **F.** NO CHANGE
   G. Recently, a mishap that involved
   H. A recent mishap involved
   J. A recent mishap involving

209. Which of the following sequences of sentences makes this paragraph most logical?
   A. NO CHANGE
   B. 1, 3, 4, 2
   C. 2, 1, 3, 4
   D. 4, 1, 3, 2

Question 210 asks about the preceding passage as a whole.

210. Upon reviewing this essay, the writer is thinking about deleting the opening paragraph. Should that paragraph be kept or deleted?
   F. Kept, because it helps establish both the subject and the tone of the essay.
   G. Kept, because it identifies the narrator's friend and the problem that person faces.
   H. Deleted, because it introduces a character that is not developed later in the essay.
   J. Deleted, because the essay fails to explain how this situation was resolved.

PASSAGE XV

Working and Living under the Sea

[1]

Underwater explorer Jacques Cousteau, exploring under the sea, predicted
211
that one day humans would be "freed from the bondage of the surface" to work and even live underwater. In the 1960s, this became reality when the U.S. Navy deployed it's first
212

undersea habitat, *SeaLab*. [213]

[2]

An undersea habitat allowed divers to remain on the ocean floor for extended periods between dives. Because the pressure inside is matched to the pressure of the ocean depth outside, divers can enter and exit at will without
214
fear of decompression sickness—the dangerous bends.

211. A. NO CHANGE
    B. Cousteau—exploring under the sea—
    C. Cousteau who explored under the sea,
    D. Cousteau

212. F. NO CHANGE
    G. there
    H. its
    J. its'

213. The writer is considering adding the following phrase to the end of the preceding sentence (replacing the period after *SeaLab* with a comma):

    an underwater environment where people can live and work.

    Should the writer add this phrase here?
    A. Yes, because it offers a brief definition of the *SeaLab* habitat.
    B. Yes, because it helps the reader envision what the Navy deployed.
    C. No, because the *SeaLab* has already been described.
    D. No, because it provides a digression that leads the paragraph away from its primary focus.

214. F. NO CHANGE
    G. at the exterior,
    H. on the reverse side,
    J. beyond,

This ability extends the time that scientists

can work <u>greatly</u> underwater.
      ₂₁₅

[216] For example, at a

depth of sixty feet. Work would be
         ₂₁₇
limited to one hour per day if the dives

had to start from the water <u>surface, using SeaLab,</u>
                                      ₂₁₈
divers can work each day for as long as they desire.

[3]

     Not long ago, the most advanced in a

series of undersea habitats, *Aquarius*, was rested

on the ocean floor in the Florida Keys. Bolted to a

two-hundred-ton platform sixty-six feet below sea level at

Conch Reef, <u>scientists at this research outpost are offered</u>
                                    ₂₁₉
a unique opportunity to study the impact of pollution on

coral reefs. [220]

---

215. The best placement for the underlined portion would be:
 - **A.** where it is now.
 - **B.** after the word *ability*.
 - **C.** after the word *time*.
 - **D.** after the word *scientists*.

216. The writer is considering adding the following clause to the end of the preceding sentence (replacing the period after the word *underwater* with a comma):

> and they can reminisce casually about the pleasant memories from previous missions.

Should the writer add this clause here?
 - **F.** Yes, because it suggests the camaraderie that is shared among marine scientists.
 - **G.** Yes, because it suggests that an undersea habitat is capable of providing the comforts of home.
 - **H.** No, because it provides a digression that leads the paragraph away from its focus.
 - **J.** No, because it does not specifically describe any of the memories.

217. A. NO CHANGE
 - **B.** depth, of sixty feet, work
 - **C.** depth of sixty feet; work
 - **D.** depth of sixty feet, work

218. F. NO CHANGE
 - **G.** surface using *SeaLab*
 - **H.** surface using *SeaLab*,
 - **J.** surface. Using *SeaLab*,

219. A. NO CHANGE
 - **B.** this research outpost offers scientists
 - **C.** scientists researching at this outpost are offered
 - **D.** research scientists at this outpost are offered

220. Which of the following true statements, if added here, would best point out the governing bodies from which the *Aquarius* project receives its orders?
 - **F.** *Aquarius* is operated jointly by the National Oceanic and Atmospheric Administration and the University of North Carolina.
 - **G.** University of North Carolina professors worked on the *Aquarius* project.
 - **H.** University professors and scientific researchers were often at odds while collaborating on the *Aquarius* habitat.
 - **J.** Many interested groups and organizations support research related to the *Aquarius* habitat project.

[4]

Hidden under the waves, *Aquarius* is a bright yellow, forty-three-foot-long cylinder. Inside, scientists live in homey if cramped quarters, with bunks, a shower and toilet, a microwave, and an array of scientific instruments.
                          221
They can watch marine life through large portholes, and enter and exit their pressurized domicile through the

moonpool, a special air pocket that keeps the ocean
        222
outside.

[5]

[1] At a depth of sixty-six feet, this decompression takes seventeen hours. [2] When the mission is complete and it is time for the aquanauts to return to land, the pressure inside the habitat must be gradual and returned
                                                        223
to that of sea level before divers can ascend. [3] A small price, Cousteau would likely have said, for being freed from the surface for so long. 224

221. Which of the following alternatives to the underlined portion would be LEAST acceptable?

  A. a classification
  B. an assortment
  C. a collection
  D. a supply

222. **F.** NO CHANGE
  G. *moonpool.* A
  H. *moonpool;* a
  J. *moonpool* a

223. **A.** NO CHANGE
  B. gradually and
  C. gradually
  D. gradual

224. Which of the following sequences of sentences will make Paragraph 5 most logical?

  F. NO CHANGE
  G. 1, 3, 2
  H. 2, 1, 3
  J. 2, 3, 1

Question 225 asks about the preceding passage as a whole.

225. Suppose the writer had intended to write a brief essay about Jacques Cousteau's contributions to life under the sea. Would this essay fulfill that purpose?

  A. Yes, because the essay describes Cousteau's research of various underwater habitats he discovered in the 1960s.
  B. Yes, because the essay describes the first underwater habitat Cousteau deployed in the 1960s.
  C. No, because the essay is about the *moonpool* and the role the University of North Carolina played in its research.
  D. No, because the essay focuses more generally on underwater habitats and how long scientists can work underwater.

PASSAGE XVI

A Problem Solver and an Inventor

Dr. George Franklin Grant was a brilliant, innovative dentist and a professor at Harvard University. But the achievement <u>that he is most widely remembered for today</u>
226

is his <u>invention and creation</u> of the wooden golf tee.
227

An avid golfer, Dr. Grant invented and patented the tee in 1899. Before <u>his</u> invention, golfers preparing to tee
228
off (hit their first shot) had to shape a mound of moist dirt

or sand to raise the golf ball off the turf in order to <u>hit it</u>
229
cleanly. Unfortunately, the ball would often roll off the handmade mound before the golfer could complete his or her swing. By both raising and stabilizing the ball, Grant's invention <u>remedied</u> this problem.
230

<u>The tee Dr. Grant invented was not marketed for</u>
231
<u>commercial use.</u> After earning his doctor of dental surgery
231
degree from Harvard University in 1870, Grant became one of Harvard's first African American professors. An internationally recognized expert in mechanical dentistry, he designed a new style of dental bridge, a device that provides support for individuals who have lost or broken teeth. Those constructed according to <u>Grants design</u> fit
232
so well and so comfortably that the general health of his

patients <u>have been</u> measurably improved.
233

226. Which of the following alternatives to the underlined portion would NOT be acceptable?
   F. in which he is most widely remembered for
   G. that he is remembered most widely for
   H. for which he is most widely remembered
   J. he is most widely remembered for

227. A. NO CHANGE
   B. invention, which was the creation
   C. invention, that is, the creation
   D. invention

228. F. NO CHANGE
   G. their
   H. its'
   J. it's

229. A. NO CHANGE
   B. for hitting
   C. to hitting
   D. that hit

230. Which of the following alternatives to the underlined portion would be LEAST acceptable?
   F. corrected
   G. alleviated
   H. fixed
   J. rescued

231. Given that all the choices are true, which one would best introduce the new subject of this paragraph?
   A. NO CHANGE
   B. Dr. Grant's achievements in the world of dentistry are equally impressive.
   C. Dr. Grant believed that golf helped build discipline and friendships.
   D. Friends of Dr. Grant were the happy recipients of his invention.

232. F. NO CHANGE
   G. Grant's design
   H. Grant's design,
   J. Grants design,

233. A. NO CHANGE
   B. was
   C. are
   D. were

Dr. Grant's invention of the golf tee and his
                                    234
innovative dental bridge may seem to be an unlikely

pairing. However, each accomplishment exemplifies a

characteristic common to innovators: the ability to

identify and solve a problem. In both of these cases, Grant

recognized a need and focused his skills, imagination, and
             235

intelligence to devising a way to fill that need.
               236

Instead, Dr. George Franklin Grant made a lasting
  237
impression on the world as an innovative engineer in both

of the fields he loved. A brilliant professor of dentistry: he
                                                 238
is best remembered for making it possible for generations

of golfers concentrated on their swings without worrying
         239
about whether their golf balls would remain in place

as they swung.

---

234. F. NO CHANGE
   G. invention, of the golf tee,
   H. invention, of the golf tee
   J. invention of the golf tee,

235. A. NO CHANGE
   B. a lack of something that was needed
   C. that a need was in existence
   D. a need that was out there

236. F. NO CHANGE
   G. at
   H. on
   J. for

237. A. NO CHANGE
   B. In addition,
   C. In contrast,
   D. OMIT the underlined portion.

238. F. NO CHANGE
   G. dentistry;
   H. dentistry,
   J. dentistry

239. A. NO CHANGE
   B. concentrating
   C. concentrate
   D. to concentrate

Question 240 asks about the preceding passage as a whole.

240. Suppose the writer's goal had been to write a brief essay documenting key innovations in golf equipment. Would this essay successfully fulfill that goal?

   F. Yes, because it highlights an important invention that changed the way golf is played.
   G. Yes, because it tells readers how and when a key innovation was introduced to the game of golf.
   H. No, because it fails to mention any improvements to golf equipment other than the tee.
   J. No, because it does not include information about tees made of plastic or metal.

PASSAGE XVII

Here Comes the Garbage Truck!

In 1917, the year our house was built. The city
$\underline{}$
$\quad$ 241

planners had an orderly scheme about the collection
$\qquad\underline{}$
$\qquad\qquad$ 242
of trash. Garbage cans would be picked up from

the narrow alleys that ran behind the rows
$\qquad\underline{}$
$\qquad$ 243

of houses. The standard-width sidewalks
$\qquad\underline{}$
$\qquad\qquad$ 244

with which the houses faced would remain
$\underline{}$
$\quad$ 245
free of trash receptacles.

$\quad$ For six or seven decades, this is the way

things would have worked. Garbage trucks
$\underline{}$
$\quad$ 246

squeezed through the back alleys, collecting trash.
$\underline{}$
$\quad$ 247
However, the construction of new vehicles in recent years

put an end to the city designers' plans. Today's garbage

trucks are enormous, far wider than the slender alleys.

Unlike the older trucks, they are painted bright yellow.
$\underline{}$
$\qquad$ 248

241. A. NO CHANGE
B. built the
C. built, the
D. built; the

242. F. NO CHANGE
G. of
H. by
J. for

243. A. NO CHANGE
B. being that they
C. so that they
D. since they

244. Given that all the choices are true, which description of the sidewalks best supports the logic of the city planners' trash collection system, as described in this paragraph?

F. NO CHANGE
G. paved cement
H. tidy, tree-lined
J. old, familiar

245. A. NO CHANGE
B. that the houses faced
C. toward the houses faced
D. with the houses facing

246. F. NO CHANGE
G. things were to have worked.
H. that things work.
J. things worked.

247. Which choice presents this action in a way most consistent with the writer's description of the alleys?

A. NO CHANGE
B. rambled down
C. rolled along
D. traveled

248. Given that all the choices are true, which one provides the most specific support for the statement in the preceding sentence?

F. NO CHANGE
G. Twice a year, city residents pick up litter from the alleys.
H. Indeed, the new trucks can barely navigate ordinary city streets.
J. Nevertheless, the alleys remain free of trash and yard clippings.

Garbage cans must now be placed on the front sidewalk and collected from the main street. What was
249

once hidden away behind the houses are now out in the
250
open, for all to see. How disappointed those early town

leaders would be to see this public display of trash.
251

[1] Yet, the new system has an unexpected benefit. [2] It has made the mechanical gymnastics of the garbage truck much more visible to our neighborhood's young children, who delight in watching the show. [3] A fire
252
engine is bright red and loud, but it doesn't pass by often. [4] For them, the garbage truck is even better than a fire engine. [5] The garbage truck, on the other hand, is a weekly visitor and exotic in its own way. [6] Its best
253

features are hard to beat the bright yellow paint, the sound
254
of the warning horn as it backs up, and, most amazing of all, the way its mechanical arm lifts and dumps the trash cans into its open back end. [255]

Sometimes the neighbors and I complain to each other about the garbage truck. It is loud, we agree, and it blocks the street. But then whatever qualms I might have are quickly erased by the children's excitement. If those long-ago city planners could see the curiosity and amazement on the children's faces, I'm sure they would feel the same way.

249. Which of the following alternatives to the underlined portion would NOT be acceptable?

    A. street, so that what
    B. street; what
    C. street, what
    D. street: what

250. F. NO CHANGE
     G. is
     H. were
     J. have been

251. Which of the following alternatives to the underlined portion would be LEAST acceptable?

    A. exhibition
    B. attraction
    C. spectacle
    D. showing

252. F. NO CHANGE
     G. whom
     H. which
     J. whose

253. Which of the following alternatives to the underlined portion would NOT be acceptable?

    A. visitor that is
    B. visitor it's
    C. visitor and is
    D. visitor,

254. F. NO CHANGE
     G. beat:
     H. beat,
     J. beat;

255. For the sake of the logic and coherence of this paragraph, Sentence 4 should be placed:

    A. where it is now.
    B. after Sentence 1.
    C. after Sentence 2.
    D. after Sentence 6.

PASSAGE XVIII

The Hunt for Morel Mushrooms

[1]

When I close my eyes I see them. They pop up through dead leaves, emerge from under fallen logs, and sprout next to tree stumps. Even indoors, I think I spot them out of the corner of my eye. Basically, I spend every free moment in search of them.
256

[2]

I'm not talking about imaginary creatures but
257
about deliciously real morel mushrooms—

funny-looking, textured, edible fungi that appear
258
in springtime. These homely ground dwellers inspire their fans to search the woods for hours, intent on finding enough to fry up for dinner. Would it be easier to buy mushrooms at the store? Absolutely. But it wouldn't be as much fun. Once you find your first morel, maybe by a dead elm or in an old apple orchard, a person will be even more
259
determined to find the next one. And the next. And so on.

[3]

Like many morel hunters, I learned from an expert. She invited me along to see firsthand how it's done. I learned even more by reading reputable, detailed field guides about wild mushrooms.
260

That's a crucial part of the preparation to get ready for
261
morel hunting, because often the same woods that yield morels produce poisonous mushrooms, too.

256. Which of the following alternatives to the underlined portion would be LEAST acceptable?
  A. all my free time
  B. appropriate vacation time slots
  C. every moment of my leisure time
  D. whatever time I can set aside

257. F. NO CHANGE
  G. about, imaginary creatures but
  H. about, imaginary creatures, but
  J. about imaginary creatures, but,

258. Given that all the choices are true, which one most specifically describes the appearance of a morel mushroom for readers who have never seen one?
  A. NO CHANGE
  B. earthy, oddly amusing, interesting-looking
  C. odorless and unusually shaped
  D. sand-colored, cone-shaped, spongelike

259. F. NO CHANGE
  G. a morel hunter
  H. you
  J. DELETE the underlined portion.

260. Given that all the choices are true, which one provides the most relevant and specific information at this point in the essay?
  A. NO CHANGE
  B. in between trips to and from the woods.
  C. to gain the expertise I wanted and needed at this point.
  D. very carefully on the topic that pertains to the activity.

261. F. NO CHANGE
  G. to make oneself fit
  H. of someone planning to be ready
  J. DELETE the underlined portion.

[4]

262 Every spring, there's a contest where I live in northern Minnesota to see who can find the most

morels, this year, I'm going to enter. Last year, one
263

participant found over 3,000 morels becoming my hero.
264
And he's willing to talk with me about this hobby we are both passionate about. Luckily, I know what question *not* to ask. You never ask morel hunters where they made their biggest find. Keeping silent about your favorite spots, is
265
part of the mystique of this glorious pastime.

[5]

Mostly, finding morels requires

two things in particular. Smaller and
266

paler then the average pinecone, a morel
267

blends perfectly into its natural surroundings.
268

However, you can look right at one and not see it.
269

Morels fool everyone, even the experts, that's probably
270
why the saying goes that the best place to look for morels is directly behind you.

262. Which of the following statements, if added here, would provide the most effective transition from Paragraph 3 to Paragraph 4?
   A. There were many field guides to choose from.
   B. I love the texture that morels add to a meal.
   C. Outdoor activities offer so many rewards.
   D. Now I want to put my knowledge to work.

263. F. NO CHANGE
   G. morels this
   H. morels. This
   J. morels, because this

264. A. NO CHANGE
   B. morels. He's my
   C. morels, what a
   D. morels, my

265. F. NO CHANGE
   G. silent, about your favorite spots
   H. silent, about your favorite spots,
   J. silent about your favorite spots

266. Given that all the choices are true, which one provides the most specific information?
   A. NO CHANGE
   B. demonstrating two skills.
   C. patience and concentration.
   D. expertise in this hobby.

267. F. NO CHANGE
   G. more pale then
   H. paler than
   J. pale than

268. A. NO CHANGE
   B. it's
   C. their
   D. there

269. F. NO CHANGE
   G. You
   H. On the other hand, you
   J. Back and forth, you

270. A. NO CHANGE
   B. experts. That's
   C. experts say, that's
   D. experts and

PASSAGE XIX

The Amazing Monarch Migration

The orange and black monarch butterfly, which is
<u>271</u>

the <u>most easiest</u> recognized and striking butterfly species
<u>272</u>
in North America. Monarchs are particularly fascinating because they are one of the few migratory butterfly species in North America.

[1] In the fall, as daylight and temperatures decrease, migrating monarchs begin their long journey <u>south, an extended flight.</u> [2] Many
<u>273</u>

<u>monarchs, west of the Rocky Mountains</u> migrate
<u>274</u>

to the southern California coast, <u>where they</u>
<u>275</u>

overwinter in eucalyptus groves. [3] <u>Besides,</u> most
<u>276</u>

<u>monarchs,</u> millions of them across the United States and
<u>277</u>
Canada—migrate as many as three thousand miles to Oyamel fir forests near Mexico City. [4] Monarchs have smaller bodies and <u>insufficiently</u> developed nervous
<u>278</u>
systems than migratory birds. [5] The features of birds that help them accomplish their long migrations are aerodynamic design, acute vision, <u>and the ability to</u>
<u>279</u>
<u>regulate their body temperature and maintain energy.</u>
<u>279</u>
[6] Monarchs lack these features, and yet, in a way

271. **F.** NO CHANGE
G. butterfly
H. butterfly that
J. butterfly,

272. **A.** NO CHANGE
B. most easy
C. easiest
D. most easily

273. **F.** NO CHANGE
G. south, which is far-reaching.
H. south.
J. south, which encompasses many miles.

274. **A.** NO CHANGE
B. monarchs west of the Rocky Mountains,
C. monarchs west, of the Rocky Mountains,
D. monarchs west of the Rocky Mountains

275. **F.** NO CHANGE
G. there
H. while
J. DELETE the underlined portion.

276. **A.** NO CHANGE
B. However,
C. Finally,
D. Therefore,

277. **F.** NO CHANGE
G. monarchs—
H. monarchs;
J. monarchs

278. **A.** NO CHANGE
B. less
C. more insufficient
D. inadequate

279. **F.** NO CHANGE
G. and regulating body temperature and maintaining energy with their ability.
H. with their body temperature regulation and energy maintenance ability.
J. and the regulation of body temperature and their ability to maintain energy.

that defies explanation, they travel up to eighty miles in a day. [280]

For decades, scientists have studied this phenomenon, hoping to learn how monarchs are able to fly such distances. Researchers have tagged migrating monarchs to study their flight patterns, and they've hiked

to the overwintering sites on the Mexican Plateau, where
          ‾‾‾‾
          281
twenty thousand monarchs are sometimes found clustered on a single Oyamel fir bough.

Scientists are starting to learn more about the monarch's life cycle. When monarchs that don't
                              ‾‾‾‾
                              282

migrate to Mexico live only four to six weeks;
                                      ‾‾‾‾‾
                                      283
the migrating generations live at least eight months.

After becoming reproductively active in the spring, monarchs that have migrated begin their return journey. They lay their eggs on milkweed plants along the way and then die. Their offspring hatch, feed on the milkweed, and the migration is eventually continued.
       ‾‾‾‾‾‾‾‾‾‾‾‾‾‾‾‾‾‾‾‾‾‾‾‾‾‾‾‾‾‾
                   284
Researchers know they have much to learn, but with the help of new tracking devices and Internet technology that makes data available worldwide, they are ready to move ahead.
‾‾‾‾‾‾‾‾‾‾‾‾‾‾‾‾‾‾‾‾‾‾‾‾
         285

280. The writer would like to divide this paragraph into two in order to signal the shift in focus from monarchs' migrating habits to the differences between monarchs and migratory birds. To accomplish this goal, the best place to start the new paragraph would be at the beginning of Sentence:
   A. 2.
   B. 3.
   C. 4.
   D. 5.

281. F. NO CHANGE
   G. site's
   H. sites'
   J. sites,

282. A. NO CHANGE
   B. If
   C. While
   D. So that

283. F. NO CHANGE
   G. weeks and
   H. weeks, and while
   J. weeks,

284. A. NO CHANGE
   B. continuing the migration is eventual.
   C. eventually continue the migration.
   D. continuing eventually the migration.

285. Which choice would best conclude the sentence and support one of the main points of the essay?
   F. NO CHANGE
   G. they are excited about learning how to use these new research tools.
   H. they hope to solve the mysteries of the monarch migration.
   J. they look forward to collaborating with other researchers who are more knowledgeable in the mysteries of monarch migration.

PASSAGE XX

> The following paragraphs may or may not be in the most logical order. Each paragraph is numbered in brackets, and question 45 will ask you to choose where Paragraph 3 should most logically be placed.

Yo-Yos Spinning through Time

[1]

Historians speculate that one of the world's oldest toys is the yo-yo, though they know <u>for sure that the oldest toy is the doll.</u> Drawings
286

<u>of objects</u> adorn ancient Greek vases and the walls of
287

Egyptian temples, <u>if</u> written mention of yo-yos goes
288
back to the fifth century B.C.

[2]

While many cultures had their variations of the yo-yo, the American version can be traced to the Philippines, where yo-yos <u>have been a national pastime for centuries.</u>
289
In fact, the name *yo-yo* is a Tagalog word that translates

as "come back." In the 1920s Pedro Flores, a Filipino
290

immigrant, introduced the toy in the United <u>States and</u>
291
soon started a yo-yo manufacturing company in California. Flores's design was different because the yo-yo's string wasn't tied to the axle of the toy, but rather looped around it. This allowed a skilled handler to make the toy spin at the end of its string, or "sleep."

286. **A.** NO CHANGE
     B. yo-yo, but it is hard to know for sure, considering the yo-yo's history.
     C. yo-yo, though no one is certain why some ancient yo-yos were made out of terra cotta, a fragile clay.
     D. yo-yo.

287. **F.** NO CHANGE
     G. that call attention to objects that look something like the toy that I have just mentioned
     H. that include objects that almost slightly resemble yo-yos
     J. of objects resembling yo-yos

288. **A.** NO CHANGE
     B. and
     C. since
     D. because

289. Given that all the choices are true, which one provides the most effective evidence of the long history of enthusiasm for the yo-yo in the Philippines?
     F. NO CHANGE
     G. have been a popular hobby for years.
     H. were carved out of fine wood or animal horns.
     J. resembled a toy that was popular in ancient China.

290. **A.** NO CHANGE
     B. by
     C. with
     D. from

291. Which of the following alternatives to the underlined portion would NOT be acceptable?
     F. States. Flores
     G. States, and he
     H. States; he
     J. States he

[3]

Yo-yo technology really progressed substantially by making
a leap forward in the 1970s when designers added
weighted rims so the toy would spin for a longer time.
In 1980, another innovation led to the development of
the "yo-yo with a brain," which featured a spring-loaded
mechanism that caused the yo-yo to return to its owner's
hand.

[4]

The American craze for the toy began when the
entrepreneur Donald Duncan saw a demonstration of

Flores's new yo-yo. Noticing the large crowd who
watched, Duncan quickly realized the yo-yo's potential.
Flores sold his yo-yo company and all rights to Duncan
in 1932, after deciding that he was more interested in
teaching people how to handle yo-yos than he was
in manufacturing them. Duncan immediately launched
an elaborate national advertising campaign to promote
the toy. He also sent Duncan Yo-Yo Professionals
around the country, demonstrating tricks and sponsoring

contests. [297] Millions of the toys were sold.

[5]

In 1985, this most ancient of toys, went into

space. Astronauts aboard the space shuttle *Discovery*
demonstrated that while a yo-yo would spin in a near-zero
gravity environment, it refused to sleep.

292. A. NO CHANGE
    B. advanced as a result of progressively making
    C. jumped ahead and made
    D. made

293. F. NO CHANGE
    G. begins
    H. begun
    J. had began

294. A. NO CHANGE
    B. whom
    C. whose
    D. who's

295. Which of the following alternatives to the underlined portion would NOT be acceptable?
    F. 1932, after his decision
    G. 1932. He had decided
    H. 1932, upon deciding
    J. 1932. Deciding

296. A. NO CHANGE
    B. in order to demonstrate
    C. who demonstrated
    D. yet demonstrating

297. If the writer were to delete the preceding sentence, the essay would primarily lose information that:
    F. proves Duncan was uncertain what would be the best way to promote the yo-yo.
    G. reveals how quickly demonstrations by Duncan Yo-Yo Professionals gained popularity.
    H. illustrates one creative strategy that Duncan used to promote the yo-yo.
    J. suggests how Duncan Yo-Yo Professionals were chosen for the job.

298. A. NO CHANGE
    B. toys went
    C. toys had went
    D. toys, had gone

299. F. NO CHANGE
    G. shuttle, *Discovery;*
    H. shuttle *Discovery,*
    J. shuttle, *Discovery*

Question 300 asks about the preceding passage as a whole.

300. For the sake of the logic and coherence of this essay, Paragraph 3 should be placed:

- **A.** where it is now.
- **B.** before Paragraph 1.
- **C.** before Paragraph 2.
- **D.** before Paragraph 5.

PASSAGE XXI

Swimming in Open Water

Immersed in the icy water off the Antarctic Peninsula, Lynne Cox wasn't sure if she could accomplish her goal to be the first person to swim a mile through the glacier-strewn sea. At forty-five, she would of been training for
₃₀₁

two years for this event, which she hoped her preparations
₃₀₂
would pay off.

Cox grew up swimming in the cold lakes of New Hampshire and Maine. When
₃₀₃
she was fifteen, she broke the men's and women's

record's for swimming the English Channel by finishing
₃₀₄

the twenty-seven-mile swim in less than ten hours. [305]

She could swim in open water and had swum across
₃₀₆
the Cook Strait in New Zealand, around the Cape of Good Hope at the southern tip of Africa, and across Lake Titicaca from Bolivia to Peru.

301. **F.** NO CHANGE
- **G.** had
- **H.** have
- **J.** had to of

302. **A.** NO CHANGE
- **B.** and
- **C.** then
- **D.** DELETE the underlined portion.

303. **F.** NO CHANGE
- **G.** cold, lakes of New Hampshire
- **H.** cold lakes, of New Hampshire
- **J.** cold, lakes of New Hampshire,

304. **A.** NO CHANGE
- **B.** records
- **C.** records'
- **D.** records,

305. At this point, the writer is considering adding the following true statement:

> At its widest, the English Channel spans a distance of 150 miles.

Should the writer make this addition here?

- **F.** Yes, because it reinforces the point that Cox swam a great distance across the English Channel.
- **G.** Yes, because it provides a logical transition to the rest of the paragraph.
- **H.** No, because the English Channel is only one place that Cox had swum before going to Antarctica.
- **J.** No, because it is irrelevant to the focus of the essay at this point.

306. Given that all the choices are true, which one best conveys Cox's attitude toward swimming and helps bring into focus the kind of swimming that appeals to her?

- **A.** NO CHANGE
- **B.** loved the challenge of
- **C.** had racked up many miles in
- **D.** astounded many by her swimming feats in

[1] Cox is fortunate that she has a natural tolerance for cold temperatures, but swimming the Antarctic—in water only slightly above freezing—demanded serious preparation. [2] This athlete studied how Antarctic animals adapt to the frigid environment. [3] Penguins' double layer of feathers acts as insulation, so she grew her hair long and piled it under her swim cap. [4] Antarctic seals rely on body fat for warmth, so Cox gained twelve pounds, <u>it was weight</u> that she hoped would keep her warm in the
₃₀₇

icy water. [308]

In November 2002, a <u>crew of</u> physicians,
₃₀₉
sailors, and expedition experts, Cox headed for Neko Harbor on the Antarctic Peninsula. There she dove into water chilled by melting glaciers and began to swim. <u>Without proper training, she would have been in peril.</u>
₃₁₀

Her initial <u>fatigue and exhaustion</u> turned into
₃₁₁
exhilaration as she moved through water that was clearer and <u>blue as</u> any she'd swum in before. For a moment at
₃₁₂
the end, she considered going even farther. Cox knew, however, that the longer she stayed in the water, the

307. **F.** NO CHANGE
 G. she put on weight
 H. she gained it so
 J. weight

308. Which of the following sequences of sentences makes this paragraph most logical?
 A. NO CHANGE
 B. 1, 4, 2, 3
 C. 3, 1, 4, 2
 D. 4, 3, 2, 1

309. **F.** NO CHANGE
 G. a crew made up of
 H. with a crew of
 J. DELETE the underlined portion.

310. The writer wants to end this paragraph with a physical detail about the swim that emphasizes that Cox was in a harsh environment. Given that all the choices are true, which one best accomplishes the writer's purpose?
 A. NO CHANGE
 B. Her amazing feat was described in a feature article in *The New Yorker* magazine.
 C. Bits of ice brushed against her arms and legs.
 D. Photographs of her in her goggles, swim cap, and bathing suit appeared in a national publication.

311. **F.** NO CHANGE
 G. exhaustion
 H. exhaustion that left her feeling fatigued
 J. exhausting fatigue

312. **A.** NO CHANGE
 B. more blue then
 C. bluer than
 D. bluer then

longer it would take to bring her body temperature—

which fell to 95.5 degrees Fahrenheit by the end of

the swim—<u>back to normal.</u> A mile was good
                     313

<u>enough as Cox closed in on the shore—and her goal—</u>
    314

<u>penguins splashed in the water with the great athlete.</u>
                     315

313. **F.** NO CHANGE
     G. back to a normal body temperature.
     H. in other words, back to normal.
     J. which was normal.

314. **A.** NO CHANGE
     B. enough. As
     C. enough, as
     D. enough,

315. Given that all the choices are true, which one best concludes the essay with an image that emphasizes the location and indicates the completion of Cox's feat?
     F. NO CHANGE
     G. birds splashed in the water as if to cheer her on toward the goal of the entire expedition.
     H. wildlife displayed their natural ability to swim in waters that truly tested Cox's ability to meet her goal.
     J. a flock of penguins jumped into the water and joined her for the last thrilling strokes.

PASSAGE XXII

"All I Can Do Is Take a Picture"

[1]

Ernest C. Withers has been recording history with his camera for more than sixty years. For most of his life, Withers has lived and worked as a photojournalist in Memphis, Tennessee, where he covered newsworthy events, both local and national, over some six decades. 316

316. The writer is thinking about deleting the phrase "over some six decades" from the preceding sentence (and replacing the comma after the word *national* with a period). Should that phrase be kept or deleted?
     A. Kept, because it gives readers some idea of Withers's longevity.
     B. Kept, because it helps readers to figure out when Withers began working as a photojournalist.
     C. Deleted, because it repeats information presented earlier in the essay.
     D. Deleted, because the length of Withers's career is not relevant to the focus of this essay.

As an African American intimately familiar with the geography and people of the South, he was often the first photographer present as historic moments took place. Using his hometown as his base and documenting the key people and events of
₃₁₇

the world in which he grew up, observed, and learned.
₃₁₈

[2]

[1] When his older sister's boyfriend showed no
₃₁₉
interest in using a camera that she had bought for him, Withers took it to school and photographed his classmate. [2] Years later, while serving as a jeep driver in World War II, he received permission from his company commander to train at the photography school at Camp Sutton, North Carolina. [3] Withers started taking pictures in his youth. [4] In 1946, he left the Army and
₃₂₀

began working at a job that was a self-employed
₃₂₁

photographer. 322

[3]

Withers's profession gave him access to famous people. He has photographed seven of the last eight U.S. presidents and every major civil rights leader since the 1950s. Thus, he is well known and well
₃₂₃
liked, Withers often traveled with and photographed

317. **F.** NO CHANGE
  G. base. Withers documented
  H. base, Withers documented
  J. base, documenting

318. Given that all the choices are true, which one provides the most effective and most specific support for the statement made in the preceding sentence?
  A. NO CHANGE
  B. the Memphis music scene, baseball's Negro Leagues, and the civil rights movement.
  C. his world, which have become memorable because of their significance.
  D. this place that he thought would be important or newsworthy.

319. Which of the following alternatives to the underlined portion would be LEAST acceptable?
  F. Whereas
  G. Since
  H. As if
  J. After

320. **A.** NO CHANGE
  B. with
  C. of
  D. at

321. **F.** NO CHANGE
  G. for himself as
  H. as
  J. DELETE the underlined portion.

322. For the sake of the logic and coherence of this paragraph, Sentence 3 should be placed:
  A. where it is now.
  B. before Sentence 1.
  C. after Sentence 1.
  D. after Sentence 4.

323. **F.** NO CHANGE
  G. In fact, he is well
  H. He is well
  J. Well

such historic figures as Martin Luther King Jr., Medgar
324

Evers, and James Meredith. For instance, his photos of
325

Memphis's Beale Street jazz and blues musicians includes
326
the likes of B. B. King, Aretha Franklin, and Elvis Presley.

[4]

In addition to capturing many public personages
on film, Withers also photographed: waitresses, church
327
congregations, nightclub audiences, and Little League
baseball games. "I can't play a piano, I can't play a guitar,
all I can do is take a picture," Withers said in a recent
interview. At long last, Ernest C. Withers had recorded
328
some five million photographic images.

324. Which of the following alternatives to the underlined portion would NOT be acceptable?
   A. such historical figures as
   B. historical figures such as
   C. such historic figures
   D. historic figures like

325. F. NO CHANGE
   G. As a result, his
   H. However, his
   J. His

326. A. NO CHANGE
   B. does include
   C. including
   D. include

327. F. NO CHANGE
   G. photographed waitresses,
   H. photographed: waitresses
   J. photographed waitresses

328. Which choice best expresses the fact that Withers is still taking photographs at the time this essay was written?
   A. NO CHANGE
   B. At last count,
   C. To sum up,
   D. All in all,

Questions 329 and 330 ask about the preceding passage as a whole.

329. Upon reviewing the essay and realizing that some information has been left out, the writer composes the following sentence incorporating that information:

   He immortalized his subjects in the middle of their performances as well as in quiet moments backstage.

   This sentence would most logically be placed at the end of Paragraph:
   F. 1.
   G. 2.
   H. 3.
   J. 4.

330. Suppose the writer's goal had been to write a biographical sketch of a photojournalist that would portray the person in the context of the world he or she photographed. Does this essay successfully accomplish that goal?
   A. Yes, because it describes Ernest Withers's career as a photojournalist and relates that career to his hometown of Memphis and the South.
   B. Yes, because it explains how Ernest Withers first developed his interest in photography and photojournalism.
   C. No, because it fails to make any connection between Ernest Withers and the world that he photographed.
   D. No, because it doesn't sufficiently describe Ernest Withers's achievements, honors, and awards.

PASSAGE XXIII

Parachuting

You do what you are told. You have had plenty of training. You strap on the equipment and squeeze on the helmet. You follow your instructor and the other two first-time jumpers into the big twin-propeller plane and take your assigned place in front of them all. You will be the first one to go.

The plane has been stripped of all its seats, so everyone is kneeling on the bare metal floor <u>on their knees</u>. The gigantic
331

engines, <u>which</u> on either side catch and roar
332

into action. <u>You now</u> can entertain any
333

second thoughts, the plane has taxied and <u>taken</u>
334

off and is circling upward into the huge cobalt sky. <u>Its</u>
335

headed to <u>an altitude of three thousand feet.</u>
336
It is impossible to talk—or protest—over the

engines' <u>roar; and the</u> noise of the wind that blasts through
337

331. **A.** NO CHANGE
    B. down on their knees.
    C. resting on their knees.
    D. OMIT the underlined portion and end the sentence with a period.

332. **F.** NO CHANGE
    G. engines, where
    H. engines
    J. engines that

333. **A.** NO CHANGE
    B. You
    C. Then you
    D. Before you

334. **F.** NO CHANGE
    G. took
    H. had taken
    J. had took

335. **A.** NO CHANGE
    B. Its'
    C. It is
    D. It was

336. **F.** NO CHANGE
    G. three thousand feet up in altitude.
    H. an altitude of three thousand feet up.
    J. an altitude of three thousand feet up in the air.

337. **A.** NO CHANGE
    B. roar and the
    C. roar. As the
    D. roar. The

the open doorways on either side of the narrow fuselage.

338 But your instructor smiles confidently. She gives you the thumbs-up sign.

[1] Despite your instincts, you fly chest first out the door of the plane. [2] When the proper altitude is reached and the signal is given, you crawl to the door. [3] As taught, you climb into the open doorway and stand so that your body is half in and half out of the plane, the wind slamming against you, the sweat soaking the rented jumpsuit you're wearing. [4] The instructor signals. [5] Despite your instincts, you nod. 339

You panic. You scream, though no one can hear you. You <u>think, you</u> might become ill.
340

<u>Furthermore,</u> only seconds pass before the static line,
341
which is a rope attached to you and to the floor of the plane, <u>becomes tight and opens</u> your chute automatically.
342
You feel like you are soaring upward, though actually you have <u>only slowed down.</u>
343
You are sitting in a snug little harness. All is quiet as you begin to drift gently in the great blue sky and to appreciate your accomplishment. <u>Thus you</u> are dangling
344
half a mile above the earth! 345

338. The writer wants to add a sentence to emphasize the narrator's growing sense of nervousness at this point in the essay. Which of the following sentences would best achieve this effect?
F. The wind rushing in is loud.
G. This is just as well, because if you could protest, you might.
H. You keep your mouth shut.
J. You wonder whether the other first-time jumpers are having as good a time as you are.

339. For the sake of unity and coherence, Sentence 1 should be placed:
A. where it is now.
B. after Sentence 3.
C. after Sentence 4.
D. after Sentence 5.

340. F. NO CHANGE
G. think, that you
H. think you
J. think, you then

341. A. NO CHANGE
B. However,
C. Thus
D. Consequently,

342. The writer wants to emphasize the violent action of the parachute opening at this point in the essay. Which of the choices would most successfully achieve this effect?
F. NO CHANGE
G. tightens and opens
H. becomes taut and yanks open
J. quickly becomes taut and opens

343. A. NO CHANGE
B. only, slowed down.
C. only slowed down?
D. only slowed, down!

344. F. NO CHANGE
G. When you
H. Since you
J. You

345. The writer wants to end the essay with a sentence that indicates that the narrator feels relaxed floating to earth. Which of the following sentences would most successfully achieve this effect?
A. You realize with relief that jumping from a plane was a fine idea after all.
B. You are relieved that the jump went well, but you still worry about landing.
C. Well, you jumped.
D. You are fine until the next time you have to jump from a plane.

PASSAGE XXIV

Harmonica Blues

For as long as I can remember, it is true that
346
I have wanted to play the harmonica. My father
played a few tunes marginally well. I often
asked him to teach me to play, but I quickly grew
impatient, with the wheezing, tinny notes that I
347

produced. After two weeks' effort, which I would
348

always set the harmonica aside and had went back
349
to the baseball field.

My father was able to teach me a few
things about the harmonica. For instance, he
told me that it originated in southern China around
1100 B.C., this early version, the *sheng*, consisted of long
350
reeds placed in water in a wooden bowl. At one time the

harmonica, which has its origins in ancient China,
351
was often confused with the *armonica*, a musical
instrument invented by Benjamin Franklin that
consisted of glasses played by rubbing the rims
with a wet finger. 352 While the harmonica

346. **F.** NO CHANGE
     G. it is a fact that
     H. it has always been the case that
     J. OMIT the underlined portion.

347. **A.** NO CHANGE
     B. impatient with the wheezing, tinny, notes
     C. impatient with the wheezing, tinny notes
     D. impatient, with the wheezing tinny notes,

348. **F.** NO CHANGE
     G. then
     H. in which
     J. OMIT the underlined portion.

349. **A.** NO CHANGE
     B. would of gone
     C. go
     D. would of went

350. **F.** NO CHANGE
     G. B.C. This early version, the *sheng,* consisted
     H. B.C. An early version, the *sheng,* consisting
     J. B.C., the early version, the *sheng,* consisted

351. **A.** NO CHANGE
     B. instrument I have been unable to play, which is called the harmonica,
     C. harmonica
     D. harmonica, which my father has repeatedly tried to teach me to play,

352. Given that all of the following sentences are true, which one should be added at this point to best continue the historical sketch of the harmonica?
     F. The harmonica as we know it was not introduced until 1828 in London.
     G. London, where the harmonica was introduced, is a foggy city frequented by tourists who enjoy visiting Big Ben and Buckingham Palace.
     H. The most difficult thing about playing the harmonica is pulling air in through the holes; blowing out is easy.
     J. Some of Benjamin Franklin's more famous inventions include the Franklin stove and the lightning rod.

was marketed <u>originally</u> as a child's
₃₅₃

<u>toy</u>, it eventually became a valued portable
₃₅₄
instrument for folk and blues musicians.

[355] Then, at age fifteen, I decided to enroll

in a blues harmonica class. On the first night, the

instructor, <u>whom had</u> performed in local rock bands
₃₅₆
for years, guided the class through a tortured version

of "Mary Had a Little Lamb."

[1] Then he played the same

<u>melody, but with such a pure, sad wail that,</u>
₃₅₇
the entire class sat in stunned silence when he'd

finished. [2] When we had finished, he said, "That was

'Mary Had a Little Lamb.'" [3] He picked up his own

harmonica. [4] "This, however, is 'Mary Had the Blues.'"

[5] He lifted the instrument to his lips. [358]

I returned home determined to learn to play well.

I worked to find the right mouth holes <u>and if I could</u> bend
₃₅₉
the right notes. All week I wheezed through versions of

"Jingle Bells" and "Oh, Susanna." Finally, on the night

before our next class, <u>which I believe was a Wednesday,</u>
₃₆₀
in the middle of an attempt at "Old Folks at Home," I

pursed my lips and blew a sweet, piercing note that filled

the room with lovely sound. I had finally played a proper

note on the harmonica, and maybe I'll someday play

the blues.

353. Which of the following placements for the underlined portion would be LEAST acceptable?

A. Where it is now
B. After the word *harmonica*
C. After the word *was*
D. After the word *as*

354. F. NO CHANGE
G. toy;
H. toy
J. toy, that

355. Which of the following sentences would best provide a logical transition from the preceding paragraph to the new subject in this paragraph?

A. Despite this accumulation of harmonica lore, I still couldn't play.
B. There you have some of the history of the harmonica.
C. As can be seen, I had always been interested in the harmonica.
D. As the reader can see, the harmonica isn't the simple children's toy we so often think it is.

356. F. NO CHANGE
G. whom once
H. who had
J. who did

357. A. NO CHANGE
B. melody, but with such a pure, sad wail that
C. melody, but with such a pure sad wail that,
D. melody but, with such a pure sad wail, that

358. For the sake of the unity and coherence of this paragraph, Sentence 1 should be placed:

F. where it is now.
G. after Sentence 2.
H. after Sentence 3.
J. after Sentence 5.

359. A. NO CHANGE
B. and
C. to see if I were to
D. and if I can

360. F. NO CHANGE
G. which as I recall was a Wednesday,
H. on a Wednesday,
J. OMIT the underlined portion.

PASSAGE XXV

Shaking Up the Language

It's usually hard to determine who first

<u>uttered out loud</u> a given word and almost as hard
   361

to know who first wrote it down <u>originally</u>. It is
                              362
known, however, that William Shakespeare's plays

immortalized many of the words and expressions

popular in his day. Have <u>you ever said you were</u>
                              363
tongue-tied? <u>Do you suspect</u> *foul play,* bid *good riddance,*
              364
or felt like a *laughingstock*? If so, you were using words

and phrases that Shakespeare's plays have made

enduringly popular.

   Shakespeare's *Hamlet,* one of his most widely

read and performed plays, contains many expressions

that are frequently used today, though often in new ways.

Hamlet's regard for humanity is evident in his line "What

a piece of work is a man!" <u>Nonetheless, we</u> still use the
                              365
expression *piece of work,* though now it's used to describe

someone who is hard to understand or deal with. ☐366☐

   Iago, the villain of the <u>tragedy, *Othello*</u> strives
                              367
to undo Othello, a respected general. Iago falsely hints

that Desdemona, the wife of Othello, is in love with

<u>one of Othellos'</u> officers. To further confuse Othello,
   368
Iago warns him against being consumed by doubts

361. **A.** NO CHANGE
     B. spoke
     C. said verbally
     D. gave vocalization to

362. **F.** NO CHANGE
     G. in the beginning.
     H. initially.
     J. OMIT the underlined portion and end the sentence with a period.

363. **A.** NO CHANGE
     B. you, ever said you were
     C. you ever said, you were
     D. you ever said you were,

364. **F.** NO CHANGE
     G. (Do NOT begin new paragraph) Have you suspected
     H. (Begin new paragraph) Do you suspect
     J. (Begin new paragraph) Have you suspected

365. **A.** NO CHANGE
     B. Otherwise, we
     C. While we
     D. We

366. The writer is considering deleting the second clause in the preceding sentence, ending the sentence with a period after the word *work.* If the writer did this, the paragraph would primarily lose:
     F. an example of how an expression changes in meaning over time.
     G. an irrelevant digression that undermines the paragraph's logic.
     H. information providing a key transition to the next paragraph.
     J. a detail that contradicts the statement in the first part of this sentence.

367. **A.** NO CHANGE
     B. tragedy, *Othello,*
     C. tragedy *Othello,*
     D. tragedy *Othello*

368. **F.** NO CHANGE
     G. one of Othellos
     H. one, of Othellos'
     J. one of Othello's

about his wife, calling jealousy a "green-eyed monster,"
a now-common term for that emotion.

The Globe audience heard hundreds of other
expressions that are now *household words.* In *Henry V,*
Shakespeare used this very term to describe how the
names of King Henry's war heroes <u>became</u> as well known
₃₆₉
to English people as simple words used in any household.

<u>A recent film version of *Henry V* was quite popular. Still</u>
₃₇₀

other terms that his plays have preserved <u>are including</u>
₃₇₁
birthplace, downstairs, eyeball, and *love letter.*

We also find <u>illusions of</u> Shakespeare's words
₃₇₂

in film. For instance, one of the *Star Trek* <u>movies are</u>
₃₇₃
subtitled "The Undiscovered Country," a phrase from
one of Hamlet's speeches. Given Shakespeare's
strong <u>presence, in speech and popular culture</u>
₃₇₄
it seems likely that, even in the future,

<u>he will continue to be a popular author.</u>
₃₇₅

369. **A.** NO CHANGE
    B. had became
    C. have became
    D. becoming

370. **F.** NO CHANGE
    G. The 1989 film adaptation of *Henry V* is itself well known to English and American audiences alike.
    H. Those war heroes are colorfully depicted in a recent film version of *Henry* V.
    J. OMIT the underlined portion.

371. **A.** NO CHANGE
    B. included:
    C. include
    D. OMIT the underlined portion.

372. **F.** NO CHANGE
    G. illusions to
    H. allusions of
    J. allusions to

373. **A.** NO CHANGE
    B. movies is
    C. movies,
    D. movies, which is

374. **F.** NO CHANGE
    G. presence in speech, and popular culture
    H. presence in speech and popular culture,
    J. presence, in speech, and popular culture

375. The writer wishes to conclude the sentence and the essay by referring to a main theme of the essay. Which of the following choices would best accomplish that goal?

    A. NO CHANGE
    B. readers will still be discussing and debating his fascinating ideas.
    C. there will be no escaping his influence on the English language.
    D. films will continue to borrow plot ideas from his plays.

PASSAGE XXVI

Maya Lin: Her Work

To the surprise of many, it was a college
                                    376

student, Maya Lin who won the 1981 competition to
           377
design the Vietnam Veterans Memorial. Although

Lin's nonrepresentational design initially stirred up a

controversy, the completed monument has won widespread

acclaim for a while now. Visitors to the monument in
       378
Washington, D.C., encounter two long black granite walls

that meet at an angle as they cut into the ground. Inscribed

in the highly polished walls are the names of the more

than 58,000 United States military personnel lost in

the war.

    While some sculptors suggest the magnitude of

an event by presenting larger-than-life figures, Lin relies
                                            379
on more understated methods to suggest matters of great

significance. [380] Since the unveiling of the Vietnam

Veterans Memorial, Lin has applied this approach in
                           381
different parts of the country and to different eras of

376. F. NO CHANGE
    G. She really surprised many,
    H. It was a surprise,
    J. It came as a surprise to many,

377. A. NO CHANGE
    B. student, Maya Lin,
    C. student Maya Lin
    D. student Maya Lin,

378. The writer would like to characterize the monument in general terms to lead into a more detailed discussion of its features. Which choice best accomplishes the writer's goal?

    F. NO CHANGE
    G. from many people.
    H. for Maya Lin's talent.
    J. for its simplicity and power.

379. A. NO CHANGE
    B. figures:
    C. figures.
    D. figures;

380. The writer is considering adding the following sentence at this point in the essay:

> After all, it is important to reflect on your life along the way.

Should the writer make this addition here?

    F. No, because it takes a position that is in complete opposition to the spirit of the essay's subject of public sculpture.
    G. No, because it disrupts the essay's tone and expresses an ordinary concept that adds very little to the essay's focus on Maya Lin and her work.
    H. Yes, because it is a generalization that provides readers with a lively way to identify with people who have seen Maya Lin's work.
    J. Yes, because it provides a surprising insight into the role monuments play in public life.

381. A. NO CHANGE
    B. will apply
    C. applied
    D. applying

United States history. [382] In 1988, she designed a memorial to honor individuals killed in the civil rights movement. Located in Montgomery, Alabama,

Maya Lin made this work consist of a low granite disk on
                          383
which the names of the dead appear along with references to landmark events of the movement. In addition, my research turned up the following information. [384] Behind

the disk stands a granite wall bearing their inscription:
                                              385
". . . UNTIL JUSTICE ROLLS DOWN LIKE WATERS AND

RIGHTEOUSNESS LIKE A MIGHTY STREAM." Lin selected

these words from a Dr. Martin Luther King Jr. speech,
                                              386
and in the monument, water flows down the wall, over

Dr. King's words, and out from the center of the disk. [387]

   Lin continues to challenge herself in a career that

combines an appreciation for sculpture, architecture, and

---

382. If the writer deleted the phrase "in different parts of the country and" from the preceding sentence, the essay would primarily lose:

   F. a broad claim that is not supported by information elsewhere in the essay.
   G. a broad claim that is supported by details presented later in the essay.
   H. an observation that is out of place in a sentence that focuses on the Vietnam Veterans Memorial.
   J. an observation that undermines claims made elsewhere in the paragraph.

383. **A.** NO CHANGE
   B. this work consists
   C. consisting
   D. her work on this monument consisted

384. If the writer deleted the preceding sentence, the essay would primarily lose a:

   F. sense of the writer's attention to the details of Maya Lin's career.
   G. detail about the writer's research that answers a question posed earlier in the essay.
   H. fact that establishes the credentials of the writer as someone with authority on the subject.
   J. reference to the writer of the essay that seems out of place in the absence of other such references.

385. **A.** NO CHANGE
   B. which
   C. this
   D. it's

386. Given that all the choices are true, which one adds the most specific information to the essay?

   F. NO CHANGE
   G. a speech given by Dr. King in the sixties, specifically 1963,
   H. the "I Have a Dream" speech by Dr. Martin Luther King Jr. himself,
   J. Dr. Martin Luther King Jr.'s 1963 "I Have a Dream" speech,

387. If the opening sentence of this paragraph ("While some sculptors suggest . . .") were deleted, the essay would primarily lose:

   A. a sharp criticism of the shortcomings of works by Maya Lin's colleagues in the field of sculpture.
   B. the only remark that draws an explicit comparison between Maya Lin and other sculptors.
   C. the only reason Maya Lin gives for choosing to work in a fashion unlike that of many other sculptors.
   D. the writer's opinion of who has influenced Maya Lin in her career of designing memorials.

the complexity of human experience. A public library in
388
Ohio, a chapel in Pennsylvania, a train station in New

York—these had been only some of the places that have
389
been influenced by Maya Lin. It is possible to come away
from her work with the sense that the distinctions we
sometimes make between public and personal life are
blurred in moments of genuine reflection.

388. **F.** NO CHANGE
G. complexity of the nature and character
H. characteristically complex and inherent complications
J. complicated character and complex nature

389. **A.** NO CHANGE
B. were
C. are
D. having been

Question 390 asks about the preceding passage as a whole.

390. Suppose the writer had intended to write an essay focusing on public reaction to the Vietnam Veterans Memorial. Would this essay fulfill the writer's goal?

F. Yes, because the reaction of the public to the Vietnam Veterans Memorial is described in great detail.
G. Yes, because the author clearly avoids limiting the essay to a view of the monument based on firsthand experience.
H. No, because the essay describes the monument as part of a broader concern with its creator, who has produced numerous public structures.
J. No, because public reaction to the monument is downplayed in the essay in favor of objective information.

PASSAGE XXVII

Zora Neale Hurston, Folklorist

The Harlem Renaissance author Zora Neale Hurston
is well known for her novels, especially *Their Eyes Were
Watching God,* however, she was also a devoted chronicler
391

of African American folklore. In her collection of Southern
392
folktales, *Mules and Men,* Hurston, who was born and
raised in Eatonville, Florida, suggested her unique
qualification for this study when she said she had "the
map of Dixie on my tongue."

While she was studying anthropology at
393
Barnard College in New York that Hurston decided

391. **A.** NO CHANGE
B. even so,
C. but
D. OMIT the underlined portion.

392. **F.** NO CHANGE
G. with
H. for
J. on

393. **A.** NO CHANGE
B. During the time that she was
C. It was while
D. While

to hook up again with the customs, songs, stories,
  394
and games she had learned as a child. By her own

account, she took the wrong approach to gathering

folklore when, in 1927, she first returned to the South.
          395

When she asked them if they knew any folktales, they
              396
glanced at her nice car and "city" clothes, shook their

heads, and told her to look elsewhere. On her next trip,

she headed straight to her hometown, where she already

knew the people and the people knew her.

    In Eatonville, her hometown, Hurston went
         397

to places where she knew the oral tradition would be
                                              398
thriving. She eagerly sought out the porch of the general

store. 399 As people gathered at the store her first day

there, a wonderful outpouring of tales begun as members
                                         400
of the crowd vied for their turn to tell stories.

    Hurston also visited Polk County, Florida, where

she sponsored contests for the most imaginative tall tale.

The winners received prizes, and Hurston collected a

wide vastness of folklore. After the contests, people came
401

394. F. NO CHANGE
    G. reconnect
    H. unite
    J. bind

395. A. NO CHANGE
    B. that,
    C. and,
    D. OMIT the underlined portion.

396. F. NO CHANGE
    G. some of them
    H. people
    J. OMIT the underlined portion.

397. A. NO CHANGE
    B. Eatonville, where she had grown up,
    C. her hometown, Eatonville,
    D. Eatonville,

398. F. NO CHANGE
    G. has been
    H. will be
    J. is

399. The writer is considering adding the following true statement to the end of the preceding sentence (changing the period after *store* to a comma):

    where she had lingered as a child, absorbing what she would later call a "love of talk and song."

Should the writer make this addition at that point?

    A. Yes, because it helps explain why Hurston chose to visit the porch of the general store as part of her research.
    B. Yes, because it is the only indication that the general store had an important role in Hurston's work.
    C. No, because it has already been established that Hurston was interested in talk and song, making the proposed addition unnecessary.
    D. No, because it is irrelevant given the essay's focus on Hurston's work as an adult rather than on her childhood.

400. F. NO CHANGE
    G. would begun
    H. had began
    J. began

401. A. NO CHANGE
    B. tremendous prosperity
    C. major chunk
    D. wealth

to her on their own to share even more stories.
₄₀₂

Many of the tales Hurston heard during her Southern trips revealed interesting information:
₄₀₃
why the woodpecker has a red head, why the alligator is black, or how the snake got its rattles.

Other tales were exaggeratedly and humorous accounts
₄₀₄
of harsh bosses and smarter workers, or of trickster animals such as, Brer Rabbit and his cousins. In part
₄₀₅
because of Hurston's work, these vibrant stories live on.

402. Which of the following alternatives to the underlined portion would NOT be acceptable?
  F. still
  G. many
  H. much
  J. OMIT the underlined portion.

403. Which choice provides the clearest and most precise preview of the tales listed later in this sentence?
  A. NO CHANGE
  B. explained the origins of animal characteristics:
  C. offered important insight into the past:
  D. concerned long-ago events:

404. F. NO CHANGE
  G. exaggeratedly humorously
  H. exaggerated humorously
  J. exaggerated, humorous

405. A. NO CHANGE
  B. as Brer Rabbit
  C. as Brer Rabbit,
  D. as, Brer Rabbit,

PASSAGE XXVIII

Taking Wing

The view must have been a thrill each time: everything below so tiny and perfect, an eagle's-eye view of the landscape. From her wooden seat in the cramped cockpit. Facing the fuel gauges and compass that helped
₄₀₆
her plot her course, Amelia Earhart was on top of the world. In her goggles and leather flight cap, she must have grinned every time she banked the wings and headed into a cloud, on her way toward new records and destinations.

[1] Born in Kansas in 1897, Earhart broke what were
₄₀₇
then the rules for girls right from the start. [2] She was considered a tomboy and belly flopped downhill on sleds, climbed trees, and hunted. [3] Before long she was taking lessons and then her first plane had been bought. [4] By
₄₀₈
1928 she had become the first woman to cross the Atlantic

406. A. NO CHANGE
  B. cockpit; facing
  C. cockpit. She faced
  D. cockpit, facing

407. F. NO CHANGE
  G. Following being born
  H. After her mother gave birth to her
  J. After having been born

408. A. NO CHANGE
  B. bought her first plane.
  C. buys her first plane.
  D. her first plane is bought.

Ocean in an airplane. [5] She went on to set record after
record, <u>showing what a person from Kansas could do.</u>
₄₀₉
[6] She became fascinated with flying as a young

<u>woman whom</u> she took her first flight—with a stunt
₄₁₀

pilot. ☐411☐

In 1937 she <u>sat about</u> from Miami, Florida, with
₄₁₂
her copilot, hoping to become the first woman to
circumnavigate the globe by airplane. They had reached
New Guinea and completed three-quarters of their flight
<u>because</u> the outside world lost contact with them on July 2,
₄₁₃
1937, as they were en route to their next island destination.

[A] <u>In contrast, the</u> U.S. Navy searched the Pacific for the
₄₁₄
plane and its occupants for weeks before giving up.

[B] <u>Rumor's</u> have abounded ever since: perhaps Earhart
₄₁₅
was on a spy mission for President Roosevelt, or perhaps
she crashed and lived for years undiscovered on an
island. ☐416☐ It is most commonly assumed that she ran out

409. Given that all the choices are true, which one best
summarizes this paragraph's description of how Earhart
"broke what were then the rules"?

F. NO CHANGE
G. graduating from high school in 1915.
H. defying expectations and shattering gender stereo-
types.
J. having seen her first airplane when she was only ten
years old.

410. A. NO CHANGE
B. woman that
C. woman when
D. woman, however,

411. For the sake of the logic and coherence of this paragraph,
Sentence 6 should be placed:

F. where it is now.
G. between Sentences 1 and 2.
H. between Sentences 2 and 3.
J. between Sentences 3 and 4.

412. A. NO CHANGE
B. set about
C. sat out
D. set out

413. F. NO CHANGE
G. when
H. while
J. after

414. A. NO CHANGE
B. However, the
C. The
D. Furthermore, the

415. F. NO CHANGE
G. Rumors
H. Rumors'
J. Rumor

416. Which of the following true statements, if it were to be
added here, would best develop the point being made in
the preceding sentence?

A. A Coast Guard cutter, the *Itasca*, was stationed in the
Pacific to receive Earhart's radio transmissions.
B. After Earhart's first flight across the Atlantic, she
had been met with a ticker tape parade in New York
City.
C. Still another theory is that Earhart landed on a vol-
canic island that later sank into the sea.
D. Earhart's previous attempt to fly around the world
had started in Oakland, California.

of fuel and was lost at sea. [C] Amelia Earhart passed into

history, and from there into myth. The legend of her

achievements and of her mysterious disappearance still

captivates us. [D] Her much-photographed face, with its

chiseled cheekbones and daring eyes, remains a familiar

image. We may never know what happened to her, but in

our imaginations she continues to be very cool high above

the earth. 420

417.
F. NO CHANGE
G. past into
H. passed over
J. past over

418.
A. NO CHANGE
B. image, we
C. image we
D. image, while we

419.
F. NO CHANGE
G. still soars
H. continues to manifest her aviation skills
J. still exhibits expertise in monitoring her altitude and velocity, using various cockpit gauges

420. The writer wants to divide the preceding paragraph into two, so that the first paragraph discusses Earhart's final trip and speculates about what may have happened, while the second focuses on how she is remembered. The best place to begin the second paragraph would be at Point:
A. A.
B. B.
C. C.
D. D.

PASSAGE XXIX

Edmonia Lewis and Her Marble Cleopatra

In 1988, during a routine inspection of a salvage yard in the Chicago area, firefighter Harold Adams made a discovery that helped solve a 100-year-old mystery. Amid the debris, he came face to face with a monumental statue of a queen in the salvage yard. The work of art had such a commanding presence that he felt compelled to bring it to

the attention of people who might be able to identify, repair, and permanently protect it.

421. Given that all the choices are true, which one adds new information about the physical appearance of the statue?
F. NO CHANGE
G. as he looked around.
H. during his rounds.
J. on her throne.

422. Given that all the choices are true, which one provides the most specific information?
A. NO CHANGE
B. appropriate individuals that he could identify in the hope of making a difference.
C. persons with knowledge pertaining to the relevant subject at hand.
D. others with expertise in their professional fields, like he was a professional, but in a different field.

Eventually, the <u>statues identity</u> emerged. The
$\overline{}$
₄₂₃

woman depicted was none other than the Egyptian ruler

Cleopatra. The <u>artist was</u> Edmonia Lewis, born in 1840
$\overline{}$
₄₂₄

to an Ojibway mother and African American father. As

a young person, Lewis had studied at Oberlin College

before moving to Boston and later Rome, where she

joined a community of American sculptors living

abroad. <u>Carving Italian marble by hand,</u> Lewis
₄₂₅

portrayed <u>Cleopatra taking, her last</u> breath. *The Death*
₄₂₆

of Cleopatra was hailed by many critics as the most

impressive sculpture at the 1876 Centennial Exposition in

Philadelphia, the event for which it had been created. $\boxed{427}$

Shortly after the exposition, the statue

fell into mysterious circumstances that frustrated

the art lovers who tried over the years <u>to locate it.</u>
₄₂₈

Decades passed before the story of <u>it's</u> journey
₄₂₉

<u>were</u> pieced together. For a while, the marble
₄₃₀

<u>queen had resided</u> in a Chicago saloon. Later, it
₄₃₁

marked the grave of a racehorse named Cleopatra. By

the time Adams stumbled upon the two-ton statue, it was

---

423. F. NO CHANGE
   G. statues' identity
   H. statue's identity
   J. identity of the statues

424. A. NO CHANGE
   B. artist,
   C. artist, whose name was
   D. artist

425. The writer would like to provide information here about the method used by the artist to create the sculpture. Given that all the choices are true, which one best accomplishes the writer's purpose?
   F. NO CHANGE
   G. An experienced and accomplished artist,
   H. Though others had depicted the Egyptian queen in marble,
   J. To complete her worthwhile project,

426. A. NO CHANGE
   B. Cleopatra, taking her last
   C. Cleopatra taking her last
   D. Cleopatra taking her last,

427. The writer is considering deleting the phrase "the 1876 Centennial Exposition in Philadelphia," from the preceding sentence. Should the phrase be kept or deleted?
   F. Kept, because it indicates where the statue was made.
   G. Kept, because it identifies the event referred to in the sentence.
   H. Deleted, because it repeats information that is already provided in the sentence.
   J. Deleted, because it provides information that shifts the focus away from the sculpture.

428. A. NO CHANGE
   B. in an effort to
   C. to attempt to
   D. regarding efforts that would

429. F. NO CHANGE
   G. its'
   H. its
   J. whose

430. A. NO CHANGE
   B. was
   C. were to be
   D. would of been

431. F. NO CHANGE
   G. queen had resided,
   H. queen, had resided
   J. queen, had resided,

chipped, cracked, and covered with graffiti. Until it could be shipped to restoration experts, Lewis's masterpiece was
₄₃₂
stored—alongside paper turkeys, tinsel streamers, and

half-empty cans of paint—in a back room somewhere.
₄₃₃
    The Death of Cleopatra returned to the limelight in the 1990s when, after being meticulously restored, the sculpture went on display at the National Museum of American Art in Washington, D.C. Where it continues to
₄₃₄

inspire renewed appreciation all over again for a bold and
₄₃₅
gifted American artist, Edmonia Lewis.

PASSAGE XXX

A Peachy Winter Game

    One winteringly New England day in 1891, a
₄₃₆

Massachusetts YMCA teacher puzzled over how to handle
₄₃₇

a difficult situation. Outside, the air was frigid inside, the
₄₃₈
students were bursting with energy and ignoring their

lessons. They were, however, being quite disruptive.
₄₃₉

    The teacher, James Naismith, was a physical

education instructor and an ordained minister. He
₄₄₀

432. Which of the following alternatives to the underlined portion would be LEAST acceptable?

  A. sent
  B. delivered
  C. transported
  D. evacuated

433. Given that all the choices are true, which one provides information that is new and specific?

  F. NO CHANGE
  G. at a shopping mall.
  H. until it could be repaired.
  J. with assorted objects.

434. A. NO CHANGE
  B. When
  C. There
  D. The point that

435. F. NO CHANGE
  G. admiration and positive appreciation
  H. attention to its worth again
  J. appreciation

436. A. NO CHANGE
  B. wintering
  C. wintry
  D. winterishly

437. F. NO CHANGE
  G. puzzled, over how to handle
  H. puzzled over, how to handle
  J. puzzled, over how to handle,

438. A. NO CHANGE
  B. frigid inside
  C. frigid, inside,
  D. frigid. Inside,

439. F. NO CHANGE
  G. as the case may be,
  H. in fact,
  J. regardless of time,

440. Which of the following alternatives to the underlined portion would NOT be acceptable?

  A. instructor. Naismith was also
  B. instructor, he was also
  C. instructor; he was also
  D. instructor. In addition, Naismith was

believed that exercising the body was as important

as exercising <u>the mental capacities of</u> the mind.

441

Both, <u>in his opinion</u> nourished the human spirit

442
and built character.

Aware of Naismith's philosophy, a supervisor

challenged the instructor to <u>invent</u> an indoor game

443
that would encourage the use of mental and

physical skills. He gave Naismith fourteen days

to accomplish this task. In tackling his assignment,

<u>popular ball game elements were borrowed</u> of the day.

444

<u>The decision of his to start the competition</u> in the center

445
of the playing territory, as in polo. He would place a goal

at each end, as in football. A referee would return out-of-

bounds balls to the <u>players,</u> as in rugby.

446

Naismith wanted the goals placed high above the

players. This setup would require the players to throw the

ball in an arc to make a goal. A janitor gave Naismith two

large wooden peach baskets to use as goals. Naismith

attached the baskets to a running track elevated ten feet

above the gymnasium floor.

Before the start of the first game, Naismith developed

thirteen rules to encourage <u>competition the rules reward</u>

447

both physical ability and strategic planning. <u>Instead, he</u>

448
created an indoor game people could play vigorously and

competitively, one that exercises body and mind.

441. F. NO CHANGE
G. the thinking apparatus of
H. the mental attributes pertaining to
J. DELETE the underlined portion.

442. A. NO CHANGE
B. Both, in his opinion,
C. Both in his opinion;
D. Both in his opinion,

443. Which of the following alternatives to the underlined portion would be LEAST acceptable?
F. design
G. come up with
H. develop
J. bring forth

444. A. NO CHANGE
B. elements from popular ball games were borrowed
C. Naismith borrowed elements from popular ball games
D. Naismith's borrowing of elements from popular ball games

445. F. NO CHANGE
G. He decided the competition would start
H. Making the decision to start the competition
J. His decision, starting the competition,

446. A. NO CHANGE
B. player's,
C. players'
D. player's

447. F. NO CHANGE
G. competition and reward
H. competition, and he also made those rules to reward
J. competition. Rewarding it with

448. A. NO CHANGE
B. Nevertheless, he
C. On the other hand, he
D. He

With excitement in the air, Naismith divided his class into two teams. In a historic moment, he tossed the ball straight up at center court. Players then dribbled the ball, aimed at the baskets, and scored <u>points and his</u> students loved the new sport. What had started as a challenge on a winter <u>day had quickly evolved</u> into the first game of basketball.

449. F. NO CHANGE
    G. points and obviously his
    H. points and that day his
    J. points. His

450. A. NO CHANGE
    B. day, had quickly evolved
    C. day had quickly evolved,
    D. day; had quickly evolved

PASSAGE XXXI

An Evening Walk in Washington

During the day, Washington, D.C., bustles with visitors, but even after sundown many people gather at <u>they're</u> famous buildings and monuments. I'd heard that the city's attractions appear even more impressive after dark, <u>not only the historic monuments but also the excellent museums.</u>

Beams of light <u>enlightened</u> the exterior of the

White House, <u>and</u> every window glowed as the work of governing continued into the night. Tourists peered through the fence, pointing when they saw a figure passing by one of the windows. Could that be the president? Families from all over the world—<u>speaking</u> in a wonderful variety of languages and dialects—posed for photographs with the brightly lit White House as the backdrop.

451. F. NO CHANGE
    G. there
    H. it's
    J. its

452. Given that all the choices are true, which one most effectively leads readers into the rest of the essay?
    A. NO CHANGE
    B. and it's one of the most historic cities in the United States.
    C. so one evening I took a walk to see if this was true.
    D. the city having no skyscrapers to obstruct the view.

453. F. NO CHANGE
    G. illuminated
    H. irradiated
    J. inflamed

454. A. NO CHANGE
    B. which
    C. who's
    D. DELETE the underlined portion.

455. Which of the following alternatives to the underlined portion would NOT be acceptable?
    F. communicating
    G. conversing
    H. talking
    J. saying

A few blocks away, in the National Mall, I climbed the long flight of marble stairs to the portico of the Lincoln Memorial, located here even though Abraham Lincoln is buried in Illinois. The statue appeared to gaze down on the Reflecting Pool, where a little girl watched as her father twirled a flashlight to make its beam dance across the still
456 456

water. 457

[1] Across from the Lincoln Memorial, I joined a group of visitors heading toward the Korean War Veterans
458

Memorial. [2] Spotlights near the soldiers' feet, lit up the
459
men's faces, showing expressions of fatigue, concern, and determination. [3] The surrounding darkness enhanced the drama of the scene. [4] The memorial featured nineteen statues of soldiers arranged in a triangular formation. 460

456. Given that all the choices are true, which one provides information most relevant to the essay's purpose and links the sentence most effectively to the paragraph's concluding sentence?
   A. NO CHANGE
   B. which was authorized by Congress in 1911 and dedicated on May 30, 1922.
   C. where spotlights shone on the enormous statue of Abraham Lincoln.
   D. which, like other monuments on the Mall, is administered by the National Park Service.

457. The writer is considering deleting the phrase "to make its beam dance across the still water" from the preceding sentence. Should this phrase be kept or deleted?
   F. Kept, because its imagery adds effectively to the mood of the scene being described.
   G. Kept, because it provides an effective transition to the next paragraph.
   H. Deleted, because it is irrelevant to this paragraph about the Lincoln Memorial.
   J. Deleted, because its removal would eliminate redundant information from the sentence.

458. Which of the following alternatives to the underlined portion would NOT be acceptable?
   A. headed toward
   B. heading off
   C. heading to
   D. headed to

459. F. NO CHANGE
   G. soldiers' feet
   H. soldiers feet,
   J. soldiers feet

460. For the sake of the logic and coherence of this paragraph, Sentence 4 should be placed:
   A. where it is now.
   B. before Sentence 1.
   C. after Sentence 1.
   D. after Sentence 2.

Nearby, light reflected off the polished surface of the Vietnam Veterans Memorial's black granite wall. [461]

Etched with the names of fallen soldiers, <u>visitors had adorned the wall with flowers and American flags left</u> in remembrance.
₄₆₂

   <u>Indeed, evening</u>
   ₄₆₃

<u>proved as</u> an excellent time
₄₆₄
to visit the White House and the Mall.

<u>Many of the city's most important historic sites are located in this area.</u> What remained visible were the
₄₆₅
buildings and monuments that represented some of the most significant events of this nation.

461. If the writer were to delete the words *polished*, *black*, and *granite* from the preceding sentence, the paragraph would lose descriptive details that primarily:

F. support the writer's case for improving the lighting at national monuments.
G. describe the artistic process used to create the Vietnam Veterans Memorial.
H. reveal the narrator's frame of mind upon viewing the wall at the Vietnam Veterans Memorial.
J. help depict what the narrator saw at the Vietnam Veterans Memorial.

462. A. NO CHANGE
B. adorning the wall were flowers and American flags that visitors had left
C. flowers and American flags adorned the wall, left by visitors
D. the wall was adorned with flowers and American flags that visitors had left

463. F. NO CHANGE
G. Nevertheless,
H. Furthermore,
J. Lastly,

464. A. NO CHANGE
B. proven to be
C. proved to be
D. proven

465. Given that all the choices are true, which one provides the best transition from the opening sentence of this paragraph to its final sentence?

F. NO CHANGE
G. Darkness drew much of the landscape into the background.
H. This allowed me to visit other parts of Washington during the day.
J. One must actually walk around Washington to appreciate it.

PASSAGE XXXII

Drought—In My Front Yard

My house in Santa Fe, New Mexico, was shaded by an enormous blue spruce. It was a tall, elegant tree that kept the house cool in <u>summer, if</u> a bit chilly in winter.
₄₆₆
The tree was not native to the city; rather, it had been transplanted from the mountains east of the city.

466. Which of the following alternatives to the underlined portion would NOT be acceptable?

A. summer, even so
B. summer and even
C. summer, though
D. summer, while

Santa Fe is in one of the most arid regions in the United States, but last year conditions were so dry that a drought emergency was declared. We were on strict water rationing, and there was a ban on outdoor watering. [467]
By spring the needles of the blue spruce started to turn

brown and were dropped off. I watered it with every
_____
468
precious drop of water I could find. I carried dirty
dishwater to the tree. I kept a plastic bucket in the
shower and watered the tree in there. All my
_____
469

efforts failed the tree died.
_____
470

The dead tree was a horrific depressing
_____
471

sight, it continued to shed its dry needles all over
____
472
the yard. I called an arborist. In my neighborhood, you
couldn't simply chop a tree down and yell "Timber!" as
it fell. The tree would have to be "topped"—a delicate
job. [473] The arborist came and shook his head. "I feel like

467. At this point, the writer is considering adding the following true statement:

> Some cities restrict outdoor watering to "low demand times" as an alternative to a complete ban.

Should the writer make this addition here?

- **F.** Yes, because it provides an explanation of the terms used in the preceding sentence.
- **G.** Yes, because it suggests a method that could have prevented the event described later in this paragraph.
- **H.** No, because it contradicts the point made earlier that this city was under a "drought emergency."
- **J.** No, because it creates a digression that may distract the reader from the main focus of this paragraph.

468. **A.** NO CHANGE
- **B.** drop
- **C.** dropping
- **D.** are dropping

469. **F.** NO CHANGE
- **G.** from that.
- **H.** in that.
- **J.** DELETE the underlined portion and end the sentence with a period.

470. **A.** NO CHANGE
- **B.** failed but the
- **C.** failed. The
- **D.** failed then the

471. **F.** NO CHANGE
- **G.** horrified
- **H.** horrible
- **J.** horribly

472. **A.** NO CHANGE
- **B.** sight
- **C.** sight, therefore
- **D.** sight, as

473. If the writer were to delete the quotation marks around the word *topped* in the preceding sentence, the sentence would primarily lose an indication that the narrator is:

- **F.** using a technical term.
- **G.** making a sarcastic comment.
- **H.** feeling angry about losing the tree.
- **J.** directly quoting a neighbor.

an undertaker," he said. "Trees are dying all over town."

Then he cut off a section at a time and dropped the pieces
<u>onto the yard, climbing the old spruce.</u> He counted the
474
rings and told me the tree was fifty years old. Santa Fe's

last fifty years had been unusually wet; the next fifty

promised not to be.

   Without the tree, the front yard changed. 475 Some

cacti, which I'd never given much attention to went
476
wild, blossoming in crimson flowers. Four little piñon

trees—trees <u>more better suited</u> to the conditions of
477

<u>drought</u>—volunteered where the spruce had grown.
478
Best of all was the effect on a dwarf peach tree that had

struggled to grow. In the shade of the spruce, it had borne

two or three peaches a season. Now in full sunlight, <u>I</u>
479
produced forty. Each peach was succulent—a welcome

harvest in a dry season.

---

474. A. NO CHANGE
   B. Then he climbed the old spruce and cut off a section at a time, dropping the pieces onto the yard.
   C. Dropping the pieces onto the yard, he then cut off a section at a time and climbed the old spruce.
   D. Dropping the pieces onto the yard, he climbed the old spruce and then cut off a section at a time.

475. At this point, the writer is considering adding the following statement:

   I expected the changes would all be for the worse, but pleasantly they weren't.

   Should the writer make this addition here?
   F. Yes, because it gives evidence that, contrary to the arborist's warning, the drought was close to an end.
   G. Yes, because it provides a logical transition between the preceding sentence and the rest of the paragraph.
   H. No, because it creates a digression and therefore does not logically fit in the essay.
   J. No, because it conflicts with the narrator's feelings about the changes to the yard expressed in the rest of this paragraph.

476. A. NO CHANGE
   B. cacti, that
   C. cacti,
   D. cacti

477. F. NO CHANGE
   G. more better suitable
   H. much better suited
   J. much better suitable

478. A. NO CHANGE
   B. drought had
   C. drought, had
   D. drought

479. F. NO CHANGE
   G. they
   H. you
   J. it

Question 480 asks about the preceding passage as a whole.

480. Suppose the writer's goal had been to write a brief persuasive essay describing the devastating effects that poor drought management can have on an area's ecosystem. Would this essay accomplish that goal?

A. Yes, because it effectively uses the example of the dying spruce tree to illustrate the greater devastation to the area.

B. Yes, because it criticizes the Santa Fe government's response to the drought for compounding the damage to the surrounding ecosystem.

C. No, because it connects the effects on the narrator's yard with climate conditions rather than with drought management practices.

D. No, because it fails to connect the area's drought to the death of the blue spruce tree.

Chapter 15:
Answers and Explanations

Check your answers to the questions in chapter 14 with the following answer key. If you missed a question, review the answer explanations on the following pages.

Answer Key

1.	C	46.	G	91.	H	136.	D	181.	C
2.	F	47.	B	92.	B	137.	H	182.	H
3.	D	48.	J	93.	J	138.	D	183.	B
4.	J	49.	C	94.	B	139.	G	184.	G
5.	A	50.	F	95.	J	140.	A	185.	D
6.	G	51.	B	96.	D	141.	F	186.	H
7.	A	52.	G	97.	F	142.	D	187.	A
8.	J	53.	A	98.	A	143.	G	188.	H
9.	C	54.	H	99.	H	144.	A	189.	A
10.	F	55.	C	100.	C	145.	F	190.	G
11.	A	56.	H	101.	F	146.	C	191.	D
12.	G	57.	B	102.	D	147.	H	192.	F
13.	D	58.	F	103.	J	148.	C	193.	C
14.	J	59.	C	104.	B	149.	H	194.	G
15.	A	60.	F	105.	J	150.	D	195.	B
16.	H	61.	C	106.	B	151.	A	196.	F
17.	D	62.	H	107.	J	152.	G	197.	C
18.	F	63.	B	108.	C	153.	C	198.	F
19.	C	64.	G	109.	F	154.	H	199.	D
20.	J	65.	C	110.	D	155.	B	200.	H
21.	C	66.	H	111.	G	156.	J	201.	D
22.	F	67.	A	112.	B	157.	C	202.	G
23.	B	68.	F	113.	G	158.	J	203.	C
24.	J	69.	B	114.	A	159.	B	204.	F
25.	A	70.	F	115.	F	160.	F	205.	D
26.	J	71.	D	116.	A	161.	D	206.	J
27.	B	72.	J	117.	J	162.	F	207.	D
28.	H	73.	D	118.	C	163.	A	208.	F
29.	D	74.	G	119.	J	164.	G	209.	B
30.	F	75.	D	120.	A	165.	D	210.	F
31.	B	76.	C	121.	J	166.	A	211.	D
32.	F	77.	G	122.	B	167.	H	212.	H
33.	C	78.	A	123.	H	168.	A	213.	C
34.	F	79.	F	124.	A	169.	J	214.	F
35.	D	80.	C	125.	J	170.	B	215.	B
36.	H	81.	G	126.	C	171.	F	216.	H
37.	D	82.	C	127.	F	172.	C	217.	D
38.	J	83.	F	128.	B	173.	H	218.	J
39.	B	84.	D	129.	F	174.	D	219.	B
40.	F	85.	J	130.	D	175.	F	220.	F
41.	C	86.	B	131.	F	176.	C	221.	A
42.	J	87.	J	132.	B	177.	G	222.	F
43.	D	88.	B	133.	G	178.	D	223.	C
44.	G	89.	H	134.	C	179.	G	224.	H
45.	B	90.	C	135.	J	180.	C	225.	D
								226.	F
								227.	D
								228.	F
								229.	A

230.	J	281.	F	332.	H	383.	B	434.	C
231.	B	282.	C	333.	D	384.	J	435.	J
232.	G	283.	J	334.	F	385.	C	436.	C
233.	B	284.	C	335.	C	386.	J	437.	F
234.	F	285.	H	336.	F	387.	B	438.	D
235.	A	286.	D	337.	B	388.	F	439.	H
236.	H	287.	J	338.	G	389.	C	440.	B
237.	D	288.	B	339.	D	390.	H	441.	J
238.	H	289.	F	340.	H	391.	C	442.	B
239.	D	290.	A	341.	B	392.	F	443.	J
240.	H	291.	J	342.	H	393.	C	444.	C
241.	C	292.	D	343.	A	394.	G	445.	G
242.	J	293.	F	344.	J	395.	A	446.	A
243.	A	294.	A	345.	A	396.	H	447.	G
244.	H	295.	J	346.	J	397.	D	448.	D
245.	B	296.	A	347.	C	398.	F	449.	J
246.	J	297.	H	348.	J	399.	A	450.	A
247.	A	298.	B	349.	C	400.	J	451.	J
248.	H	299.	F	350.	G	401.	D	452.	C
249.	C	300.	D	351.	C	402.	H	453.	G
250.	G	301.	G	352.	F	403.	B	454.	A
251.	B	302.	B	353.	D	404.	J	455.	J
252.	F	303.	F	354.	F	405.	B	456.	C
253.	B	304.	B	355.	A	406.	D	457.	F
254.	G	305.	J	356.	H	407.	F	458.	B
255.	C	306.	B	357.	B	408.	B	459.	G
256.	B	307.	J	358.	J	409.	H	460.	C
257.	F	308.	A	359.	B	410.	C	461.	J
258.	D	309.	H	360.	J	411.	H	462.	D
259.	H	310.	C	361.	B	412.	D	463.	F
260.	A	311.	G	362.	J	413.	G	464.	C
261.	J	312.	C	363.	A	414.	C	465.	G
262.	D	313.	F	364.	G	415.	G	466.	A
263.	H	314.	B	365.	D	416.	C	467.	J
264.	B	315.	J	366.	F	417.	F	468.	B
265.	J	316.	C	367.	C	418.	A	469.	G
266.	C	317.	H	368.	J	419.	G	470.	C
267.	H	318.	B	369.	A	420.	C	471.	J
268.	A	319.	H	370.	J	421.	J	472.	D
269.	G	320.	A	371.	C	422.	A	473.	F
270.	B	321.	H	372.	J	423.	H	474.	B
271.	G	322.	B	373.	B	424.	A	475.	G
272.	D	323.	J	374.	H	425.	F	476.	D
273.	H	324.	C	375.	C	426.	C	477.	H
274.	D	325.	J	376.	F	427.	G	478.	A
275.	F	326.	D	377.	B	428.	A	479.	J
276.	B	327.	G	378.	J	429.	H	480.	C
277.	G	328.	B	379.	A	430.	B		
278.	B	329.	H	380.	G	431.	F		
279.	F	330.	A	381.	A	432.	D		
280.	C	331.	D	382.	G	433.	G		

Explanatory Answers

ENGLISH • EXPLANATORY ANSWERS

Passage I

Question 1. The best answer is C because the comma after *tribe* sets off what follows as a nonrestrictive appositive that describes what "the Miami tribe" is: "a Native American people with strong ties to territory in present-day Ohio, Indiana, and Illinois."

The best answer is NOT:

A because it is missing the comma needed after *tribe* to set off the following nonrestrictive appositive from the noun *tribe* and because it places an unnecessary and confusing comma between the noun *people* and the series of prepositional phrases starting with "with strong ties" that follows and describes *people*.

B because it pointlessly separates with a comma the adjective *Native American* from the noun *people*.

D because it misuses the semicolon. The semicolon inappropriately implies that what will follow is an independent clause, as in "My family is part of the Miami tribe; we are a Native American people. . ."

Question 2. The best answer is F because "making freezer jam or researching tribal history" gives the most specific and vivid glimpse of what the grandmother was interested in.

The best answer is NOT:

G because "being actively involved in her pursuits" is vague and gives no suggestion of what those pursuits are.

H because "things I really hope she'll teach me one day" gives no suggestion of what those things are.

J because "historical research as well as domestic projects" offers only a general notion of the interests that are more pointedly described in **F**.

Question 3. The best answer is D because the word *rushed* by itself is sufficient to express the idea "urged to hasten."

The best answer is NOT:

A because the word *rushed* and the phrase "in a hurry" are redundant.

B because the words *hurried* and *rushed* are redundant.

C because the phrase "made to go faster" and the word *rushed* are redundant.

Question 4. The best answer is **J** because a comma is appropriate between the long introductory adverbial clause "if we were running late for an appointment" and the sentence's main clause, which begins with *she.*

The best answer is NOT:

F because placing a period after the word *appointment* makes the introductory adverbial clause (subordinated by the conjunction *if*) into a sentence fragment and because doing so obscures how the ideas are related.

G because placing a semicolon after the word *appointment* makes the introductory adverbial clause into a sentence fragment and obscures how the ideas are related.

H because the coordinating conjunction *and* should not be used to join two unequal sentence elements, such as a subordinate clause and a main clause, as would be the case here.

Question 5. The best answer is **A** because it opens this paragraph with a general statement about the concept of Miami time and serves as the most logical link between the preceding paragraph and the subject of this paragraph.

The best answer is NOT:

B because the reference to the doctor's appointment is only loosely related to the end of the preceding paragraph and to the subject of this paragraph, which is defining and describing the concept of Miami time.

C because the general reference to the relationship between the narrator and the grandmother is only loosely related to the subject of this paragraph, which is defining and describing the concept of Miami time.

D because the general reference to the son being curious about and having never met the grandmother is only loosely related to the subject of this paragraph, which is defining and describing the concept of Miami time.

Question 6. The best answer is **G** because the dependent clause "when time seemed to slow down or stand still" is necessary information to explain which moments are being referred to and thus should not be set off from the rest of the sentence by a comma.

The best answer is NOT:

F because the comma between the words *moments* and *when* identifies the information in the dependent clause "when time seemed to slow down or stand still" as unnecessary information when, in fact, the clause is vital to defining the moments of Miami time.

H because the comma between the words *moments* and *as if* identifies the information in the dependent clause "as if time seemed to slow down or stand still" as unnecessary information and because the conjunction *as if* does not appropriately link the ideas in this sentence.

J because the comma between the words *moments* and *because* identifies the information in the dependent clause "because time seemed to slow down or stand still" as unnecessary information and because the conjunction *because* does not appropriately link the ideas in this sentence.

Question 7. The best answer is **A** because the word *words* by itself is a sufficient, clear, and appropriate way to refer to what the grandmother had said.

The best answer is NOT:

B because the phrase "spoken statements to my ears" is clumsy, wordy, and overly formal for the tone of the essay.

C because the phrase "expressed opinions on the matter" is wordy and overly formal for the tone of the essay.

D because the phrase "verbal remarks in conversation" is wordy, redundant, and overly formal for the tone of the essay.

Question 8. The best answer is **J** because the past tense verb *slipped* appropriately describes an event that occurred in the past and is consistent with the other past tense verbs used throughout the essay.

The best answer is NOT:

F because the verb *will slip* describes a past event in future tense.

G because the verb *slip* describes a past event in present tense.

H because the verb *are slipping* describes a past event in present progressive tense.

Question 9. The best answer is **C** because *thinking* is the second half of a compound verb (*was pushing and . . . thinking*). The words *I was* are implied in front of *thinking*.

The best answer is NOT:

A because the plural verb *were thinking* doesn't agree with the singular subject *I*.

B because the plural verb *were having* doesn't agree with the singular subject *I*.

D because deleting the underlined portion would leave the second part of the sentence without a verb ("I was pushing Jeremy in his stroller and of the day ahead . . .").

Question 10. The best answer is **F** because no punctuation should interrupt the compound subject "two does and three fawns" or separate it from the rest of the sentence.

The best answer is NOT:

G because it places an unnecessary comma between parts of the compound subject.

H because it places an unnecessary comma between the compound subject and the verb *stood*.

J because it places an unnecessary comma between parts of the compound subject.

Question 11. The best answer is **A** because sentence 3, which introduces the deer, fits logically between sentence 2's reference to Jeremy squealing and pointing at the clearing and sentence 4's reference to the movement of the deer's ears.

The best answer is NOT:

B because the word *there* in sentence 3 would have no logical antecedent, leaving unclear where the deer are. Also, the setting for the paragraph, revealed in Sentence 1 ("a familiar trail near our house"), would not yet have been established.

C because the narration in the first part of the paragraph involves a surprise: the pair are out for a walk (sentence 1), then Jeremy suddenly squeals and points (sentence 2), and then the surprise is explained (sentence 3). Placing the revelation in sentence 3 ahead of what happens "suddenly" in sentence 2 removes the surprise.

D because the word *there* in sentence 3 would have no logical antecedent in sentence 4, leaving unclear what *there* refers to. Also, the more general introduction to the deer in sentence 3 ("two does and three fawns") should occur before the more specific reference to the deer in sentence 4 ("five pairs of ears").

Question 12. The best answer is **G** because the word *rustling* is parallel in form to *lazing* earlier in the sentence. Together, these two words help form the compound subject of the verb *surprised* ("Lizards lazing . . . and quail rustling . . . surprised us").

The best answer is NOT:

F because *rustled* isn't parallel in form to *lazing* previously in the sentence, and this lack of parallelism creates an ungrammatical sentence ("Lizards lazing in the sun and quail rustled through grasses surprised us").

H because *were rustling* isn't parallel in form to *lazing* previously in the sentence, and this lack of parallelism creates an ungrammatical sentence ("Lizards lazing in the sun and quail were rustling through grasses surprised us").

J because deleting the underlined portion creates an ungrammatical, nonsensical sentence ("Lizards lazing in the sun and quail through grasses surprised us").

Question 13. The best answer is **D** because no transition word or phrase is necessary here to make the sentence part of a list of sensory experiences the narrator and son had: seeing lizards and quail, eating wild blackberries, and smelling crushed eucalyptus leaves.

The best answer is NOT:

A because the phrase "For example" illogically suggests that the aroma of crushed eucalyptus leaves is an example of the taste of wild blackberries rather than being the third item in a list of sensory experiences.

B because the phrase "On the other hand" illogically suggests that the aroma of crushed eucalyptus leaves is somehow in opposition to the taste of wild blackberries rather than being the third item in a list of sensory experiences.

C because the phrase "Just in case" makes no sense in this context; it is unclear what smelling the aroma of crushed eucalyptus leaves would be designed to prevent.

Question 14. The best answer is **J** because "shorter than" is the correct comparative form to use to contrast how long the 3-hour hike seemed to take with how long the normal-length hike usually seemed.

The best answer is NOT:

F because the adverb *then* is incorrectly used instead of the preposition *than* to introduce the second part of the comparison.

G because *more shorter* is an incorrectly formed comparative term and because the adverb *then* is incorrectly used instead of the preposition *than* to introduce the second part of the comparison.

H because *shortest* is a superlative term used here incorrectly to compare two things.

Question 15. The best answer is **A** because most of the essay narrates a hike that took a long time but seemed short, the rhetorical aim being to illustrate one of the narrator's personal experiences with Miami time because that concept is defined in the early part of the essay.

The best answer is NOT:

B because although the essay has met the goal specified in the question, which was to convey a personal experience with Miami time, the reason given here is inaccurate. The essay doesn't reveal whether the narrator decided to live in Miami time, nor is it clear that one can actually choose to live always in Miami time.

C because the essay has met the goal specified in the question, which was to convey a personal experience with Miami time. That the grandmother's view of Miami time is represented doesn't detract from the fact that the essay still relates the narrator's personal experience.

D because the essay has met the goal specified in the question, which was to convey a personal experience with Miami time. It is unclear what it would mean for the term *Miami time* to *belong* to the grandmother; in any case, the essay indicates that the narrator and the grandmother came to share a similar sense of Miami time.

Passage II

Question 16. The best answer is **H** because the meaning here is clearest when the ideas are divided into two sentences, with the first sentence giving a general description of the artwork and the second describing the eight women in the artwork more specifically.

The best answer is NOT:

F because the relative pronoun *that* should be used to connect an adjectival clause to a main clause, not two main clauses. *That* in this position would logically refer to the immediately preceding noun, *flowers*, which makes no sense here.

G because the coordinating conjunction *and* creates a rambling sentence in which it's difficult to tell where one thought ends and the next begins, especially without a comma before *and*.

J because using only the comma after the word *flowers* to join two independent clauses creates a comma splice.

ENGLISH • EXPLANATORY ANSWERS

Question 17. The best answer is **D** because no transition word is necessary here to link the two questions posed at the end of the essay's first paragraph with the answers that unfold beginning in the second paragraph.

The best answer is NOT:

A because the word *thus* illogically suggests that the fact that the answers to the questions posed at the end of the essay's first paragraph can be found in the artwork itself is a result of the questions being posed.

B because the word *instead* illogically sets up a contrast between the questions posed at the end of the essay's first paragraph and the fact that the answers can be found in the artwork itself.

C because the word *furthermore* illogically suggests that something additional but similar to the questions posed at the end of the essay's first paragraph is coming next (mostly likely, more questions), when, in fact, the essay switches to discussing the answers to the questions.

Question 18. The best answer is **F** because the word order creates a clear, understandable sentence.

The best answer is NOT:

G because the placement of the phrase "the story" creates a nonsensical statement.

H because the placement of the phrase "of text" creates a nonsensical expression ("this gathering of text").

J because the placement of the phrase "on two horizontal panels of text" divides the phrase "the story" from the prepositional phrase that describes the story, "of this gathering."

Question 19. The best answer is **C** because *its* is the correct form of the singular possessive pronoun and agrees with its singular antecedent, understood to be the noun *piece*.

The best answer is NOT:

A because *it's* is a contraction meaning "it is" rather than the singular possessive pronoun *its*, which is needed here.

B because *its'* is an incorrect form of the singular possessive pronoun *its*, which is needed here.

D because *their* is the plural possessive pronoun, which doesn't agree with its singular antecedent, understood to be the noun *piece*.

Question 20. The best answer is **J** because the interposed explanatory phrase "the story explains" is properly set off from the rest of the sentence by two commas, indicating that the phrase could be omitted without changing the basic meaning of the sentence.

The best answer is NOT:

F because the interposed explanatory phrase "the story explains" is not preceded by a comma, which would be needed to set the phrase off properly from the rest of the sentence.

G because the interposed explanatory phrase "the story explains" is improperly set off from the rest of the sentence by a comma before the phrase and a dash after the phrase. Either two commas or two dashes would be appropriate, but not one of each.

H because the interposed explanatory phrase "the story explains" is not preceded by a dash, which would be needed to set the phrase off properly from the rest of the sentence.

Question 21. The best answer is **C** because placing the underlined portion after the word *cause* is the only one of the four choices that wouldn't be acceptable. This placement of the phrase "in their various ways" divides the phrase "the cause" from the prepositional phrase that describes the cause, "of justice." Therefore, all of the choices would be acceptable EXCEPT **C**.

The best answer is NOT:

A because keeping the underlined portion where it is now creates a clear and correct sentence in English.

B because placing the underlined portion after the word *support* creates a clear and correct sentence in English.

D because placing the underlined portion after the word *world* (and before the period) creates a clear and correct sentence in English.

Question 22. The best answer is **F** because the rest of the paragraph explains that the women depicted in the artwork lived at different times and so couldn't have sat together and made a quilt.

The best answer is NOT:

G because the phrase "in summary" illogically suggests that the sentence summarizes the preceding text, which it does not do.

H because the phrase "in addition" illogically suggests that the sentence directly adds to the preceding text, which it does not do.

J because the phrase "in contrast" illogically suggests that the sentence provides a direct contrast to the preceding text, which it does not do.

ENGLISH • EXPLANATORY ANSWERS

Question 23. The best answer is **B** because Ringgold is the only artist being referred to at this point; the singular possessive form of the noun *artist's* is therefore required.

The best answer is NOT:

A because *artists* is a plural noun, not the singular possessive form of the noun *artist's* that is required.

C because *artists'* is a plural possessive form of the noun, not the singular possessive form *artist's* that is required.

D because the phrase "artists imagination" uses the plural form of the noun *artists* instead of the singular possessive, *artist's*, that is required, and because **D** includes an unnecessary comma after the word *imagination*.

Question 24. The best answer is **J** because the plural verb *were* agrees with the plural compound subject, "Sojourner Truth and Harriet Tubman."

The best answer is NOT:

F because the singular verb *was* doesn't agree with the plural compound subject "Sojourner Truth and Harriet Tubman."

G because the singular verb *was* doesn't agree with the plural compound subject "Sojourner Truth and Harriet Tubman."

H because the singular verb *was* doesn't agree with the plural compound subject "Sojourner Truth and Harriet Tubman."

Question 25. The best answer is **A** because information about Wells speaking out for social and racial justice is highly relevant, given that the paragraph focuses on the causes championed by the women, including Wells, depicted in Ringgold's artwork.

The best answer is NOT:

B because information about the man Wells married is only marginally relevant to the topic of the paragraph: the historical reality behind Ringgold's artwork.

C because information about which newspapers Wells wrote for isn't as relevant to the topic of the paragraph as the information in **A**.

D because information about Wells's birthplace, birth year, and siblings is only marginally relevant to the topic of the paragraph.

Question 26. **The best answer is J** because the word *business* is sufficient, together with the words *her own* earlier in the sentence, to indicate that Madam C. J. Walker established her own business.

The best answer is NOT:

F because the intensive pronoun *herself* is awkward and redundant with *her own* and because the comma between the noun *business* and the intensive *herself* is unnecessary and confusing.

G because the phrase "belonging to her" is awkward and redundant with "her own."

H because the intensive pronoun *herself* is awkward and redundant with "her own" and because an intensifier, even when appropriate in a sentence, doesn't need to be set off by commas from the rest of the sentence.

Question 27. **The best answer is B** because this sentence structure makes "Madam C. J. Walker" the subject of the sentence, which is necessary in order to have the introductory participial phrase "establishing her own hair products business in the first decade of the twentieth century" refer clearly to Walker.

The best answer is NOT:

A because this sentence structure makes the introductory participial phrase a dangling modifier that refers to "millions of dollars," which doesn't make sense.

C because this sentence structure makes the introductory participial phrase a dangling modifier that refers to "charities and educational institutions," which doesn't make sense.

D because this sentence structure makes the introductory participial phrase a dangling modifier that refers to "millions of dollars," which doesn't make sense.

Question 28. The best answer is H because no punctuation is warranted in this underlined portion. "Among the schools that benefited from this generosity" is an introductory adverbial phrase that, because it immediately precedes the verb it modifies, should not be set off by a comma. Had the sentence elements been arranged in the more typical subject-verb-object order ("Those [schools] that Mary McLeod Bethune opened and ran in order to provide a better education for Black students were among the schools that benefited from this generosity"), it would've been more obvious that no internal punctuation is required.

The best answer is NOT:

F because the comma after the word *generosity* is an unwarranted break between the prepositional phrase and the verb it modifies.

G because the semicolon after the word *generosity* creates two inappropriate sentence fragments, as neither what precedes nor what follows the semicolon is an independent clause.

J because the colon after the word *were* is unwarranted; what follows the colon is not a series, a list, an explanation, or a clarification.

Question 29. The best answer is D because the phrase "movement of" creates a clear, complete sentence, with the preposition *of* heading the phrase *of the 1950s and 1960s.*

The best answer is NOT:

A because "movement, it happened in" forms a second independent clause in the sentence joined to the original independent clause by only a comma, creating a comma splice.

B because "movement, it took place in" forms a second independent clause in the sentence joined to the original independent clause by only a comma, creating a comma splice.

C because "movement, that happened in" forms a second independent clause in the sentence joined to the original independent clause by only a comma, creating a comma splice.

Question 30. The best answer is F because the sentence under consideration interprets what the flowers represent ("seem to celebrate") and makes a concluding reference to the main focus of the essay ("the women's accomplishments and the beauty of their shared vision").

The best answer is NOT:

G because the sentence under consideration makes no comparison of Ringgold to the women depicted in the artwork.

H because the sentence under consideration says nothing about a brushwork technique.

J because the sentence under consideration offers no evaluation of Ringgold's artistic talent, only an interpretation of what the flowers represent ("seem to celebrate").

Passage III

Question 31. **The best answer is B** because the plural present perfect verb *have allowed* agrees with the plural subject *times* and indicates appropriately that the creation of spectacular science fiction films continues.

The best answer is NOT:

A because the singular present perfect verb *has allowed* doesn't agree with the plural subject *times*.

C because the singular verb *allows* doesn't agree with the plural subject *times*.

D because the singular past progressive verb *was allowing* doesn't agree with the plural subject *times* and incorrectly indicates that the creation of spectacular science fiction films ended in the past.

Question 32. **The best answer is F** because the relative adverb *when* is appropriately used to follow a time expression ("in 1902"); no punctuation is needed.

The best answer is NOT:

G because the coordinating conjunction *and* treats a dependent clause ("when audiences first saw . . .") as a second independent clause, creating a nonsensical sentence.

H because the relative pronoun *which* logically refers to *1902*, both implying that audiences first saw the year 1902 (rather than first seeing a groundbreaking movie) and creating a garbled sentence.

J because the relative adverb *where* doesn't fit logically into this context, since *1902* refers to time rather than place.

Question 33. **The best answer is C** because *his* is the appropriate masculine singular pronoun to refer to the male magician Méliès.

The best answer is NOT:

A because the singular pronoun *its* refers to things, not people, and in the sentence would illogically refer to the camera rather than Méliès.

B because the plural pronoun *their* has no logical antecedent in the sentence.

D because *it's* is a contraction meaning "it is," which makes no sense in the sentence.

Question 34. **The best answer is** F because when a conjunctive adverb such as *however* is used in the middle of a sentence, it needs to be set off by commas.

The best answer is NOT:

G because the semicolon after the word *however* creates an abbreviated main clause ("he found out, however;") followed by an inappropriate sentence fragment ("that the public preferred live magic acts to filmed versions").

H because the phrase "out, however" lacks the comma after the word *however* needed to set off the conjunctive adverb from the rest of the sentence.

J because the phrase "out however," lacks the comma after the word *out* needed to set off the conjunctive adverb from the rest of the sentence.

Question 35. **The best answer is** D because sentence 1 explains what Méliès did after he was *undaunted* by the discovery that people didn't like filmed magic acts (sentence 5). He began *instead* to tell fantasy stories.

The best answer is NOT:

A because keeping sentence 1 where it is now would weaken the logic and coherence of the paragraph. The paragraph would begin with a reference to Méliès being *undaunted* and turning to fantasy stories *instead* before Méliès had been formally described in sentence 2 and before the incident that caused him to turn away from filmed magic acts had been related (sentences 3 to 5).

B because placing sentence 1 after sentence 2 would weaken the logic and coherence of the paragraph. The words *undaunted* and *instead* in sentence 1 would make no sense, because there's nothing in sentence 2 to suggest that Méliès had met with any problems.

C because placing sentence 1 after sentence 3 would weaken the logic and coherence of the paragraph. The words *undaunted* and *instead* in sentence 1 would make no sense, because there's nothing in sentences 2 or 3 to suggest that Méliès had met with any problems.

Question 36. The best answer is **H** because the sentence under consideration should NOT be deleted; it creates a transition between the preceding paragraph, about Méliès the magician, and this paragraph, which focuses on Méliès's exploration of special film effects.

The best answer is NOT:

F because the sentence under consideration mentions Méliès's "magician's eye" but doesn't otherwise describe his ability as a magician.

G because the sentence under consideration mentions "the basics of special effects" but doesn't begin to explain any of the techniques of trick photography.

J because the sentence under consideration doesn't indicate "that Méliès's interest in learning about trick photography existed before his interest in magic." The preceding paragraph, in fact, describes Méliès's interests as beginning with magic, then moving into filmmaking.

Question 37. The best answer is **D** because perfecting "eerie film entrances and exits" is a specific example of Méliès's skill and inventiveness.

The best answer is NOT:

A because the clause "he was able to do interesting things" is vague and doesn't give any specific illustration of Méliès's skill and inventiveness.

B because the clause "he used effects commonly seen in his stage productions" doesn't suggest that Méliès was particularly skillful or inventive; on the contrary, it suggests that the best Méliès could do as a filmmaker was to copy himself.

C because "his actors could enter and leave the scene" shifts the focus away from Méliès to his actors, which doesn't effectively highlight Méliès's skill and inventiveness and because relative to **D**, **C** is imprecise.

Question 38. The best answer is **J** because the phrase "exceedingly high" appropriately uses the adverb *exceedingly* in front of the adjective it modifies, *high*, which in turn modifies the noun *costs*.

The best answer is NOT:

F because an adjective is needed to modify the noun *costs*, whereas the phrase "highly excessively" consists of two adverbs.

G because an adjective is needed to modify the noun *costs*, whereas the phrase "exceeding highly" consists of a participle and an adverb.

H because the phrase "high excessively" reverses conventional word order.

Question 39. The best answer is B because the verb *fired* is sufficient to indicate the action clearly.

The best answer is NOT:

A because the words *fired*, *launched*, and *projected* mean essentially the same thing in this context, making the phrasing redundant.

C because the words *fired* and *projected* mean essentially the same thing in this context, making the phrasing redundant.

D because the words *fired* and *propelled* mean essentially the same thing in this context, making the phrasing redundant.

Question 40. The best answer is F because the noun *creatures* is sufficient to indicate clearly what the terrain was filled with.

The best answer is NOT:

G because the clause "who they now realize live there" adds only wordiness to the sentence, which already strongly implies that the space travelers realize that the hostile creatures they encounter live in the strange terrain.

H because the clause "whom they are encountering" adds only wordiness to the sentence, which already clearly indicates that the space travelers encounter hostile creatures in the strange terrain.

J because the clause "who are found there" adds only wordiness to the sentence, which already clearly indicates that hostile creatures are found in the strange terrain.

Question 41. The best answer is C because for clarity this sequence of events should be divided into two sentences, the first indicating that the travelers fall off the edge of the moon to escape and the second establishing that the travelers land in the ocean and are eventually rescued.

The best answer is NOT:

A because using only a comma after the word *moon* to join two independent clauses creates a comma splice. (Alternatively, it's possible to see the error here as a comma splice created by the comma after the word *ocean*.)

B because the phrase "moon after landing" creates a fused sentence. (Alternatively, it's possible to see the error here as a comma splice created by the comma after the word *ocean*, with the sentence then suggesting illogically that the space travelers fell off the edge of the moon after landing in the ocean.)

D because using only a comma after the word *moon* to join two independent clauses creates a comma splice. (Alternatively, it's possible to see the error here as a comma splice created by the comma after the word *ocean*.)

Question 42. The best answer is **J** because the past perfect verb *had begun* is made up of the past tense form *had* and the past participle *begun*. Past perfect is called for here because Méliès produced *A Trip to the Moon* long before interplanetary explorations had taken place.

The best answer is NOT:

F because *had began* is an improperly formed past perfect verb that uses the past tense form *began* instead of the past participle *begun*.

G because *would of begun* is an improperly formed verb that uses the word *of* instead of *have*.

H because *have began* is an improperly formed present perfect verb that uses the past tense form *began* instead of the past participle *begun*. (Even if the present perfect verb had been formed properly, it still wouldn't work in this context because the past perfect is needed to indicate that producing *A Trip to the Moon* occurred before interplanetary explorations had taken place.)

Question 43. The best answer is **D** because *disturb* is the only one of the four alternatives that, in the context of the sentence, can't reasonably be used as a substitute for the underlined word (*arouse*). "Disturb his audience's curiosity" is neither a conventional expression in standard English nor an appropriate innovation here. Therefore, *disturb* is the LEAST acceptable alternative to *arouse*.

The best answer is NOT:

A because the word *whet*, meaning here to stimulate or excite curiosity, is an acceptable, idiomatically appropriate alternative to the word *arouse*.

B because the word *stimulate*, meaning here to encourage or increase curiosity, is an acceptable, idiomatically appropriate alternative to the word *arouse*.

C because the word *awaken*, meaning here to stir up or stimulate curiosity, is an acceptable, idiomatically appropriate alternative to the word *arouse*.

Question 44. **The best answer is G** because the writer's assertion that *A Trip to the Moon* "provided the genesis for a film genre"—science fiction—"that still packs theaters" is both specific and consistent with the writer's point, made throughout the essay, that Méliès produced a landmark movie.

The best answer is NOT:

F because the assertion that "People are still going to theaters to see science fiction films" has no clear tie to Méliès's role in science fiction filmmaking.

H because the assertion that "Méliès made an important contribution to filmmaking many years ago" is vague and doesn't clearly express the writer's viewpoint about Méliès's role in science fiction filmmaking.

J because the assertion that "In Méliès's production even the film crew knew a lot about space" shifts the focus away from Méliès's own role in science fiction filmmaking.

Question 45. **The best answer is B** because the essay fulfills the specified goal by focusing on a single artist, Méliès, and explaining how he used his talents as a magician and filmmaker to produce the landmark film *A Trip to the Moon* and thereby inaugurated the genre of science fiction films.

The best answer is NOT:

A because although the essay fulfills the goal specified in the question, which was to highlight the contributions a single artist can make to a particular art form, the essay doesn't assert that Méliès's work as a magician never would have succeeded without the contributions of the artists in the film industry. Instead, the essay indicates that Méliès was a successful magician prior to having any association with film and filmmaking.

C because the essay fulfills the goal specified in the question and because the main focus of the essay is on a single artist, Méliès, and a specific film, *A Trip to the Moon*, not on the general process of making science fiction films.

D because the essay fulfills the goal specified in the question and because the essay doesn't suggest that it took many artists working together to create Méliès's success. Rather, the essay stresses Méliès's accomplishments as a magician and his central role in creating the film *A Trip to the Moon*.

Passage IV

Question 46. The best answer is G because the past perfect verb *had gone* is made up of the past tense form *had* and the past participle *gone*. Past perfect is called for here because if the Nancy Drew mystery series had gone out of style, it would have occurred prior to the events narrated here in past tense ("I thought . . ."). Furthermore, "gone out of style" is a conventional, idiomatic expression indicating that something has become unfashionable.

The best answer is NOT:

F because *had went* is an improperly formed past perfect verb that uses the past tense form *went* instead of the past participle *gone*.

H because *had went* is an improperly formed past perfect verb that uses the past tense form *went* instead of the past participle *gone* and because "went from style" isn't a conventional, idiomatic expression in standard English.

J because "gone from style" isn't a conventional, idiomatic expression in standard English.

Question 47. The best answer is B because the context calls for the auxiliary verb *would* to express the presumption expressed by "I was sure" (and to parallel *would have* earlier in the sentence) and calls for the present perfect verb *have been retired* in the passive voice to indicate the idea that the "sleuth" received the action of being "retired" to the library's back rooms.

The best answer is NOT:

A because *would of been* is an improperly formed verb that uses the word *of* instead of *have*.

C because *would of* is an improperly formed verb that uses the word *of* instead of *have*.

D because deleting the underlined portion leaves just the simple past tense verb *retired*, which isn't parallel to the other verb in the sentence, *would have*.

Question 48. The best answer is **J** because the possessive form of the word *library* (*library's*) is needed to indicate "the dusty back rooms of the library" and because no comma is needed between the words *dusty* and *back* since *back rooms* functions as a single unit (a compound noun) and *dusty* and *back* aren't coordinate adjectives.

The best answer is NOT:

F because the comma between *dusty* and *back* is unnecessary since *back rooms* functions as a single unit (a compound noun) and *dusty* and *back* aren't coordinate adjectives. (You couldn't say "the library's dusty *and* back rooms," for example.)

G because the plural form *libraries* is incorrectly used in place of the possessive form *library's* and because the comma between *dusty* and *back* is unnecessary since *back rooms* functions as a single unit (a compound noun) and *dusty* and *back* aren't coordinate adjectives.

H because the plural form *libraries* is incorrectly used in place of the possessive form *library's*.

Question 49. The best answer is **C** because of the four choices, the word *hundreds* provides the most specific information about the number of Nancy Drew novels in existence.

The best answer is NOT:

A because the word *heaps* is vague and too informal for the style and tone of the essay.

B because the phrase "a high number" is vague.

D because the word *plenty* is vague.

Question 50. The best answer is **F** because the comma after the word *novels* is needed to finish setting off the nonrestrictive appositive "the teenaged heroine of hundreds of young adult mystery novels" from *Nancy Drew*, the noun the appositive describes.

The best answer is NOT:

G because the comma after the word *alive* is unnecessary since the list of adjectives "alive and well and still on the job" is already linked by the coordinating conjunction *and*.

H because a comma is needed after the word *novels* to finish setting off the nonrestrictive appositive "the teenaged heroine of hundreds of young adult mystery novels" from *Nancy Drew*, the noun the appositive describes, and because the comma after the word *alive* is unnecessary since the list of adjectives "alive and well and still on the job" is already linked by the coordinating conjunction *and*.

J because a comma is needed after the word *novels* to finish setting off the nonrestrictive appositive "the teenaged heroine of hundreds of young adult mystery novels" from *Nancy Drew*, the noun the appositive describes.

Question 51. The best answer is B because the phrase "the mysteries" makes clear that the girls were reading Nancy Drew novels all summer long.

The best answer is NOT:

A because the pronoun *that* has no clear, logical antecedent. Though *that* is obviously intended to refer to the Nancy Drew novels the girls were reading all summer long, *that* is singular and *novels* is plural.

C because the pronoun *that* has no clear, logical antecedent. Though *that* is obviously intended to refer to the Nancy Drew novels the girls were reading all summer long, *that* is singular whereas *novels* is plural. Furthermore, "reading up on that" is an idiomatic phrase but one that doesn't work in this context. To "read up on" something means to learn about a topic, not to read a number of novels for pleasure.

D because "Liana and her friends were reading it over all summer long" is confusing in more than one way. First, we again have to ask what they were reading, because *it* doesn't logically refer to anything in the preceding sentence. Then "over all summer long" is a redundant phrase, with *over* being an extra, or superfluous, word.

Question 52. The best answer is G because the main clause of the sentence must have a subject (*she*) and a verb (*had followed*), and the verb must be in past perfect tense to indicate that Liana had already read the Nancy Drew novels *The Spider Sapphire Mystery* and *The Secret of the Crossword Cipher* before she went back to school.

The best answer is NOT:

F because "school and had" leaves the sentence without a main clause, creating an inappropriate sentence fragment.

H because "school, having" leaves the sentence without a main clause, creating an inappropriate sentence fragment.

J because "school, she" creates an inappropriate verb tense shift. The words "By the time" and "went back" signal that the past perfect verb *had followed*, rather than the simple past form *followed*, is needed to indicate that Liana had already read the Nancy Drew novels *The Spider Sapphire Mystery* and *The Secret of the Crossword Cipher* before she went back to school.

Question 53. The best answer is A because no punctuation is warranted between the verb *solve* and its direct object, *The Spider Sapphire Mystery*.

The best answer is NOT:

B because the colon between the verb *solve* and its direct object, *The Spider Sapphire Mystery*, is unnecessary and confusing.

C because the semicolon between the verb *solve* and its direct object, *The Spider Sapphire Mystery*, is unnecessary and confusing.

D because the comma between the verb *solve* and its direct object, *The Spider Sapphire Mystery*, is unnecessary and confusing.

Question 54. The best answer is H because this sentence names some specific settings for the Nancy Drew novels (Arizona, Argentina, Nairobi, New York) and uses the verb *had chased*, which suggests that Liana was so caught up in what she was reading that she felt like she was solving the mysteries along with Nancy Drew.

The best answer is NOT:

F because this sentence refers generally to "different places and various cultures all over the world" but doesn't specify any settings for the Nancy Drew novels and because the verb *had read* doesn't make clear that Liana was particularly interested in the novels.

G because this sentence refers generally to "many breathtaking adventures involving all sorts of colorful characters" but doesn't specify any settings for the Nancy Drew novels.

J because this sentence refers generally to "many new places around the world" but doesn't specify any settings for the Nancy Drew novels and because the phrases *through her exposure to* and *learned about* don't make clear that Liana was particularly interested in the novels.

Question 55. **The best answer is** C because the proposed sentence, concerning how many books are in one of the series featuring Nancy Drew, shouldn't be added at this point in the essay because it distracts the reader from the main point of the paragraph, which is about why the narrator and her childhood friends loved Nancy Drew so much.

The best answer is NOT:

A because while the proposed sentence does attest to the longevity and popularity of the Nancy Drew Mystery Story series, the sentence is out of place and largely irrelevant at this point in a paragraph mainly about the place Nancy Drew held in the narrator's childhood and that of her friends.

B because the proposed sentence, with its facts and figures, addresses the history of the Nancy Drew Mystery Story series, not why the narrator loved Nancy Drew, which is why the sentence is out of place and largely irrelevant at this point in a paragraph mainly about the place Nancy Drew held in the narrator's childhood and that of her friends.

D because while the proposed sentence shouldn't be added at this point, adding in information about the author of the Nancy Drew Mystery Story series would only make the sentence more out of place and irrelevant, given that the paragraph is mainly about the place Nancy Drew held in the narrator's childhood and that of her friends.

Question 56. **The best answer is** H because "her freedom to do what she wanted" is clear and is parallel with "her loyal companions" and "her bravado," used previously in the sentence to identify two other things the narrator and her friends loved about Nancy Drew.

The best answer is NOT:

F because "there was a love for her freedom to do what she wanted" is not parallel with the two similar structures in the sentence ("her loyal companions," "her bravado") and is awkward, wordy, and redundant with "we loved."

G because "a love for her freedom to do what she wanted" is not parallel with the two similar structures in the sentence ("her loyal companions," "her bravado") and is awkward and redundant with "we loved."

J because "the freedom to do as one wants" is not parallel with the two similar structures in the sentence ("her loyal companions," "her bravado") and because the impersonal and rather formal pronoun *one* is stilted and out of place in a sentence focused on Nancy Drew's qualities.

Question 57. The best answer is B because the word *therefore* is the only one of the four alternatives that, in the context of the sentence, can't reasonably be used as a substitute for the underlined portion (*also*). *Therefore* introduces something that is a result of something else, but *also* only signals the addition of one or more things. Thus, *therefore* is the LEAST acceptable alternative to *also*.

The best answer is NOT:

A because the word *furthermore*, meaning "in addition," is an acceptable alternative to the word *also*, as the two mean essentially the same thing in this context.

C because the word *likewise*, meaning "in a similar manner," is an acceptable alternative to the word *also*, as the two mean essentially the same thing in this context.

D because deleting the underlined portion doesn't change the meaning of the sentence much if at all. Even without the word *also*, the sentence is clearly adding to the list of qualities that the narrator and her friends loved about Nancy Drew.

Question 58. The best answer is F because the phrase "was able to solve crimes" effectively sets up a grammatically parallel list of notable things Nancy Drew was able to do: "solve crimes," "win golf tournaments," "kick bad guys in the shins," and "impress her father's distinguished clients."

The best answer is NOT:

G because the phrase "was capable of solving crimes" doesn't set up a parallel list of notable things Nancy Drew was able to do, as *solving* isn't parallel with *win*, *kick*, and *impress*, nor is it standard to say that Drew "was capable of . . . win golf tournaments," and so on.

H because the phrase "was good at crime solving" doesn't set up a parallel list of notable things Nancy Drew was able to do, as *solving* isn't parallel with *win*, *kick*, and *impress*, nor is it standard to say that Drew "was good at . . . win golf tournaments," and so on.

J because the phrase "solved crimes" doesn't set up a parallel list of notable things Nancy Drew was able to do, as *solved* isn't parallel with *win*, *kick*, and *impress*.

Question 59. The best answer is **C** because the semicolon after the word *successful* is appropriately used to divide this sentence into two closely related independent clauses.

The best answer is NOT:

A because the lack of appropriate punctuation and/or a conjunction between the words *successful* and *they* creates a fused sentence.

B because the lack of appropriate punctuation and/or a conjunction between the words *successful* and *they* creates a fused sentence.

D because "successful, knowing" creates a confusing, possibly redundant sentence, as it's not clear who knows what.

Question 60. The best answer is **F** because the phrase "those exciting adventure tales spiced with mystery" effectively supports the point in the first part of the sentence that what the girls in Liana's generation "need and love" is entertaining fiction ("the stories themselves").

The best answer is NOT:

G because the phrase "the answers to the mysteries of their lives" suggests that what the girls in Liana's generation "need and love" are stories that teach the girls about themselves, whereas "the stories themselves," used in the first part of the sentence, suggests that what the girls really want is entertaining fiction.

H because the phrase "a strong role model for their generation" suggests that what the girls in Liana's generation "need and love" are stories that inspire them, whereas "the stories themselves," used in the first part of the sentence, suggests that what the girls really want is entertaining fiction. The preceding two sentences in the paragraph also make the point that girls today don't need a "successful girl detective" as a role model.

J because the phrase "the ability to overcome obstacles" clumsily suggests that what the girls in Liana's generation "need and love" are stories that show a "successful girl detective" rising above adversity, whereas "the stories themselves," used in the first part of the sentence, suggests that what the girls really want is entertaining fiction. The preceding two sentences in the paragraph also make the point that girls today don't need a "successful girl detective" as a role model.

Passage V

Question 61. The best answer is C because the preposition *from* effectively sets up the long introductory phrase "From ancient Babylonian astronomers . . . to twentieth-century science fiction writers" that begins the sentence.

The best answer is NOT:

A because the words "there were" introduce another independent clause into the sentence, resulting in ungrammatical and confusing sentence structure.

B because the subordinating conjunction *when* creates a nonsensical introductory phrase and an ungrammatical sentence.

D because the adjective *those* creates a nonsensical introductory phrase and an ungrammatical sentence.

Question 62. The best answer is H because the clause "who penned spine-tingling stories of 'little green men from Mars'" is the most relevant to helping make the point that Mars "has often been a symbol of ill will and danger."

The best answer is NOT:

F because the fact that there are twentieth-century science fiction writers "whose works become best-sellers" isn't relevant to making the point that Mars "has often been a symbol of ill will and danger."

G because the comment that there are twentieth-century science fiction writers who have "wild imaginations about outer space" is too vague to help explain why Mars "has often been a symbol of ill will and danger."

J because the fact that there are twentieth-century science fiction writers "who created images of Mars in literature" doesn't say anything specific about the nature of those images or help explain why Mars "has often been a symbol of ill will and danger."

Question 63. The best answer is B because this sentence effectively ties together the bad reputation Mars has often had ("such negative associations"), described in the preceding paragraph, and the more recent interest in robotic and human missions to Mars, discussed in this paragraph.

The best answer is NOT:

A because this sentence about the United States competing with other countries to explore space is at best only loosely relevant to the topic of this paragraph, which is recent interest in robotic and human missions to Mars, and is unconnected to the topic of the preceding paragraph, which is Mars's impact on thought and culture.

C because this sentence about which year the United States founded its space agency is loosely relevant to the topic of this paragraph, which is recent interest in robotic and human missions to Mars, but is unconnected to the topic of the preceding paragraph, which is Mars's impact on thought and culture.

D because this sentence about Earth and Mars being planets in the inner solar system offers encyclopedia- or textbook-style information that is only loosely related to the topic of this paragraph, which is recent interest in robotic and human missions to Mars, and the topic of the preceding paragraph, which is Mars's impact on thought and culture.

Question 64. The best answer is G because the past perfect tense verb *had sent* is made up of the past tense form *had* and the past participle *sent*. Past perfect is called for here to indicate that one event in the past (NASA sending its thirtieth spacecraft to Mars) took place before another past event ("By 2003").

The best answer is NOT:

F because *would of sent* is an improperly formed verb that uses the word *of* instead of *have*.

H because the simple past tense verb *send* is inappropriate given that a past perfect verb is needed to make clear that NASA had already sent its thirtieth spacecraft to Mars "by 2003."

J because the present perfect tense verb *have sent* is inappropriate given that a past perfect verb is needed to make clear that NASA had already sent its thirtieth spacecraft to Mars "by 2003."

ENGLISH • EXPLANATORY ANSWERS

Question 65. **The best answer is** C because the participial phrase "prompting speculation" modifies in a clear way the preceding clause: by sending thirty spacecraft to Mars by 2003, NASA had led people to think seriously about the possibility of a human mission to Mars.

The best answer is NOT:

A because the subject *speculation* and the verb *has been prompted* begin a second independent clause joined to the first by only the comma after the word *planet*, creating a comma splice.

B because the words "to which speculation has prompted" create a confusing and ungrammatical construction, partly because "speculation has prompted" isn't a conventional, idiomatic expression and partly because the pronoun *which* has no logical antecedent.

D because the words "which is speculation" create a confusing construction because the pronoun *which* has no logical antecedent.

Question 66. **The best answer is** H because the phrase "Although few" begins a subordinate introductory clause that is set off from the sentence's main clause with a comma, resulting in a complete and logical sentence.

The best answer is NOT:

F because the lack of a subordinating conjunction in front of the word *Few* turns the introductory clause into an independent clause joined to the sentence's main clause by only the comma after the word *exciting*. The result is a comma splice.

G because the lack of a subordinating conjunction in front of the words "Maybe a few" turns the introductory clause into an independent clause joined to the sentence's main clause by only the comma after the word *exciting*. The result is a comma splice.

J because the lack of a subordinating conjunction in front of the words "Few, if any," turns the introductory clause into an independent clause joined to the sentence's main clause by only the comma after the word *exciting*. The result is a comma splice.

Question 67. **The best answer is A** because the nonrestrictive appositive "the most ambitious NASA project yet" is nonessential explanatory information that needs to be set off by commas from the rest of the sentence.

The best answer is NOT:

B because a comma is needed after the word *yet* to finish setting off the nonrestrictive appositive "the most ambitious NASA project yet" from the rest of the sentence.

C because a comma, not a colon, is needed after the word *yet* to finish setting off the nonrestrictive appositive "the most ambitious NASA project yet" from the rest of the sentence.

D because a comma, not a dash, is needed after the word *yet* to finish setting off the nonrestrictive appositive "the most ambitious NASA project yet" from the rest of the sentence. Although a pair of dashes could have been used to set off the nonrestrictive appositive, the writer uses a comma after the word *Station*, so parallelism requires that a second comma follow the word *yet*.

Question 68. **The best answer is F** because the information should be added to the sentence; the explicit detail about the amount of money actually spent on constructing the space station—nearly double the already high projected cost of $17 billion—strengthens the sentence's assertion that "NASA overspent on the International Space Station."

The best answer is NOT:

G because although the information should be added to the sentence, nothing in the information suggests, let alone proves, that space flight will be more affordable in the future.

H because the information would strengthen, rather than weaken, the point made in the paragraph about the high cost of human flight to Mars. If the actual cost of constructing the International Space Station was almost double the projected cost, it's reasonable to worry about the accuracy of the already high projections of the cost of sending humans to Mars. Thus, the information should be added to the sentence.

J because the essay's focus isn't on the human experience in travel to Mars but rather on the costs of manned and unmanned missions to the planet. The information isn't a digression but instead strengthens the point made in the paragraph about the high cost of human flight to Mars. Thus, the information should be added to the sentence.

ENGLISH • EXPLANATORY ANSWERS

Question 69. The best answer is **B** because *what* is the logical introductory word in the noun clause functioning as the direct object of the verb *imagine*, resulting in "what the final price of a human voyage to Mars would be." Turning this clause around reinforces the idea that *what* is the best answer: "The final price of a human voyage to Mars would be *what*?"

The best answer is NOT:

A because *if* is an illogical introductory word in the noun clause functioning as the direct object of the verb *imagine*. Turning the clause around makes this clear: "The final price of a human voyage to Mars would be *if*?"

C because *how* is an illogical introductory word in the noun clause functioning as the direct object of the verb *imagine*. Turning the clause around makes this clear: "The final price of a human voyage to Mars would be *how*?"

D because deleting the underlined portion results in an illogical, incomplete-sounding sentence: "One can only imagine the final price of a human voyage to Mars would be."

Question 70. The best answer is **F** because "robotic spacecraft launched in 2003" offers an effective description of the Mars Rovers.

The best answer is NOT:

G because "which captured the imagination of the general public" doesn't offer any specific description of the Mars Rovers.

H because "the products described at length in the media" doesn't offer any specific description of the Mars Rovers.

J because "familiar to many who watched the news coverage at the time" doesn't offer any specific description of the Mars Rovers.

Question 71. The best answer is **D** because the word *capacity* is sufficient to refer to the capability of the Mars Rovers to examine soil and rocks.

The best answer is NOT:

A because the words *capacity* and *ability* are redundant; they mean basically the same thing in this context.

B because the adjective *genuine* in the phrase "genuine capacity" creates a confusing expression; *genuine* suggests there might be some doubt about the Rovers' capability, but no doubts have been raised.

C because the phrase "potential capacity" is a confusing expression; *potential* suggests there might be some conditions or limits on the Rovers' capability, but no conditions or limits have been mentioned.

Question 72. The best answer is **J** because *age-old*, which means having been around for a long time, is a conventional, idiomatic expression that makes sense in this context.

The best answer is NOT:

F because the words *aging* and *older* are redundant; they mean basically the same thing in this context. "Aging or older visions" is also not likely what the writer intends to say here, because the writer suggests in the essay that there's a timeless appeal to the notion of human spaceflight.

G because "old age" creates a silly expression ("old age visions") that implies that visions of human space travel are held only by old people.

H because "aging old" creates a nonsensical expression ("aging old visions").

Question 73. The best answer is **D** because the phrase "Even so," meaning "despite that," effectively signals the contrast between the preceding sentence, which says that using only machines to explore Mars may take some of the romance out of space travel, and this sentence, which says that we nevertheless need to remember that the right machines can do as much as if not more than humans can and at a fraction of the cost.

The best answer is NOT:

A because the phrase "In other words" incorrectly indicates that this sentence restates or summarizes the preceding sentence. Instead, this sentence offers a contrast to the preceding one.

B because the phrase "For that reason alone" incorrectly indicates that this sentence offers a consequence following from a circumstance identified in the preceding sentence. Instead, this sentence offers a contrast to the preceding one.

C because the phrase "In that time frame" makes no sense in context, as no time frame is indicated in the preceding sentence. Instead, this sentence offers a contrast to the preceding one.

Question 74. The best answer is G because the word *at* creates a conventional, idiomatic expression ("at a fraction of the cost") that makes sense in the context of the writer identifying an additional consideration (machines doing as much as if not more than humans *and* at a much lower cost).

The best answer is NOT:

F because the phrase *such as* creates a nonsensical expression ("such as a fraction of the cost").

H because the phrase "but only" is missing the word *at* that would make it a conventional, idiomatic expression ("but only at a fraction of the cost") and because *but* suggests a contrast with what precedes it in the sentence when what follows is an additional consideration (machines doing as much as if not more than humans and at a much lower cost). (The writer here might have used "at only," for example, but not "but only.")

J because deleting the underlined portion creates a nonsensical expression. "A fraction of the cost" suggests that what precedes it in the sentence identifies a cost (e.g., ". . . less than one billion dollars—a fraction of the cost [of a human mission]"), but this isn't the case.

Question 75. The best answer is D because concluding the essay with the proposed sentence would blur the essay's focus on Mars and the cost of sending humans there.

The best answer is NOT:

A because although the proposed sentence may capture the emotion that is the basis for the space exploration described in the essay, the sentence is out of place as a conclusion to an essay focused mainly on the expense of a human mission to Mars.

B because although the proposed sentence may invite the reader to reflect on the insignificance of money in relation to the mystery of space, the sentence is out of place as a conclusion to a paragraph and essay on the expense of a human mission to Mars.

C because although the proposed sentence shouldn't be added at this point, the essay doesn't contain a chronological history of people who traveled in space.

Passage VI

Question 76. The best answer is C because it appropriately uses the relative pronoun *who* to introduce the clause that modifies *students* —"who join our senior class." Besides introducing that clause, the pronoun *who* also functions as the subject of the clause.

> **The best answer is NOT:**
>
> **A** because it creates a comma splice (two or more complete sentences separated only by a comma). The phrase "those teenagers" is the subject of the second complete sentence.
>
> **B** because it, too, produces a comma splice. In addition, it creates grammatical disagreement between the plural *students* and the singular *he or she*.
>
> **D** because it creates a run-on, or fused, sentence. There is no punctuation or conjunction (connecting word) between the two statements.

Question 77. The best answer is G because it provides the predicate *was,* which produces a complete sentence. Remember that a statement that has no predicate verb is a sentence fragment (an incomplete sentence).

> **The best answer is NOT:**
>
> **F** because it uses the verb form *being,* which is a participle. Because it is a verb form, a participle is often mistaken for the main verb in a sentence. This statement has no predicate, so it is a sentence fragment.
>
> **H** because it has no predicate verb. Without a predicate, the statement is a sentence fragment and does not express a complete thought.
>
> **J** because it lacks a verb and therefore creates another sentence fragment.

Question 78. The best answer is A because it correctly uses the pronoun *who* to introduce the clause that describes Ligia Antolinez. In this sentence, *who* is required because it refers to a person. The pronoun *who* is also appropriate because it functions as the subject of the clause.

> **The best answer is NOT:**
>
> **B** because it uses the object pronoun *whom* instead of the subject pronoun *who*.
>
> **C** because it uses the pronoun *which* when the personal pronoun *who* is required. In general, *who* refers to people and *which* refers to objects, events, or animals.
>
> **D** because it inserts an unnecessary pronoun, *she.* Because *who* is the subject of the descriptive clause, the pronoun *she* has no function in this sentence.

372 The Official ACT English Guide

ENGLISH • EXPLANATORY ANSWERS

Question 79. The best answer is **F** because this short sentence expresses a complete thought and is clear, concise, and grammatically sound. It also logically fits between the preceding sentence and the sentence that follows.

The best answer is NOT:

G because it creates a statement that is not logical. The conjunction (connecting word) *therefore* suggests a cause–effect relationship that makes no sense. The fact that the narrator "was a junior then" was not the cause of her not being in classes with Ligia.

H because it makes no sense. It illogically suggests that the narrator was a junior because she "wasn't in any of Ligia's classes."

J because it creates the same error as **H** does by illogically suggesting that the narrator was a junior because she "wasn't in any of Ligia's classes."

Question 80. The best answer is **C** because it adds a relevant detail that fits with the point of the rest of the sentence. The narrator didn't know Ligia but knew of her. The narrator "saw her at school events and had read a story about her." Considering the other choices, C provides the most relevant information about the narrator's familiarity with Ligia.

The best answer is NOT:

A because the phrase "which are sometimes supported financially by local business" is not relevant with regard to the narrator's knowledge of Ligia.

B because the information that the school paper "is written by students interested in journalism" is irrelevant to the writer's purpose here.

D because information about the narrator checking the paper "for local movie listings" is a detail that distracts the reader from the main point of the sentence.

Question 81. The best answer is **G** because the plural possessive form *hosts'* is the correct punctuation here. The phrase "her hosts' house" shows possession and requires an apostrophe.

The best answer is NOT:

F because it fails to use the required apostrophe to show possession.

H because again, it fails to use an apostrophe after the plural *hosts*.

J because although it does use the required apostrophe after *hosts,* it fails to use the required apostrophe to show possession in *Ligia's.*

Question 82. The best answer is C because it correctly inserts a comma after the word *year*. Notice that this comma is necessary to set off the nonessential clause "who had volunteered to move." A nonessential clause adds information that is not necessary to the main idea. Nonessential clauses are set off with commas on both ends.

The best answer is NOT:

A because it inserts an unnecessary and confusing comma after *move*.

B because it fails to insert the required comma after *year*. This comma is necessary to set off the nonessential clause that begins with "who had volunteered ...."

D because it inserts an unnecessary and confusing comma after *volunteered*.

Question 83. The best answer is F because it provides the best explanation of the host family's situation and why Ligia needed a place to stay. This choice provides relevant information to show that after the storm, the two brothers needed their upstairs room back— the same room that Ligia had been using.

The best answer is NOT:

G because it adds irrelevant information. The detail that the upstairs room "had been freshly painted" distracts the reader from the main point of the sentence, which is to show why Ligia needed another place to live.

H because the statement in parentheses, "it was a two-story house," is also irrelevant to the writer's purpose here.

J because if the sentence simply ended with "had to be moved," it would not clearly explain why Ligia needed a new place to live.

Question 84. The best answer is D because, of the four choices, **D** makes the point in the clearest, most concise way.

The best answer is NOT:

A because it is redundant; that is, it repeats an idea that has already been stated. The sentence states that the narrator was aware of "Ligia's problem." Adding that this problem "needed to be solved" is overstating the obvious. It is better to end the sentence with the word *problem*.

B because it, too, is unnecessarily wordy. The word *problem* already implies a *dilemma*.

C because it is incorrect in the same way that **A** and **B** are. That Ligia's problem "needed a solution" overstates the obvious and lacks conciseness.

ENGLISH · EXPLANATORY ANSWERS

Question 85. The best answer is J. You need to pay close attention to the stated question. It asks you for the choice that does *not* show that the narrator's "family felt confident about inviting Ligia to live in their home." In other words, the question tells you that the best answer is the *worst* word choice with respect to the writer's purpose. The verb *supposed* is the only choice that does not show that "the family felt confident," so it is the best answer to this question.

The best answer is NOT:

F because it does indicate the family's confidence. Because the family *agreed* to host Ligia, they "felt confident about inviting Ligia to live in their home."

G because it, too, does indicate the family's confidence.

H because the word *knew* is appropriate in this context and, like **F** and **G**, does indicate confidence.

Question 86. The best answer is B because it correctly uses the correlative conjunctions *not only* and *but*. Correlative conjunctions connect similar ideas and are always used in pairs. In this sentence, the pair is *"not only* did we have a room…, *but…* the house had seemed too quiet." The conjunctions *not only* and *but* logically connect the two reasons that the family agreed to host Ligia.

The best answer is NOT:

A because "not only … and" does not logically connect the two reasons, and it is not idiomatic (it does not conform to standard written English).

C because it is incorrect in the same way that **A** is. It creates a statement that is not logical.

D because it is incorrect in the same way that **A** and **C** are. It also fails to use proper correlative conjunctions.

Question 87. The best answer is J because it is the clearest and most logical, and it is the most structurally sound. The two clauses in this sentence are parallel and logically follow one another. The second clause, "she started teaching me … dance steps," logically follows "I introduced Ligia to my favorite music."

The best answer is NOT:

F because using the passive voice ("I started being taught by Ligia") makes the sentence confusing. It is difficult for the reader to tell what the subject and object of this sentence are. The arrangement of the sentence elements is also confusing and garbled.

G because it has an incorrect modifier. When a modifying phrase containing a verb comes at the beginning of a sentence, the phrase is followed by a comma. The word that the phrase modifies should immediately follow the comma. In this case, the modifying phrase "Introducing Ligia to my favorite music, at top volume," is followed by the pronoun *she,* instead of the pronoun *I* (to refer to the narrator).

H because the modifying word after the introductory phrase is correct, but the rest of the sentence is weak because it relies on the passive voice ("was introduced by me"). In addition, the phrase at the end of the sentence, "at top volume," is misplaced.

Question 88. The best answer is B because it uses the correct verb form. The entire essay is in the past tense, so the past tense *took* is required here.

The best answer is NOT:

A because it uses an incorrect verb form here—the past participle *taken* without an auxiliary (helping) verb (for example, *had).*

C because *had took* is an incorrect verb form.

D because it uses an incorrect verb form—the past participle *begun* without an auxiliary verb.

Question 89. The best answer is H because it appropriately uses the past tense verb form *(went)* to show that the event (Ligia's going home) occurred at a specific past time.

The best answer is NOT:

F because it inappropriately uses the past perfect tense. The perfect tenses are mainly used to show that one event happened before another event, which is not the case here.

G because it uses a future tense (in this case, the future perfect) to refer to a past event. You can tell that this is a past event by reading the sentence that follows.

J because it uses the present tense *goes* to refer to an event that happened in the past.

Question 90. **The best answer is C** because it concludes the essay by referring back to topics that were previously mentioned: that Ligia spoke Spanish and that she taught the narrator Colombian dance steps. In addition, it logically follows the preceding sentence by explaining how the narrator continues to make plans for a visit to Ligia.

The best answer is NOT:

A because it does somewhat follow the preceding sentence, but it does not refer back to any of the ideas mentioned in the essay. It is therefore a poor conclusion when compared with **C**.

B because this is a poor conclusion for the essay because it introduces an entirely new topic: joining the workforce.

D because although the essay does refer earlier to "senior activities," this is also a weak conclusion because it is a vague generalization. In addition, it does not logically follow the statement that the narrator is "trying to save enough to go see my new sister next year."

Passage VII

Question 91. **The best answer is H** because it uses a comma after *attend* to appropriately set off the introductory phrase from the main clause. Without this comma, the reader might be confused and think that the narrator attended the laundromat.

The best answer is NOT:

F because it adds an unnecessary and confusing comma between *college* and *I*.

G because it, too, adds an unnecessary and confusing comma between *college* and *I*. In addition, it fails to add the appropriate comma after *attend*.

J because, like **G**, it omits the comma after *attend,* producing a potentially confusing statement for readers.

Question 92. **The best answer is B** because it appropriately uses the present tense to describe an event that is happening in the present time. Notice that the writer begins the essay in the present tense ("the Save-U Laundromat *is* always open").

The best answer is NOT:

A because it makes a confusing tense shift from present (*is*) to past *(was)*.

C because it makes another confusing tense shift—this time from the present tense to the past perfect tense.

D because, like **A**, it makes a confusing tense shift from present to past.

Question 93. The best answer is **J** because no punctuation is needed here. The absence of punctuation creates the clearest and most understandable sentence.

> **The best answer is NOT:**

> **F** because it places a semicolon between two descriptive phrases, which is a misuse of the semicolon.

> **G** because it inserts an unnecessary and confusing comma between a preposition and its object.

> **H** because it places an unnecessary comma between the two descriptive phrases. There is no pause or separation between the phrases "across the street" and "from a drugstore." They belong together as one description.

Question 94. The best answer is **B** because it is grammatically correct. In this sentence, *cool* is used as an adjective to modify the noun *magnificence*.

> **The best answer is NOT:**

> **A** because *coolly* is an adverb, and an adverb cannot be used to modify a noun. (Adverbs generally modify verbs or adjectives.)

> **C** because it uses an adjective phrase—"magnificently cool"—where a noun is required. The complete phrase "The magnificently cool of the shade trees" is both ungrammatical and confusing.

> **D** because it uses an adjective phrase—"cool magnificent"—where a noun is called for. The phrase "the cool magnificent of the shade trees" is ungrammatical.

Question 95. The best answer is **J** because it states the idea most clearly and concisely. It does not repeat the same idea twice, and it does not add unnecessary words to the sentence.

> **The best answer is NOT:**

> **F** because it is redundant (repeats the same idea) and wordy (adds unnecessary words). The descriptive phrase "who wrongfully enter the property" is really a repetition of the same idea expressed by the use of the word *trespassers*. In other words, the descriptive phrase restates the obvious.

> **G** because it has the same problem that **F** does. The phrase "who trespass by walking on private property" adds wordiness and redundancy.

> **H** because it, too, is wordy. It is not necessary to state the obvious. It is already clear to readers that people "who ignore the signs and walk on the grass" are trespassers.

Question 96. The best answer is D because placing Sentence 5 after Sentence 3 makes the paragraph logical and coherent. If you read Sentences 3, 4, and 5 carefully, you will notice that Sentence 4 does not logically follow Sentence 3. The opening clause in Sentence 4, "But no one is ever around to enforce the threats," has no antecedent to connect it back to Sentence 3. The *threats* in Sentence 4 refer to the "signs … posted all over the lawn" that are referred to in Sentence 5. Therefore, Sentence 4 makes the best sense when it follows Sentence 5 rather than precedes it.

The best answer is NOT:

A because leaving Sentence 5 where it is now is not logical for the reasons explained above.

B because Sentence 5 would be a poor and illogical introduction to this paragraph because the reader would not know to what lawn the writer was referring. In addition, the paragraph would make no sense if Sentence 1 followed Sentence 5.

C because this arrangement of the sentences is also illogical and would confuse the reader. Placing Sentence 5 after the description of the laundromat in Sentence 1 makes no sense because the signs on the lawn are on the grounds of a school and are not part of the laundromat.

Question 97. The best answer is F because the singular verb *has* agrees with the singular noun *paneling*. Remember that the verb must agree in number with its subject (in this case, *paneling*) and not the object of the preposition (in this case, the plural noun *walls*).

The best answer is NOT:

G because the plural verb *have* does not agree in number with the singular noun *paneling*.

H because, like **G**, it has an agreement problem. The plural verb *were* does not agree in number with the singular noun *paneling*.

J because, like **G** and **H,** it has an agreement problem. The plural verb *are* does not agree in number with the singular noun *paneling*.

Question 98. The best answer is **A** because it provides the added detail asked for in the question. Pay close attention to the stated question. It asks for the sentence that would best accomplish the writer's wish to "further describe the laundromat's paneling." **A** is the only choice that accomplishes this goal. It further describes the "artificial wood grain finish" by showing that it was intended to resemble wood grain but doesn't.

The best answer is NOT:

B because it does *not* provide a detail that further describes the paneling. Although **B** mentions the paneling, it does not offer a further description of it. Rather, it adds a detail that is irrelevant to the paragraph.

C because it, too, fails to further describe the paneling. Instead, it offers an opinion about the color of the paneling.

D because it is incorrect in the same way that **C** is. It offers an opinion about the person who "chose that color scheme," but it does not further the description of the paneling.

Question 99. The best answer is **H** because it effectively links the new paragraph to the question implied by the preceding paragraph: Why does the neon sign promise friendly service? **H** also provides the most effective introduction to the information in the new paragraph.

The best answer is NOT:

F because it does not link the theme of friendly service that is questioned in the preceding paragraph to the description of the machines in this new paragraph. In addition, it shifts to a more formal tone.

G because it makes no sense. Being "across the street from a park" has nothing to do with friendly service. Besides, in the first paragraph, the writer states that "the park isn't really a park at all."

J because it misleads the reader into thinking that the topic of the new paragraph will be "washing machines."

Question 100. The best answer is **C** because it provides the correct adjectives *(many, few)* to describe the quarters. The phrase "too many or too few quarters" describes a relationship of number.

The best answer is NOT:

A because it is ungrammatical. It incorrectly uses an adjective of quantity *(much)* when an adjective of number *(many)* is required.

B because it incorrectly adds the modifier *too* to the comparative adjective *fewer*.

D because it is incorrect in the same way that **A** is. It incorrectly uses an adjective of quantity *(much)* when an adjective of number *(many)* is required.

Question 101. **The best answer is F** because the phrase "mostly older people from around the neighborhood" specifically describes the group of "regular customers" mentioned in the first part of the sentence. If the phrase were deleted, specific descriptive material would be lost.

The best answer is NOT:

G because the phrase is not a detail that provides a logical transition because the sentence that follows describes a different group of customers.

H because the phrase does not foreshadow the conclusion. The writer does not conclude the essay with "older people from around the neighborhood"; rather, the essay ends with all the people who frequent the laundromat.

J because this information is not understated. Also, it is not "important information"—essential to the essay—but, rather, an interesting and relevant side note.

Question 102. **The best answer is D** because it results in a complete sentence. The complete subject of the sentence is "a crowd of thirteen-year-old kids." The predicate *is* immediately follows this subject.

The best answer is NOT:

A because it creates an incomplete sentence. It improperly inserts the pronoun *that* between the subject and predicate, which results in a sentence fragment.

B because it is incorrect in the same way that A is. It inserts the relative pronoun *who* between the subject and the predicate and creates an incomplete sentence.

C because the use of the comma and the conjunction *and* generally indicates that the sentence contains two independent clauses, but in this case, there is only one independent clause. "Usually a crowd of thirteen-year old kids" is a phrase, not a clause, because it has no verb. Meanwhile, in the main clause, the predicate *is* disagrees in number with the subject *they*.

Question 103. **The best answer is J** because it is clear, concise, and structurally sound. It clearly expresses the idea that it is the writer who is imagining.

The best answer is NOT:

F because it has an ineffective sentence structure that results in a dangling modifier. When a modifying phrase containing a verb comes at the beginning of a sentence, the phrase is followed by a comma ("Imagining all these people,"). Following the comma is the word that this phrase modifies. Notice in this sentence that the pronoun *it* incorrectly follows the introductory phrase. The modifying word should be the pronoun *I*.

G because it creates a confusing and unclear statement. In the clause "It being that I imagine all these people," the reader does not know to what the pronoun *It* refers.

H because it has a dangling modifier. It has a problem that is similar to the one in **F**. The pronoun *I* should follow the introductory clause, not the pronoun *they*.

Question 104. **The best answer is B** because it is grammatically correct, and the verbs in the sentence are parallel (maintain the same verb tense). The appropriate verbs here are "nod and smile" because they correctly follow the auxiliary (helping) verb *would:* "someone *would* look up … and [would] nod and smile at me." Although the helping verb *would* is not repeated before "nod and smile," it is implied.

The best answer is NOT:

A because is ungrammatical. It incorrectly uses the third-person singular verb form ("nods and smiles") after the implied helping verb *would*.

C because the use of the present participle ("nodding and smiling") after the helping verb *would* is ungrammatical. Note also that that sentence lacks parallelism: "someone would look up … and nodding and smiling at me." There is an illogical tense shift from the present tense ("would look") to the present participle ("nodding and smiling").

D because it makes the same mistake as **A**. In addition, it results in an illogical statement.

Question 105. The best answer is **J** because it is the only choice that is a complete sentence with appropriate sentence structure. Notice that this sentence has a compound subject ("the Save-U Laundromat" and "its people"). This construction makes the subject of the sentence clear.

The best answer is NOT:

F because it inserts incorrect punctuation (a period) that results in two sentence fragments (incomplete sentences).

G because it also inserts incorrect punctuation. The clause after the period does create a complete sentence, but the opening phrase "It is comforting to know that the Save-U Laundromat" is *not* a complete sentence; the relative clause does not contain a predicate.

H because it has a confusing and ineffective sentence structure. Inserting the relative pronoun *that* between the conjunction *and* and the pronoun *its* results in a sentence with faulty parallelism. The first of these two relative clauses ("that the Save-U Laundromat") is incomplete.

Passage VIII

Question 106. The best answer is **B** because it correctly uses the relative pronoun *whose* to introduce the clause that describes the company that the narrator admires. The pronoun *whose* indicates possession and is appropriate here.

The best answer is NOT:

A because it uses a contraction *(who's)* instead of the required pronoun *(whose)*. The contraction *who's* means "who is" and does not indicate possession.

C because it has a problem that is similar to the one in **A**. It incorrectly uses the contraction *that's,* which means "that is."

D because it is creates an unclear statement, and it fails to use the proper relative pronoun *whose* to indicate possession.

Question 107. The best answer is **J** because it provides the best punctuation to set off the appositive "Bill Williams." An appositive is a noun or pronoun that identifies and follows another noun or pronoun. In this sentence, "Bill Williams" identifies "Glory Foods' president and founder." Appositives are set off by commas (except when the apposition is restrictive, such as in the phrase "my sister Sue" when I have three sisters).

The best answer is NOT:

F because it inserts an unnecessary and confusing comma between *president* and *and.* In addition, it fails to set off the appositive with a necessary comma between *founder* and *Bill.*

G because, like **F**, it inserts an unnecessary and confusing comma between *president* and *and.*

H because it fails to set off the appositive by adding the necessary comma between *founder* and *Bill.*

Question 108. The best answer is **C** because the third-person plural pronoun *they* clearly refers back to the plural noun *foods.*

The best answer is NOT:

A because the singular pronoun *it* has no logical antecedent. An antecedent is the word or phrase to which a pronoun refers. In this sentence, the antecedent *foods* is plural and requires a plural pronoun *(they).*

B because it has the same problem described in **A.**

D because it creates faulty coordination and a confusing statement. The phrase "and that they" does not effectively coordinate with "that while he knows."

Question 109. The best answer is **F** because it provides the clearest, most concise statement, and it uses modifiers correctly. Note that the pronoun *he* directly follows and correctly modifies the adjective phrase "as a young adult."

The best answer is NOT:

G because it creates a dangling modifier. The phrase "as a young adult" does not logically refer to or modify the noun phrase it precedes ("his cooking skills"). This arrangement of sentence elements results in a confusing statement.

H because although the wording is somewhat different, the problem here, a dangling modifier, is the same as that in **G.** Here, "his skill" is not "a young adult."

J because the problem is much like that in both **G** and **H.** In this statement, "the refinement of his cooking skills" is not "a young adult."

Question 110. The best answer is D because it is the clearest and most concise statement. The writer logically describes the Culinary Institute of America as "prestigious."

The best answer is NOT:

A because it is redundant. That is, it repeats the same idea twice: *prestigious* and *acclaimed* mean the same thing.

B because it, too, is redundant. It repeats the same idea three times: *famed, renowned,* and *notable* all have similar meanings.

C because the adjective *luscious* makes no sense in this context. Food might be "luscious," but an institute would not be.

Question 111. The best answer is G because the sentence parts are arranged in a logical order so that they modify the appropriate elements. This results in the clearest word order for this sentence.

The best answer is NOT:

F because the clauses are put together in a way that confuses the reader. The noun phrase "a line of Southern-inspired cuisine" doesn't connect logically with the noun and the clause that immediately follows it: "a time when there were no convenience foods designed for African American consumers."

H because it is ambiguous. It is unclear what is meant by the opening clause "He came up in 1989."

J because, like **F,** it strings clauses together in a confusing way.

Question 112. The best answer is B because it creates the clearest, most logical, and most concise statement. This is another case (like question 35) where the least wordy choice is best.

The best answer is NOT:

A because it is redundant. It states the same idea twice. The introductory word *Initially* is redundant because the sentence later states that "Glory Foods were *first* offered for sale in Ohio in 1992."

C because it is redundant. In this case, the words *originally* and *first* mean the same thing.

D because it is both wordy and redundant. The phrases "At the outset" and "the earliest" both imply the same thing.

Question 113. The best answer is **G** because it most effectively concludes this paragraph by continuing the theme of Glory Foods' business success. That Glory Foods "were being distributed in twenty-two states" logically follows the information that "sales were twice the original projections."

The best answer is NOT:

F because it changes the topic by discussing recipes instead of the company's success.

H because it shifts to an entirely new topic, that of "several other companies."

J because the use of the word *however* makes this statement illogical. As it is used here, *however* indicates that this sentence is going to contradict the statement in the preceding sentence, but this sentence does not do that.

Question 114. The best answer is **A** because no punctuation is needed here. The absence of commas makes this the clearest sentence.

The best answer is NOT:

B because it adds unnecessary commas and incorrectly treats " professional, advisers, and subcontractors" as if they were items in a series, but *professional* functions as an adjective modifying the noun *advisers*.

C because the unnecessary comma between the two parts of the compound direct object "advisers and subcontractors" adds confusion to the sentence.

D because it inserts an inappropriate and confusing semicolon between *advisers* and *and*.

Question 115. The best answer is **F** because without the qualifying phrases the sentence would give the impression that all the subcontractors and farmers were African Americans. These phrases clarify the writer's point that Glory Foods employs African Americans "whenever possible."

The best answer is NOT:

G because even without the phrases, Paragraph 4 clearly explains Glory Foods' attempt to employ African American contractors.

H because the phrases "whenever possible" and "much of" are not examples of wordiness; rather, they clearly inform the reader.

J because the phrases do not describe the subcontractors or farmers yet they are essential to the meaning of the sentence.

Question 116. **The best answer is A** because it correctly uses the infinitive form of the verb *(to evoke)* after the verb of intention *(is meant)*.

The best answer is NOT:

B because the verb phrase "is meant at evoking" is not an idiom of standard written English and confuses the reader.

C because it is incorrect in a way that is similar to the problem in **B**. The verb phrase "is meant in evoking of" is not idiomatic English and results in an unclear statement.

D because omitting the infinitive *to evoke* also results in a phrase that is not standard written English. The verb *is meant* needs to be followed by an infinitive verb form—in this case *to evoke*.

Question 117. **The best answer is J** because it is the clearest, most logical statement. The prepositional phrase "during the Civil War" clearly modifies "a black regiment." Modifying phrases should be placed as near as possible to the words they modify, which is why "during the Civil War" is best placed at the end of this sentence.

The best answer is NOT:

F because the phrase "during the Civil War" appears to modify "the movie." This placement wrongly suggests that the movie was filmed and shown during the Civil War. In addition, the phrase "of the same name" appears to modify "the Civil War" instead of "the movie."

G because the phrase "during the Civil War" appears to modify "the same name," which makes no sense.

H because the phrase "during the Civil War" appears to modify "of a black regiment." Again, the resulting statement "which tells the story during the Civil War of a black regiment" reads as though the movie was shown during the war.

Question 118. **The best answer is C** because it clearly explains why the writer should not add the information about the actor who starred in the film *Glory*. This information is not in keeping with the main point of the paragraph, which is to explain how the company got its name. Adding information about an actor distracts the reader from the focus of the paragraph and the essay as a whole.

The best answer is NOT:

A because it suggests that the sentence belongs in the paragraph when it clearly does not. Information about the actor who starred in *Glory* is not relevant at this point in the essay.

B because it, too, wrongly suggests that the sentence belongs in the paragraph.

D because even though it does indicate that the writer should not add the sentence, the reason given for not making this addition makes no sense. Including additional information saying that Bill Williams had met the actor Denzel Washington would also be irrelevant to the essay.

Question 119. The best answer is **J** because it maintains the present tense *(are)*. Notice that present tense is used throughout the essay. A tense shift here would be illogical.

The best answer is NOT:

F because it makes an illogical and confusing shift from present tense to past tense.

G because it makes an illogical and confusing shift from present tense to past perfect tense.

H because it makes an illogical and confusing shift from the present tense to the past conditional.

Question 120. The best answer is **A** because it provides the most effective introductory paragraph. This is the best opening for the essay because it introduces the main topic, which is Bill Williams and his company, Glory Foods.

The best answer is NOT:

B because Paragraph 2 would be an ineffective and confusing opening for this essay. Look at its first sentence: "Even as a child, Williams loved to prepare food." The clue that this is not a good opening sentence is that most essays would not begin this abruptly. The reader would not know who this Williams person was.

C because it has the same problem that **B** does. Placing Paragraph 1 after Paragraph 3 makes Paragraph 2 the opening paragraph, but that paragraph begins too abruptly to provide an effective introduction.

D because it is incorrect for the same basic reason that **B** and **C** are.

Passage IX

Question 121. The best answer is **J** because the paragraph is more focused when the underlined portion is omitted. Mentioning the writer's trip to the movies diverts the reader's attention from the focus of the paragraph, which is a description of the game arcade.

The best answer is NOT:

F because adding information about the writer's trip to the movies is irrelevant to this paragraph and should be omitted. If you read the entire paragraph, you will see that this information does not belong.

G because it is incorrect in the same way that **F** is. It adds information that distracts the reader from the main focus of this introductory paragraph.

H because it is incorrect in the same way that **F** and **G** are. Even though this information is set off by parentheses, it still distracts the reader and is irrelevant.

Question 122. **The best answer is B** because the past tense *(was)* is consistent with the rest of the paragraph. In addition, the singular verb *was* is in agreement with the singular subject *one*.

The best answer is NOT:

A because the subject and verb do not agree in number. The subject *one* is singular and therefore requires a singular verb. The verb *were* is plural.

C because, again, the subject and verb do not agree. The subject *one* is singular, and the verb *were* is plural and therefore incorrect.

D because the past conditional tense *(would have been)* is inappropriate and confusing. In addition, adding the adjective *actual* would make the sentence unnecessarily wordy.

Question 123. **The best answer is H** because it provides the predicate *are,* which produces a complete sentence. A statement that has no predicate is a sentence fragment (an incomplete sentence).

The best answer is NOT:

F because placing the relative pronoun *which* between the subject ("Video screens") and predicate ("have been populated") creates a sentence fragment.

G because it is incorrect in the same way that **F** is. In this case, the relative pronoun *that* is placed between the subject and predicate.

J because it fails to provide a predicate, which creates another incomplete sentence.

Question 124. **The best answer is A** because it provides the most logical sequence of sentences for this paragraph. Sentence 4 provides a necessary link between the description of the video games in Sentences 1 through 3 and the description of the pinball machines in Sentence 5. In Sentence 4, the phrase "on the other hand" signals that this sentence is going to provide a contrasting point of view. In this case, the writer contrasts video games and pinball machines.

The best answer is NOT:

B because if Sentence 4 were placed right after Sentence 1, the paragraph would be incoherent, illogical, and confusing. Placing Sentence 4 here would interrupt the description of the video games with a comment about pinball machines.

C because placing Sentence 4 after Sentence 5 would confuse readers. They would not understand that the phrase "Some machines" in Sentence 5 actually refers to pinball machines. Also, the transitional phrase "on the other hand" in Sentence 4 does not logically follow the information in Sentence 5.

D because omitting Sentence 4 would confuse readers. The transition that Sentence 4 provides is a necessary link between the description of the video games in Sentences 1 through 3 and the description of the pinball machines in Sentence 5.

Question 125. The best answer is **J** because information about the durability of video games is not relevant to the writer's argument in this paragraph. The main point of the paragraph is that video games are more predictable than pinball machines. Adding information about how video games are "built to last" or are "constructed durably" distracts the reader.

The best answer is NOT:

F because, as stated above, information about how the machines have been "built to last" diverts the reader from the main focus of the paragraph.

G because it is incorrect in the same way that **F** is. Adding the irrelevant information that the machine "is constructed durably" is distracting to the reader.

H because it is incorrect in the same way that **G** and **F** are.

Question 126. The best answer is **C** because it maintains the second-person (*you*) perspective that is used throughout this paragraph. It is important to note that the writer is using the second-person point of view in this paragraph to speak directly to and draw in the reader. Consider the sentence preceding this one: "As *you* guide *your* character through the game's challenges, *you* come to know how the machine will respond to *your* every move."

The best answer is NOT:

A because it fails to maintain a consistent viewpoint. It makes an illogical shift from the second person (*you*) to the third-person singular (*he or she*).

B because it makes an illogical shift from the second person (*you*) to the first-person plural (*we*).

D because it not only shifts from second person (*you*) to third person (*people*), but it also illogically shifts from present tense (*learn*) to past tense (*learned*).

Question 127. The best answer is **F**. Notice that this question asks for the *least* acceptable answer. In other words, the best answer is the *weakest* choice. If you read the paragraph carefully, you will see that the idea presented in this sentence (pinball is unpredictable) is meant to contrast with the idea in the preceding sentence (video games are predictable). Given this context, using the transitional word *therefore* at this point is illogical and confusing.

The best answer is NOT:

G because it is an acceptable alternative to *though,* providing the same logical transition.

H because it also provides an acceptable alternative to *though.*

J because, along with **G** and **H**, it provides an acceptable alternative to *though.*

Question 128. The best answer is **B** because the absence of a comma here creates the clearest and most understandable sentence.

The best answer is NOT:

A because it places an unnecessary and distracting comma between the subject clause ("a ball you thought was lost") and the predicate ("will … bounce").

C because it sets off the auxiliary (helping) verb *will* for no logical reason.

D because it places an unnecessary and distracting comma between the auxiliary verb *will* from the main verb *bounce*.

Question 129. The best answer is **F** because it most effectively links the topic of Paragraph 3 (pinball is less predictable than video games) and the topic of Paragraph 4 (the element of chance makes pinball more interesting than video games).

The best answer is NOT:

G because it fails to provide an effective link between the topics of the two paragraphs, as described above. This choice undermines the writer's argument by saying that pinball games are similar to video games.

H because it, too, fails to provide an effective transition from Paragraph 3 to Paragraph 4. **H** also contradicts the writer's previously stated point that pinball is challenging.

J because, like **G** and **H,** it provides an ineffective transition between the ideas presented in the two paragraphs. In addition, if you inserted this sentence at the beginning of Paragraph 4, the next sentence would not logically follow.

Question 130. The best answer is **D** because it results in the clearest and most concise response. In other words, it avoids redundancy (repeating the same idea) and wordiness.

The best answer is NOT:

A because it is redundant. At this point in the sentence, it is already clear that the writer is referring to "these video games."

B because it is incorrect for the same reason that **A** is.

C because it is incorrect in the same way that **A** and **B** are.

Question 131. The best answer is **F** because it maintains the second-person *(you)*, present-tense perspective that is used in the surrounding text. Notice that the preceding sentence establishes the second-person point of view: "Once *you* have mastered a game." (This question is similar to question 51.)

The best answer is NOT:

G because it makes a confusing tense shift in this sentence from the present perfect tense ("you have mastered") to the past tense ("you then looked").

H because it makes an illogical shift from the second-person plural (you) to the third person *(one)*.

J because it, too, makes an illogical shift from the second-person plural (you) to the third person *(one)*.

Question 132. The best answer is **B** because the comma between these two noun phrases ("sometimes your enemy" and "sometimes your ally") provides clarity for this sentence.

The best answer is NOT:

A because without the comma there, the statement becomes ambiguous and confusing. It's hard to tell whether the second *sometimes* is modifying *your enemy* or *your ally*.

C because it improperly uses a semicolon between these two noun phrases. By the way, those phrases are called "predicate nouns" because they follow the linking verb *is*.

D because even though the conjunction *and* could be used between these two sentence elements, setting off the conjunction with commas is inappropriate and confusing.

Question 133. The best answer is **G** because it provides the most concise way to make the writer's point.

The best answer is NOT:

F because it is vague and unnecessarily wordy. In addition, it creates a clause that lacks subject-verb agreement. The subject *times* is plural and requires a plural verb, not the singular verb *is*.

H because it is redundant (it repeats the same idea). In this sentence, *each, single,* and *unique* all mean the same thing.

J because the phrases "every single time" and "each" make this sentence wordy and repetitive.

Question 134. The best answer is C because it provides an adjective *(continual)* for the noun that it precedes *(challenge)*.

The best answer is NOT:

A because the adverb *continually* lacks a neighboring sentence element that it can modify (a verb or an adjective).

B because the adverb *continuously* faces the same problem of lacking something to modify.

D because the verb form *continue* is simply out of place here between the article *a* and the noun *challenge*.

Question 135. The best answer is J because throughout the essay, the writer suggests that "pinball is superior" by making the argument that pinball requires more skill and is more challenging than video games. It is reasonable to conclude, then, that this essay fulfilled the writer's goal.

The best answer is NOT:

F because the writer does suggest in this essay that video games "might seem more attractive than pinball," but this has nothing to do with the writer's goal of writing an essay that shows pinball as being superior to video games.

G because this choice can be ruled out for two reasons: first, the essay does fulfill the writer's goal, and second, the writer does not say that video games challenge the skills of the player.

H because this answer states that the essay does fulfill the writer's goal, but the reason given is not accurate. The writer never states that pinball games "are more visually attractive than video games."

Passage X

Question 136. The best answer is D because the absence of commas here creates the clearest and most understandable sentence.

The best answer is NOT:

A because it inserts an unnecessary and confusing comma between the noun *letters* and the preposition *in*. The phrase "in front of you" modifies *letters,* and these elements should not be separated by any punctuation.

B because it inappropriately and confusingly inserts a comma between the verb *tumbles* and the preposition *to*.

C because it inserts an unnecessary and confusing comma between the complete subject phrase ("each of the letters in front of you") and the verb *tumbles*.

Question 137. **The best answer is H** because it effectively and logically uses the coordinating conjunction (linking word) *and* to connect the two independent clauses in this sentence.

The best answer is NOT:

F because the use of the conjunction *unless* here creates an illogical statement. It makes no sense to say, "The computer is probably sick, *unless* … [it] has a virus."

G because the use of the conjunction *except* also creates an illogical statement. A computer with a virus is *not* an exception to a computer being sick.

J because the use of the conjunction *as if* creates a confusing and ambiguous sentence.

Question 138. **The best answer is D** because it appropriately sets off the conjunctive adverb *however* with commas. When a conjunctive adverb or transitional expression interrupts a clause, as *however* does in this sentence, it should usually be set off with commas.

The best answer is NOT:

A because it places a comma after *however* but omits the corresponding comma before the word.

B because it inappropriately uses a semicolon instead of a comma before the adverb *however*.

C because it is incorrect because it places a comma before *however* but omits the corresponding comma after the word.

Question 139. **The best answer is G** because it provides the most effective introductory sentence for Paragraph 3. The topic of the paragraph is the serious computer viruses known as "bombs." Notice that the second sentence in this paragraph logically follows and further defines these "bombs."

The best answer is NOT:

F because the information is too broad. The topic of the paragraph is not all computer viruses; rather, it is the much narrower topic of viruses called "bombs." In addition, if this sentence opened the paragraph, the reader would not understand, later in the paragraph, what "these bombs" referred to.

H because it introduces a topic other than the "bombs." If you read the paragraph with this sentence as the introduction, the paragraph makes no sense.

J because it, too, strays from the main topic of the paragraph, which is the computer viruses referred to as "bombs."

Question 140. The best answer is A because it most clearly and concisely expresses the point being made in this sentence.

The best answer is NOT:

B because the phrase "devastative disaster" is redundant (repeating information). In this case, the use of the adjective *devastative* is redundant because the noun *disaster* expresses the same thought.

C because this phrasing is confusing if not nonsensical. How can something be "devastation to the operating of a computer"?

D because it is redundant and unclear. The redundancy occurs in the phrase "can be possibly." Also, the phrase "operating of a computer" is not idiomatic English; that is, it's not the way English speakers would normally say or write the phrase.

Question 141. The best answer is F because it is the clearest and most concise of the four choices given.

The best answer is NOT:

G because the phrase "that detect computer viruses" is redundant. The phrase is not necessary because the reader already knows that detection programs, by definition, "detect computer viruses." In addition, the phrase "computer viruses" appears a second time at the end of the sentence.

H because it is also unnecessarily wordy and redundant. The phrase "computer viruses" appears twice in this short sentence.

J because it, too, unnecessarily repeats the phrase "computer viruses."

Question 142. The best answer is D because both verbs in the subordinate, or dependent, clause of this sentence agree in number with the subject *programs,* which the clause modifies. The subject *programs* is plural, so the verbs *search* and *destroy* must also be plural.

The best answer is NOT:

A because the singular verb forms *(searches, destroys)* do not agree with their plural subject, *programs.*

B because it is incorrect in the same way that **A** is; the singular verb forms do not agree with their plural subject.

C because it is ungrammatical. Although the verb *search* is plural and agrees with the subject *programs,* the verb *destroys* is singular and does not agree.

Question 143. The best answer is **G** because it provides a predicate verb *(is found)* for the main clause of this sentence. ("Evidence … is found in the names of their programs.")

The best answer is NOT:

F because it creates an incomplete sentence, a fragment. The participle *being found* cannot function as the predicate verb of the main clause of this sentence.

H because, like **F**, it creates a fragment because the participle *having been found* cannot function as a predicate verb.

J because, in this case, the verb form *found* reads as if it were a past participle, not a predicate verb. This too is a sentence fragment because it lacks a predicate for the sentence's main clause.

Question 144. The best answer is **A** because it appropriately uses a colon to introduce the list of names of the programs. Introducing a list is one function of the colon.

The best answer is NOT:

B because it improperly uses the semicolon, which is generally used to separate two independent clauses.

C because it omits the necessary punctuation. The colon is needed here to signal to readers that a list of "the names of their programs" will follow.

D because the comma is not a "strong" enough punctuation mark here. Is this comma the same as or part of the series of commas that follow in this sentence?

Question 145. The best answer is **F** because it is the clearest and most logical of the four choices. It also provides a proper idiom of standard written English. The phrase "As with all diseases" indicates that the best cure for computer viruses is that same as that for all diseases: prevention.

The best answer is NOT:

G because it results in an ambiguous and illogical statement. It states that "the best cure" is "similarly to all diseases," which is illogical and ungrammatical.

H because it is unclear. The use of the phrase "In the same way as" suggests that the writer is trying to compare apples ("all diseases") and oranges ("the best cure").

J because "According with" is not an idiom of standard written English. Even if the sentence began "According to all diseases," which *is* idiomatic, the sentence still wouldn't make sense.

ENGLISH • EXPLANATORY ANSWERS

Question 146. The best answer is **C** because the question states that the writer's intention is to recommend "ways to protect computer data against viruses." **C** provides a recommendation by advising the reader to use antivirus programs frequently.

The best answer is NOT:

A because stating that many "viruses are quite sophisticated" does not provide a recommendation and, thus, does not accomplish the writer's stated intention.

B because it does provide a recommendation of sorts, but not the recommendation stated in the question. Adding software that checks spelling does not "protect computer data against viruses."

D because although this choice makes a broad recommendation ("be aware of the various ways to prevent viruses"), it does *not* recommend "specific ways to protect to protect computer data," which is the writer's stated intention.

Question 147. The best answer is **H** because placing the word *better* into the phrasing "you had better hope" provides the clearest statement and best clarifies the meaning of the sentence.

The best answer is NOT:

F because here, *better* inappropriately modifies *responds,* which confuses the meaning of the sentence. Also, the resultant phrase "you had hope" sounds wrong in this sentence along with its two present tense verbs *(is* and *responds).*

G because in this arrangement, *better* modifies *system* and implies a comparison that does not exist. "If there is a virus in your *better* system" wrongly suggests that there are two systems.

J because it is incorrect for the same reason that **F** is.

Question 148. The best answer is **C** because the most logical and effective placement for this sentence is after Paragraph 4. The last sentence of this paragraph lists the names of the virus detection programs; the new sentence, which refers to those names, logically follows. Also, this new sentence states that the "Names … suggest that the problem is serious." The names identified in Paragraph 4 *(Vaccine, Checkup, Antitoxin,* and *Disinfectant)* do imply a level of seriousness.

The best answer is NOT:

A because Paragraph 2 provides a description of what a computer virus can do and does not refer to any "names" of viruses. Adding the sentence here makes no sense.

B because the main topic of Paragraph 3 is computer "bombs." As with **A,** there is no reference to particular "names."

D because it, too, would be an illogical placement. Although there are "names" in the last sentence of Paragraph 5 *(Internet* and *World Wide Web),* these names do not suggest a serious problem in the way that the "names" in Paragraph 4 do.

Question 149. The best answer is **H** because the second-person pronouns (*you, your*) do directly address the reader. Revising the essay so that it used the third-person pronouns *one* and *one's* would sacrifice that sense of addressing and advising the reader.

The best answer is NOT:

F because, although shifting to the third-person pronouns *one* and *one's* may change the tone of the essay, a polite and formal tone is clearly not appropriate to the purpose of this piece.

G because changing the pronouns in the essay from second to third person would not suggest that the writer is "speaking to a broader and more inclusive audience."

J because, in this essay, the setting is not a prominent element, and a shift in pronouns from second to third person would not change the sense of that setting.

Question 150. The best answer is **D** because the essay does limit itself "to describing computer viruses and the basic precautions to be taken against them." The essay does not discuss the ethics of tampering with a computer system, so it would not meet the writer's goal as described in this question.

The best answer is NOT:

A because the essay does not explain any moral or ethical consequences resulting from computer viruses.

B because the process of ridding a computer system of viruses is not explained in detail.

C because a reader would not necessarily have to know how a virus is programmed in order to make a judgment about the morality or ethics of programming a virus.

Passage XI

Question 151. The best answer is **A** because it provides punctuation (in this case, a period) that appropriately separates these two complete thoughts or statements: "My grandfather is not known for embracing technological change" and "He still drives his '59 Chevy Impala."

The best answer is NOT:

B because it creates a run-on, or fused sentence. There is no punctuation or conjunction (connect word) between the two statements.

C because the phrase "still driving his '59 Chevy Impala" is not a complete statement (because there is no stated subject). It could work in this sentence if it were set off from the main clause with a comma. It would then modify "My grandfather," the subject of the main clause. But this answer doesn't provide that punctuation.

D because the conjunction *and* that connects the phrase "still driving his '59 Chevy Impala" to the main clause creates confusion by linking groups of words that are not grammatically parallel.

Question 152. **The best answer is G** because it correctly punctuates this sentence, which is actually a fairly simple subject-verb-direct object sentence except that the direct object is a noun clause. The sentence could also be written with the word *that* introducing the clause.

The best answer is NOT:

F because it inserts an unnecessary comma between the verb *says* and the direct object, which is what he says ("he can't imagine needing frivolous options like automatic transmission or power steering"). It's worth pointing out that the comma would be correct if what followed the verb were a direct quotation, as in speech: He says, "I can't imagine needing frivolous options."

H because it inserts an unnecessary comma between the verb and the direct object clause.

J because it adds the same unnecessary comma as H does, plus it places an unnecessary comma between the pronoun *that* and the clause it introduces.

Question 153. **The best answer is C** because it provides the correct past tense form of the irregular verb *go*.

The best answer is NOT:

A because the verb *has went* is grammatically incorrect. It should be *has gone* (which would still be incorrect here because it would create an awkward tense shift).

B because the verb *had went* is grammatically incorrect. It should be *had gone*.

D because it is in the present tense, creating a shift in verb tense in this sentence. The three verbs that follow this one in the sentence are all in the past tense: *had quit, tried,* and *resisted.*

Question 154. **The best answer is H** because the coordinating word *because* clearly and concisely links this parenthetical clause ("because his old black-and-white model had finally quit") to the preceding clause ("he went to buy a new color television").

The best answer is NOT:

F because it is excessively wordy and clunky. The phrase "owing to the knowledge that his old black-and-white model had finally quit" doesn't express anything that the clause "because his old black-and-white model had finally quit" doesn't express more clearly and more precisely.

G because it is unnecessarily wordy. The clause "due to the understandable fact that his old black-and-white model had finally quit" seems, on first glance, impressive. But it is empty, pretentious language, and not consistent with the style of the rest of this essay.

J because the coordinating word *so* does not logically link this parenthetical clause to the preceding clause.

Question 155. The best answer is **B** because it adds an appropriate and relevant detail here. In this sentence, the writer is expressing that the grandfather believed he was still healthy and had no need of a remote control for his television—"He said that he had two good legs and was perfectly capable of getting out of his chair." The addition of "when he wanted to change the channel" fits with the point of the rest of the sentence.

The best answer is NOT:

A because the fact that the chair "was made of black leather" is irrelevant to the writer's purpose here.

C because the fact that the chair is located "by the south window in the family room" is a pointless digression in this sentence.

D because, again, the fact that the grandfather "liked to sit" in his chair is an insignificant detail here. Since it was "his chair," he would presumably like to sit there.

Question 156. The best answer is **J** because, here, no adverb or phrase is needed to make a connection between these two sentences. The essay works fine here without that kind of help.

The best answer is NOT:

F because the adverb *however*, as it is used here, indicates that this sentence is going to contradict or contrast with the statement in the preceding sentence. This sentence does not do that.

G because the adverb *additionally* indicates that this sentence is going to add a point that builds on the statement in the preceding sentence. This sentence does not do that.

H because the adverb *conversely* expresses the same general idea that *however* does. This sentence does not provide a contrast to the statement in the preceding sentence.

Question 157. The best answer is **C** because the absence of commas here creates the clearest and most understandable sentence. This is another case (like question 6) where less is more.

The best answer is NOT:

A because it inserts a comma that confounds your ability to understand the sentence. The comma after the word *time* makes you think that Grandpa punched in the time and then he punched in the channel of his favorite news program, when actually he punched in the time that the program came on and the channel it was on.

B because it also inserts an unnecessary and confusing comma, this time after the conjunction *and* rather than just before it.

D because the comma after the word *channel* indicates that the phrase "of his favorite daily news program" is not essential. It's set off from the rest of the sentence with commas, as if it were parenthetical—a nice piece of information but not necessary to the meaning of the sentence. But if you try reading the sentence without this phrase, the meaning of the sentence is no longer clear.

Question 158. The best answer is J because the phrase *On the other hand* signals that this sentence is going to provide a contrasting point or a different perspective. Grandpa's logic goes like this: The remote control's volume button is great for drowning out someone he doesn't want to hear; on the other hand (from another perspective), the mute button is great for silencing the television when he doesn't want to hear it.

The best answer is NOT:

F because the phrase *For example* indicates that this sentence will offer an example of the statement expressed in the sentence before it. This sentence does not provide that payoff.

G because it is incorrect for the same reason that F is. The phrase *To illustrate* is fairly close in meaning to *For example*.

H because the phrase *On the one hand* suggests that the writer is going to make a point here and then make another point. But the other point never gets made here; this is the last sentence in this paragraph.

Question 159. The best answer is B because *advertisers* is a specific noun that clearly communicates who Grandpa wants to be able to cut off in midsentence.

The best answer is NOT:

A because the pronoun *them* does not have a clear antecedent (a noun that it refers to and stands in for).

C because the pronoun *it* seems to refer back to the noun *sound*, but that is nonsensical. How do you "cut sound off in midsentence"?

D because the possessive pronoun *its* might refer back to the noun *sound* or to the noun *button*, but both of those would be nonsensical. What do you make of "the button that mutes the sound lets him cut the button's function off in midsentence"?

Question 160. The best answer is F because it appropriately punctuates this complex sentence. A complex sentence, by definition, contains an independent clause ("This option automatically turns the TV off after a preset amount of time") and one or more dependent clauses ("which is very convenient" and "when he falls asleep while watching a show").

The best answer is NOT:

G because by inserting a comma before the clause "when he falls asleep while watching a show" and setting it off from the rest of the sentence, the writer is signaling that the clause is not essential to the meaning of the rest of the sentence. But that is not so. Try reading the sentence without that final clause. The option of automatically turning off the TV is not always convenient, but it's sure handy when Grandpa falls asleep in the middle of a show.

H because it creates a sentence fragment. "When he falls asleep while watching a show" cannot stand alone. It's not a complete thought. Readers want to know more.

J because it is incorrect for the same reason that H is wrong. As it is used here, the semicolon is signaling that the statements on either side of the semicolon should be independent clauses (complete thoughts).

Question 161. The best answer is D. Think of this sentence as a jigsaw puzzle. Each puzzle piece is a phrase or clause. In this version, all the pieces of this sentence fit together well. And the "picture" that results looks like something that we can understand.

The best answer is NOT:

A because the parts of this complex sentence are poorly arranged—to the point of nonsense. Perhaps the best way of answering this question is to listen carefully to each wording as you read it out loud to yourself. The clause "what he wants his TV doing … is to know a source of both pleasure and power" is pretty funny, but it's probably not what the writer meant to say here.

B because of a similarly flawed arrangement of the elements of this sentence. Placing the introductory clause "Even when he sleeps" directly before the statement "Grandpa says" gives readers the wrong impression that Grandpa is talking in his sleep.

C because of its clumsiness. The following makes little or no sense at all: "Doing what he wants … is to know his TV is a source of both pleasure and power for him."

Question 162. The best answer is **F** because it provides a main clause for this sentence: "Grandpa points his finger at the TV and … seemingly turns it on." Notice that the phrase introducing the sentence (which is often called a participial phrase) cannot be a main clause because it has no stated subject.

The best answer is NOT:

G because it creates a sentence fragment. There is no stated subject and no main clause.

H because it is incorrect for the same reason that G is incorrect—no subject, no main clause.

J not because of a fragment problem but because of a tense shift problem. Both the verb in the preceding sentence (*uses*) and the second verb in the compound predicate in this sentence (*turns*) express action in the present. It doesn't make sense to place a verb here (*has pointed*) that expresses action that began in the past and continues in the present.

Question 163. The best answer is **A** because it provides a fitting ending for this personal essay because it refers to Grandpa's continuing discovery of creative ways of using his new television remote control.

The best answer is NOT:

B because it provides a description of Grandpa as uninterested in learning how to use his remote control. That's inconsistent with the rest of the essay's portrayal of him as embracing this new technology.

C because it introduces elements that are insignificant in terms of the rest of the essay. The 200-page manual had not been mentioned elsewhere in the story, and the salesperson had only a minor role early in the story.

D because it suggests that the grandmother's feelings or thoughts are central to the essay, but the rest of the essay has focused on the actions and opinions of the grandfather.

Question 164. The best answer is **G** because the placement that creates the most logical order is between Sentences 1 and 2. First, the statement that Grandpa likes to use the programming function to play jokes on his grandchildren. Then, the explanation of how he does it: He programs the TV to turn on at a certain time; in the grandchildren's presence, he points his finger at the TV when it's programmed to turn on.

The best answer is NOT:

F because it is not the most logical place to add this information. It doesn't make sense to explain Grandpa's TV programming trick before the reader even knows that Grandpa likes to use the programming function to play jokes on his grandchildren.

H because it reverses the chronological order of how Grandpa's joke works. He can't play the trick on the grandchildren and then program the TV to turn on at a certain time.

J because it is incorrect for the same reason that H is. The chronological order of the setup of the remote control–finger joke is out of whack.

Question 165. The best answer is **D** because it provides an effective transition from the first part of the essay to the second part. The opening paragraphs focus on Grandpa's resistance to but eventual acquisition of a new TV with a remote control. The last sentence of Paragraph 2 indicates that Grandpa overcame his resistance to technology and began to use the remote. The first sentence of Paragraph 3 points out that Grandpa has actually grown interested in the uses of the remote, and this leads into the rest of the essay's description of the uses that he discovers, many of which wouldn't be found in that 200-page manual.

The best answer is NOT:

A because the first sentence of Paragraph 3 is "Grandpa is intrigued by the various uses for that remote." This sentence suggests that the remote control might have intriguing uses, but it doesn't provide any *information* about those uses.

B because, again, the sentence does suggest that Grandpa liked using the remote, but it doesn't provide any *details* that support that as a fact.

C because it would be a vast overstatement to say that this sentence is "a humorous blend of descriptive details and relevant information."

Passage XII

Question 166. The best answer is **A** because it provides the punctuation (a comma) that best indicates the relationship between the introductory prepositional phrases ("During the early morning hours of October 28, 1965") and the main clause ("engineers stationed 630 feet above the ground made careful measurements").

The best answer is NOT:

B because the connecting word *and* creates confusion here. A word like *and* usually connects similar kinds of grammatical units—nouns (Tom and Mary), verbs (wander and search), adverbs (high and low), etc. Here, the word tries to connect an introductory phrase and a main clause.

C because placing a period here creates a sentence fragment: "During the early morning hours of October 28, 1965."

D because it is incorrect for the same reason that C is wrong. A semicolon is normally used to connect two independent clauses (that is, clauses that could each stand alone as complete sentences).

Question 167. **The best answer is H** because it shows the correct use of the apostrophe in expressions of time. You're probably more familiar with the uses of the apostrophe to express possession or ownership or to indicate a contraction (letters left out when words are combined). But you've probably seen phrases such as "yesterday's news" and "tomorrow's headlines" and "an hour's delay" —they all follow the same punctuation rule as "the day's work."

The best answer is NOT:

F because it leaves out that necessary apostrophe. Without the apostrophe, a reader might misread "the days" as a subject and "work" as a predicate.

G because it places the apostrophe in the wrong location. The rest of this sentence makes it clear that this is *one* day's work.

J because one would never use an apostrophe like this—by adding 's to the end of a plural noun.

Question 168. **The best answer is A** because this story of the last step in the construction of the Gateway Arch is told in the past tense. The past tense verb threatened is consistent with the other predicate verbs used in this paragraph—*stationed, made, indicated.*

The best answer is NOT:

B because the passive voice of the verb *had been threatened* doesn't make sense in this sentence.

C because the future perfect tense verb *will have threatened* creates an awkward and confusing shift from the past tense used elsewhere in this essay.

D because the present tense verb *threatens* creates a similarly awkward and confusing shift in tense.

Question 169. **The best answer is J** because it provides the most concise wording for this sentence and avoids the pointless repetition of the other choices.

The best answer is NOT:

F because it is pointlessly repetitive. The word *delay* doesn't add any information here that's not already clearly expressed by the word *postpone.*

G because the phrase "postpone to a later time" is pointlessly wordy. Can you postpone something to an earlier time? The information "to a later time" is already clearly expressed by the word *postpone.*

H because it is incorrect for the same reason that **F** is. The phrase "postpone by delaying" is another example of verbal overkill. Readers can sometimes feel disrespected when an essay tells them the same thing over and over.

ENGLISH • EXPLANATORY ANSWERS

Question 170. **The best answer is B** because this sentence explains that the topping-out ceremony being referred to here is "the placement of the final section between the two freestanding legs of the St. Louis Gateway Arch." Without this phrase, we wouldn't be able to figure out what "topping out" meant until we were halfway into the essay.

The best answer is NOT:

A because the essay would *not* lose a minor detail if this phrase were deleted. This is a key piece of information.

C because the wording of this phrase is straightforward and factual—there's nothing to suggest that the writer is expressing his or her opinion on the significance of anything.

D because the phrase does not state the ceremony's importance to St. Louis residents. Readers might draw a conclusion about the ceremony's importance based on the essay as a whole, but that's something else entirely.

Question 171. **The best answer is F** because the phrase "Luther Ely Smith" is an appositive for (renames or explains) the phrase it follows, "attorney and civic leader." Most appositive phrases are set off by commas, but this one should not be, because it is essential to the meaning of the sentence. Try reading the sentence without "Luther Ely Smith"—doesn't it sound strange or clunky?

The best answer is NOT:

G because the comma between the nouns *attorney* and *civic leader* is unnecessary and distracting. The word *and* is linking up these two nouns; the comma just gets in the way of that.

H because there should not be a comma separating the noun phrase "attorney and civic leader" and the noun phrase that defines and specifies it, "Luther Ely Smith."

J because it is incorrect for the reasons given for G and H, and because the proliferation of commas just totally confuses things: "In 1933, attorney, and civic leader" starts looking like it might be a series of three items.

Question 172. The best answer is **C** because this sentence states, "In 1933, attorney and civic leader Luther Ely Smith envisioned a memorial that would recognize St. Louis's major role in the westward expansion of the United States." It does provide some helpful background about the history leading up to the construction of the Gateway Arch, and it's the only place in the essay where such background is provided.

The best answer is NOT:

A because the sentence does state that St. Louis played a role in the westward expansion, but it does not explain why St. Louis played that role.

B because the sentence does state that Smith envisioned a memorial, but it does not mention what the memorial that he envisioned might look like.

D because the sentence does provide some biographical facts about Smith—he was an attorney and a civic leader, and he had an idea about a memorial. However, this information is not particularly crucial. The information that is most relevant and meaningful to this paragraph is that a memorial to St. Louis's role in the U.S. westward expansion (that is, the Gateway Arch) was first envisioned in 1933.

Question 173. The best answer is **H** because it is the only choice that makes this a complete sentence.

The best answer is NOT:

F because it creates a sentence fragment—a noun phrase ("Architect Eero Saarinen") and a dependent clause that modifies the noun phrase ("who created the design that symbolized the memorial's theme").

G because it too creates a sentence fragment—that same noun phrase and an appositive phrase that renames the noun phrase ("creator of the design that symbolized the memorial's theme").

J because it too creates a sentence fragment—that same noun phrase and a participial phrase modifying the noun phrase ("creating the design that symbolized the memorial's theme").

Question 174. The best answer is D because this question asks you to decide which word would provide the most logical and effective transition from one sentence to another. The best decision here is to use no transitional adverb at all. The preceding sentence states that Saarinen designed the Gateway Arch. This sentence is the first of three that describe the details of that design.

The best answer is NOT:

A because the sense of *Meanwhile* is that this event takes place at the same time that the preceding event takes place. That sense doesn't work logically here.

B because the sense of *Therefore* is that this condition exists or event takes place as a result of the preceding condition or event. That sense would work here only if we'd already been told that Saarinen's designs always look like the description that follows.

C because the sense of *However* is that this condition exists or event takes place in contrast to the preceding condition or event. That sense would work only if we'd already been told that Saarinen's designs never look like the description that follows.

Question 175. The best answer is F. All of these word choices are similar in meaning, having something to do with "decreasing or reducing in size," but they are not interchangeable synonyms. The context of this sentence helps us to decide the best choice: "spraying the [metal and concrete] leg [of the Gateway Arch] with water to cool it would make it contract." *Merriam-Webster's Collegiate Dictionary* (11th ed.) supports the accuracy of this choice, stating that "CONTRACT applies to a drawing together of surfaces or particles or a reduction of area or length" (p. 271).

The best answer is NOT:

G because *reduce* has more of a sense of "bringing down or lowering in size or degree or intensity," which is not exactly the action being described in this sentence. It's a much less precise word choice than *contract* is.

H because *decrease* has more of a sense of "declining in size or number or amount," which is not exactly the action being described here. It's a much less precise word choice than *contract* is.

J because *compress* primarily means "to reduce in size by pressing or squeezing," which is not the action being described here.

Question 176. The best answer is **C** because this phrasing uses the correct forms of the possessive pronouns *their* and *its*: "in their attempt to reduce its expansion."

The best answer is NOT:

A because it uses the contraction *they're* (meaning "they are") where the possessive pronoun *their* is called for.

B because it uses the contraction *they're* and the contraction *it's* (meaning "it is") where the possessive pronouns *their* and *its* are called for.

D because it uses the contraction *it's* where the possessive pronoun *its* is called for.

Question 177. The best answer is **G** because it provides the most logical and fluent arrangement of the possible parts of this sentence: an introductory dependent clause ("as the crowd cheered") followed by a main clause with a compound predicate ("the final section was hoisted up and welded to the two legs of the arch").

The best answer is NOT:

F because this arrangement of the pieces of information provides us with the nonsensical image of the final section being hoisted up *after* it had been welded to the legs of the arch.

H because this arrangement of the pieces of information provides us with the absurd image of the crowd being welded to the legs of the arch.

J because this arrangement of the pieces of information provides us with the confusing image of the crowd either doing some of the welding or being welded to the legs of the arch.

Question 178. The best answer is **D** because it offers the most concise wording and avoids the redundancy of the other choices. (Have you ever heard of the Department of Redundancy Department? That might be a handy way to remember what the word *redundant* means.)

The best answer is NOT:

A because, since a decade is ten years and three decades are thirty years, the phrase "Over three decades and more than thirty years" is redundant.

B because its phrasing is redundant and pointless. "Over three decades" do amount to "more than thirty years," but there's no reason to inform readers of that here.

C because the parenthetical phrase "over thirty years" merely repeats the time span just reported in a different measure of time (decades).

Question 179. The best answer is G because this is the LEAST acceptable alternative to the underlined portion. The sentence with the underlined portion reads, "Over three decades of planning and building had come to a conclusion, and the tallest monument in the United States was now complete." Replacing the word *conclusion* with *halt* creates a meaning problem in the context of this sentence because "coming to a halt" expresses the idea of stopping or suspending before or without completion.

The best answer is NOT:

F because it provides an acceptable wording. The phrase "reached completion" works in the context of this sentence just as well as "come to a conclusion" does.

H because it provides an acceptable wording. The phrase "come to an end" works in this sentence just as well as "come to a conclusion" does.

J because it provides an acceptable wording. The word "ended" works in this sentence just as well as "come to a conclusion" does.

Question 180. The best answer is C because the title of this essay—" 'Topping Out' the Gateway Arch"—is a fairly good summary of the piece and actually helps us to arrive at the answer. The essay does *not* do a good job of describing the entire process of designing and building the Gateway Arch because it focuses instead on telling the story of this one step in the process.

The best answer is NOT:

A because this essay does mention the materials used to make the exterior and interior structural supports, but that doesn't mean it has described the entire design and construction process.

B simply because it presents an inaccurate description of this essay. An essay that does what B claims to do would indeed fulfill the intended goal.

D because it is incorrect for the same reason as B is—it inaccurately describes this essay. This essay devotes just a few sentences to the early stages in the development of the arch.

Passage XIII

Question 181. The best answer is **C** because it correctly inserts a period between two independent clauses. "Many viewers" is the subject of the compound verb "stood and applauded."

The best answer is NOT:

A because it creates a comma splice (two or more complete sentences separated only by a comma).

B because it creates a run-on sentence. There is no punctuation or conjunction (joining word) between the two independent clauses.

D because the subordinating conjunction *while* creates a sentence fragment. When an introductory clause begins with a subordinating conjunction, it must be followed by a comma, a subject, and a verb.

Question 182. The best answer is **H** because it provides a clear and convincing reason the statement should *not* be added. This statement interrupts the introduction of Amalia Hernández with a loosely related detail that expands the focus of the essay to include other famous Mexican dancers who began their careers with Ballet Folklórico. The essay that follows focuses on just one dancer: Amalia Hernández.

The best answer is NOT:

F because it does *not* provide a clear and convincing reason the statement should be added. This statement expands the focus of the essay to include other famous Mexican ballet dancers. The essay focuses on just one dancer: Amalia Hernández.

G because this statement does not emphasize how difficult it is to become a professional dancer. Instead, it emphasizes that Amalia Hernández is one of many famous dancers who got their start in Ballet Folklórico. The path to becoming a professional dancer is portrayed as accessible.

J because it does *not* contradict information offered elsewhere in the essay.

Question 183. **The best answer is B** because the introductory phrase "growing up in Mexico in the 1920s" is appropriately set off from the main clause with a comma.

The best answer is NOT:

A because it inserts a confusing and unnecessary comma between the participial phrase "Growing up" and the location where Amalia Hernández grew up: "in Mexico." These elements should not be separated by any punctuation. Additionally, this answer lacks a necessary comma after *1920s*.

C because it inserts a confusing and unnecessary comma between the participial phrase "Growing up" and the location where Amalia Hernández grew up: "in Mexico." These elements should not be separated by any punctuation. Additionally, this answer lacks a necessary comma after *1920s*.

D because it inserts a confusing and unnecessary comma between the participial phrase "Growing up" and the time when Amalia Hernández grew up in Mexico: in the 1920s. These elements should not be separated by any punctuation.

Question 184. **The best answer is G** because the transition word *finally* appropriately indicates that Amalia Hernández's father eventually acquiesced to her persistent efforts to gain his support for her dance career.

The best answer is NOT:

F because the phrase "despite this" signals contrast. Amalia Hernández's father acquiesced to her expectations because of rather than despite Amalia's persistence.

H because the phrase "in fact" is an emphasizer. It does not logically fit within the context of the paragraph. If the phrase "in fact" were appropriate, it would be followed by an example of how Amalia was persistent in her efforts to gain her father's support of her dance career.

J because the phrase "On the other hand" signals contrast. It is typically used to introduce two different perspectives. Amalia Hernández's father acquiesced to her expectations because of her persistence. His acquiescing does not contrast with the concept that Amalia was persistent in her efforts to convince her father to support her dance career.

Question 185. **The best answer is D** because omitting the underlined portion eliminates redundancy and wordiness.

The best answer is NOT:

A because it is needlessly wordy and redundant. The word *acquiesced* means to give in.

B because it is needlessly wordy and redundant. The word *acquiesced* means to give in.

C because the word *acquiesced* means to agree with someone else's position, typically after a good deal of persuasion.

Question 186. **The best answer is H** because no punctuation is needed here. The absence of commas creates the clearest sentence.

The best answer is NOT:

F because it inserts an inappropriate and confusing colon between *in* and *classical*. An independent clause must precede a colon. In this answer, a sentence fragment precedes the colon.

G because it inserts an inappropriate and confusing comma between *in* and *classical*.

J because *classical* and *modern* ballet are just two items in a list and, therefore, no comma is needed.

Question 187. **The best answer is A** because this sentence indicates why Amalia Hernández felt that "something wasn't right." Additionally, this sentence connects logically with the first sentence of the subsequent body paragraph, which explains that Hernández began studying Mexico's folklore because of her dissatisfaction with her studies with Europe's finest teachers.

The best answer is NOT:

B because this sentence indicates that Hernández wished to no longer dance, but the very next paragraph emphasizes how Hernández continued to pursue her passion for dance with a focus on her country's folklore. Additionally, this answer emphasizes how Hernández does not like the music she had been dancing to. Later, the essay states that Hernández cherished songs that chronicle life, death, and rebirth, so clearly a distaste for music does not cause her to reject dance.

C because this does not fit logically into the essay. This paragraph emphasizes Hernández's dissatisfaction with the instruction she receives in the studios her father built for her. This sentence emphasizes Hernández's appreciation for the dance studio where she studied, but the paragraph actually emphasizes what Hernández's training lacks and how it fails to inspire her.

D because the paragraph that follows does not focus on Amalia's Hernández's study of modern ballet. Instead, it focuses on her study of Mexican folklore, which is connected to the country's history more so than to its modern situation.

Question 188. **The best answer is H** because it correctly uses an apostrophe to signify possession. The folklore belongs to the country. Country is singular.

The best answer is NOT:

F because *countrys* is incorrect in any context. The plural of the noun *country* is *countries*. Additionally, this answer leaves out a necessary apostrophe. The folklore belongs to the country.

G because it places the apostrophe in the wrong location. Country is singular, and, therefore, it should be followed by *'s* to signify possession. *-s'* is reserved for plural possession. The plural of country is countries, and the essay makes it clear that Hernández is from the country of Mexico.

J because it leaves out a necessary apostrophe. The folklore belongs to the country. *Countries* is the plural of the noun *country*. The essay makes it clear that Hernández is from the country of Mexico.

Question 189. **The best answer is A** because this is the LEAST acceptable alternative to the underlined portion. The word *grouping* implies that the different influences remain separated. The point of this sentence is that Aztec, Mayan, Spanish, French, Dutch, and African influences are *fused,* or integrated. The word *grouping* does not capture that concept as well as the other word choices do.

The best answer is NOT:

B because the word *combination* appropriately conveys that the influences are integrated rather than separate.

C because the word *blend* appropriately conveys that the influences are integrated rather than separate.

D because the word *mixture* appropriately conveys that the influences are integrated rather than separate.

Question 190. **The best answer is G** because the noun *rebirth* is parallel with the nouns *life* and *death*.

The best answer is NOT:

F because the phrase "to have a rebirth" is not parallel with the nouns *life* and *death*.

H because the phrase "to have a rebirth" is not parallel with the nouns *life* and *death*.

J because the phrase "to have a rebirth" is not parallel with the nouns *life* and *death*.

Question 191. **The best answer is D** because it avoids introducing a needless and illogical transition word. The phrase "this lore" logically refers to the Mexican songs and dances that celebrated the seasons and the harvest.

The best answer is NOT:

A because the word *however* incorrectly indicates that this sentence contrasts with the previous sentence.

B because the word *nevertheless* incorrectly indicates that this sentence contrasts with the previous sentence.

C because the word *instead* incorrectly indicates that this sentence contrasts with the previous sentence.

Question 192. **The best answer is F** because it provides a clear and convincing reason that the clause should be added to the preceding sentence. This detail illustrates how prolific Hernández was, which supports the paragraph's focus on Hernández's success after she started her own dance company.

The best answer is NOT:

G because it provides an inaccurate justification for adding this clause. The clause does *not* describe what Hernández's ballets were like.

H because the paragraph does not focus on Hernández's job at Mexico's Institute of Fine Arts. The paragraph's main point is that Hernández found success after leaving her job at Mexico's Institute of Fine Arts.

J because this clause does not disrupt the description of Hernández's role in Ballet Folklórico. It provides elaborating details that indicate how many ballets she choreographed for her dance company.

Question 193. The best answer is C because em-dashes appropriately set off "Ballet Folklórico." The phrase "her legacy" is synonymous with Ballet Folklórico. Therefore, "Ballet Folklórico" could be cut out of this sentence without affecting its meaning. Framing commas would also be appropriate here.

The best answer is NOT:

A because two em-dashes should be used to set off "Ballet Folklórico."

B because two em-dashes should be used to set off "Ballet Folklórico." Two commas could also be used to set off "Ballet Folklórico," but a comma and an em-dash should not be combined to set off a nonessential piece of information.

D because it is missing a necessary em-dash before the word "the." Two em-dashes should be used to set off "Ballet Folklórico."

Question 194. The best answer is G because it emphasizes how Ballet Folklórico's performances have created greater awareness of Mexican culture. These performances share Mexico's cultural heritage with the world. As the previous paragraph indicates, Ballet Folklórico was "an official cultural ambassador" of Mexico.

The best answer is NOT:

F because it simply emphasizes the quality of Ballet Folklórico but does not emphasize its value as a method for globally communicating Mexico's culture.

H because it simply emphasizes Ballet Folklórico's fame but does not emphasize its value as a method for globally communicating Mexico's culture.

J because it emphasizes Ballet Folklórico's potential staying power but does not emphasize its value as a method for globally communicating Mexico's culture.

Passage XIV

Question 195. The best answer is B because the essay describes how Hernández translated Mexican folklore into ballet performances. She drew upon songs and dances that chronicled life, death, and rebirth.

The best answer is NOT:

A because this justification does not emphasize how Hernández's work was influenced by Mexican folklore. The essay briefly notes that Hernández's Ballet Folklórico "won hundreds of awards," but the awards do not illustrate how the traditions and customs of an artist's culture can be the foundation for his or her art.

C because though the essay focuses on Hernández, the essay illustrates how the traditions and customs of Hernández's culture were the foundation of her art.

D because the passage indicates that Hernández studied classical and modern ballet with Europe's finest teachers, but that Hernández's traditions and customs were the foundation for her art.

Question 196. The best answer is F because it correctly uses an apostrophe to signify possession. The pen belongs to someone else. *Else* is an adjective that modifies the pronoun *someone.* The resulting compound "someone else" is singular and possessive and, therefore, receives *-'s.*

G because it places the apostrophe in the wrong location. *-s'* is reserved for plural possession.

J because it leaves out a necessary apostrophe. The pen belongs to *someone else.* Therefore, an apostrophe is needed to signify possession.

Question 197. **The best answer is C** because a period is appropriately used between two independent clauses.

The best answer is NOT:

A because it incorrectly inserts a relative pronoun: *which*. This leads the verb *assume* to no longer function as a verb in the context of the sentence. Relative clauses, which begin with relative pronouns, are often used in incorrect answers to questions that test your understanding of what constitutes a sentence. In this sentence, the subject is *I* and the verb should be *assume*. Adding the relative pronoun *which* before *I assume* makes the verb *assume* no longer function as a verb within the context of the sentence. Instead, the verb functions as part of a descriptive clause that functions like an adjective.

B because it incorrectly inserts a relative pronoun: *that*. This leads the verb *assume* to no longer function as a verb in the context of the sentence. Relative clauses, which begin with relative pronouns, are often used in incorrect answers to questions that test your understanding of what constitutes a sentence. In this sentence, the subject is *I* and the verb should be *assume*. Adding the relative pronoun *that* before "I assume" makes the verb *assume* no longer function as a verb within the context of the sentence. Instead, the verb functions as part of a descriptive clause that functions like an adjective.

D because it creates a run-on, or fused, sentence. There is no punctuation or conjunction (connecting word) between the two independent clauses.

Question 198. **The best answer is F** because deleting these words would make it seem as though the narrator is intentionally attempting to walk away with pens that belong to others, consciously assuming "all pens belong to me." These adverbs clarify that the narrator doesn't mean to take others' pens.

The best answer is NOT:

G because these adverbs are not describing the narrator's deception. Instead, they underscore that the narrator absentmindedly and unintentionally walks off with pens that belong to others.

H because the narrator does not feel *threatened*. This word is too extreme in relation to the content of the passage. The narrator seems embarrassed by this repeated pattern of inadvertently taking others' pens.

J because the narrator is not indecisive. The narrator does not consciously deliberate over whether or not to take pens that belong to others. Instead, the narrator unconsciously takes others' pens.

Question 199. **The best answer is D** because the contraction *I'm* means "I am." This correctly creates two independent clauses joined by the coordinating conjunction *and*.

The best answer is NOT:

A because it uses the verb form *being*, which is a participle. Because it is a verb form, a participle is often mistaken for the main verb in a clause. The statement "perhaps this is because being a writer," has no verb, so it is a sentence fragment. It is not an independent clause, and therefore, it is incorrect to use the conjunction *and* to join it with the independent clause that follows it. The use of the word *and* in this sentence suggests that it will provide two separate reasons why the narrator inadvertently takes others' pens.

B because it uses the verb form *being*, which is a participle. Because it is a verb form, a participle is often mistaken for the main verb in a clause. The statement "perhaps this is because being that I'm a writer" has no verb, so it is a sentence fragment. It is not an independent clause, and, therefore, it is not appropriate to use the conjunction *and* to join it with the independent clause that follows it. The use of the word *and* in this sentence suggests that it will provide two separate reasons why the narrator inadvertently takes others' pens.

C because it uses the verb form *being*, which is a participle. Because it is a verb form, a participle is often mistaken for the main verb in a clause. The statement "perhaps this is because my being a writer" has no verb, so it is a sentence fragment. It is not an independent clause, and, therefore, it is not appropriate to use the conjunction *and* to join it with the independent clause that follows it. The use of the word *and* in this sentence suggests that it will provide two separate reasons why the narrator inadvertently takes others' pens.

Question 200. **The best answer is H** because this question asks what alternative would NOT be acceptable. It is not idiomatic for the word *many* to be followed by *of*. The phrase "many of pens" is awkward. It would be acceptable to say "many pens." In the context of this sentence, *many* functions as a determiner, meaning that it quantifies the amount pens. Determiners should be followed directly by a plural noun. Determiners can also refer to certain nouns. Other determiners include *fewer, every,* and *these*.

The best answer is NOT:

F because it is idiomatically correct to say "a large number of pens." Additionally, this effectively conveys that the narrator always has a pen nearby in case a writing opportunity presents itself.

H because it is idiomatically correct to say, "a handful of pens." Additionally, this effectively conveys that the narrator always has a pen nearby in case a writing opportunity presents itself.

J because it is idiomatically correct to say, "a lot of pens." Additionally, this effectively conveys that the narrator always has a pen nearby in case a writing opportunity presents itself.

Question 201. The best answer is **D** because it appropriately uses the verb form *knowing* to modify the subject: *knowing* is a participle, which functions as part of the descriptive phrase "knowing that a pen is handy."

The best answer is NOT:

A because the infinitive "to know" is not appropriate with the context of this sentence. This is because the adjective *better* is not appropriately followed by an infinitive. Other adjectives like *careful, fortunate*, and *sorry* are often followed by infinitives. For example, in this sentence, the infinitive *to know* explains what the subject is eager about: "I feel eager *to know* if I was cast as the lead in the play."

B because the infinitive "to know" is not appropriate with the context of this sentence. This is because it is not idiomatic for the adjective *better* to be followed by an infinitive. Other adjectives like *careful, fortunate*, and *sorry* are often followed by infinitives. For example, in this sentence, the infinitive "to know" explains what the subject is eager about: "I feel eager *to know* if I was cast as the lead in the play."

C because *known*, the past participle of the verb *to know*, is not appropriate within the context of the sentence.

Question 202. The best answer is **G** because this creates the most logical sentence within the context of the paragraph. The narrator talks about always having many pens and feeling better knowing that a pen is handy.

The best answer is NOT:

F because it uses the plural pronoun *they*, which does not have a logical antecedent in the previous sentence because the previous sentence talks about having *a pen handy*. The article *a* indicates a single pen. If the previous sentence described having *pens handy*, then it would be appropriate to use the plural pronoun *they* here.

H because the word *something* is too vague.

J because the word *either* implies that the previous sentence refers to two pens when, in fact, the sentence only refers to "a pen."

ENGLISH • EXPLANATORY ANSWERS

Question 203. The best answer is **C** because it appropriately sets off the nonessential phrase ("as if of their own accord") with commas.

The best answer is NOT:

A because it omits a necessary comma before the word *as*. Two commas are needed to set off the nonessential phrase "as if of their own accord" —one before the word *as* and another after the word *accord*.

B because a semicolon should be used to separate two independent clauses. A semicolon is incorrectly used here before a nonessential phrase ("as if of their own accord") that should be set off by commas.

D because a colon is incorrectly used here before a nonessential phrase ("as if of their own accord") that should be set off by commas.

Question 204. The best answer is **F** because this detail emphasizes how many pens the narrator has, which is a detail that is relevant to the paragraph.

The best answer is NOT:

G because this sentence does not explain a statement made in the preceding sentence. The previous sentence describes how there are piles of ballpoint pens on the narrator's night table.

H because it does not distract readers from the main focus of the paragraph.

J because this sentence is not vague and pointless.

Question 205. The best answer is **D** because it appropriately uses the possessive pronoun *its*. The word *it* refers to the narrator's habit. The negative consequences figuratively belong to the habit. *Its* without an apostrophe is used to signify possession.

The best answer is NOT:

A because *it's* means "it is," which is not logical within the context of this sentence.

B because *there* specifies a certain place or topic. The word *there* is not appropriate within the context of this sentence.

C because the plural possessive pronoun *their* does not agree with the singular antecedent *habit*.

Question 206. The best answer is **J** because the adverb *also* logically introduces an additional negative consequence of having so many pens.

The best answer is NOT:

F because the adverb *still* means *even* and incorrectly implies that several negative consequences have been listed when this paragraph has only listed one negative consequence thus far in the essay.

G because the adverb *consequently* incorrectly indicates that this sentence offers a consequence following from a circumstance identified in the preceding sentence. Instead, this sentence offers an additional negative consequence of having so many pens.

H because the adverb *instead* incorrectly indicates contrast. The ideas here are not contradictory. This sentence and the previous one give examples of the negative consequences of having so many pens.

Question 207. The best answer is **D** because the plural present tense verb *are* agrees with the plural subject *clothes*. This answer also correctly uses the adjective *decorated* to describe the condition of the clothes.

The best answer is NOT:

A because the verb phrase "have been decorating" is illogical within the context of this sentence. It implies that the clothes have the agency and consciousness to decorate something with ink stains.

B because it incorrectly uses the *singular* verb phrase "had been." The singular auxiliary (helping) verb *had* does not agree with the plural subject *clothes*.

C because the verb phrase "are decorating" is illogical within the context of this sentence. It implies that the clothes have the agency and consciousness to decorate something with ink stains.

Question 208. The best answer is F because a comma is appropriate after the introductory phrase "After a recent mishap involving half of my travel wardrobe" and the sentence's main clause, which begins with "my father."

The best answer is NOT:

G because it creates a sentence fragment. It only includes the adverb *recently* as a transition word followed by the noun phrase "a mishap that involved half of my travel wardrobe." This fragment does not include a subordinating conjunction that makes it dependent on the independent clause "my father convinced me not to pack pens in my suitcase."

H because this creates a comma splice, meaning that a comma is used where a period is needed between two independent clauses. "A recent mishap involved half of my travel wardrobe" is an independent clause because it contains a subject (*mishap*) and a past tense verb (*involved*).

J because it creates a sentence fragment. It only includes the noun phrase "a recent mishap involving half of my travel wardrobe." This fragment does not include a subordinating conjunction that makes it dependent on the following independent clause: "my father convinced me not to pack pens in my suitcase." The word *involving* is a participle, which is often mistaken for the main verb in a clause. Participles function essentially as adjectives. In this case, the participial phrase "involving half my wardrobe" modifies the noun *mishap*.

Question 209. The best answer is B because placing Sentence 1 first makes sense because it introduces an anecdote about how a mishap involving half of the narrator's travel wardrobe prompted the decision to no longer pack pens in his or her suitcase. Sentence 3 logically comes next, explaining that the pens leaked due to low air pressure. Sentence 4 includes the phrase *such calamities*, which logically refers back to the leaking pens in Sentence 3. Sentence 2 sums up the narrator's view on the choice to only pack pens in his or her pocket.

The best answer is NOT:

A because leaving Sentence 2 where it is now is not logical because Sentence 2 must come last. It sums up the narrator's feeling about the experience of no longer packing pens in his or her suitcase after several leaked.

C because this arrangement of the sentences is illogical. Sentence 2 must come last because it sums up the narrator's feeling about the experience of no longer packing pens in his or her suitcase after several leaked in her suitcase.

D because this arrangement of the sentences is illogical. Sentence 4 includes the phrase "such calamities," which logically refers back to the leaking pens in Sentence 3. Therefore, Sentence 4 must be placed after Sentence 3.

Question 210. The best answer is F because this quote cleverly grabs the reader's attention by relaying a snippet of dialogue about the narrator's tendency to inadvertently take others' pens. It helps establish that the essay will address the narrator's love of pens, and it conveys the essay's conversational tone.

The best answer is NOT:

G because the friend is not the focus of the essay. Additionally, the word *problem* is somewhat extreme to describe how this quote portrays the friend's feelings about the narrator inadvertently taking his or her pens. The essay indicates that the friend *gently* asks for the pen back.

H because it is not necessary for this character to be developed later in the essay.

J because it is not necessary for the essay to indicate how this situation was resolved. The function of this anecdote is simply to introduce the narrator's love of pens.

Passage XV

Question 211. The best answer is D because it states the idea clearly and concisely. It does not repeat the same idea twice, and it does not add unnecessary words to the sentence.

The best answer is NOT:

A because it would add redundant information to the essay. The phrase "exploring under the sea" is redundant with "underwater explorer."

B because it would add redundant information to the essay. The phrase "exploring under the sea" is redundant with "underwater explorer."

C because it would add redundant information to the essay. "Who explored under the sea" is redundant with "underwater explorer."

Question 212. The best answer is H because it appropriately uses the possessive pronoun *its*. The word *it* refers to the U.S. Navy. The undersea habitat belongs to *the U.S. Navy. Its* without an apostrophe is used to signify possession. "The U.S. Navy" is singular. Organizations are typically treated as singular nouns even though they refer to groups of people.

The best answer is NOT:

F because *it's* means "it is," which is not logical within the context of this sentence.

G because *there* specifies a certain place or topic. The word *there* is not appropriate within the context of this sentence. Additionally, *there* is plural, and there is no logical plural antecedent earlier in the sentence. "The U.S. Navy" is singular.

J because *its'* is never correct in any context. *It* is singular and *s'* signifies plural possession as in "the students' teachers taught them well."

Question 213. The best answer is C because the *SeaLab* has already been described earlier in the essay as a place where "one day humans would be 'freed from the bondage of the surface' to work and even live underwater."

The best answer is NOT:

A because this brief definition is redundant with Jacques Cousteau's prediction that "one day humans would be 'freed from the bondage of the surface' to work and even live underwater."

B because it is not needed to help the reader envision what the Navy deployed. This phrase is redundant with Jacques Cousteau's prediction that "one day humans would be 'freed from the bondage of the surface' to work and even live underwater."

D because it is not a digression that leads the paragraph away from its primary focus. It would be relevant if it weren't redundant.

Question 214. The best answer is F because the word *outside* concisely and appropriately forms the counterpoint to *inside*.

The best answer is NOT:

G because the phrase "the ocean depth at the exterior" is needlessly wordy.

H because the phrase "the ocean depth on the reverse side" is needlessly wordy.

J because the word *beyond* is not as logical as the word *outside* to describe the way the pressure is balanced inside and outside the underwater habitat. Additionally, the pressure being described is immediately outside the habitat. The phrase "the ocean depth beyond" implies a broader scope than is ideal within the context of this sentence.

Question 215. The best answer is B because the adverb *greatly* appropriately modifies the verb *extends*. The word *greatly* answers the question "to what extent?" Adverbs should ideally be placed as close as possible to the verbs they modify.

The best answer is NOT:

A because adverbs should ideally be placed as close as possible to the verbs they modify. The adverb *greatly* modifies the verb *extends*.

C because adverbs should ideally be placed as close as possible to the verbs they modify. The adverb *greatly* modifies the verb *extends*.

D because adverbs should ideally be placed as close as possible to the verbs they modify. The adverb *greatly* modifies the verb *extends*.

ENGLISH • EXPLANATORY ANSWERS

Question 216. The best answer is **H** because the proposed clause is a digression. Additionally, the next sentence begins with the phrase "for example," and what follows is not an example of what this clause describes.

The best answer is NOT:

F because this addition would emphasize camaraderie, but it does not logically fit within the context of the paragraph.

G because this clause does not suggest that an undersea habitat is capable of providing the comforts of home.

J because while it is accurate that this clause does not specifically describe any of the memories, this clause should not be included because it is a digression from the focus of the paragraph. It would continue to be a digression even if it included more specific details about the content of the memories.

Question 217. The best answer is **D** because it appropriately sets off the nonessential phrase "at a depth of sixty feet" with commas.

The best answer is NOT:

A because it creates a sentence fragment by inserting a period after the introductory phrase "For example, at a depth of sixty feet."

B because it inserts an unnecessary and confusing comma before the prepositional phrase "of sixty feet."

C because it creates a sentence fragment by inserting a semicolon after the introductory phrase "For example, at a depth of sixty feet."

Question 218. The best answer is **J** because it correctly inserts a period between two independent clauses. The second sentence begins with the participial phrase "using SeaLab," which modifies the subject: divers. The verb phrase for the second sentence is "can work."

The best answer is NOT:

F because it creates a comma splice (two or more complete sentences separated only by a comma).

G because it creates a run-on sentence. The word *using* begins a second independent clause, and, therefore, it should have a period before it.

H because it creates a run-on sentence. The word *using* begins a second independent clause, and, therefore, it should have a period before it.

Question 219. The best answer is **B** because the introductory description "bolted to a two-hundred-ton platform sixty feet below sea level at Conch Reef," clearly refers to the subject of the sentence "this research outpost."

The best answer is NOT:

A because this makes the introductory description "bolted to a two-hundred-ton platform sixty feet below sea level at Conch Reef" refer to scientists, which does not make sense.

C because this makes the introductory description "bolted to a two-hundred-ton platform sixty feet below sea level at Conch Reef" refer to scientists, which does not make sense.

D because this makes the introductory description "bolted to a two-hundred-ton platform sixty feet below sea level at Conch Reef" refer to research scientists, which does not make sense.

Question 220. The best answer is **F** because it specifies the governing bodies that give orders to the Aquarius project: The National Oceanic and Atmospheric Administration and the University of North Carolina.

The best answer is NOT:

G because it doesn't clearly indicate that the University itself is a governing body—it only states that professors from the university were involved with the project.

H because it does not point out the governing bodies from which the *Aquarius* project receives its orders. It only highlights the conflict between university professors and scientific researchers working on the *Aquarius* habitat.

J because this statement is vague and does not specify any governing bodies.

Question 221. **The best answer is A** because the word *classification* is the least appropriate alternative to the original word *array*. Classification means labeling according to a system. The main point here is that scientists had access to a variety of scientific instruments.

The best answer is NOT:

B because the word *assortment* is an appropriate alternative to the original word *array*. The word *assortment* means a collection of items. The main point here is that scientists had access to a variety of scientific instruments, so the word *assortment* makes sense here.

C because the word *collection* is an appropriate alternative to the original word *array*. The word *array* means a collection of items. The main point here is that scientists had access to a variety of scientific instruments, so the word *collection* makes sense here.

D because the word *supply* is an appropriate alternative to the original word *array*. The word *supply* means an accumulation of resources. The main point here is that scientists had access to a variety of scientific instruments, so the word *supply* makes sense here.

Question 222. **The best answer is F** because a comma appropriately sets off the appositive phrase "a special air pocket that keeps the ocean outside," which renames *moonpool*.

The best answer is NOT:

G because it creates a sentence fragment by inserting a period before the appositive phrase "a special air pocket that keeps the ocean outside." The verb *keeps* does not function as a verb within the context of this sentence because it is part of the relative clause "that keeps the ocean outside."

H because it creates a sentence fragment by inserting a semicolon before the appositive phrase "a special air pocket that keeps the ocean outside." The verb *keeps* does not function as a verb within the context of this sentence because it is part of the relative clause "that keeps the ocean outside."

J because it does not include a comma before the appositive phrase "a special air pocket that keeps the ocean outside."

Question 223. The best answer is C because the adverb *gradually* appropriately modifies the verb *returned*. It answers the question "*how* is the pressure inside the habitat returned to that of sea level?"

The best answer is NOT:

A because the adjective *gradual* and the verb *returned* are not parallel sentence elements. It does not make sense to say that the "pressure inside the habitat must be *gradual* and *returned* to that of sea level."

B because the adverb *gradually* and the verb *returned* are not parallel sentence elements. It does not make sense to say that the "pressure inside the habitat must be *gradually* and *returned* to that of sea level."

D because the adjective *gradual* cannot be used to modify the verb *returned*. Adjectives modify nouns whereas adverbs modify verbs, adverbs, and other adjectives.

Question 224. The best answer is H because Sentence 1 includes the phrase "this decompression," which logically refers back to the gradual decompression process described in Sentence 2. Sentence 3 fits logically as the conclusion of the essay.

The best answer is NOT:

F because leaving Sentence 1 where it is now is not logical because it includes the phrase "this decompression," which does not have a logical antecedent. Sentence 1 must logically follow Sentence 2. Additionally, Sentence 3 fits logically as the concluding sentence of the essay.

G because leaving Sentence 1 where it is now is not logical because it includes the phrase "this decompression," which does not have a logical antecedent. Sentence 1 must logically follow Sentence 2. Additionally, Sentence 3 fits logically as the concluding sentence of the essay.

J because Sentence 1 must come after Sentence 2 because the phrase "this decompression," logically refers back to the gradual decompression process described in Sentence 2. Additionally, Sentence 3 fits logically as the concluding sentence of the essay.

Question 225. The best answer is D because the reference to Jacques Cousteau only indicates that he predicted that "one day humans would be 'freed from the bondage of the surface' to work and even live underwater." The essay does not indicate that Cousteau himself contributed directly to making life under the sea a reality.

The best answer is NOT:

A because the essay does not indicate that Cousteau researched various underwater habitats.

B because Cousteau himself was not involved in the U.S. Navy's deployment of its first undersea habitat.

C because the essay describes several underwater habitats including the *SeaLab* and the *Aquarius*, but Cousteau was not involved in their development.

Passage XVI

Question 226. The best answer is F because the phrase "the achievement *in* which he is most widely remembered for" is not idiomatically correct. The preposition *in* should be deleted to clearly describe which accomplishment Dr. Grant is most widely remembered *for*.

The best answer is NOT:

G because "that he is remembered most widely for" is a relative clause that makes sense in this context.

H because "for which he is most widely remembered" is a prepositional phrase that makes sense in this context. This word order is sometimes used to avoid ending a sentence with a preposition such as *for*.

J because "he is most widely remembered for" modifies the noun *achievement* and makes sense in this context.

Question 227. The best answer is D because it states the idea clearly and concisely. It does not repeat the same idea twice, and it does not add unnecessary words to the sentence.

The best answer is NOT:

A because the phrase "invention and creation" is wordy. In this context the word *invention* is redundant with the word *creation*.

B because in this context the clause "which was the creation" is wordy and redundant with the word *invention*.

C because in this context the phrase "that is, the creation" is wordy and redundant with the word *invention*.

Question 228. **The best answer is F** because the singular possessive pronoun *his* is appropriate within the context of the sentence. Dr. Grant invented the golf tee, so it is *his* invention.

The best answer is NOT:

G because the plural possessive pronoun *their* does not agree with the singular subject of the sentence: *Dr. Grant*.

H because *its'* is never correct in any context because *it* is singular and *s'* signifies plural possession as in "the *students'* teachers taught them well."

J because *it's* means "it is," which is not logical within the context of this sentence.

Question 229. **The best answer is A** because "in order" is appropriately followed by the infinitive form of the verb: *to hit*.

The best answer is NOT:

B because it is not idiomatic for "for hitting" to follow the phrase "in order." The phrase "in order" must be followed by an infinitive, which begins with the word *to*.

C because it is not idiomatic for "to hitting" to follow the phrase "in order." The phrase "in order" must be followed by an infinitive. The word *to* is typically only used in the infinitive form of a verb. "Hitting" is a participle, not the infinitive form. "To hit" is the infinitive.

D because it is not idiomatic for "that hit" to follow the phrase "in order." The phrase "in order" must be followed by an infinitive, which begins with the word *to*.

Question 230. **The best answer is J** because this is the LEAST acceptable alternative to the underlined portion. The word *rescued* implies that a person or object is being saved from danger. "Rescuing" a problem sounds strange. The tone is somewhat melodramatic within the context of this essay.

The best answer is NOT:

F because the word *corrected* appropriately describes how Dr. Grant's invention of the golf tee fixed the problem of golf balls rolling away before they could be hit.

G because the word *alleviated* appropriately describes how Dr. Grant's invention of the golf tee fixed the problem of golf balls rolling away before they could be hit. The word *alleviate* implies that an obstacle is overcome or that the effect of a negative influence has been lightened.

H because the word *fixed* appropriately describes how Dr. Grant's invention of the golf tee remedied the problem of golf balls rolling away before they could be hit.

Question 231. The best answer is B because it shifts the focus away from Dr. Grant's invention of the golf tee. This sentence appropriately introduces this paragraph, which describes Dr. Grant's contributions to the field of dentistry.

The best answer is NOT:

A because this sentence is irrelevant to the focus of this paragraph, which describes Dr. Grant's contributions to the field of dentistry.

C because this sentence is irrelevant to the focus of this paragraph, which describes Dr. Grant's contributions to the field of dentistry. This sentence focuses on Dr. Grant's appreciation for golf and the role it can play in building relationships.

D because this sentence is not logically connected to the focus of this paragraph, which describes Dr. Grant's contributions to the field of dentistry. It is not logical to begin this paragraph by stating that Dr. Grant's friends were "the happy recipients of his invention" when this paragraph focuses on Dr. Grant's invention of a new style of dental bridge, a device that provides support for individuals who have lost or broken teeth. There is no mention of the doctor's friends in the paragraph.

Question 232. The best answer is G because it correctly uses an apostrophe to signify possession. The design belongs to Dr. Grant.

The best answer is NOT:

F because it leaves out a necessary apostrophe before the *s* in *Grant's*. An apostrophe is needed to signify possession. The design belongs to Dr. Grant.

H because although it forms the possessive correctly, it inserts an unnecessary and confusing comma between the subject "Grant's design" and the verb *fit*.

J because it leaves out a necessary apostrophe before the *s* in *Grant's*. An apostrophe is needed to signify possession. The design belongs to Dr. Grant. Additionally, this answer inserts an unnecessary and confusing comma between the subject *Grant's design* and the verb *fit*.

Question 233. The best answer is **B** because the singular past tense verb *was* agrees with the singular subject "general health." The subject of a verb cannot be found in a prepositional phrase such as "of his patients."

The best answer is NOT:

A because the plural verb phrase *have been* does not agree with the singular subject "general health."

C because the plural verb *are* does not agree with the singular subject "general health."

D because the past tense plural verb *were* does not agree with the singular subject "general health."

Question 234. The best answer is **F** because no punctuation is needed. The prepositional phrase "of the golf tee" should not be separated from the noun it modifies (*invention*) by a comma.

The best answer is NOT:

G because the prepositional phrase "of the golf tee" should not be separated from the noun it modifies (*invention*) by a set of framing commas.

H because the prepositional phrase "of the golf tee" should not be separated from the noun it modifies (*invention*) by a comma.

J because the prepositional phrase "of the golf tee" should not be separated from the noun it modifies (*invention*) by a comma.

Question 235. The best answer is **A** because it states the idea clearly and concisely. It does not repeat the same idea twice, and it does not add unnecessary words to the sentence.

The best answer is NOT:

B because the phrase "a lack of something that was needed" is unnecessarily wordy.

C because the phrase "that a need was in existence" is unnecessarily wordy.

D because the phrase "a need that was out there" is unnecessarily wordy and vague.

Question 236. **The best answer is H** because it is idiomatic for the preposition *on* to follow the verb *focused* in the phrase "focused his skills, imagination, and intelligence *on* devising a way to fill that need."

The best answer is NOT:

F because it is not idiomatic for the preposition *to* to follow the verb *focused* in the phrase "focused his skills, imagination, and intelligence *to* devising a way to fill that need."

G because it is not idiomatic for the preposition *at* to follow the verb *focused* in the phrase "focused his skills, imagination, and intelligence *at* devising a way to fill that need."

J because it is not idiomatic for the preposition *for* to follow the verb *focused* in the phrase "focused his skills, imagination, and intelligence *for* devising a way to fill that need."

Question 237. **The best answer is D** because it avoids introducing an unnecessary and illogical transition word.

The best answer is NOT:

A because the word *instead* incorrectly indicates that this sentence will contrast with the previous one.

B because the phrase *in addition* incorrectly indicates that this sentence will provide an additional example of Dr. Grant's contributions. Instead, this sentence emphasizes the lasting impression Dr. Grant made on golf and dentistry.

C because the phrase *in contrast* incorrectly indicates that this sentence contradicts the previous one. This is not accurate. Instead, the previous sentence describes how Dr. Griffin was innovative, and this sentence describes the influence of his work in the fields of golf and dentistry.

Question 238. The best answer is **H** because it appropriately sets off the introductory appositive phrase "a brilliant professor of dentistry" with a comma.

The best answer is NOT:

F because it creates a sentence fragment because a colon follows a noun phrase: "a brilliant professor of dentistry." It does not include a subordinating conjunction such as *although* that could make this introductory phrase dependent on the independent clause "he is best remembered…"

G because it creates a sentence fragment because a semicolon follows a noun phrase: "a brilliant professor of dentistry." It does not include a subordinating conjunction such as *although* that could make this introductory phrase dependent on the independent clause "he is best remembered…"

J because the appositive phrase "a brilliant professor of dentistry" must be set off from the main clause (beginning with *he*) with a comma.

Question 239. The best answer is **D** because "making it possible for" should be followed by the infinitive form of the verb: *to concentrate*. "Making it possible for generations of golfers *to concentrate* on their swings" is grammatically correct.

The best answer is NOT:

A because the phrase "making it possible for generations of golfers *concentrated* on their swings" is grammatically incorrect. An infinitive phrase is required here.

B because the phrase "making it possible for generations of golfers *concentrating* on their swings" is grammatically incorrect. An infinitive phrase is required here.

C because it omits the word *to*, which is needed here to create the infinitive *to concentrate*. The phrase "making it possible for generations of golfers *concentrate* on their swings" is grammatically incorrect. An infinitive phrase is required here.

Question 240. **The best answer is H** because the essay focuses on just one of Dr. Griffin's inventions related to golf: the golf tee. The essay does not broadly describe key innovations in golf equipment.

The best answer is NOT:

F because the essay only highlights one key innovation in golf: the golf tee. Exploring one innovation does not mean "documenting key innovations in golf equipment."

G because while it is true that the essay describes when the golf tee was introduced, the essay only highlights one key innovation in golf: the golf tee.

J because while the essay does not describe tees made of plastic or metal, this omission is not the main reason that this essay does not achieve the goal of documenting key innovations in golf equipment. The main issue is that the essay only highlights one key innovation in golf: the golf tee.

Passage XVII

Question 241. **The best answer is C** because it appropriately sets off the nonessential element "in 1917, the year our house was built" with commas. This phrase does not provide information that is essential to the meaning of the sentence. The main clause includes the subject "the city planners" and the verb *had*.

The best answer is NOT:

A because it creates a sentence fragment by incorrectly inserting a period after the introductory cause "In 1917, the year our house was built." This nonessential element should be set off from the main clause whose subject is "the city planners" and whose verb is *had*.

B because it lacks a necessary comma to set off the nonessential element "In 1917, the year our house was built."

D because it creates a sentence fragment by incorrectly inserting a semicolon after the nonessential element "In 1917, the year our house was built." This should be set off from the main clause whose subject is "the city planners" and whose verb is *had*.

Question 242. **The best answer is J** because the phrase "had a scheme for" is idiomatically correct.

The best answer is NOT:

F because the phrase "had a scheme *about* the collection of trash" is not idiomatically correct.

G because the phrase "had a scheme *of* the collection of trash" is not idiomatically correct.

H because the phrase "had a scheme *by* the collection of trash" is not idiomatically correct.

Question 243. The best answer is **A** because the relative pronoun *that* appropriately introduces the relative clause "that ran behind the rows of houses," which modifies the noun phrase it follows: "the narrow alleys."

The best answer is NOT:

B because in the context of this sentence, the phrase "being that" means *because.* This incorrectly indicates a cause-and-effect relationship. The garbage cans are not picked up from the narrow alleys *because* they ran behind the rows of houses.

C because *so* incorrectly indicates a cause-and-effect relationship. The garbage cans are not picked up from the narrow alleys *because* they ran behind the rows of houses.

D because *since* incorrectly indicates a cause-and-effect relationship. The garbage cans are not picked up from the narrow alleys *because* they ran behind the rows of houses.

Question 244. The best answer is **H** because it conveys that the city planners' trash collection system prioritizes orderliness and tidy appearances. The garbage cans were placed behind the houses, which suggests that these garbage cans were viewed as an eyesore that should ideally remain out of sight. Describing the sidewalks as *tidy* and *tree-lined* emphasizes how the city aims to project an orderly image.

The best answer is NOT:

F because the sidewalk's width does not support the idea that the city hoped that their trash collection system would be orderly.

G because the sidewalks being paved with cement does not support the idea that the city hoped that their trash collection system would be orderly. It just provides a detail about the material used to create the sidewalks.

J because the adjectives *old* and *familiar* do not support the logic of the city planners' trash collection system, which prioritizes orderliness.

Question 245. **The best answer is B** because the relative clause "that the houses faced" appropriately modifies the noun *sidewalks*. It provides descriptive detail about the location of the house in relation to the sidewalk.

The best answer is NOT:

A because it is wordy and awkward. The phrase "with which" is not idiomatically correct within the context of this sentence. This phrase is sometimes used to avoid ending a sentence with the preposition *with* as is true in the following sentence: "Fortunately, the school was able to develop a policy *with which* the teachers agreed." This phrase also emphasizes that one noun (often a trait or capacity) is used to achieve a certain purpose. For example, the following sentence includes an idiomatically correct use of this phrase: "I was amazed by the confidence *with which* she scaled the rock wall."

C because the syntax is awkward. The subject of this sentence is *the sidewalks*. Typically, a subject is followed by a verb and the verb's direct object (the receiver of the action), but this sentence inverts the verb and the direct object: "the sidewalks toward the houses faced." The correct expression is "the sidewalks faced toward the houses."

D because this sentence inserts an awkward prepositional phrase that modifies the subject of the sentence: "the sidewalks with the houses facing." This is not an idiomatic way to indicate that sidewalks are facing the houses.

Question 246. **The best answer is J** because the simple past tense verb *worked* is appropriate within the context of the paragraph, which describes how the trash collection system has worked for the past six or seven decades. Additionally, this verb tense is parallel with the past tense verb *squeezed* in the sentence that follows.

The best answer is NOT:

F because the verb phrase "would have worked" is not appropriate within the context of the paragraph. It suggests that this trash collection system was not actually implemented. Additionally, this verb tense is not parallel with the past tense verb *squeezed* in the sentence that follows.

G because the verb phrase "were to have worked" is not appropriate within the context of the paragraph. It suggests that this trash collection system was not actually implemented. Additionally, this verb tense is not parallel with the past tense verb *squeezed* in the sentence that follows.

H because the present tense verb *work* is not logical here because this sentence describes how the trash collection system has worked for the past six or seven decades. Additionally, this verb is not parallel with the past tense verb *squeezed* in the sentence that follows.

Question 247. The best answer is A because *squeezed* appropriately describes how the garbage trucks navigated the back alleys, collecting trash for several decades. This word choice is supported by the indication that the alleys are *narrow* earlier in the essay.

The best answer is NOT:

B because the phrase "rambled down" suggests traveling without a sense of purpose or direction. This does not connect well with the passage's earlier indication that the alleys are narrow and that they were part of the city planners' orderly scheme for the collection of trash.

C because the phrase "rolled along" suggests steady unimpeded progress. This does not connect well with the passage's earlier indication that the alleys are narrow and that they were part of the city planners' orderly scheme for the collection of trash.

D because the word *travelled* does not provide any further information that connects well with the passage's earlier indication that the alleys are narrow and that they were part of the city planners' orderly scheme for the collection of trash.

Question 248. The best answer is H because this sentence notes that today's garbage trucks can barely even fit down ordinary city streets. This underscores that today's garbage trucks are too wide for the narrow alleys that were originally constructed in 1917.

The best answer is NOT:

F because this sentence focuses on the garbage truck's color. It does not relate to the previous sentence, which focuses on the trucks' difficulties navigating the narrow alleys that were originally constructed in 1917.

G because this sentence describes how residents pick up litter from the alley twice a year. It does not support the previous sentence, which emphasizes that modern garbage trucks are too wide to fit down narrow alleys.

J because this sentence describes how the alleys remain free of trash and yard clippings. It does not support the previous sentence, which emphasizes that modern garbage trucks are too wide to fit down narrow alleys.

Question 249. The best answer is C because this question asks which alternative is NOT acceptable. This answer creates a comma splice (two or more complete sentences separated only by a comma).

The best answer is NOT:

A because the conjunction *so* correctly joins two independent clauses. In the context of this sentence, the word *so* means *therefore*.

B because it correctly inserts a semicolon between two independent clauses.

D because it correctly inserts a colon between two independent clauses.

Question 250. The best answer is G because the singular verb *is* agrees with the singular subject *what*.

The best answer is NOT:

F because the present plural verb *are* does not agree with the singular subject *what*.

H because the past plural verb *were* does not agree with the singular subject *what*.

J because the plural verb *have been* does not agree with the singular subject *what*.

Question 251. The best answer is B because it is the LEAST appropriate word in the context of this sentence. The word *attraction* has a positive connotation and implies that people are drawn to observe the trash cans left on the sidewalk. The context calls for a word with neutral or negative connotation.

The best answer is NOT:

A because the word *exhibition* means a display. This word has a neutral connotation, so it could describe trash cans being left on the sidewalks in front of houses.

C because the word *spectacle* means a powerful scene. This word has a neutral connotation, so it could describe trash cans being left on the sidewalks in front of houses.

D because the word *showing* means a display. This word has a neutral connotation, so it could describe trash cans being left on the sidewalks in front of houses.

Question 252. **The best answer is F** because the relative pronoun *who* appropriately begins this relative clause, which provides nonessential detail describing the neighborhood's young children "who delight in watching the show." Additionally, *who* is used when the noun referred to by the pronoun is the subject of the verb in the relative clause.

The best answer is NOT:

G because the direct object *whom* is not appropriate within the context of this sentence. The word *whom* typically follows prepositions such as *of, from,* or *to. Whom* functions as the receiver of the verb's action. For example, *whom* is used correctly in the following sentence "You threw the pie at *whom*?"

H because the relative pronoun *who* should modify the noun phrase "young children" since *who* is generally used to refer to people. The relative pronoun *which* primarily modifies thing rather than people. *Which* is also sometimes used to refer to animals.

J because the possessive pronoun *whose* is illogical within the context of the sentence. Inserting *whose* creates a sentence fragment because the relative clause "whose delight in watching the show" should, within the context of the sentence, be followed by a verb explaining what their *delight* does. For example, the sentence could appropriately end in the following manner: "whose delight in watching the show *is* a joy to observe."

Question 253. **The best answer is B** because *it's* means "it is," which does not make sense within the context of this sentence.

The best answer is NOT:

A because the relative clause "that is exotic in its own way" appropriately modifies the visitor (the garbage truck).

C because the conjunction *and* appropriately introduces a parallel sentence element "is exotic in its own way." This parallels the earlier part of the sentence that states that the garbage truck "is a weekly visitor." It is appropriate for the conjunction *and* to not have a comma before it because it is not followed by a subject and verb. If the sentence read, "and it is exotic in its own way," then the conjunction *and* would need a comma before it.

D because the nonrestrictive phrase "exotic in its own way" appropriately modifies the noun *visitor* (the garbage truck).

Question 254. **The best answer is G** because a colon appropriately introduces a list of the positive qualities of today's garbage trucks. A colon must have an independent clause before it, which it does here: "Its best features are hard to beat."

The best answer is NOT:

F because it lacks appropriate punctuation. A colon is needed to provide clarity. The colon indicates that a list of features will follow. A colon must have a complete sentence before it.

H because a colon, not a comma, is needed to introduce this list of the positive qualities of today's garbage trucks. What comes before the list is a complete sentence, and therefore a colon is the most appropriate choice. If the list were preceded by the phrase "such as," then a colon would *not* be appropriate because placing the phrase "such as" before the list creates a sentence fragment: "Its best features are hard to beat, such as . . ." If that were the case, a comma before the phrase "such as" or no punctuation would be clearest and most appropriate.

J because a semicolon should, in most contexts, have a complete sentence before *and* after it. The one exception is when semicolons are used to create clarity by separating complex phrases in a list. This answer creates a sentence fragment that lists the positive qualities of today's garbage trucks.

Question 255. **The best answer is C** because the plural pronoun *them* in Sentence 4 refers to the "young children" in Sentence 2. Additionally, the "fire engine" at the end of the sentence is repeated at the beginning of Sentence 3, which creates cohesion.

The best answer is NOT:

A because leaving Sentence 4 where it is now is not logical because the plural pronoun *them* in sentence 4 does not have a logical antecedent in Sentence 3. In fact, Sentence 3 does not even contain a plural noun.

B because placing Sentence 4 after sentence 1 is not logical because the plural pronoun *them* in Sentence 4 does not have a logical antecedent in Sentence 1. In fact, Sentence 1 does not even contain a plural noun.

D because placing Sentence 4 after Sentence 6 is not logical because the plural pronoun *them* in Sentence 4 does not have a logical antecedent in Sentence 6. Additionally, Sentence 6 contains the plural nouns *features* and *cans* but neither of these words fits the description in Sentence 4 "for them, the garbage truck is even better than a fire engine."

Passage XVIII

Question 256. The best answer is B because this question asks you to choose the LEAST acceptable alternative. "I spend appropriate vacation time slots" is the *least* acceptable alternative because the narrator's search for mushrooms is not limited to vacation time slots. In addition, this phrase does not fit stylistically with the rest of the essay—it is more formal than the rest of the essay.

The best answer is NOT:

A because "all my free time" is an acceptable alternative (in meaning and style) to "every free moment."

C because "every moment of my leisure time" is an acceptable alternative (in meaning and style) to "every free moment."

D because "whatever time I can set aside" is an acceptable alternative (in meaning and style) to "every free moment."

Question 257. The best answer is F because the absence of punctuation creates the clearest and most understandable sentence.

The best answer is NOT:

G because it incorrectly inserts a comma between *about* and *imaginary creatures* (*about* is not the end of an introductory phrase).

H because it incorrectly inserts a comma between *about* and *imaginary creatures* (*about* is not the end of an introductory phrase).

J because it incorrectly inserts a comma after the coordinating conjunction *but*.

Question 258. The best answer is D because it provides the most specific description of the appearance of morel mushrooms. It describes the color, shape, and appearance of the texture of morel mushrooms.

The best answer is NOT:

A because the description of "funny-looking" is based on the judgment of the writer and may be visualized differently by someone else. The descriptions "textured" is vague. "Edible" addresses usefulness and safety rather than physical appearance.

B because the description of "earthy" is vague, and the descriptions "amusing" and "interesting" are based on the judgment of the writer. Again, these are vague descriptions that could be visualized differently by different people.

C because it only gives one visual descriptor "unusually shaped," which is vague. The description "odorless" is used with the sense of smell rather than with the sense of sight.

Question 259. The best answer is H because the word *you* maintains agreement with the use of the second person pronoun *you* earlier in the passage.

The best answer is NOT:

F because "a person" does not maintain agreement with the use of the word *you* earlier in the essay.

G because the phrase "a morel hunter" does not maintain agreement with the word *you* earlier in the essay.

J because it deletes the subject of the verb phrase *will be*.

Question 260. The best answer is A because it provides information about what the writer read and specific details on how the writer chose the reading material. This connects well with the next sentence, which indicates that the narrator searches "the same woods that yield morels produce poisonous mushrooms, too."

The best answer is NOT:

B because it does not provide specific details about what the writer reads. It only provides vague information about when the writer reads.

C because it does not provide specific details about what the writer reads. It only provides vague information about why the writer was reading.

D because it does not provide specific details about what the writer reads. It only provides vague information on how the writer reads.

Question 261. The best answer is J because it creates the clearest and most concise sentence, eliminating redundancy.

The best answer is NOT:

F because "preparation to get ready for" is redundant.

G because "make oneself fit for" is redundant with "preparation."

H because "of someone planning to be ready" is redundant with "preparation."

Question 262. The best answer is **D** because it serves as a transition between the writer researching morel mushrooms and what the writer plans to do after learning about mushrooms—enter a mushroom-hunting contest.

The best answer is NOT:

A because while the previous paragraph describes the writer using field guides, this sentence does not effectively transition to the current paragraph, as there is no mention of mushroom hunting.

B because this sentence about eating morels does not connect to the previous or the current paragraph; it mentions neither preparing for mushroom hunting nor mushroom-hunting activities.

C because this detail about outdoor activities does not fit logically at this point in the essay. While it loosely connects to the current paragraph in that a mushroom-hunting contest is a rewarding outdoor activity, it does not connect to the previous paragraph's topic on preparing for mushroom hunting.

Question 263. The best answer is **H** because it correctly inserts a period between two independent clauses.

The best answer is NOT:

F because it creates a comma splice (two or more complete sentences separated only by a comma). "This year, I'm going to enter" is an independent clause.

G because it creates a run-on sentence.

J because inserting the word *because* incorrectly indicates a cause-effect relationship.

Question 264. The best answer is **B** because it correctly inserts a period before the sentence "He's my hero."

The best answer is NOT:

A because it lacks a necessary comma before *becoming*.

C because it creates a comma splice (two or more complete sentences separated only by a comma). "What a hero" is a complete thought.

D because the phrase "my hero" should be placed after the noun it modifies (one participant). Modifying phrases should be placed as near as possible to the words they modify.

Question 265. The best answer is J because the absence of commas here creates the clearest and most understandable sentence.

The best answer is NOT:

F because it incorrectly inserts a single comma between the subject "keeping silent about your favorite spots" and verb *is*.

G because it incorrectly inserts a comma between the subject "keeping silent" and the preposition *about*. The phrase "about your favorite spots" modifies *keeping silent*, and these elements should not be separated by any punctuation.

H because it inserts an unnecessary comma between the subject "keeping silent" and the preposition *about*. The phrase "about your favorite spots" modifies "keeping silent," and these elements should not be separated by any punctuation.

Question 266. The best answer is C because it provides the most specific information about what is needed in order to find morel mushrooms: "patience and concentration."

The best answer is NOT:

A because "two things in particular" is vague and does not specify what is needed in order to find morel mushrooms.

B because "demonstrating two skills" is vague and does not specify what is needed in order to find morel mushrooms.

D because "expertise in this hobby" is vague and does not specify what is needed in order to find morel mushrooms.

Question 267. The best answer is H because "paler than" is the correct comparative form to use to contrast a pinecone and a mushroom.

The best answer is NOT:

F because the adverb *then* is incorrectly used instead of the preposition *than* to introduce the second part of the comparison. *Then* is used to indicate sequence.

G because the adverb *then* is incorrectly used instead of the preposition *than* to introduce the second part of the comparison. *Then* is used to indicate sequence. Additionally, the phrase "more pale" is not the correct comparative term in the context of the contrast of two things: a pinecone and a mushroom.

J because the word *pale* is not the correct comparative term in the context of the contrast of two things: a pinecone and a mushroom.

Question 268. The best answer is **A** because it uses the correct form of the possessive pronoun *its*.

The best answer is NOT:

B because it uses the contraction *it's* (meaning "it is") where the possessive pronoun *its* is called for.

C because it uses the plural possessive pronoun *their* when the singular possessive pronoun *its* is called for to refer to the singular noun "a morel."

D because it uses the pronoun *there,* which should be used to refer to locations or to introduce a clause.

Question 269. The best answer is **G** because no transition word or phrase is needed here.

The best answer is NOT:

F because the transition word *however* incorrectly signals contrast from the previous sentence. The information in this sentence is used to support the previous sentence.

H because the phrase "on the other hand" incorrectly signals contrast. The information in this sentence is used to support the previous sentence.

J because the phrase "back and forth" does not serve as a logical introduction to the idea that follows: "you can look right at one [a morel mushroom] and not see it."

Question 270. The best answer is **B** because it correctly inserts a period between two independent clauses.

The best answer is NOT:

A because it creates a comma splice (two or more complete sentences separated only by a comma). "Morels fool everyone, even the experts" is a complete thought.

C because it creates a comma splice (two or more complete sentences separated only by a comma). "Morels fool everyone" is a complete thought. Additionally, if the word *say* is followed by a comma (as it is here), then it introduces a direct quotation that should be framed by quotation marks. If the word *say* were not followed by a comma, then it would be introducing an indirect quotation that would not require quotation marks.

D because the coordinating conjunction *and* is lacking the necessary comma before it that would correctly join the two independent clauses. The second independent clause begins with the subject *that's*.

Passage XIX

Question 271. The best answer is **G** because it creates the clearest and most understandable sentence with a clear subject (*butterfly*) and a clear verb (*is*).

The best answer is NOT:

F because it attaches the main verb *is* to the relative pronoun *which*, creating a clause that interrupts the sentence and creates a sentence fragment (an incomplete sentence).

H because it attaches the main verb *is* to the relative pronoun *that*, creating a clause that interrupts the sentence and creates a sentence fragment (an incomplete sentence).

J because it incorrectly inserts a comma between the subject *butterfly* and the verb *is*.

Question 272. The best answer is **D** because *most* is a superlative term used correctly here to compare "black monarch butterflies" to other butterfly species in North America. The adverb *easily* correctly modifies the verb *recognized*.

The best answer is NOT:

A because it incorrectly uses the adjective *easiest* to modify the verb *recognized*. In addition, it is incorrect to use the superlative adverb *most* with the superlative adjective *easiest*.

B because it incorrectly uses the adjective *easy* to modify the verb *recognized*.

C because it incorrectly uses the adjective *easiest* to modify the verb *recognized*.

Question 273. The best answer is **H** because it creates the clearest and most concise sentence.

The best answer is NOT:

F because "an extended flight" is redundant with "their long journey."

G because "which is far-reaching" is redundant with "their long journey."

J because "which encompasses many miles" is redundant with "their long journey."

Question 274. **The best answer is D** because the absence of commas here creates the clearest and most understandable sentence.

The best answer is NOT:

A because it incorrectly inserts a comma between the subject *monarchs* and the prepositional phrase that modifies it: "west of the Rocky Mountains." These elements should not be separated by any punctuation.

B because it incorrectly inserts a comma between the prepositional phrase "west of the Rocky Mountains" (which modifies the subject of the sentence) and the verb *migrate*. These elements should not be separated by any punctuation.

C because it incorrectly inserts a comma that interrupts the phrase ("west of the Rocky Mountains") that modifies the subject: "many monarchs." In addition, it incorrectly inserts a comma between the prepositional phrase "west of the Rocky Mountains" (which modifies the subject of the sentence) and the verb "migrate." These elements should not be separated by any punctuation.

Question 275. **The best answer is F** because it appropriately uses the relative pronoun *where* to introduce the sentence element that modifies "the southern California coast."

The best answer is NOT:

G because it creates a comma splice (two or more complete sentences separated only by a comma). "There they overwinter in eucalyptus groves" is an independent clause.

H because it creates a nonsensical sentence. The monarchs cannot simultaneously *migrate* and "overwinter [stay] in eucalyptus groves." The monarchs overwinter *after* their migration to the southern California coast.

J because it creates a comma splice (two or more complete sentences separated only by a comma). "They overwinter in eucalyptus groves" is an independent clause.

Question 276. The best answer is **B** because the word *however* correctly contrasts the description of the migration patterns of many monarchs within the United States to the migrations of monarchs that travel far beyond the United States, "as many as three thousand miles," to Mexico City.

The best answer is NOT:

A because the word *besides* indicates that a previous idea is being elaborated upon, which is not the case here.

C because the word *finally* indicates the end of a long process. This sentence focuses on a new subset of the monarch population that migrates to Mexico City.

D because the word *therefore* indicates a cause-effect relationship, which isn't the case here.

Question 277. The best answer is **G** because a dash, not a comma, is needed before the word *millions* to set off the phrase "millions of them across the United States and Canada." Although a pair of commas could have been used to set off this nonessential phrase, the writer uses a dash after the word *Canada*, so parallelism requires that a dash precede the word *millions*.

The best answer is NOT:

F because a dash, not a comma, is needed before the word *millions* to set off the phrase "millions of them across the United States and Canada."

H because a dash, not a semicolon, is needed before the word *millions* to set off the phrase "millions of them across the United States and Canada." Using a semicolon results in a sentence fragment: "Besides, most monarchs."

J because a dash is needed before the word *millions* to set off the phrase "millions of them across the United States and Canada."

Question 278. The best answer is **B** because it provides the correct adjective (*less*) to contrast the development of the monarchs' and migratory birds' nervous systems. In addition, *less* is the logical connector when using *than*.

The best answer is NOT:

A because the sentence sets up a comparison between the nervous systems of monarchs and those of birds. The adverb *insufficiently* does not correctly compare the development of the monarchs' and migratory birds' nervous systems.

C because the adjective *insufficient* does not correctly modify the verb *developed*. An adverb (*insufficiently*) is needed in this context.

D because the adjective *inadequate* does not correctly modify the verb *developed*. An adverb (*inadequately*) is needed in this context.

Question 279. The best answer is **F** because the noun *ability* is parallel in form to the nouns *design* and *vision* earlier in the sentence.

> The best answer is NOT:

> **G** because the gerunds (verbs that act as nouns by adding *-ing*) *regulating* and *maintaining* are not parallel with the nouns listed earlier in the sentence (*aerodynamic design* and *acute vision*).

> **H** because the phrase "with their body temperature regulation and energy maintenance ability," is not parallel in form to the nouns *design* and *vision* earlier in the sentence.

> **J** because the phrase "and the regulation of body temperature and their ability to maintain energy" is not parallel in form to the nouns *design* and *vision* earlier in the sentence. To maintain parallelism, the word *their* (before *ability*) would need to be changed to "the."

Question 280. The best answer is **C** because Sentence 4 introduces the idea that monarchs and migratory birds have important differences, including body size and a difference in nervous system development.

> The best answer is NOT:

> **A** because Sentence 2 maintains focus on the monarchs' migration.

> **B** because Sentence 3 maintains focus on the monarchs' migration.

> **D** because Sentence 5 should follow Sentence 4 since Sentence 4 describes differences between monarchs and migratory birds and Sentence 5 describes the similarities that help both migrate successfully.

Question 281. The best answer is **F** because the context of the sentence requires the word *sites* in the main clause to be plural but not possessive. No punctuation is necessary at this point in the sentence.

> The best answer is NOT:

> **G** because the word *site* should be plural but not be possessive.

> **H** because the word *sites* should not be possessive.

> **J** because no comma is needed between the word *sites* and the preposition *on*.

Question 282. The best answer is C because the word *while* effectively introduces the contrast between monarchs that migrate and those that do not.

The best answer is NOT:

A because the word *when* does not effectively introduce the contrast between monarchs that migrate and those that do not. The word *when* is used with time and sequence relationships.

B because the word *if* does not effectively introduce the contrast between monarchs that migrate and those that do not. The word *if* establishes a cause-effect relationship.

D because the phrase "so that" does not effectively introduce the contrast between monarchs that migrate and those that do not. The phrase "so that" establishes a cause-effect relationship.

Question 283. The best answer is J because when an introductory clause begins with a subordinating conjunction, it must be followed by a comma and a subject and a verb.

The best answer is NOT:

F because when an introductory clause begins with a subordinating conjunction, it must be followed by a comma, not a semicolon. A semicolon is typically used to separate two independent clauses. Using a semicolon here creates a sentence fragment.

G because the use of the word *and* at this point in the sentence creates a sentence fragment.

H because the use of the word *and* at this point in the sentence creates a sentence fragment. Additionally, the subordinating conjunction *while* should be followed by a comma, a subject, and a verb.

Question 284. The best answer is C because the present tense plural verb *continue* maintains parallelism with the use of the present tense verb *feed* earlier in the passage.

The best answer is NOT:

A because the past tense verb *continued* does not maintain parallelism with the use of the present tense verb *feed* earlier in the passage.

B because *continuing* does not maintain parallelism with the use of the present tense verb *feed* earlier in the passage.

D because *continuing* does not maintain parallelism with the use of the present tense verb *feed* earlier in the passage.

Question 285. The best answer is H because it supports the main point that some aspects of the monarch's migration continue to be mysterious.

The best answer is NOT:

F because "they are ready to move ahead" is vague and does not directly support one of the main points of the essay.

G because it does not directly support one of the main points of the essay. Research tools are mentioned for the first time in this sentence.

J because the author refers generally to *researchers* throughout the essay, but it does not indicate that one group of researchers is more knowledgeable than another.

Passage XX

Question 286. The best answer is D because it creates the clearest and most concise sentence.

The best answer is NOT:

A because it introduces an irrelevant detail about the doll being the oldest toy.

B because it is redundant with the word *speculate* earlier in the sentence.

C because it discusses a material used in making yo-yos, which interrupts the topic of the yo-yo as an ancient toy.

Question 287. The best answer is J because "of objects resembling yo-yos" clearly and concisely describes the content of the ancient drawings.

The best answer is NOT:

F because the word *objects* is vague.

G because it is awkward and wordy.

H because the phrase "almost slightly resemble" is wordy and redundant. The word *resemble* alone indicates that the drawings are not exact renderings of modern yo-yos.

Question 288. The best answer is **B** because the conjunction *and* effectively joins two independent clauses. "Written mention of yo-yos goes back to the fifth century B.C." is an independent clause.

> The best answer is NOT:

> **A** because it creates a statement that is not logical. The word *if* implies a cause-effect relationship where one does not exist.

> **C** because it creates a statement that is not logical. The word *since* implies a cause-effect relationship where one does not exist.

> **D** because it creates a statement that is not logical. The word *because* implies a cause-effect relationship where one does not exist.

Question 289. The best answer is **F** because it states that "yo-yos have been a national pastime for *centuries*," which demonstrates that there has been a long history of enthusiasm for the yo-yo in the Philippines. Widespread interest is indicated by the words "national pastime."

> The best answer is NOT:

> **G** because the yo-yo's popularity for *years* is not the most effective evidence of the long history of enthusiasm for the yo-yo in the Philippines.

> **H** because it provides a largely irrelevant detail about the materials used to make yo-yos.

> **J** because it provides a largely irrelevant detail about the yo-yo's similarities to a toy that was once popular in ancient China.

Question 290. The best answer is **A** because "translates *as*" is an idiomatically correct expression in context.

> The best answer is NOT:

> **B** because "translates *by*" creates an idiomatically nonstandard expression in context.

> **C** because "translates *with*" creates an idiomatically nonstandard expression in context.

> **D** because "translates *from*" creates an idiomatically nonstandard expression in context.

Question 291. **The best answer is J** because the lack of punctuation creates a run-on sentence. Therefore, this answer is NOT acceptable.

    The best answer is NOT:

    F because it correctly inserts a period between two independent clauses. "Flores soon started a yo-yo manufacturing company in California" is an independent clause.

    G because it correctly inserts a comma and a coordinating conjunction (*and*) between two independent clauses. "He soon started a yo-yo manufacturing company in California" is an independent clause.

    H because it correctly inserts a semicolon between two closely related independent clauses. "He soon started a yo-yo manufacturing company in California" is an independent clause.

Question 292. **The best answer is D** because it creates the clearest and most concise sentence.

    The best answer is NOT:

    A because "really progressed substantially" is redundant with "making a leap forward."

    B because "advanced as a result of progressively making" is redundant with "making a leap forward."

    C because "jumped ahead" is redundant with "made a leap forward."

Question 293. **The best answer is F** because the simple past tense verb *began* is consistent with the verb tense in the rest of the paragraph.

    The best answer is NOT:

    G because the present tense verb *begins* is inconsistent with the verb tense in the rest of the paragraph.

    H because the past participle *begun* must be preceded by the auxiliary verb *had*. Additionally, it is inconsistent with the verb tense in the rest of the paragraph.

    J because *begun* (not began) is the past participle of the verb "to begin."

Question 294. The best answer is **A** because the relative pronoun *who* correctly introduces the relative clause "who watched."

The best answer is NOT:

B because the relative pronoun *whom* is used incorrectly here; whom is the object pronoun, but the sentence requires a subject pronoun (*who*).

C because the possessive pronoun *whose* is used incorrectly here.

D because the contraction *who's* means "who is," which is not logical within the context of this sentence.

Question 295. The best answer is **J** because it creates a sentence fragment. "Deciding that he was more interested in teaching people how to handle yo-yos than he was in manufacturing them" is a participial phrase, not a complete sentence. A statement that has no predicate verb is a sentence fragment (an incomplete sentence).

The best answer is NOT:

F because it produces a complete sentence.

G because "He had decided that he was more interested in teaching people how to handle yo-yos than he was in manufacturing them" is a complete sentence.

H because it produces a complete sentence.

Question 296. The best answer is A because the participle *demonstrating* is parallel with *sponsoring*. Additionally, the participial phrase "demonstrating tricks and sponsoring contests" modifies in a clear way the Yo-Yo Professionals' trips around the country.

The best answer is NOT:

B because the verb *demonstrate* is not parallel with the participle *sponsoring*. Additionally, no comma is needed before "in order to demonstrate."

C because the verb *demonstrated* is not parallel with the participle *sponsoring*. Additionally, the phrase "who demonstrated tricks" should directly follow the noun it modifies: *professionals*.

D because the word *yet* signals contrast, which is not logical within the context of this sentence.

Question 297. The best answer is H because "sending Yo-Yo Professionals around the country" is one creative strategy that Duncan used to promote the yo-yo.

The best answer is NOT:

F because the preceding sentence does not indicate how Duncan felt about any yo-yo advertising.

G because the preceding sentence does not reveal how quickly demonstrations by Duncan Yo-Yo Professionals gained popularity.

J because there is no indication of how Duncan Yo-Yo Professionals were chosen.

Question 298. The best answer is B because the simple past tense verb *went* is consistent with the verb tense in the rest of the paragraph.

The best answer is NOT:

A because no comma is needed between the subject *toys* and the verb *went*.

C because the auxiliary verb *had* should be followed by the past participle *gone*, not *went*.

D because the past perfect tense verb *had gone* is inconsistent with the verb tense in the rest of the paragraph.

Question 299. The best answer is **F** because there should be no punctuation following *shuttle* or *Discovery*. Since *Discovery* is the name of the specific shuttle, there should be no comma following *shuttle*.

The best answer is NOT:

G because the semicolon after *Discovery* creates a sentence fragment (an incomplete sentence). A semicolon must be preceded by an independent clause. In addition, there should be no comma after *shuttle* when the shuttle is specifically named.

H because the comma after *Discovery* is unnecessary.

J because *Discovery* is the name of the specific shuttle. There should be no comma following *shuttle*.

Question 300. The best answer is **D** because placing Paragraph 3 before Paragraph 5 puts the events in chronological order. Paragraph 3, which describes the yo-yos of the 1970s and early 1980s, fits chronologically within the context of the essay. The 4th paragraph describes how the yo-yo craze began in the 1930s, and the 5th paragraph describes how a yo-yo was sent into outer space in 1985.

The best answer is NOT:

A because Paragraph 3 is about the yo-yo in the 1970s and 1980, while Paragraph 4 mentions the year 1932. Paragraph 3 should be placed after, not before Paragraph 4.

B because Paragraph 1 describes ancient references to the yo-yo. Paragraph 3, which is about yo-yos in the 1970s and 1980s, should come later in the essay.

C because Paragraph 2 mentions the 1920s, while Paragraph 3 is about the yo-yo in the 1970s and 1980s. Therefore, Paragraph 3 should be placed after, not before, Paragraph 2.

Passage XXI

Question 301. The best answer is **G** because the singular past tense auxiliary verb *had* forms the past perfect progressive tense verb phrase "had been training." The context calls for this tense because this sentence describes how Lynne Cox had been training for two years prior to attempting to swim a mile through the glacier-strewn sea.

The best answer is NOT:

F because "would of" is an improperly formed verb that uses the word *of* instead of *have*.

H because the plural verb *have* does not agree in number with the singular noun *she*.

J because "had to of" is an improperly formed verb that uses the word *of* instead of *have*.

Question 302. **The best answer is B** because the conjunction *and* effectively joins two independent clauses. "At forty-five, she had been training for two years for this event" is an independent clause.

The best answer is NOT:

A because the relative clause "which she hoped her preparations would pay off" does not logically modify the noun directly before it: *event*.

C because it creates a comma splice (two or more complete sentences separated only by a comma). "Then she hoped her preparations would pay off" is an independent clause.

D because it creates a comma splice (two or more complete sentences separated only by a comma). "She hoped her preparations would pay off" is an independent clause.

Question 303. **The best answer is F** because no punctuation is needed here. The absence of commas makes this the clearest sentence.

The best answer is NOT:

G because the adjective *cold* should not be separated from the noun it modifies: *lakes*.

H because the comma after the word *lakes* is an unwarranted break between the prepositional phrase "of New Hampshire and Maine" and the noun it modifies: *lakes*.

J because the adjective *cold* should not be separated from the noun it modifies: *lakes*. Additionally, no comma is needed to separate two items in a list.

Question 304. **The best answer is B** because the plural noun *records* makes sense within the context of the sentence, which refers to men's and women's records broken by Cox.

The best answer is NOT:

A because it uses an incorrect apostrophe after *record*, suggesting that the record possesses something. No such possession is supported by the essay.

C because it uses an incorrect apostrophe after *records*, suggesting that the record possesses something. No such possession is supported by the essay.

D because the comma after the word *records* is an unwarranted break between the prepositional phrase "for swimming the English Channel" and the noun it modifies: *records*.

Question 305. The best answer is J because the proposed statement is irrelevant at this point in a paragraph mainly about Lynne Cox's experiences swimming long distances.

The best answer is NOT:

F because the essay already indicates that Cox completed a "twenty-seven-mile swim" in the English Channel. This sufficiently conveys that Cox swam a great distance.

G because this statement does not provide a logical transition to the rest of the paragraph.

H because Cox's swim in across the English Channel is relevant. What makes the proposed sentence irrelevant is that a more relevant measurement has already been given by this point in the essay.

Question 306. The best answer is B because the phrase "loved the challenge" emphasizes Cox's passion for swimming long distances under challenging conditions.

The best answer is NOT:

A because the phrase "could swim" does not indicate an attitude.

C because the phrase "had racked up many miles" does not indicate an attitude.

D because the phrase "astounded many by her swimming feats" does not emphasize Cox's passion for swimming long distances in challenging conditions. Instead, it emphasizes how others perceive Cox's accomplishments.

Question 307. The best answer is J because "weight that she hoped would keep her warm in the icy water" provides further information about the "twelve pounds" that Cox gained without creating a comma splice.

The best answer is NOT:

F because it creates a comma splice. "It was weight that she hoped would keep her warm in the icy water" is an independent clause.

G because it creates a comma splice. "She put on weight that she hoped would keep her warm in the icy water" is an independent clause.

H because it creates a nonsensical sentence: "She gained it so that she hoped would keep her warm in the icy water."

Question 308. The best answer is A because the sentences flow in a logical order. First, the paragraph introduces the idea that Cox needed to prepare to swim the Antarctic. Then, the paragraph explains steps Cox took to prepare.

The best answer is NOT:

B because placing Sentence 4 before Sentence 2 is not logical. Sentences 3 and 4 should be placed after Sentence 2, which introduces the idea that Cox studied how Antarctic animals adapt to the frigid environment. Sentences 3 and 4 provide specific examples of the Antarctic animals' adaptations to frigid environments.

C because placing Sentence 3 before Sentence 1 is not logical. Sentence 1 introduces the idea that Cox needed to prepare to swim the Antarctic. Additionally, placing Sentence 2 after Sentences 3 and 4 is not logical. Sentences 3 and 4 should be placed after Sentence 2, which introduces the idea that Cox studied how Antarctic animals adapt to the frigid environment. Sentences 3 and 4 provide specific examples of the Antarctic animals' adaptations to frigid environments.

D because placing Sentence 4 first is not logical because it provides a specific detail about how Antarctic seals tolerate cold temperatures. This detail should not appear until after Sentence 2, which introduces the idea that Cox studied how Antarctic animals adapt to the frigid environment.

Question 309. The best answer is H because the prepositional phrase "with a crew of physicians, sailors, and expedition experts" correctly modifies the subject of the sentence: *Cox*.

The best answer is NOT:

F because the subject of the sentence is *Cox* alone. Without *with*, the sentence makes both *crew* and *Cox* the subject of the sentence, which isn't logical.

G because the subject of the sentence is *Cox* alone. Without *with*, the sentence makes both *crew* and *Cox* the subject of the sentence, which isn't logical.

J because the subject of the sentence is *Cox* alone. This sentence makes it sound like *physicians*, *sailors*, *expedition leaders*, and *Cox* are the subject of the sentence. To make this sentence logical, the *and* would need to be moved in front of *Cox*.

Question 310. The best answer is **C** because this physical detail about brushing up against ice best emphasizes that Cox was in a harsh environment.

The best answer is NOT:

A because it does not offer a physical detail. Rather, it is vague about the perils of the swim.

B because it describes publicity surrounding the event rather than offering a physical detail about Cox during the swim.

D because it describes publicity surrounding the event rather than offering a physical detail about Cox during the swim.

Question 311. The best answer is **G** because it creates the clearest and most concise sentence.

The best answer is NOT:

F because the word *fatigue* is redundant with the word *exhaustion*.

H because the phrase "that left her feeling fatigued" is redundant with the word *exhaustion*.

J because the word *exhausting* is redundant with the word *fatigue*.

Question 312. The best answer is **C** because it uses the correct comparative adjective *bluer* and the correct conjunction *than* to compare the Antarctic water to other water she had swum in.

The best answer is NOT:

A because the phrase "blue as" should be preceded by the word *as*. Additionally, the phrase "blue as" is not parallel with the comparative adjective *clearer* earlier in the sentence.

B because the phrase "more blue then" is an incorrect use of the comparative adjective *more* in combination with *blue*. Additionally, the conjunction *than* must be used to set up the comparison in the sentence, not the adverb *then*.

D because the conjunction *than* must be used to set up the comparison in the sentence, not the adverb *then*.

Question 313. **The best answer is F** because it creates the clearest and most concise sentence.

The best answer is NOT:

G because "body temperature" is redundant.

H because the phrase "in other words" is illogical within the context of the sentence. The nonessential phrase "which fell to 95.5 degrees Fahrenheit by the end of the swim" is framed by dashes and therefore you should be able to cut it out of the sentence without creating awkwardness or confusion.

J because it is not logical with the first part of the sentence. "… the longer it would take to bring her body temperature which was normal" is illogical.

Question 314. **The best answer is B** because it correctly begins the sentence with the subordinating conjunction *as*. "A mile was good enough" is an independent clause.

The best answer is NOT:

A because it creates a run-on sentence. "A mile was good enough" is an independent clause, and, therefore, it should end with a period.

C because it creates a comma splice (two or more complete sentences separated only by a comma). "A mile was good enough" is an independent clause.

D because it creates a comma splice (two or more complete sentences separated only by a comma). "A mile was good enough" is an independent clause.

Question 315. **The best answer is J** because it best concludes the essay with a specific image (of a flock of penguins) that emphasizes the location. The phrase "last thrilling strokes" indicates the completion of Cox's historic swim.

The best answer is NOT:

F because it does not indicate the completion of Cox's feat.

G because the word *birds* does not best conclude the essay with an image that emphasizes the location of Cox's feat. The correct answer's use of the word *penguins* emphasizes the location of Cox's feat.

H because the use of the word *wildlife* does not best conclude the essay with an image that emphasizes the location of Cox's feat. Additionally, this answer does not emphasize the completion of Cox's feat.

ENGLISH • EXPLANATORY ANSWERS

Passage XXII

Question 316. The best answer is C because the phrase "over some six decades" is redundant with the phrase "for more than sixty years."

The best answer is NOT:

A because the phrase "over some six decades" is redundant.

B because the phrase "over some six decades" is redundant. Additionally, this detail does not indicate *when* Withers began working as a photojournalist.

D because this phrase is relevant. It is just redundant.

Question 317. The best answer is H because it results in a complete sentence with a comma separating the main clause from the participial phrase that begins with *using*.

The best answer is NOT:

F because it lacks a subject, creating a sentence fragment.

G because it creates a sentence fragment: "using his hometown as his base."

J because it does not contain a main clause. The participial phrase beginning with *using* is followed by a second participial phrase that lacks a subject: "documenting the key people and events…"

Question 318. The best answer is B because it provides the most effective and most specific support for the statement made in the preceding sentence.

The best answer is NOT:

A because it is vague about what historic moments took place. It also doesn't indicate that the neighborhood or area in which Withers grew up included historic moments.

C because it is vague about what historic moments took place.

D because it is vague about what historic moments took place.

Question 319. The best answer is **H** because the phrase "as if" is the only one of the four alternatives that, in the context of the sentence, can't reasonably be used as a substitute for the underlined portion (*when*). "As if" is the only option that is not logical in the context of the sentence.

The best answer is NOT:

F because the word *whereas* is an acceptable alternative to the word *when*. The word *whereas* emphasizes the different reactions to the camera.

G because the word *since* is an acceptable alternative to the word *when*. The word *since* emphasizes that Withers was able to take the camera to school *because* his sister's boyfriend showed no interest in using it.

J because the word *after* is an acceptable alternative to the word *when*. The word *after* emphasizes that Withers takes the camera once his sister's boyfriend showed no interest in using it.

Question 320. The best answer is **A** because "taking pictures in his youth" is the correct, idiomatic phrase needed in order to make this sentence the most understandable. This idiomatic phrase means that Withers started taking pictures when he was young.

The best answer is NOT:

B because the phrase "taking pictures *with* his youth" is not idiomatic.

C because the phrase "taking pictures *of* his youth" is not idiomatic. This implies that Withers is documenting his own childhood, which is not accurate within the context of the essay.

D because the phrase "taking pictures *at* his youth" is not idiomatic.

Question 321. The best answer is **H** because it creates the clearest and most concise sentence.

The best answer is NOT:

F because "at a job that was" is unnecessarily wordy.

G because "for himself" is redundant with *self-employed*.

J because it creates confusion about who is working as a photographer. It suggests that Withers has hired a self-employed photographer.

Question 322. The best answer is B because placing Sentence 3 before Sentence 1 creates the most logical progression of ideas. Sentence 3 introduces the idea that Withers began taking pictures in his youth. Sentence 1 explains how Withers acquired his first camera. Sentences 2 and 4 explain how Withers used his photography skills later in life.

The best answer is NOT:

A because keeping Sentence 3 where it is now illogically presents the idea that Withers began taking pictures in his youth after Sentence 1, which explains how Withers acquired his first camera.

C because placing Sentence 3 after Sentence 1 illogically presents the idea that Withers began taking pictures in his youth after Sentence 1, which explains how Withers acquired his first camera.

D because placing Sentence 3 after Sentence 4 illogically presents the idea that Withers began taking pictures in his youth after Sentences 2 and 4, which explains how Withers used his photography skills later in life.

Question 323. The best answer is J because "well known" correctly modifies the subject of the sentence: Withers. Additionally, it is parallel with "well liked." Each of the other choices creates a comma splice (two or more complete sentences separated only by a comma).

The best answer is NOT:

F because the word *thus* incorrectly indicates a cause-effect relationship. In addition, it creates a comma splice (two or more complete sentences separated only by a comma). "Thus, he is well known and well liked" is an independent clause.

G because it creates a comma splice. (two or more complete sentences separated only by a comma). "In fact, he is well known and well liked" is an independent clause.

H because it creates a comma splice (two or more complete sentences separated only by a comma). "He is well known and well liked" is an independent clause.

Question 324. **The best answer is** C because the phrase "such historic figures" creates an idiomatically nonstandard expression in context. It lacks a word like *as* or *like* to introduce the list of historical figures.

The best answer is NOT:

A because "such historical figures as" is an idiomatically correct expression in context. It includes the word *as* to introduce the list of historical figures.

B because "historical figures such as" is an idiomatically correct expression in context. It includes the word *as* to introduce the list of historical figures.

D because "historic figures like" is an idiomatically correct expression in context. It includes the word *like* to introduce the list of historical figures.

Question 325. **The best answer is** J because the singular pronoun *his* begins a clear and logical sentence within the context of the paragraph.

The best answer is NOT:

F because "for instance" incorrectly implies that what follows will be an example of the photos Withers took of Martin Luther King Jr., Medgar Evers, or James Meredith. Instead, this sentence focuses on photographs of famous musicians.

G because "as a result" incorrectly indicates a cause-effect relationship.

H because the word *however* incorrectly signals contrast.

Question 326. **The best answer is** D because the plural verb *include* agrees in number with the plural subject *photos.*

The best answer is NOT:

A because the singular verb *includes* does not agree in number with the plural subject *photos.*

B because the singular verb phrase *does include* does not agree in number with the plural subject *photos.*

C because it creates a sentence fragment. It does not contain a main clause. The word *including* functions as a participle, not a verb.

Question 327. **The best answer is G** because no punctuation is needed between the word *photographed* and the list of subjects that Withers photographed. Additionally, a comma should follow each item in a list of three or more items. Therefore, the word *waitresses* should be followed by a comma.

The best answer is NOT:

F because a colon should not separate the verb (*photographed*) from its objects (*waitresses, church congregations, nightclub audiences, and Little League baseball games*).

H because a colon should not separate the verb (*photographed*) from its objects (*waitresses, church congregations, nightclub audiences, and Little League baseball games*). Additionally, a comma should follow each item in a list of three or more items. Therefore, the word *waitresses* should be followed by a comma.

J because a comma should follow each item in a list of three or more items. Therefore, the word *waitresses* should be followed by a comma.

Question 328. **The best answer is B** because the phrase "at last count" expresses that Withers's photographs are still being counted. He was still taking pictures when this essay was written.

The best answer is NOT:

A because the phrase "at long last" implies that Withers finally recorded five million photographic images, but it does not suggest that Withers continued to take photographs at the time this essay was written.

C because the phase "to sum up" does not suggest that Withers continued to take photographs at the time this essay was written. "To sum up" indicates that what follows in the sentence is a summary of the essay.

D because the phrase "all in all" does not suggest that Withers continued to take photographs at the time this essay was written.

Question 329. The best answer is **H** because placing this sentence at the end of Paragraph 3 logically elaborates on the types of photographs Withers took of jazz and blues musicians.

The best answer is NOT:

F because this sentence would disrupt the essay's introduction of Withers and his work as a photographer with a specific detail about Withers's photographs of musicians.

G because this sentence would disrupt the essay's description of how Withers first became interested in photography with a specific detail about his photography later in his career.

J because this sentence would disrupt the fourth paragraph's focus on Withers's photography of everyday subjects such as waitresses, church congregations, and nightclub audiences.

Question 330. The best answer is **A** because this essay portrays a biographical sketch of Ernest Withers's career as a photojournalist and the context of the world he photographed.

The best answer is NOT:

B because this essay goes beyond simply describing how Ernest Withers first developed his interest in photography and photojournalism. It also describes his photography career, which was based in the town where grew up.

C because this essay draws connections between Ernest Withers and the world he photographed. The essay focuses on Withers work within his hometown.

D because this essay portrays a biographical sketch of Ernest Withers's career as a photojournalist and the context of the world he photographed. The essay does not specifically describe Withers's awards, but it notes his achievements such as recording some five million photographic images and his honors such as photographing seven of the last eight U.S. presidents.

ENGLISH • EXPLANATORY ANSWERS

Passage XXIII

Question 331. The best answer is D because omitting the underlined portion eliminates redundancy.

The best answer is NOT:

A because "on their knees" is redundant with "kneeling."

B because "down on their knees" is redundant with "kneeling."

C because "resting on their knees" is redundant with "kneeling."

Question 332. The best answer is H because it is the only option that forms a complete sentence.

The best answer is NOT:

F because the word *which* creates a sentence fragment.

G because the word *where* creates a sentence fragment.

J because the word *that* creates a sentence fragment.

Question 333. The best answer is D because beginning the sentence with *before you* creates a correct introductory subordinating clause "before you can entertain any second thoughts." Notice that the comma is followed directly by a subject and a verb: "the plane has taxied." An introductory clause that begins with a subordinating conjunction should be followed by a comma, a subject, and a verb.

The best answer is NOT:

A because this creates a comma splice (two or more complete sentences separated only by a comma) since an independent clause "You now can entertain any second thoughts" precedes a comma.

B because this creates a comma splice (two or more complete sentences separated only by a comma) since an independent clause "You can entertain any second thoughts" precedes a comma.

C because this creates a comma splice (two or more complete sentences separated only by a comma) since an independent clause "Then you can entertain any second thoughts" precedes a comma.

Question 334. The best answer is F because the use of the past participle *taken* maintains parallelism with the past participle *taxied*. Notice that the present-perfect verb tense is used earlier in this sentence "the plane has taxied." The correct verbs here are *taxied* and *taken* because they correctly follow the auxiliary (helping) verb *has*: "The plane has *taxied*… and [has] *taken* off."

The best answer is NOT:

G because it uses the simple past tense, which does not maintain parallelism with *has taxied*.

H because it uses the past perfect tense (*had* + the past participle), which does not maintain parallelism with *has taxied*.

J because this uses the simple past tense verb *took* paired with the helping verb *had*, which does not maintain parallelism with *has taxied*. *Had took* is not correct in any context.

Question 335. The best answer is C because the singular pronoun *it* is the subject of this sentence. The word *is* is part of the verb phrase *is headed*.

The best answer is NOT:

A because nothing is being possessed. *Its* without an apostrophe is used to signify possession.

B because nothing is being possessed. The use of an apostrophe here implies possession. *Its'* is not correct in any context because *it* is singular and *s'* signifies plural possession.

D because the verb *was* describes a present event in the past tense.

Question 336. The best answer is F because this answer choice states the idea the most clearly and concisely.

The best answer is NOT:

G because the word *up* is redundant with the phrases "circling upward" and "headed to an altitude."

H because the word *up* is redundant with the phrases "circling upward" and "headed to an altitude."

J because the phrase "up in the air" is redundant with the phrases "circling upward" and "headed to an altitude."

Question 337. **The best answer is B** because "the engines' roar" and "the noise of the wind that blasts through the open doorway" are two items in a list of what it is "impossible to talk over." Therefore, *and* is an appropriate conjunction to join these sentence elements, and no comma is needed.

The best answer is NOT:

A because it creates a sentence fragment following a semicolon. A semicolon divides two closely related independent clauses. What follows the semicolon does not include a verb.

C because it creates a sentence fragment. *As* is a subordinating conjunction. Accordingly, what follows *as* is a subordinate clause, which must be followed by a comma and an independent clause in order to create a complete sentence.

D because the word *that* in this sentence creates a sentence fragment.

Question 338. **The best answer is G** because this logically connects with the first sentence of the paragraph, which indicates that "it is impossible to talk— or protest—over the engines' roar." The phrase "this is just as well" implies that it does not matter that you cannot be heard over the sound of the engine. In addition, the idea that the narrator is thinking about protesting indicates that the narrator is reconsidering (probably from nervousness) parachuting.

The best answer is NOT:

F because "the wind rushing in is loud" is redundant with "the noise of the wind blasts." This phrase does not necessarily indicate the narrator's nervousness.

H because inserting "You keep your mouth shut" here is not logical because the subsequent sentence reads "But your instructor smiles confidently." The word *but* signifies contrast, but the ideas here are not directly contradictory. Keeping one's mouth shut is not necessarily an indication of nervousness.

J because the tone is too positive. This does not capture the sense of nervousness that the narrator clearly feels.

Question 339. The best answer is **D** because this paragraph describes a sequence of events leading up to the narrator jumping out of the door of the plane. Sentence 1 describes the final step in the sequence: jumping. Therefore, it should come last.

The best answer is NOT:

A because leaving Sentence 1 where it is now is not logical because Sentences 2, 3, 4, and 5 all describe actions that take place *before* the narrator jumps out of the plane.

B because this arrangement of the sentences is illogical. The instructor must signal *before* the jump occurs. Additionally, the narrator would not nod, as is stated in Sentence 5, *after* jumping out of the plane.

C because this arrangement of the sentences is illogical. The narrator would not nod, as is stated in Sentence 5, *after* jumping out of the plane. Therefore, Sentence 1 must be placed after Sentence 5.

Question 340. The best answer is **H** because no punctuation is needed here. The absence of punctuation creates the clearest and most understandable sentence.

The best answer is NOT:

F because the comma between the verb *think* and the pronoun *you* is unnecessary.

G because the comma between the verb *think* and the relative pronoun *that* is unnecessary.

J because combining "You think" and "you then might become ill" creates a comma splice (two or more complete sentences separated only by a comma).

Question 341. The best answer is **B** because the word *However* introduces contrast. Just when the narrator thinks "you might become ill," the parachute yanks open, and the narrator is relieved to gently drift through the sky.

The best answer is NOT:

A because the word *furthermore* incorrectly indicates that this sentence elaborates on the preceding sentence. Instead, this sentence contrasts with the previous sentence.

C because the word *thus* incorrectly indicates that this sentence offers a consequence following from a circumstance identified in the preceding sentence. Instead, this sentence offers a contrast to the preceding one.

D because the word *consequently* incorrectly indicates that this sentence offers a consequence following from a circumstance identified in the preceding sentence. Instead, this sentence offers a contrast to the preceding one.

Question 342. **The best answer is H** because the word *yank* emphasizes the violent action of the parachute opening at this point in the essay. The word *taut* also emphasizes that the parachute was under a great deal of tension before it opened.

The best answer is NOT:

F because the word *opens* does not emphasize the violent action of the parachute opening.

G because the word *opens* does not emphasize the violent action of the parachute opening.

J because the phrase "quickly becomes taut and opens" does not emphasize the violent action of the parachute opening as much as the phrase "yanks open" does.

Question 343. **The best answer is A** because no punctuation is needed here. The absence of punctuation creates the clearest and most understandable sentence.

The best answer is NOT:

B because it places an unnecessary comma between the subject *you* and the verb *slowed*.

C because it ends the sentence with a question mark when this sentence is a statement.

D because it places an unnecessary comma between the verb *slowed* and the adverb *down*.

Question 344. **The best answer is J** because this creates the clearest sentence within the context of the paragraph.

The best answer is NOT:

F because the word *Thus* incorrectly indicates that this sentence offers a consequence following from a circumstance identified in the preceding sentence. Dangling above the earth is not *caused* by the narrator's appreciation of this accomplishment.

H because the word *since* is a subordinating conjunction in this context, making this a sentence fragment.

G because the word *when* is a subordinating conjunction in this context, making this a sentence fragment.

Question 345. **The best answer is A** because it indicates that the narrator feels relief and looks back on the decision to jump out of a plane with appreciation, saying it "was a fine idea after all." In this context, the word *fine* has a positive connotation.

The best answer is NOT:

B because it indicates that the narrator is still worried about the landing while floating to earth. This does not suggest that the narrator feels *relaxed*.

C because it suggests that the narrator accepts and perhaps is even proud of having jumped, but there is no indication that the narrator feels *relaxed* floating to earth.

D because the word *fine* in this context does not suggest that the narrator is *relaxed* while floating to earth. Here, the word *fine* means that the narrator is only okay until jumping from a plane again.

Passage XXIV

Question 346. **The best answer is J** because it provides the most concise way to make the writer's point.

The best answer is NOT:

F because it is not necessary to emphasize the writer's truthfulness with the clause "it is true that."

G because it is not necessary to emphasize the writer's truthfulness with the clause "it is a fact that."

H because it is not necessary to emphasize the narrator's truthfulness with the clause "it has always been the case that." Additionally, this answer is particularly wordy.

Question 347. **The best answer is C** because *wheezing* and *tinny* are coordinate adjectives, meaning that they have equal weight, and both modify the same noun: *notes*. Coordinate adjectives need to be separated by a comma. Additionally, no comma is needed between *impatient* and *with*. The preposition *with* connects the narrator's impatience to its source: the wheezing, tinny notes.

The best answer is NOT:

A because it incorrectly places a comma between *impatient* and *with*. The preposition *with* connects the narrator's impatience to its source: the *wheezing, tinny notes*.

B because it incorrectly places a comma between the adjective *tinny* and the noun it modifies: *notes*.

D because it incorrectly places a comma between the noun *notes* and the relative clause "that I produced." The relative pronoun *that* introduces essential information that cannot be cut out of a sentence without affecting its meaning.

Question 348. **The best answer is J** because this creates the clearest sentence. It allows the verb phrase *would set* to function as a verb in relation to the sentence's subject *I*.

The best answer is NOT:

F because the relative pronoun *which* makes the sentence illogical.

G because the word *then* is redundant with the introductory clause "After two weeks' effort."

H because "in which" makes the sentence illogical. It also creates a sentence fragment.

Question 349. **The best answer is C** because it is grammatically correct, and the verbs in the sentence maintain the same verb tense. The correct verbs here are *set* and *go* because they correctly follow the auxiliary (helping) verb *would*: "I would set… and [would] go." Although the helping verb *would* is not repeated before *go*, it is implied.

The best answer is NOT:

A because "had went" is not parallel with "would set." In addition, *had* and *went* are never used together. "Had gone" can be used together but uses the wrong verb tense in the context of this sentence.

B because "would of gone" is not parallel with "would set." Additionally, this answer incorrectly uses *of* in place of the helping verb *have*.

D because "would of went" is not parallel with *would set*. Additionally, this answer incorrectly uses *of* in place of the helping verb *have*.

Question 350. **The best answer is G** because "this early version" is synonymous with "the *sheng*." It is appropriate to set off "the *sheng*" with commas because it is nonessential information that repeats the idea "this early version." Additionally, a period is used correctly between two independent clauses.

The best answer is NOT:

F because it creates a comma splice (two or more complete sentences separated only by a comma).

H because it creates a sentence fragment. The word *consisting* functions as part of a participial phrase, which modifies the noun *the sheng*. This leaves the sentence without a verb.

J because it creates a comma splice (two or more complete sentences separated only by a comma).

Question 351. The best answer is C because it creates the clearest and most concise sentence.

The best answer is NOT:

A because "which has its origins in ancient China" is redundant with "it originated in southern China in 1100 B.C."

B because "the instrument I have been unable to play" is redundant with the author's description of repeatedly giving up on playing the harmonica: "After two weeks' effort, I would always set the harmonica aside and go back to the baseball field."

D because "I often asked him to teach me to play" is redundant with "which my father repeatedly tried to teach me to play."

Question 352. The best answer is F because this answer retains a focus on the harmonica and its origin: "The harmonica as we know it was not introduced until 1828 in London."

The best answer is NOT:

G because this answer focuses on providing loosely related elaborating information about London, which disrupts the paragraph's focus on the harmonica.

H because this specific fact about the challenges of playing a harmonica disrupts the paragraph's focus on the general introduction of the modern harmonica.

J because this answer provides loosely related elaborating information about Benjamin Franklin and his inventions, which disrupts the paragraph's focus on the harmonica.

Question 353. The best answer is D because placing the word *originally* after the word *as* is illogical because the adverb *originally* describes when the harmonica was marketed as a children's toy. Modifiers should be placed as near as possible to the words they modify. In this case, the verb phrase "was marketed" is modified by *originally*.

The best answer is NOT:

A because it provides an acceptable placement of *originally*. Placing the word *originally* after the word *marketed* is logical because the adverb *originally* describes when the harmonica was marketed as a children's toy.

B because it provides an acceptable placement of *originally*. Placing the word *originally* after the word *harmonica* is logical because the adverb *originally* describes when the harmonica was marketed as a children's toy.

C because it provides an acceptable placement of *originally*. Placing the word *originally* after the word *was* is logical because the adverb *originally* describes when the harmonica was marketed as a children's toy.

Question 354. **The best answer is F** because a comma is appropriate after the subordinating clause "While the harmonica was originally marketed as a children's toy," and the sentence's main clause, which begins with *it*.

The best answer is NOT:

G because placing a semicolon after the word *toy* causes the introductory adverbial clause to become a sentence fragment.

H because a comma is needed between *toy* and *it* in order to separate the introductory clause from the main clause of the sentence.

J because inserting the relative pronoun *that* creates an illogical sentence with *it*.

Question 355. **The best answer is A** because the introductory phrase "despite this accumulation of harmonica lore" correctly reiterates the information from the previous paragraph, and the main clause "I still couldn't play" serves as a bridge to this paragraph, which focuses on how the author finally learned how to play harmonica.

The best answer is NOT:

B because it connects only to the previous paragraph. In addition, it offers no new information.

C because the previous paragraph primarily focuses on how the author's father provides education about the history of the harmonica. There isn't a clear indication that the author was enthusiastic about learning about the harmonica. Additionally, this sentence does not provide any content that serves as a bridge to this paragraph, which focuses on how the author finally learned how to play harmonica.

D because the previous paragraph doesn't emphasize the complexity or potential of the harmonica as an instrument. Instead, it describes the history of instruments that led to the development of the harmonica.

Question 356. The best answer is **H** because it includes the correct helping verb *had* with the past participle, which properly indicates that one past tense event (performing in rock bands) occurred *before* another past tense event "guided the class." In addition, it uses *who*, which is the correct pronoun case.

The best answer is NOT:

F because *whom* is a direct object (the receiver of an action). The word *who* functions as the subject of a sentence: the doer of the action. Therefore, it is incorrect to place *whom* directly before the verb phrase "had performed."

G because *whom* is a direct object (the receiver of an action). The word *who* functions as the subject of a sentence. Therefore, it is incorrect to place *whom* directly before the adverb *once*.

J because the past perfect verb tense uses *had* rather than *did* with the past participle. *Did* and *performed* should never be used together.

Question 357. The best answer is **B** because *pure* and *sad* are coordinate adjectives, meaning that they have equal weight and modify the same noun: *wail*. Coordinate adjectives should have a comma between them.

The best answer is NOT:

A because the relative pronoun *that* should not have a comma directly after it in this sentence since it connects the instructor's melody with the class's reaction.

C because the coordinate adjectives *pure* and *sad* should have a comma between them. In addition, the relative pronoun *that* should not have a comma directly after it in this sentence since it connects the instructor's melody with the class's reaction.

D because the coordinate adjectives *pure* and *sad* should have a comma between them. In addition, a comma is never placed directly after the coordinating conjunction *but*.

Question 358. **The best answer is J** because Placing Sentence 1 after Sentence 5 makes the paragraph logical and coherent. Sentence 1 describes a song whose melody has "such a pure, sad wail that the entire class sat in stunned silence." This logically follows Sentence 5, which introduces the song "Mary had the Blues."

The best answer is NOT:

F because leaving Sentence 1 where it is now is not logical because Sentence 2 describes the traditional folk song "Mary had a Little Lamb," which cannot be accurately described as sounding like a "pure, sad wail." Sentences 3, 4, and 5 build anticipation surrounding the moment when the teacher plays "Mary had the Blues." Therefore, Sentence 1 should be placed after Sentence 5.

G because this arrangement of the sentences is illogical. Sentences 3, 4, and 5 logically occur before the teacher plays "Mary had the Blues."

H because this arrangement of the sentences is illogical. Sentences 4 and 5 logically occur before the teacher plays "Mary had the Blues."

Question 359. **The best answer is B** because it is grammatically correct, and the verbs in the sentence maintain the same verb tense. The correct verbs here are *find* and *bend* because they correctly follow *worked to*: "I worked to *find*… and [worked to] *bend*."

The best answer is NOT:

A because "if I could bend" is not parallel with *find*.

C because "to see if I were to" is not parallel with *find*.

D because "if I can" is not parallel with *find*.

Question 360. **The best answer is J** because it creates the clearest sentence within the context of the paragraph. The day of the week is not relevant to this passage, particularly given that the narrator has already indicated that he finally played harmonica "on the night before our next class."

The best answer is NOT:

F because the day of the week is not relevant to this passage.

G because the day of the week is not relevant to this passage.

H because the day of the week is not relevant to this passage.

Passage XXV

Question 361. The best answer is B because the word *spoke* creates the clearest and most concise statement.

The best answer is NOT:

A because *uttered out loud* is redundant. One cannot *utter* silently.

C because *said verbally* is redundant. The word *said* implies communication through verbalization.

D because *gave vocalization to* is unnecessarily wordy and does not fit with the style and tone of the essay.

Question 362. The best answer is J because it is the clearest and most concise statement. It avoids needlessly repeating the concept expressed earlier in the sentence by the word *first*.

The best answer is NOT:

F because the word *originally* is redundant with the word *first* used earlier in the sentence.

G because the phrase "in the beginning" is redundant with the word *first* used earlier in the sentence.

H because the word *initially* is redundant with the word *first* used earlier in the sentence.

Question 363. The best answer is A because no punctuation is needed here. The absence of punctuation creates the clearest sentence.

The best answer is NOT:

B because there should not be a comma between the adverb *every* and the verb phrase it modifies: "have said."

C because there should not be a comma after the verb *said* unless it is followed immediately by a direct quotation.

D because a comma should not be used before the introduction of a specialized term even if that term appears in quotation marks. In this case, the specialized term *tongue-tied* is italicized, but it could have also correctly appeared within quotation marks.

Question 364. The best answer is **G** because the auxiliary (helping) verb *have* is needed before the past participles *suspected* and *felt*. This should not begin a new paragraph because this sentence logically provides an additional example of Shakespearean phrases that are still used today.

> The best answer is NOT:
>
> **F** because the auxiliary (helping) verb *have* is needed before the past participle *felt*.
>
> **H** because the auxiliary (helping) verb *have* is needed before the past participle *felt*. This should not begin a new paragraph because this sentence logically provides an additional example of Shakespearean phrases that are still used today.
>
> **J** because this should not begin a new paragraph since this sentence logically provides an additional example of Shakespearean phrases that are still used today.

Question 365. The best answer is **D** because it avoids the use of an illogical transition word.

> The best answer is NOT:
>
> **A** because the word *nonetheless* most nearly means *despite this* or *still*. This conjunctive adverb illogically signals contrast.
>
> **B** because the conjunctive adverb *otherwise* illogically signals contrast.
>
> **C** because the subordinating conjunction *while* illogically signals contrast.

Question 366. The best answer is **F** because the second clause states that the phrase "piece of work" is now "used to describe someone who is hard to understand or deal with." This provides an example of how an expression changes in meaning over time. The previous sentence explains that Shakespeare used the phrase to mean that mankind is a marvel.

> The best answer is NOT:
>
> **G** because the second clause provides a relevant example of how Shakespeare's phrase has changed in meaning over time.
>
> **H** because the second clause does *not* provide a key transition to the next paragraph. The subsequent paragraph provides an additional example ("green-eyed monster") of how Shakespeare's words and phrases are still commonly used today.
>
> **J** because the second clause explains that the expression "piece of work" is now "used to describe someone who is hard to understand or deal with." This does not contradict the statement in the first part of this sentence: "We still use the expression *piece of work*."

Question 367. The best answer is C because the phrase "the villain of the tragedy *Othello*," is an appositive for (renames or explains) the term it follows: *Iago*. This appositive should be set off by commas because it is not essential to the meaning of the sentence. *Iago* is synonymous with "the villain of the tragedy *Othello*." No punctuation is needed between *tragedy* and *Othello* because the word tragedy is restrictive: it specifies one certain tragedy.

The best answer is NOT:

A because placing a comma after the word *tragedy* separates the descriptor *tragedy* from the noun it modifies: *Othello*.

B because placing a comma after the word *tragedy* separates the descriptor *tragedy* from the noun it modifies: *Othello*.

D because the phrase "the villain of the tragedy *Othello*," is an appositive for (renames or explains) the term it follows: *Iago*. This appositive should be set off by commas because it is not essential to the meaning of the sentence.

Question 368. The best answer is J because the singular possessive form *Othello's* is the correct punctuation here. The officer figuratively belongs to Othello.

The best answer is NOT:

F because it uses the plural possessive *Othellos'* where the singular possessive *Othello's* is called for.

G because the singular possessive form *Othello's* is called for. This answer fails to correctly use an apostrophe before the *s* in *Othellos*.

H because it uses the plural possessive *Othellos'* where the singular possessive *Othello's* is called for. Additionally, it inserts a confusing and unnecessary comma between the noun *one* and the preposition *of*. The phrase "one of Othello's officers" is the object of the prepositional phrase *in love with*, and these elements should not be separated by any punctuation.

Question 369. The best answer is A because the simple past tense verb *became* is called for here to describe an event that began and ended in the past.

The best answer is NOT:

B because adding *had* before *became* creates a grammatically incorrect sentence. *Had become* is the correct *past perfect* form of the verb *to become*.

C because *have became* creates a grammatically incorrect sentence. *Have become* is the present perfect form of the verb *to become*.

D because the verb form *becoming* creates a sentence fragment.

Question 370. The best answer is J because references to the film version of *Henry V* are not relevant to this passage.

The best answer is NOT:

F because the reference to the film version of *Henry V* is not relevant to this passage. Including this sentence disrupts the paragraph's focus on words and phrases that Shakespeare's plays have popularized.

G because the reference to the 1989 film version of *Henry V* is not relevant to this passage. Including this sentence disrupts the paragraph's focus on words and phrases that Shakespeare's plays have popularized.

H because the reference to the film version of *Henry V* is not relevant to this passage. Including this sentence disrupts the paragraph's focus on words and phrases that Shakespeare's plays have popularized.

Question 371. The best answer is C because the present tense plural verb *include* agrees with the plural subject *terms*.

The best answer is NOT:

A because the present continuous verb form *are including* is not called for here. The verb in this sentence needs to agree with the subject: *terms*.

B because the past tense verb *included* describes a present event in the past tense.

D because it eliminates the verb *include* and creates a sentence fragment.

Question 372. The best answer is J because the word *allusion* means a reference to a text, person, place, or event. "Allusion to" is a conventional, idiomatic expression that makes sense in this context.

The best answer is NOT:

F because the word *illusion* means a deception. *Illusion* is illogical in this sentence.

G because the word *illusion* means a deception. The word *illusion* is illogical in this sentence.

H because "allusion of" is not an idiom of standard English.

Question 373. The best answer is B because no punctuation is needed here. The singular verb *is* agrees with the singular subject *one*.

The best answer is NOT:

A because the plural verb *are* does not agree with the singular subject *one*.

C because it does not have a verb. Therefore, it is a sentence fragment.

D because inserting *which* before *is* creates a sentence fragment because the verb is no longer functioning as a verb.

Question 374. The best answer is H because no punctuation is needed before or after "in speech." A comma is not needed in a list of only *two* items. The comma after the word *culture* correctly sets off the introductory phrase "Given Shakespeare's strong presence in speech and popular culture," from the main clause.

The best answer is NOT:

F because the preposition *in* indicates where Shakespeare's presence is found: in speech and popular culture. The prepositional phrase "in speech and popular culture" should not be separated from the noun it modifies: *presence*.

G Because when two items appear in a list, a comma should not be used. This sentence provides *two* places where Shakespeare's influence is present: speech and popular culture. A comma is not needed in a list of only *two* items.

J because the preposition *in* indicates two places where Shakespeare's presence is found: in speech and popular culture. The prepositional phrase "in speech and popular culture" should not be separated from the noun it modifies: *presence*. No punctuation is needed before or after "in speech." Additionally, when two items appear in a list, a comma should not be used.

Question 375. The best answer is C because it emphasizes Shakespeare's ongoing influence on speech and popular culture.

The best answer is NOT:

A because the essay does not emphasize Shakespeare's *popularity* as an author. Instead, it emphasizes the lasting relevance of his words and phrases.

B because the essay does not emphasize that Shakespeare's plays have prompted discussions and debates about his fascinating ideas.

D because the essay does not focus on how films borrow plot ideas from Shakespeare's plays.

Passage XXVI

Question 376. The best answer is **F** because the introductory phrase "To the surprise of many," avoids creating a comma splice.

The best answer is NOT:

G because the subject *she* and the verb *surprised* create a comma splice (two or more complete sentences separated only by a comma).

H because the subject *It* and the verb *was* create a comma splice (two or more complete sentences separated only by a comma).

J because the subject *It* and the verb *came* create a comma splice (two or more complete sentences separated only by a comma).

Question 377. The best answer is **B** because the name "Maya Lin" is an appositive for (renames or explains) the phrase it follows: "a college student." This appositive should be set off by commas because it is not essential to the meaning of the sentence. Additionally, it correctly inserts a comma before the relative pronoun *who*.

The best answer is NOT:

A because it is missing a comma after *Lin*. The name "Maya Lin" is an appositive for (renames or explains) the phrase it follows: "a college student." This appositive phrase should be set off by commas because it is not essential to the meaning of the sentence.

C because it does not include commas that set off the appositive "Maya Lin." The name "Maya Lin" is an appositive for (renames or explains) the phrase it follows: "a college student." This appositive phrase should be set off by commas because it is not essential to the meaning of the sentence.

D because it is missing a comma before *Maya*. The name "Maya Lin" is an appositive for (renames or explains) the phrase it follows: "a college student." This appositive phrase should be set off by commas because it is not essential to the meaning of the sentence.

Question 378. The best answer is **J** because the details that follow describe a *simple* and *powerful* monument: "two long black granite walls" that are inscribed with "the names of more than 58,000 United States military personnel lost in the war."

The best answer is NOT:

F because it only provides vague information about the length of time that the monument has received acclaim. It does not discuss the monument's features in any way.

G because it only indicates that "many people" now acclaim the monument. It does not discuss the monument's features in any way.

H because it only points to Maya Lin's talent, as shown through the memorial. It does not discuss the monument's features in any way.

Question 379. The best answer is **A** because beginning the sentence with *while* creates a correct subordinating clause "While some sculptors suggest the magnitude of an event by presenting larger-than-life figures." In addition, this is the only option that prevents a sentence fragment.

The best answer is NOT:

B because placing a colon after the word *figures* makes the introductory subordinating clause into a sentence fragment.

C because placing a period after the word *figures* makes the introductory subordinating clause into a sentence fragment.

D because placing a semicolon after the word *figures* makes the introductory subordinating clause into a sentence fragment.

Question 380. The best answer is **G** because adding the proposed sentence disrupts the essay's content and tone. The previous sentence describes Lin's artistic approach of relying on "understated methods to suggest matters of great significance." The next sentence then refers back to this idea, stating that Lin has "applied *this approach* in different parts of the country." Additionally, this proposed statement expresses a general concept (reflecting on life) that adds very little to the essay's focus on Maya Lin and her work.

The best answer is NOT:

F because it offers an incorrect reason to delete information and incorrectly describes the relationship between the sentence in question and the surrounding text. It is not accurate to characterize this possible addition as being in "complete opposition to the spirit of the essay's subject of public sculpture." The essay highlights the power of a minimalist, nonrepresentational monument. The position of the essay does not directly contradict the notion that "it is important to reflect on your life along the way."

H because this addition is out of place at this point in the essay. It is a generalization, but it does not "provide readers with a lively way to identify with people who have seen Maya Lin's work."

J because this addition is out of place at this point in the essay. This generalization does not provide "surprising insight into the role monuments play in public life."

Question 381. The best answer is **A** because the present perfect verb tense *has applied* is correct here. Lin began applying her approach in the past and continues to do so today.

The best answer is NOT:

B because the future verb tense *will apply* is incorrect within the context of this paragraph. Lin began applying her approach in the past and continues to do so today.

C because the simple past tense verb *applied* is incorrect within the context of this paragraph. It suggests that Maya Lin no longer applies her approach today, but Lin *has applied* her approach to sculpture "since the unveiling of the Vietnam Memorial."

D because the participle *applying* creates a sentence fragment.

Question 382. **The best answer is G** because this phrase claims that Lin has applied her approach to sculpture "in different parts of the country and to different eras of United States history." The essay later indicates that Maya Lin's work can also be found at "a public library in Ohio, a chapel in Pennsylvania, and a train station in New York."

The best answer is NOT:

F because this broad claim *is* supported by information elsewhere in the essay. The essay later indicates that Maya Lin's work can also be found at "a public library in Ohio, a chapel in Pennsylvania, and a train station in New York."

H because this sentence focuses on Lin's work following the "unveiling of the Vietnam Memorial." The rest of the essay details some of the work Lin did after the Vietnam Memorial, so this phrase serves as a transition.

J because this sentence does not *undermine* claims made elsewhere in the paragraph. In fact, this sentence *supports* claims made elsewhere in the paragraph. The next sentence provides an example of Lin applying her approach in a different context. In 1988, she designed a memorial in Montgomery, Alabama "to honor individuals killed in the civil rights movement."

Question 383. **The best answer is B** because this sentence structure makes "this work" the subject of the sentence, which is necessary in order to have the introductory phrase "Located in Montgomery, Alabama," refer clearly to Lin's work.

The best answer is NOT:

A because this sentence structure makes the introductory phrase a misplaced modifier that refers to "Maya Lin," which doesn't make sense.

C because the word *consisting* creates a sentence fragment.

D because this sentence structure makes the introductory phrase a misplaced modifier that refers to "her work on this monument," rather than the monument itself, which doesn't make sense.

Question 384. The best answer is **J** because this sentence oddly highlights the author by using the personal possessive pronoun *my*. This reference to the writer seems out of place and irrelevant in the absence of other such references.

The best answer is NOT:

F because the writer's attention to the details of Maya Lin's career is clear even if this sentence is deleted. The author incorporates specific details throughout the essay, including various monuments' materials, locations, and purposes.

G because no questions arise earlier in the passage. Additionally, this sentence only vaguely refers to the author's research. It does not provide meaningful details.

H because simply completing research does not establish a person as an authority on a matter.

Question 385. The best answer is **C** because in context, the pronoun *this* specifies a certain inscription that follows immediately after the word *this*: "…Until justice rolls down like waters and righteousness like a mighty stream."

The best answer is NOT:

A because the possessive plural pronoun *their* does not have a logical antecedent. It is unclear what the word *their* would refer to.

B because the relative pronoun *which* is not logical within the context of this sentence.

D because *it's* means *it is*, which is not logical in the context of this sentence.

Question 386. The best answer is **J** because it provides the specific speech from which this quote is taken and the exact year when it was delivered.

The best answer is NOT:

F because it does not specify the title of the speech or the year it was delivered.

G because it does not provide specific information about what exact speech this quote was taken from. Instead, it only specifies what year the speech was given and who gave the speech.

H because it does not provide the specific year when the speech was delivered.

Question 387. The best answer is B because this sentence compares Lin's minimalist, nonrepresentational style to that of sculptors who "suggest the magnitude of an event by presenting larger-than-life figures." It is the only place in the essay that draws an explicit comparison between Maya Lin and other sculptors.

The best answer is NOT:

A because the author is only describing how Lin's work differs from that of other sculptors. The author is not critical of "the shortcomings of works by Maya Lin's colleagues in the field of sculpture."

C because there is no indication that Maya Lin's style emerged as a conscious deviation from the work of other sculptors. The essay does not present the reasons for Lin's artistic sensibilities.

D because the author does not indicate that Maya Lin has been directly influenced by any other artists or artistic movements.

Question 388. The best answer is F because the phrase "the complexity of human experience" is a sufficiently clear and appropriate way to describe how Lin's artwork addresses the broad range of human experiences.

The best answer is NOT:

G because the phrase "complexity of the nature and character of human experience" is wordy and repetitive. *Nature* and *character* are synonyms in the context of this sentence.

H because the phrase "characteristically complex and inherent complications of human experience" is wordy and repetitive.

J because the phrase "complicated character and complex nature of human experience" is wordy and repetitive. "Complicated character" and "complex nature" are essentially expressing the same idea.

Question 389. **The best answer is C** because the plural present tense verb *are* agrees with the plural subject *these*. The present tense is correct here given that the monuments influenced by Lin still exist today.

The best answer is NOT:

A because the past-perfect tense is not called for here. This tense is used to describe one past tense event that occurs before another past tense event.

B because the simple plural past-tense verb *were* is incorrect because the sculptures influenced by Lin still exist today. Additionally, the past tense verb *were* does not fit logically within the context of the sentence, which also states that various places "*have been* influenced by Maya Lin."

D because "having been" creates a sentence fragment.

Question 390. **The best answer is H** because the essay does not focus on the public reaction to the Vietnam War. It only briefly mentions that initially her work stirred up controversy. The essay focuses on Lin's creation of simple, powerful, understated, nonrepresentational sculptures.

The best answer is NOT:

F because the essay does not describe the public reaction to the Vietnam War "in great detail." It only briefly notes that the Vietnam Memorial was originally considered controversial but that it later received acclaim. The public reaction to Lin's work is not the focus of the essay.

G because the author does not incorporate "a firsthand experience" of viewing one of Lin's sculptures.

J because the public reaction to the monument is not "downplayed in favor of objective information." The public reaction is briefly mentioned. The author seems to admire Lin's approach to sculpture and does not strive to focus on "objective information."

Passage XXVII

Question 391. **The best answer is C** because it correctly uses the coordinating conjunction *but* to join two contradictory independent clauses.

The best answer is NOT:

A because *however* creates a comma splice (two or more complete sentences separated only by a comma).

B because "even so" creates a comma splice (two or more complete sentences separated only by a comma).

D because omitting the underlined portion creates a comma splice (two or more complete sentences separated only by a comma).

Question 392. The best answer is F because "chronicler of" provides a proper idiom of standard English. The phrase "chronicler of" indicates that Hurston documented African American folklore.

The best answer is NOT:

G because the phrase *chronicler with* is not idiomatic English.

H because the phrase *chronicler for* is not idiomatic English.

J because the phrase *chronicler on* is not idiomatic English.

Question 393. The best answer is C because it correctly uses the correlative conjunctions "It was while" and *that*. The conjunctions "It was while" and *that* logically connect Hurston's experience at Bard College with the community engagement she pursued while studying there.

The best answer is NOT:

A because "While she was studying" does not logically connect with *that*.

B because it creates a sentence fragment since it does not contain a verb. The introductory clause "during the time that she was" does not logically connect with *that*.

D because "While she was studying" does not logically connect with *that*.

Question 394. The best answer is G because it fits the tone and content of the essay. Hurston studied in New York for college after growing up in Florida. Therefore, it is accurate to describe Hurston's trip back to the south as an opportunity to *reconnect* with customs, songs, stories, and games she had learned as a child.

The best answer is NOT:

F because the phrase "hook up" is casual and does not fit the relatively academic tone of the essay.

H because the word *unite* does not convey that Hurston is returning to the South where she grew up.

J because the word *bind* does not convey that Hurston is returning to the South where she grew up. While the verb *to bond* means to unite, it does not convey the concept of connecting again in the same way that the word *reunite* does.

Question 395. **The best answer is A** because the conjunction *when* effectively combines two independent clauses. *When* connects logically with the year *1927*.

The best answer is NOT:

B because the relative pronoun *that* is used to provide essential elaborating detail about the noun it follows. The independent clause "she first returned to the South" does *not* describe the *folklore* that Hurston sought to gather.

C because the coordinating conjunction *and* is used to join two independent clauses of equal weight. The word *and* suggests that two distinct events are taking place one after the other whereas this sentence describes two events occurring simultaneously. Hurston believes she "took the wrong approach" *when* she "returned to the South."

D because this creates a comma splice (two or more complete sentences separated only by a comma) since an independent clause ("In 1927, she returned to the South") follows a comma.

Question 396. **The best answer is H** because the word *people* is adequately specific. It does not require an antecedent (a noun that it refers to and stands in for).

The best answer is NOT:

F because it is an ambiguous pronoun. It is unclear who is meant by *them*.

G because it is ambiguous. It is unclear who is meant by "some of them."

J because it is ambiguous. It is unclear who is meant by *they*. The pronoun *they* does not have a clear antecedent (a noun that it refers to and stands in for).

Question 397. **The best answer is D** because it creates the clearest and most concise sentence, avoiding needless repetition.

The best answer is NOT:

A because it would add redundant information to the essay. The previous paragraph indicates that Hurston "headed straight to her hometown."

B because it would add redundant information to the essay. The previous paragraph indicates that Hurston "headed straight to her hometown."

C because it would add redundant information to the essay. The previous paragraph indicates that Hurston "headed straight to her hometown."

Question 398. The best answer is **F** because the verb form "would be" is correctly used here to describe the ongoing oral tradition that Hurston *expected* to find thriving in Eatonville. This sentence describes a future expectation that occurred in the past.

The best answer is NOT:

G because "has been" is incorrect. "Has been" does not maintain agreement with the simple past verb *went*, which is used earlier in the sentence.

H because the future tense verb form "will be" does not maintain agreement with the simple past verb *went*, which is used earlier in the sentence.

J because this sentence describes an ongoing event that began in the past. Therefore, it is incorrect to use the simple present tense verb *is*.

Question 399. The best answer is **A** because this detail helps explain why Hurston was drawn to observe people at the porch of the general store in her town.

The best answer is NOT:

B because the proposed addition is not "the *only* indication that the general store had an important role in Hurston's work." The subsequent sentence describes "an outpouring of tales" told at the general store."

C because although the essay has already established that Hurston was interested in talk and song, the proposed statement provides elaborating detail about *why* Hurston thought that visiting the Eatonville general store would provide meaningful data for her anthropological studies.

D because the proposed statement *is* relevant to the essay's focus on Hurston's work as an adult. Her childhood experiences in Eatonville led her to appreciate the folklore passed down through the oral tradition.

Question 400. The best answer is **J** because the simple past tense verb *began* maintains agreement with the simple past tense verb *gathered* earlier in the sentence.

The best answer is NOT:

F because it uses the past participle *begun,* which does not maintain agreement with the past tense verb *gathered* earlier in the sentence. In addition, *begun* is only grammatically correct with a helping verb ("had begun," for example).

G because "would begun" does not maintain agreement with the past tense verb *gathered.* In addition, "would begun" is never grammatically correct.

H because "had began" does not maintain agreement with the past tense verb *gathered.* In addition, "had began" is never grammatically correct.

Question 401. The best answer is **D** because the word *wealth*, within the context of this sentence, means a vast amount.

The best answer is NOT:

A because *wide vastness* is wordy and redundant.

B because *prosperity* is a noun that typically refers to success or monetary wealth, not folklore. Although the word *wealth* has a similar meaning to *prosperity*, the word *wealth* is used more often to describe situations that do not involve money.

C because the word *chunk* is too informal and does not fit with the tone of the essay.

Question 402. The best answer is **H** because the word *much* functions as an adjective of quantity, which should be used to modify uncountable nouns. The noun *stories* is countable, and therefore *many*, an adjective of number, should be used rather than *much*.

The best answer is NOT:

F because the adverb *still* correctly modifies the adjective *more*. In the context of this sentence, the phrase *still more* means *even more*.

G because *many* is an adjective of number, which correctly modifies the countable noun *stories*.

J because the adjective *more* correctly modifies the noun *stories*.

Question 403. The best answer is **B** because the tales listed describe the origins of specific animal characteristics.

The best answer is NOT:

A because the phrase "revealed interesting information" is vague and does not specify that the following information will describe tales about the origins of animal characteristics.

C because the phrase "offered important insights into the past" is vague and does not specify that the information that follows will describe tales about the origins of animal characteristics.

D because the phrase "concerned long-ago events" is vague and does not specify that the information that follows will describe tales about the origins of animal characteristics.

Question 404. The best answer is J because *exaggerated* and *humorous* are coordinate adjectives, meaning that they are of equal weight and that they modify the same noun: *accounts*. Coordinate adjectives should have a comma between them.

The best answer is NOT:

F because the conjunction *and* calls for two adjectives to modify the noun that follows: *accounts.* Therefore, the adverb *exaggeratedly* does not work here.

G because adjectives should modify the noun *accounts*. The words *exaggeratedly* and *humorously* are adverbs.

H because the adverb *exaggeratedly* does not agree with the adjective *humorous*. Adjectives should be used to modify the noun *accounts*. The word *humorously* is an adverb, which can be used to modify verbs, adjectives, and other adverbs but not nouns.

Question 405. The best answer is B because no punctuation is needed here. The absence of punctuation creates the clearest and most understandable sentence. "Such as" is an idiomatic expression used to introduce examples. There should not be a comma separating "such as" from the list of examples provided.

The best answer is NOT:

A because it inserts an unnecessary comma between "such as" and *Brer Rabbit*. There should not be a comma separating "such as" from the list of examples provided.

C because this sentence includes only two items in a list: *Brer Rabbit* and "his cousins." A comma is not needed in a list of only two items.

D because the proper noun *Brer Rabbit* is essential information that should not be set off with commas. Eliminating *Brer Rabbit* creates an illogical sentence. The phrase "such as" is an idiomatic expression used to introduce examples. There should not be a comma separating "such as" from the list of examples provided.

Passage XXVIII

Question 406. The best answer is **D** because it does not create a sentence fragment.

The best answer is NOT:

A because it turns the phrase "From her wooden seat in the cramped cockpit" into a sentence fragment.

B because it incorrectly connects an independent clause, "Facing the fuel gauges and compass that helped her plot her course, Amelia Earhart was on top of the world," to a prepositional phrase "From her wooden seat in the cramped cockpit." A semicolon should be used to connect two independent clauses.

C because it turns the phrase "From her wooden seat in the cramped cockpit" into a sentence fragment. It also creates a comma splice in the subsequent sentence.

Question 407. The best answer is **F** because it conveys the information in a way that is clear and avoids wordiness and redundancy.

The best answer is NOT:

G because the phrase "following being born" is needlessly wordy. The word *born* effectively conveys the same idea.

H because the phrase "after her mother gave birth to her" is needlessly wordy. The word *born* effectively conveys the same idea.

J because the phrase "after having been born" is needlessly wordy. The word *born* effectively conveys the same idea.

Question 408. The best answer is **B** because the simple past tense verb *bought* creates an independent clause that is parallel with the independent clause that precedes the conjunction *and*: "she was taking lessons."

The best answer is NOT:

A because it uses *and* to connect two independent clauses but fails to place a comma before *and*, creating a run-on sentence. When a coordinating conjunction is used to connect two independent clauses, a comma must come after the first independent clause and before the coordinating conjunction.

C because the verb *buys* is in the present tense, while the other verb in the sentence, "was taking," is in the past. Because the sentence suggests that both events happened around the same time, both verbs should be in the past tense.

D because it uses and to connect two independent clauses but fails to place a comma before *and*, creating a run-on sentence. When a coordinating conjunction is used to connect two independent clauses, a comma must come after the first independent clause and before the coordinating conjunction. In addition, it uses the present tense verb *is*, while the other verb in the sentence, "was taking," is in the past. Because the sentence suggests that both events happened around the same time, both verbs should be in the simple past tense.

Question 409. The best answer is **H** because the statement that Earhart defied expectations and shattered gender stereotypes indicates that her behavior differed from the social norms of her time, which fulfills the writer's purpose of summarizing how Earhart broke "what were then the rules for girls."

The best answer is NOT:

F because the statement that Earhart showed what a person from Kansas could do does not illustrate how Earhart broke the rules and defied gender stereotypes.

G because the fact that Earhart graduated from high school in 1915 does not illustrate how Earhart broke the rules and defied gender stereotypes.

J because the fact that Earhart saw her first airplane when she was only ten years old does not illustrate how Earhart broke the rules and defied gender stereotypes.

Question 410. The best answer is **C** because the word *when* creates a logical connection between the first part of the sentence and the second part of the sentence, indicating that Earhart became fascinated with flying some time during her first flight.

The best answer is NOT:

A because it uses the object pronoun *whom* as if it were a subordinating conjunction, which creates an illogical connection between the first part of the sentence and the second part of the sentence. This makes the relationship between Earhart's fascination with flying and her first flight unclear.

B because the word *that* creates an illogical connection between the first part of the sentence and the second part of the sentence, which makes the relationship between Earhart's fascination with flying and her first flight unclear.

D because it uses the adverb *however* instead of a subordinating conjunction or a coordinating conjunction, which creates a run-on sentence. Also, the transition word *however* suggests that Earhart's fascination with flying as a young woman somehow contrasts with the fact that she took her first flight with a stunt pilot, which doesn't make sense in this context.

Question 411. The best answer is **H** because Sentences 1 and 2 discuss Earhart's childhood, while Sentences 3, 4, and 5 discuss her early experiences with flying. Sentence 6 refers to Earhart's first flight, when she was a young woman. Therefore, the most logical place for Sentence 6 is between Sentences 2 and 3, after the essay has finished discussing Earhart's childhood and before it has begun discussing Earhart's subsequent flying experience.

The best answer is NOT:

F because Sentences 3, 4, and 5 discuss Earhart's early experiences with flying, while Sentence 6 refers to Earhart's first flight. Because it can be inferred that the event in Sentence 6 occurred before the events in Sentences 3, 4, and 5, it is most logical to place Sentence 6 before Sentences 3, 4, and 5.

G because Sentences 1 and 2 discuss Earhart's childhood, while Sentence 6 refers to Earhart's first flight as an adult. Placing Sentence 6 between Sentences 1 and 2 would interrupt the essay's discussion of Earhart's childhood with a statement about Earhart's young adulthood.

J because Sentences 3, 4, and 5 discuss Earhart's early experiences with flying, while Sentence 6 refers to Earhart's first flight. Because it can be inferred that the event in Sentence 6 occurred before the events in Sentences 3, 4, and 5, it is most logical to place Sentence 6 before Sentences 3, 4, and 5.

Question 412. **The best answer is D** because the phrase "set out from Miami" uses the commonly accepted idiomatic expression "set out," which indicates that Earhart left from Miami in a plane.

The best answer is NOT:

A because the phrase "sat about" indicates that a person is physically sitting around. This doesn't make sense in this context, as Earhart is leaving from Miami in a plane.

B because the phrase "set about from Miami" does not create a logical phrase. "Set about from Miami" is not a commonly accepted idiomatic expression.

C because the phrase "sat out" indicates that a person is not participating in an activity. This doesn't make sense in this context, as Earhart is leaving from Miami in a plane.

Question 413. **The best answer is G** because the word *when* creates a logical connection between the first part of the sentence and the second part of the sentence, suggesting that Earhart and her co-pilot lost contact with the outside world around three-quarters into their flight.

The best answer is NOT:

F because the word *because* creates an illogical connection between the first part of the sentence and the second part of the sentence, suggesting that Earhart and her co-pilot completed three-quarters of their flight because they lost contact with the outside world.

H because the word *while* creates an unclear connection between the first part of the sentence and the second part of the sentence, suggesting that the loss of contact occurred while Earhart and her co-pilot were in the process of completing three-quarters of their flight and reaching New Guinea. If the outside world had lost contact with Earhart *while* she reached New Guinea, then no one would know that Earhart successfully made it there.

J because the word *after* creates an illogical connection between the first part of the sentence and the second part of the sentence, suggesting that Earhart and her co-pilot completed three-quarters of their flight after they had lost contact with the outside world. If the outside world had lost contact with Earhart *after* she reached New Guinea, then no one would know that Earhart successfully made it there.

Question 414. The best answer is C because it does not suggest an illogical relationship between this sentence and the previous sentence. The most logical choice is to omit the transition word.

The best answer is NOT:

A because the phrase "in contrast" indicates that the content of this sentence will contrast with the preceding sentence. Instead, this sentence describes a logical step that was taken once Earhart's plane had lost contact with the outside world.

B because the word *however* indicates that the content of this sentence will contrast with content of the preceding sentence. Instead, this sentence describes a logical step that was taken once Earhart's plane had lost contact with the outside world.

D because the word *furthermore* indicates that this sentence elaborates on a point made in the preceding sentence. Instead, this sentence describes a logical step that was taken once Earhart's plane had lost contact with the outside world.

Question 415. The best answer is G because it does not use an unnecessary possessive apostrophe. In addition, the plural noun *rumors* agrees with the plural verb phrase "have abounded."

The best answer is NOT:

F because the possessive apostrophe suggests that the subsequent phrase, "have abounded," belongs to a rumor, which is illogical. The correct choice is to omit the possessive apostrophe.

H because the possessive apostrophe suggests that the subsequent phrase, "have abounded," belongs to rumors, which is illogical. The correct choice is to omit the possessive apostrophe.

J because the singular subject *rumor* does not agree with the plural verb phrase "have abounded."

Question 416. The best answer is **C** because the preceding sentence states that "rumors have abounded" about what happened to Earhart, and this sentence provides an example of an additional rumor about what might have happened to Earhart, which further develops the point made in the preceding sentence.

The best answer is NOT:

A because it does not develop the preceding sentence's discussion of rumors about Earhart's disappearance. Instead, it indicates that the Coast Guard was ready to receive radio transmissions from Earhart.

B because it does not develop the preceding sentence's discussion of rumors about Earhart's disappearance. Instead, it indicates that Earhart received praise for her first flight across the Atlantic.

D because it does not develop the preceding sentence's discussion of rumors about Earhart's disappearance. Instead, it indicates where Earhart's previous attempt to fly around the world had started.

Question 417. The best answer is **F** because it correctly uses the verb *passed* and the preposition *into* to indicate that Amelia Earhart has become a part of history.

The best answer is NOT:

G because it incorrectly uses the noun *past*, which refers to time. A verb is needed within the context of this sentence.

H because the phrase "passed over" figuratively means that a person, thing, or idea has been overlooked or neglected. It can also indicate that somebody has physically crossed an area. Neither of these phrases make sense in the context of this sentence, which is discussing how Amelia Earhart became a part of our history.

J because it incorrectly uses the noun *past*, which refers to time. A verb is needed within the context of this sentence. In addition, the phrase "past over" is not an accepted idiomatic phrase.

Question 418. The best answer is **A** because it connects two independent clauses using a period, creating two grammatical sentences.

The best answer is NOT:

B because it connects two independent clauses with a comma, which creates a comma splice.

C because it connects two independent clauses without using any punctuation, which creates a run-on sentence.

D because it connects two independent clauses using the subordinating conjunction *while*. To connect two independent clauses without using a period or a semicolon, it is necessary to use a comma followed by a coordinating conjunction. In addition, the word *while* is redundant with the word *but* that comes later in the sentence.

Question 419. The best answer is **G** because it is consistent with the style of the rest of the essay.

The best answer is NOT:

F because the phrase "continues to be very cool" is too casual and inconsistent with the essay's style.

H because the phrase "continues to manifest her aviation skills" is too formal and inconsistent with the essay's style. It is also wordy, using overly complex language to illustrate a simple idea.

J because the phrase "still exhibits expertise in monitoring her altitude and velocity, using various cockpit gauges" is too formal and inconsistent with the essay's style. It is also wordy, using overly complex language to illustrate a simple idea.

Question 420. The best answer is C because the sentences before Point C discuss Earhart's trip and the rumors surrounding her disappearance, while the sentences after Point C discuss how Earhart has become a part of our history and how she is remembered today.

The best answer is NOT:

A because the sentences that come after Point A discuss how the U.S. Navy searched for Earhart and the rumors surrounding her disappearance. Because of this, a paragraph division at Point A would place speculation about what may have happened to Earhart in the second paragraph, rather than the first paragraph.

B because the sentences that come after Point B discuss the rumors surrounding Earhart's disappearance. Because of this, a paragraph division at Point B would place speculation about what may have happened to Earhart in the second paragraph, rather than the first paragraph.

D because the sentences that come before Point D discuss how Earhart has become a part of our history, and how the legend of her achievements continues to captivate us. Because of this, a paragraph division at Point D would place a discussion about how Earhart is remembered in the first paragraph, rather than the second paragraph.

Passage XXIX

Question 421. The best answer is J because it presents a new detail, indicating that the statue depicts the queen on her throne.

The best answer is NOT:

F because the first sentence of the paragraph indicates that Adams made a discovery while completing an inspection of a salvage yard. Therefore, the detail that the statue was in a salvage yard is not new information. In addition, the detail does not provide any information about the physical appearance of the statue.

G because the fact that Adams found the statue while he was doing his rounds does not provide any new information about the physical appearance of the statue.

H because the fact that Adams found the statue while he was looking around does not provide any new information about the physical appearance of the statue.

Question 422. The best answer is **A** because it offers specific information about what Adams hoped would be done to the statue, which provides insight into the kind of people that Adams was likely looking for.

The best answer is NOT:

B because while it does indicate that Adams was looking for people and that he wanted to make a difference, it does not say what difference he hoped to make or what he hoped these people would be able to do, which makes B a less specific statement than A.

C because while it does indicate that Adams was looking for people with knowledge, it does not say what sort of knowledge such people might have had, which makes C a less specific statement than A.

D because while it does indicate that Adams was looking for people with expertise, it does not say what sort of expertise such people might have had, which makes D a less specific statement than A.

Question 423. The best answer is **H** because it correctly uses a possessive apostrophe to indicate that the writer is discussing the identity of the statue.

The best answer is NOT:

F because it fails to use a possessive apostrophe to indicate that the writer is discussing the identity of the statue.

G because it places the possessive apostrophe after the -s, which indicates that the writer is discussing more than one statue. This is misleading, as the essay clearly indicates that Adams found a single statue.

J because it uses the plural noun *statues*, which indicates that the writer is discussing more than one statue. This is misleading, as the essay clearly indicates that Adams found a single statue.

Question 424. The best answer is **A** because it creates an independent clause with a clear subject (*artist*) and verb (*was*).

The best answer is NOT:

B because it omits the verb *was* from the sentence, which creates a sentence fragment.

C because it turns the independent clause, "The artist was Edmonia Lewis," into a dependent clause, "The artist, whose name was Edmonia Lewis," creating a sentence fragment.

D because it omits the verb *was* from the sentence, which creates a sentence fragment.

Question 425. The best answer is **F** because it states that Lewis carved the marble by hand, which offers insight into Lewis's methods for carving the statue.

The best answer is NOT:

G because the statement that Lewis was an accomplished and experienced artist does not provide information about the method Lewis used to create the sculpture.

H because the statement that others had depicted Cleopatra in marble offers some insight into the materials used by other artists, but it provides no information about the method Lewis used to create the sculpture.

J because the statement that Lewis was working to complete her project does not provide information about the method Lewis used to create the sculpture.

Question 426. The best answer is **C** because no punctuation is needed here. The absence of commas creates the clearest sentence.

The best answer is NOT:

A because it inserts an unnecessary comma between the verb *taking* and its direct object, "her last breath." Generally, a verb should not be separated from its direct object by a comma.

B because it inserts an unnecessary comma between the subject *Cleopatra* and the verb *taking*. Generally, a verb should not be separated from its subject by a comma.

D because it inserts an unnecessary comma between the adjective *last* and the noun *breath*. Generally, a comma should not separate an adjective from the noun it modifies.

Question 427. The best answer is **G** because the phrase provides the name of the event for which the statue was created, which helps identify the event referred to in the sentence.

The best answer is NOT:

F because the phrase does not indicate where the statue was made. Instead, it provides the name of the event for which the statue was created.

H because the name of the event for which the statue was create is not provided at any other point in this sentence.

J because the phrase does not shift the focus away from the statue. Rather, the phrase provides specific details about the event for which the statue was created.

Question 428. The best answer is **A** because it conveys the information in a way that is clear and avoids wordiness and redundancy.

The best answer is NOT:

B because the phrase "in an effort to" is needlessly wordy. The word *to* effectively conveys the same idea.

C because the phrase "to attempt to" is needlessly wordy. The word *to* effectively conveys the same idea.

D because the phrase "regarding efforts that would" is needlessly wordy. The word *to* effectively conveys the same idea.

Question 429. The best answer is **H** because it correctly uses the possessive pronoun *its* to indicate that the statue's journey is being discussed.

The best answer is NOT:

F because *it's* is a contraction for "it is," which is not logical in the context of this sentence.

G because *its'* is never correct in any context, as *it* is a singular pronoun and *-s'* signifies plural possession.

J because the possessive personal pronoun *whose* is typically used to describe situations when a person owns or figuratively possesses something. Here, the pronoun "its" is more appropriate, as the sentence is referring to an object (the statue).

Question 430. The best answer is **B** because the singular verb *was* agrees with the singular subject *story*.

The best answer is NOT:

A because the plural verb *were* does not agree with the singular subject *story*.

C because the plural verb *were* does not agree with the singular subject *story*.

D because the word *of* is incorrectly used here in place of the helping verb *have*.

Question 431. The best answer is **F** because no punctuation is needed here. The absence of commas creates the clearest sentence.

The best answer is NOT:

G because it inserts an unnecessary comma between the verb *resided* and the prepositional phrase "in a Chicago saloon."

H because it inserts an unnecessary comma between the subject "the marble queen" and the verb phrase "has resided."

J because it inserts an unnecessary comma between the subject "the marble queen" and the verb phrase "has resided." It also inserts an unnecessary comma between the verb *resided* and the prepositional phrase "in a Chicago saloon."

Question 432. The best answer is **D** because the word *evacuated* implies that the statue was removed from a dangerous place to a safer place, which does not make sense in this context.

The best answer is NOT:

A because the word *sent* appropriately fits the context of the sentence.

B because the word *delivered* appropriately fits the context of the sentence.

C because the word *transported* appropriately fits the context of the sentence.

Question 433. The best answer is **G** because the phrase "at the shopping mall" specifies where the backroom was located.

The best answer is NOT:

F because the word *somewhere* does not provide new or specific information, as it can already be assumed that the statue was located somewhere.

H because the same sentence indicates that the statue was stored until it could be shipped to restoration experts.

J because the same sentence indicates that the statue was stored in a back room alongside paper turkeys, tinsel streamers, and half-empty cans of paint.

Question 434. The best answer is **C** because the pronoun *there* logically refers to the National Museum of American Art, where the sculpture is on display, and creates a full sentence, rather than a sentence fragment.

The best answer is NOT:

A because the word *Where* turns the sentence into a dependent clause, which results in a sentence fragment.

B because the word *When* turns the sentence into a dependent clause, which results in a sentence fragment.

D because the phrase *The point that* turns the sentence into a dependent clause, which results in a sentence fragment.

Question 435. The best answer is **J** because it conveys the information in a way that is clear and avoids wordiness and redundancy.

The best answer is NOT:

F because the phrase "continues to inspire renewed appreciation" is redundant with the phrase "all over again."

G because the word *admiration* and the phrase "positive appreciation" are redundant.

H because the word *renewed* is redundant with the word *again*.

Passage XXX

Question 436. The best answer is **C** because the adjective *wintry* appropriately modifies the noun *day*.

The best answer is NOT:

A because the adverb *winteringly* is not an adjective and therefore does not appropriately modify the noun *day*.

B because the participle *wintering* means spending the winter in a certain location, which does not make sense in this context. Also, the word *wintering* is not an adjective and does not appropriately modify the noun *day*.

D because the adverb *winterishly* is not an adjective and therefore does not appropriately modify the noun *day*.

Question 437. **The best answer is** F because no punctuation is needed here. The absence of commas creates the clearest sentence.

The best answer is NOT:

G because it inserts an unnecessary comma between the verb *puzzled* and the prepositional phrase "over how to handle a difficult situation."

H because it inserts an unnecessary comma between the preposition *over* and its object: "how to handle a difficult situation."

J because it inserts an unnecessary comma between the verb *puzzled* and the prepositional phrase "over how to handle a difficult situation." The comma between "handle" and "a difficult situation" is also unnecessary.

Question 438. **The best answer is** D because it inserts a period between two independent clauses, creating two grammatical sentences.

The best answer is NOT:

A because it connects two independent clauses using only a comma, which creates a run-on sentence. Also, the placement of the comma creates confusion, as the sentence seems to claim that the air was frigid both outside and inside.

B because it fails to use punctuation to connect two independent clauses, which creates a run-on sentence.

C because it uses only commas to connect two independent clauses, which creates a run-on sentence.

Question 439. The best answer is H because the phrase *in fact* emphasizes the fact that the students were "bursting with energy and ignoring their lessons," which makes it a logical addition to the sentence.

The best answer is NOT:

F because the word *however* implies contrast, which does not make sense in this context, as the statement that the students were being "quite disruptive" does not contrast with the statement that the students were "bursting with energy and ignoring their lessons." Rather, the statement that the students were being disruptive logically follows from the claim that the students were ignoring their lessons.

G because the phrase "as the case may be" is generally used when two different situations may be the case. This does not make sense in this context, as the writer is discussing one instance in which the students were being disruptive.

J because it uses the phrase "regardless of the time," which is not logical within the context of the sentence, as the writer is not discussing the time. Rather the writer is discussing one instance in which the students were being disruptive.

Question 440. The best answer is B because it connects two independent clauses with a comma, rather than a period, semicolon, or a comma followed by a coordinating conjunction, which creates a comma splice and a run-on sentence.

The best answer is NOT:

A because it correctly uses a period to connect two independent clauses.

C because it correctly uses a semicolon to connect two independent clauses.

D because it correctly uses a period to connect two independent clauses.

Question 441. The best answer is J because it conveys the information in a way that is clear and avoids wordiness and redundancy.

The best answer is NOT:

F because the phrase "mental capacities of the mind" is needlessly wordy. The word *mind* effectively conveys the same idea.

G because the phrase "the thinking apparatus of the mind" is needlessly wordy. The word *mind* effectively conveys the same idea.

H because the phrase "the mental attributes pertaining to the mind" is needlessly wordy. The word *mind* effectively conveys the same idea.

Question 442. The best answer is **B** because it uses commas to set off the nonrestrictive phrase, "in his opinion."

The best answer is NOT:

A because it fails to separate the nonrestrictive phrase, "in his opinion," from the rest of the sentence.

C because it fails to separate the nonrestrictive phrase, "in his opinion," from the rest of the sentence.

D because it fails to separate the nonrestrictive phrase, "in his opinion," from the rest of the sentence.

Question 443. The best answer is **J** because the phrase "bring forth" is overly formal and not consistent with the style of the essay.

The best answer is NOT:

F because it is consistent with the style of the essay.

G because it is consistent with the style of the essay.

H because it is consistent with the style of the essay.

Question 444. The best answer is **C** because the introductory phrase, "In tackling his assignments," appropriately modifies Naismith. Because Naismith's name immediately follows this phrase, it is clear that Naismith is tackling the assignment.

The best answer is NOT:

A because it creates a misplaced modifier, which illogically suggests that "popular ball game elements" are "tackling [Naismith's] assignment."

B because it creates a misplaced modifier, which illogically suggests that "elements from popular ball games" are "tackling [Naismith's] assignment."

D because it creates a misplaced modifier, which illogically suggests that "Naismith's borrowing of elements" is "tackling [Naismith's] assignment."

Question 445. The best answer is **G** because it does not create a sentence fragment.

The best answer is NOT:

F because it does not include a verb to follow the subject, "The decision of his." This creates a sentence fragment.

H because it omits the subject, "He," creating both a sentence fragment and a dangling modifier.

J because it does not include a verb to follow the subject, "His decision," which creates a sentence fragment.

Question 446. The best answer is **A** because *players* is a plural noun.

The best answer is NOT:

B because the possessive apostrophe in *player's* suggests that the sentence is referring to something that belongs to a player, which doesn't make sense in this context.

C because the possessive apostrophe in *players'* suggests that the sentence is referring to something that belongs to the players, which doesn't make sense in this context.

D because the possessive apostrophe in *player's* suggests that the sentence is referring to something that belongs to a player, which doesn't make sense in this context.

Question 447. The best answer is **G** because the present tense verb *reward* is parallel with the verb *encourage*.

The best answer is NOT:

F because it creates a run-on, or fused, sentence. There is no punctuation or connecting word (conjunction) between the two statements. The second independent clause begins with "the rules."

H because, although the sentence is grammatical, the phrase "and he also made those rules to reward" is unnecessarily wordy, as it is already clear that the sentence is discussing Naismith's rules.

J because it turns the phrase "Rewarding it with both physical ability and strategic planning" into a sentence fragment.

Question 448. The best answer is D because no transition word or phrase is necessary here.

The best answer is NOT:

A because the word *Instead* indicates that this sentence will contrast with the preceding sentence. Instead, this sentence simply elaborates on the content of the preceding sentence by indicating that Naismith created a vigorous, competitive game that exercises both the body and the mind.

B because the word *Nevertheless* indicates that this sentence will contrast with the preceding sentence. Instead, this sentence simply elaborates on the content of the preceding sentence by indicating that Naismith created a vigorous, competitive game that exercises both the body and the mind.

C because the phrase "On the other hand" indicates that this sentence will contrast with the preceding sentence. Instead, this sentence simply elaborates on the content of the preceding sentence by indicating that Naismith created a vigorous, competitive game that exercises both the body and the mind.

Question 449. The best answer is J because it appropriately inserts a period between two independent clauses.

The best answer is NOT:

F because it connects two independent clauses with the coordinating conjunction *and* but fails to include a comma before the coordinating conjunction, creating a run-on sentence.

G because it connects two independent clauses with the coordinating conjunction *and* but fails to include a comma before the coordinating conjunction, creating a run-on sentence.

H because it connects two independent clauses with the coordinating conjunction *and* but fails to include a comma before the coordinating conjunction, creating a run-on sentence.

Question 450. The best answer is A because it omits unnecessary punctuation.

The best answer is NOT:

B because it uses an unnecessary comma to separate the subject, "What had started as a challenge on a winter day," from the verb phrase, "had quickly evolved."

C because it inserts an unnecessary comma between the verb phrase, "had quickly evolved," and the prepositional phrase, "into the first game of basketball."

D because it uses a semicolon to connect two sentence fragments. Semicolons should be used to connect two independent clauses.

Passage XXXI

Question 451. The best answer is **J** because the possessive pronoun *its* indicates that the sentence is referring to Washington, D.C.'s famous buildings and monuments.

The best answer is NOT:

F because *they're* is not a possessive pronoun. Instead, it is a contraction of "they are," which doesn't make sense in this context.

G because the word *there* is not a possessive pronoun. Rather, it is generally used as a noun and indicates a location.

H because *it's* is not a possessive pronoun. Instead, *it's* is a contraction of "it is," which doesn't make sense in this context.

Question 452. The best answer is **C** because it describes the writer's plan to take a walk through Washington D.C. to see the monuments after dark, an experience that is detailed throughout the rest of the essay.

The best answer is NOT:

A because the rest of the essay does not discuss Washington D.C.'s museums, which makes this a less effective introduction to the essay.

B because the rest of the essay does not focus on the extent to which Washington D.C. is more historic than other cities in the United States, which makes this a less effective introduction to the essay.

D because the rest of the essay does not discuss the benefits of having no skyscrapers, which makes this a less effective introduction to the essay.

Question 453. The best answer is **G** because the word *illuminated* indicates that the exterior of the White House was well lit, which makes sense in the context of the essay.

The best answer is NOT:

F because the word *enlightened* generally refers to an intellectual awakening, which does not make sense in this context.

H because the word *irradiated* generally refers to the process of treating something with heat or radiation, which does not make sense in this context.

J because the word *inflamed* generally means irritated or engulfed in flames, neither of which make sense in this context.

Question 454. The best answer is **A** because the coordinating conjunction *and* is preceded by a comma and connects two independent clauses, creating a grammatical sentence.

The best answer is NOT:

B because it incorrectly treats the second clause as a relative clause modifying the first clause, which creates an illogical sentence.

C because *who's* is a contraction for *who is*, which does not make sense within the context of the sentence.

D because it uses only a comma to separate two independent clauses, omitting the necessary coordinating conjunction *and,* which creates a comma splice.

Question 455. The best answer is **J** because the word *saying* is generally followed by a quotation or a paraphrase of what was said, which does not make sense in this context, as the writer is not referring to a specific statement. Instead, the writer is indicating that many people are exchanging words with one another in a variety of languages.

The best answer is NOT:

F because the word *communicating* is an appropriate synonym for the word *speaking*.

G because the word *conversing* is an appropriate synonym for the word *speaking*.

H because the word *talking* is an appropriate synonym for the word *speaking*.

ENGLISH • EXPLANATORY ANSWERS

Question 456. The best answer is C because the illuminated appearance of Lincoln is directly relevant to the essay's discussion of the narrator's experience of the monuments after dark. C also is directly related to the final sentence of the paragraph, which describes how a man twirls "a flashlight to make its beam dance across the still water." Both sentences emphasize the prominence of light and the city's beauty in the darkness of night.

The best answer is NOT:

A because it describes where Lincoln is buried but is not clearly related to the essay's discussion of the narrator's experience of the monuments after dark. It is also not clearly related to the final sentence of the paragraph, which describes how a man twirls "a flashlight to make its beam dance across the still water."

B because it describes the dates when the Lincoln Memorial was authorized and dedicated but is not clearly related to the essay's discussion of the narrator's experience of the monuments after dark. It is also not clearly related to the final sentence of the paragraph, which describes how a man twirls "a flashlight to make its beam dance across the still water."

D because it indicates that the monuments on the Mall are administered by the National Park Service but is not clearly related to the essay's discussion of the narrator's experience of the monuments after dark. It is also not clearly related to the final sentence of the paragraph, which describes how a man twirls "a flashlight to make its beam dance across the still water."

Question 457. The best answer is F because this detail provides a more specific image of the scene being recalled by the narrator by describing the way in which the flashlight moved across the water.

The best answer is NOT:

G because this phrase is not directly related to the content of the next paragraph, which focuses on the narrator's experience at the Korean War Veterans Memorial.

H because this phrase is relevant to the paragraph's discussion of the Lincoln Memorial, as it discusses how the Lincoln Memorial "appeared to gaze down on the Reflecting Pool." In this way, the writer's description of the Reflecting Pool is a part of the paragraph's discussion of the Lincoln Memorial.

J because this information has not been mentioned at any other point in the essay and therefore is not redundant.

Question 458. The best answer is **B** because a preposition such as *to* or *toward* is necessary to indicate that the writer is heading in the direction of a particular location. Without *to* or *toward*, the phrase "heading off the Korean War Veterans Memorial" does not make sense.

The best answer is NOT:

A because the phrase "headed toward" appropriately indicates that the visitors traveled in the direction of the Korean War Veterans Memorial.

C because the phrase "heading to" appropriately indicates that the visitors traveled in the direction of the Korean War Veterans Memorial.

D because the phrase "headed to" appropriately indicates that the visitors traveled in the direction of the Korean War Veterans Memorial.

Question 459. The best answer is **G** because it correctly uses an apostrophe to indicate that the feet belong to the soldiers.

The best answer is NOT:

F because, although it correctly uses an apostrophe to indicate that the feet belong to the soldiers, it also separates the subject, *Spotlights,* and the verb phrase, "lit up," with an unnecessary comma following the word *feet.*

H because it fails to use a possessive apostrophe to indicate that the feet belong to the soldiers. It also separates the subject, *Spotlights,* and the verb phrase, "lit up," with an unnecessary comma following the word *feet.*

J because it fails to use a possessive apostrophe to indicate that the feet belong to the soldiers.

Question 460. The best answer is C because Sentence 4 indicates that there are statues of soldiers on the memorial, while Sentence 2 discusses what the soldiers looked like. Therefore, it would be most logical to place Sentence 4 after Sentence 1 and before Sentence 2.

The best answer is NOT:

A because Sentence 4 indicates that there are statues of soldiers on the memorial, while Sentence 2 discusses what the soldiers looked like. Therefore, it would not be logical to place Sentence 4 after Sentences 2 and 3.

B because Sentence 4 provides a general description of the Korean War Veterans Memorial, while Sentence 1 describes the writer traveling to the Korean War Veterans Memorial. For this reason, it doesn't make sense to put Sentence 4 before Sentence 1.

D because Sentence 4 indicates that there are statues of soldiers on the memorial, while Sentence 2 discusses what the soldiers looked like. Therefore, it would be most logical to place Sentence 4 before Sentence 2, not after Sentence 2.

Question 461. The best answer is J because the words *polished*, *black*, and *granite* describe the physical appearance of the Vietnam Memorial, which offers insight into what the narrator saw while viewing it.

The best answer is NOT:

F because the narrator does not attempt to make a case for improving the lighting at the national monuments.

G because the words *polished*, *black*, and *granite* provide information about the physical appearance of the Vietnam Memorial but do not provide much insight into the process used to create the Vietnam Veterans Memorial.

H because the words *polished*, *black*, and *granite* primarily serve to characterize the physical appearance of the Vietnam Veterans Memorial and do not offer much insight into the narrator's frame of mind.

Question 462. The best answer is D because the phrase "etched with the names of fallen soldiers" appropriately modifies the noun that directly follows it, *the wall*, indicating that the wall was etched with the names of fallen soldiers.

The best answer is NOT:

A because it makes the introductory phrase, "etched with the names of fallen soldiers," a misplaced modifier that refers to *visitors*, suggesting that the visitors were etched with the names of fallen soldiers, which doesn't make sense.

B because it makes the introductory phrase, "etched with the names of fallen soldiers," a misplaced modifier that refers to the word *adorning*, suggesting that the participle "adorning" was etched with the names of fallen soldiers, which doesn't make sense.

C because it makes the introductory phrase, "etched with the names of fallen soldiers," a misplaced modifier that refers to *flowers and American flags*, suggesting that the flowers and American flags were etched with the names of fallen soldiers, which doesn't make sense in this context.

Question 463. The best answer is F because the word *indeed* serves to reinforce the essay's earlier claim that Washington, D.C.'s "attractions appear even more impressive after dark."

The best answer is NOT:

G because the word *nevertheless* suggests that this sentence (that evening proved to be an excellent time to visit the White House and the Mall) contrasts with the preceding sentence (a description of the Vietnam Veterans Memorial), which doesn't make sense.

H because the word *furthermore* suggests that this sentence (that evening proved to be an excellent time to visit the White House and the Mall) elaborates on a point made in the preceding sentence. Because the previous sentence is simply a description of the Vietnam Veterans Memorial, this transition suggests a relationship between this sentence and the preceding one that is not supported by the essay.

J because the word *lastly* suggests that this sentence comes at the end of a list or series of related statements, which is not the case. Rather, this sentence comes at the beginning of the narrator's reflection on why evening was an excellent time to visit the White House and the Mall.

Question 464. The best answer is **C** because the past tense verb *proved* is parallel with the verb *remained* later in the paragraph. Additionally, the phrase "proved to be" is a commonly used idiomatic expression that effectively indicates that the narrator believes evening is an excellent time to visit the White House and the mall.

The best answer is NOT:

A because the phrase "proved as an excellent time" is not a widely accepted idiomatic expression and therefore creates an illogical statement.

B because the past participle *proven* needs to be preceded by helping verbs such as *had* or *has.* It cannot stand on its own.

D because the past participle *proven* needs to be preceded by helping verbs such as *has* or *had.* It cannot stand on its own. Additionally, the past participle *proven* needs to be followed either directly by an adjective such as *excellent* or by the phrase "to be."

Question 465. The best answer is **G** because it connects the preceding sentence's statement that evening was an excellent time to visit the White House and the Mall to the subsequent sentence's claim that buildings and monuments were especially visible at night. This suggests that the darkness of the evening drew much of the landscape into the background and made the most significant buildings and monuments more visible.

The best answer is NOT:

F because it does not address the narrator's experience of the city at night, which is the main idea reinforced in the opening and closing sentences of this paragraph.

H because it does not address the narrator's experience of the city at night, which is the main idea reinforced in the opening and closing sentences of this paragraph.

J because it does not address the narrator's experience of the city at night, which is the main idea reinforced in the opening and closing sentences of the concluding paragraph.

Passage XXXII

Question 466. The best answer is **A** because the phrase "even so" is a conjunctive adverb that does not appropriately join the parallel sentence elements "cool in the summer" and "even a bit chilly in the winter."

The best answer is NOT:

B because the conjunction *and* appropriately joins the parallel sentence elements "cool in the summer" and "even a bit chilly in winter."

C because the conjunction *though* appropriately joins the parallel sentence elements "cool in the summer" and "a bit chilly in winter."

D because the conjunction *while* appropriately joins the parallel sentence elements "cool in the summer" and "a bit chilly in winter."

Question 467. The best answer is **J** because adding the sentence interrupts the paragraph's discussion of the drought emergency in Santa Fe with a statement about a tactic used by other cities to conserve water. Because this method is not mentioned again in this paragraph (or in the essay), it serves as an unnecessary digression that could distract readers from the paragraph's main focus.

The best answer is NOT:

F because the sentence does not provide a definition for any of the terms in the preceding sentence.

G because, although this sentence describes a method that would allow residents to water outdoor plants, this method is not mentioned again at any point in the essay, and it interrupts the essay's discussion of Santa Fe's response to the drought emergency.

H because this statement does not contradict the essay's claim that the city was experiencing a drought emergency. Rather, it describes a tactic used by other cities to conserve water.

Question 468. The best answer is **B** because the verb *drop* is parallel with phrase "started to turn brown."

The best answer is NOT:

A because the verb phrase "were dropped" is not parallel with the phrase "started to turn brown."

C because the verb *dropping* is not parallel with the phrase "started to turn brown."

D because the verb phrase "are dropping" is not parallel with the phrase "started to turn brown."

Question 469. The best answer is **G** because the phrase "from that" effectively conveys that the narrator is using water from the bucket to water the tree.

The best answer is NOT:

F because the phrase "in there" implies that the narrator was somehow able to water the tree in the shower, which doesn't make sense.

H because the phrase "in that" implies that the narrator was somehow able to water the tree inside the plastic bucket, which doesn't make sense.

J because deleting the underlined portion of the sentence obscures the relationship between the narrator's plastic bucket and the manner in which the narrator watered the tree.

Question 470. The best answer is **C** because it correctly uses a period to separate two independent clauses.

The best answer is NOT:

A because it fails to use any punctuation to separate two independent clauses, creating a run-on sentence.

B because it connects two independent clauses with a coordinating conjunction (*but*) that is not preceded by a comma, creating a run-on sentence. In addition, the coordinating conjunction *but* is not logical within the context of this sentence, as the death of the tree does not contrast with the narrator's statement that "All my efforts failed."

C because it fails to use any punctuation to separate two independent clauses, instead simply using the word *then,* which creates a run-on sentence.

Question 471. The best answer is **J** because the adverb *horribly* appropriately modifies the adjective *depressing.*

The best answer is NOT:

F because it uses an adjective, *horrific,* to modify another adjective, *depressing.* Adjectives can be modified by adverbs, not by adjectives.

G because it uses a verb, *horrified,* to modify an adjective, *depressing.* Adjectives can be modified by adverbs, not by verbs.

H because it uses an adjective, *horrible,* to modify another adjective, *depressing.* Adjectives can be modified by adverbs, not by adjectives.

Question 472. The best answer is **D** because it connects an independent clause to a dependent clause, creating a grammatical sentence.

The best answer is NOT:

A because it separates two independent clauses using only a comma, which creates a comma splice.

B because it fails to use any punctuation to separate two independent clauses, creating a run-on sentence.

C because it separates two independent clauses using only a comma and the adverb *therefore,* creating a comma splice.

Question 473. The best answer is **F** because the quotation marks suggest that the word "topped" is a term that might be unfamiliar to the reader, which helps indicate that the narrator is using a technical term.

The best answer is NOT:

G because there is no indication that the narrator is being sarcastic about this statement. In fact, the rest of the essay shows that an arborist did in fact have to come and "top" the tree.

H because, while the essay does make it clear that the narrator tried to save the tree, there is no indication that the narrator's statement that the tree will have to be "topped" expresses anger. Instead, the narrator seems to express respect for the difficulty of "topping" the tree, referring to the work as "a delicate job."

J because there is no mention of a neighbor in the essay, so there is not enough evidence to indicate that the narrator is quoting a neighbor here.

Question 474. The best answer is **B** because the events are described in a logical chronological order. First, the arborist climbed into the spruce; then, he began to cut off a section at a time, dropping the pieces onto the yard.

The best answer is NOT:

A because the order of events is not logical. The arborist would have needed to climb the spruce before cutting off sections and dropping the pieces onto the yard.

C because the order of events is not logical. The arborist would have needed to climb the spruce before cutting off sections and dropping the pieces onto the yard.

D because the order of events is not logical. The arborist would have needed to climb the spruce before cutting off sections and dropping the pieces onto the yard.

Question 475. The best answer is G because the sentence creates a logical transition between the narrator's indication that, without the tree, the yard had changed, and also his observations about the positive impact of the cacti, pinon trees, and the dwarf peach tree on his yard.

The best answer is NOT:

F because the sentence does not contradict the arborist's claim that trees were dying off all around town (in fact, the death of the narrator's tree provides evidence to support the arborist's statement). Rather, the sentence suggests that the narrator found pleasure in what was still able to grow in his yard.

H because the sentence creates a logical transition between the narrator's indication that, without the tree, the yard had changed, and also his observations about the impact of the cacti, pinon trees, and the dwarf peach tree on his yard. Therefore, it does not make sense to characterize the statement as a digression.

J because the sentence does not conflict with the narrator's feelings about the changes to the yard expressed in the rest of this paragraph. Rather, the narrator discusses how the other plants, which were more suited to the conditions of drought, thrived in the absence of the old spruce tree, and describes the fruit of one tree as a "welcome harvest," suggesting that he was pleased with the changes to his yard.

Question 476. The best answer is D because the sentence does not create a nonrestrictive clause that needs to be set off by commas. Rather, the sentence is grammatical without any additional punctuation.

The best answer is NOT:

A because it creates a nonrestrictive clause, "which I'd never given much attention to," that lacks a comma after the word *to* later in the sentence.

B because it introduces an unnecessary comma after the word *that*.

C because it introduces an unnecessary comma after the word *cacti*.

Question 477. The best answer is H because the adverb *much* appropriately modifies the adverb *better*. In addition, *better* appropriately modifies *suited*.

The best answer is NOT:

F because the adverb *more* does not appropriately modify the adverb *better*.

G because the adverb *more* does not appropriately modify the adverb *better*. In addition, the adverb *better* does not appropriately modify the adjective *suitable*.

J because the adverb *better* does not appropriately modify the adjective *suitable*.

Question 478. The best answer is **A** because it successfully sets off the nonrestrictive phrase "trees much better suited to the conditions of drought" using two em-dashes.

The best answer is NOT:

B because it lacks the second em-dash necessary to successfully set off the non-restrictive phrase "trees much better suited to the conditions of drought."

C because it lacks the second em-dash necessary to successfully set off the non-restrictive phrase "trees much better suited to the conditions of drought." Instead, it uses a comma, which is not parallel with the first em-dash used earlier in the sentence.

D because it lacks the second em-dash necessary to successfully set off the non-restrictive phrase "trees much better suited to the conditions of drought."

Question 479. The best answer is **J** because the singular pronoun *it* logically refers to "the dwarf peach tree" mentioned earlier in this paragraph.

The best answer is NOT:

F because the pronoun *I* suggests that the narrator produced forty peaches in the sunlight, which does not make sense in this context.

G because the pronoun *They* suggests that the narrator is referring to multiple trees, when it is clear that he only has one peach tree.

H because the pronoun *You* suggests that some second party, such as the reader, produced forty peaches in the sunlight, which doesn't make sense.

Question 480. **The best answer is C** because, while the essay does indicate that many trees have died because of the drought, it does not place the blame for these deaths on the city's drought management system. Instead, the essay primarily indicates that the drought is responsible for the deaths of the trees.

The best answer is NOT:

A because, while the essay does indicate that many trees have died because of the drought, it does not place the blame for these deaths on the city's drought management system. Instead, the essay primarily indicates that the drought is responsible for the deaths of the trees. In addition, the narrator indicates that, in the absence of the old spruce tree, new plants began to thrive, suggesting that the effects of the drought were not wholly negative.

B because, while the essay does indicate that many trees have died because of the drought, it does not place the blame for these deaths on the city's drought management system. Instead, the essay primarily indicates that the drought is responsible for the deaths of the trees.

D because the essay does suggest that the drought resulted in the spruce tree's death, explaining that the spruce "started to turn brown" after the city issued a ban on outdoor watering.

Appendix: English Test Glossary

Action verbs verbs that show what the subject does.

Adjective a word that describes a noun. It typically describes color, size, consistency, or number.

Adjective of number a modifier that describes countable nouns.

> *Example:* I don't have **many** cookies.

Adjective of quantity a modifier that describes an uncountable noun.

> *Example:* I don't have **much** cookie dough left.

Antecedent the word that a pronoun refers back to.

> *Example:* I like **puppies**. <u>They</u> are cute.

Appositive a phrase that describes a noun using nouns, pronouns, adjectives, and prepositions.

Article a word that qualifies a noun. Similar to an adjective, an article can also be said to modify a noun.

> *Examples: a, an, the*

Clause a group of words containing a subject and verb.

> *Example:* My dog ran. (This is a simple sentence.)

Comma splice a comma used where a period, colon, dash, or semicolon would be more appropriate. A comma splice occurs when a subject and a verb immediately follow a comma in a sentence that does not start with a subordinating conjunction.

Coordinate adjectives successive adjectives that modify the same noun. These adjectives will be separated by a comma or the word *and*. If there are three or more adjectives, the word *and* appears before the final adjective.

> *Example:* It was a cold, gloomy day.

Coordinating conjunction a type of conjunction that connects equal parts of a sentence, such as two independent clauses. Also known as FANBOYS conjunctions because of the first letter of each of the words: *For And Nor But Or Yet So.*

Cumulative adjectives modifiers that belong in a fixed order to describe a noun with one adjective especially linked to the noun, as in *black leather jacket* when *leather* must go closest to the noun.

Demonstrative adjective   an adjective (*this, that, these, those*) that is used to modify or point out a specific noun.

Example: This apple versus that apple.

Dependent clause   a clause that cannot stand alone as a complete sentence. A clause has a subject and a verb.

Direct object   a noun or noun phrase that functions as the recipient of the action in the sentence.

Example: She threw <u>the ball</u>. (The ball is the recipient of the action.)

Future perfect   The formula for the future perfect is the following: will have + past participle

Example: By the end of high school, <u>I will have taken</u> the ACT three times.

Gerund   the noun form of a verb. It typically ends in *-ing*. It looks exactly the same as the present participle.

Example: I enjoy running.

Indefinite pronoun   a pronoun used to a describe a noun in a nonspecific way. It refers to any noun from a group of nouns.

Examples: any, several, many, most, few

Independent clause   a clause that can stand alone. A clause has a subject and a verb.

Indirect object   the receiver of the direct object. These are rare. They require that the sentence also has a direct object, which is the receiver of an action.

Example: Michael built **his grandson** a wooden toy train. *Michael* is the subject, *built* is the verb, *a wooden toy train* is the direct object, and *his grandson* is the indirect object. This sometimes answers the question "to whom?" To whom was the train given?

Interrogative adjective   an adjective that asks questions.

Examples: What? Which? Whose? How many?

Linking verbs   verbs that show what a subject is. They connect the subject with modifiers that express a state of being or feeling.

Examples:

appear	feel	stay	smell	taste
become	remain	seem	sound	turn

Modifiers   adjectives, adverbs, and participial phrases that provide further information about a noun, verb, or adjective.

Noun   a person, place, or thing.

Noun phrase describes a person, place, or thing in more than just one word. Typically, a noun phrase is made up of an adjective and a noun the adjective modifies.

Participial phrase a phrase that typically begins with a word ending in *-ing*. It functions like an adjective to describe the noun immediately before it.

   Example: The town has installed many solar panels, <u>powering lights across the town.</u>

Past participles a part of the past perfect, future perfect, and present perfect tenses. Past participles usually end in the following: *ed, -d, -t, -en,* or *-n.*

   Examples: I had **woken** up early that morning. At the end of the month, I will have **cooked** breakfast for myself for twenty-one days. I have **taught** this book for five years.

Past perfect a verb tense that describes actions that happened in the past before another past tense event. Had + past participle.

   Example: By the time summer was over, I had read ten books.

Phrase a group of related words that does not include a subject and a verb.

Possessive adjectives an adjective that shows ownership.

   Examples: my, your, his, her, its, their, our, your, and whose

Predicate the verb phrase of a sentence that includes the main verb along with its auxiliaries, modifiers, and objects.

Present perfect this tense is used to describe a past action that was completed. The form is has/had + the past participle.

   Example: I <u>have eaten</u> octopus.

Pronoun a word that takes the place of a specific or proper noun after it is first introduced.

Referent the word that a pronoun refers back to.

Relative clause a clause that begins with relative pronouns such as *who, whose, where, when, which,* and *that.* They provide further information about a noun.

Relative pronoun a pronoun that introduces a subordinate clause that provides information about who, which, that, and when. In other words, a relative pronoun answers question about identity, specification, and timing.

Subject the noun phrase that identifies the person, place, or thing shown acting or being in a sentence. This noun phrase of the subject includes the main noun along with its modifiers.

Subordinate clause a clause that includes a subject and a verb. It is usually introduced by a subordinating conjunction and is dependent on the main independent clause

Subordinating conjunction a conjunction that introduces a subordinate clause.

NOTES